United States Foreign Oil Policy
Since World War I

United States Foreign Oil Policy Since World War I

For Profits and Security

STEPHEN J. RANDALL

Second Edition

McGill-Queen's University Press
Montreal & Kingston · London · Ithaca

ISBN 0-7735-2922-5 (cloth)

Legal deposit first quarter 2005
Bibliothèque nationale du Québec

Printed in Canada on acid-free paper that is 100%
ancient forest free (100% post-consumer recycled),
processed chlorine free.

McGill-Queen's University Press acknowledges the
support of the Canada Council for the Arts for our
publishing program. We also acknowledge the financial support of the Government of Canada through the
Book Publishing Industry Development Program
(BPIDP) for our publishing activities.

**Library and Archives Canada Cataloguing
in Publication**

Randall, Stephen J., 1944–
    United States foreign oil policy since World War I:
for profits and security / Stephen J. Randall. – 2nd ed.

First ed. published under title: United States foreign
    oil policy, 1919–1948.
Includes bibliographical references and index.
ISBN 0-7735-2922-5

    1. Petroleum industry and trade – Government policy
– United States – History – 20th century.   2. Petroleum
industry and trade – Political aspects – United States –
History – 20th century.   3. United States – Foreign
relations – 20th century.   I. Title.

HD9566.R35 2005   338.2'7282'0973   C2005–900149–6

Contents

Preface

The second edition of this study of United States foreign oil policy since World War I is designed to integrate the dramatic developments in global politics since the end of the Cold War and to bring up to date the analysis of the years between 1949 and the early twenty-first century. Many factors have provided the context for oil policy formation: a succession of crises in Iran since the 1950s, culminating in the Iranian revolution in the Carter years; two wars against Iraq; u.s. intervention in Afghanistan; the threats of international terrorism since 11 September 2001; the ongoing conflict between Israel and the Arab nations in the Middle East; political instability in Saudi Arabia and in Venezuela at the beginning of the twenty-first century; and the trend toward trade and investment liberalization in Latin America in the 1990s.

Extensive scholarship in the field has occurred since the publication of the first edition in 1985, and this edition seeks to integrate the important contributions to our understanding of United States global oil politics. The focus remains, as before, on the nature, goals, regional scope, accomplishments, and challenges of u.s. foreign oil policy, as well as on the relationship between the state and private sectors. This edition has also been informed by my move to a major natural resource-producing region of Canada, a province that, in terms of sources of non-conventional oil, rivals Saudi Arabia. Many years of discussion with leading members of the oil industry here and with a series of ministers of energy have provided me with a deeper understanding of the industry and its relationship to foreign policy.

I would like to express my appreciation to Philip Cercone and Joan McGilvray of McGill-Queen's University Press for their encouragement in preparing a new edition of this study and for their consummate professionalism. Lesley Andrassy provided outstanding editorial work on the manuscript in its final stages. I would also like to thank the many colleagues and scholars in the field who have provided insights and suggestions on the first edition over the past twenty years or who have published work that has enhanced my understanding of the critical issues. Ms Jillian Dowding, my former graduate student in strategic studies, was instrumental in identifying and collating research materials for this edition. The maps in Chapter 12 were prepared by Robin Poitras, Department of Geography, University of Calgary. As with the first edition, I alone bear responsibility for any errors or omissions as well as for the interpretation advanced in this study.

Stephen J. Randall
Calgary, 2004

Abbreviations

AD	Acción Democrática
AIMME	American Institute of Mining and Metallurgical Engineering
ANPB	Army-Navy Petroleum Board
API	American Petroleum Institute
APOC	Anglo-Persian Oil Company
BFDC	Bureau of Foreign and Domestic Commerce
DS	Department of State decimal files (all references are to Record Group 59, National Archives, unless otherwise indicated)
FDRL	Franklin Delano Roosevelt Presidential Library
FDR	Franklin Delano Roosevelt Papers
FEA	Foreign Economic Administration
FO	Foreign Office Files, Public Record Office, Great Britain
FOC	Foreign Operations Committee
FOCB	Federal Oil Conservation Board
FR	Department of State, *Papers Relating to the Foreign Relations of the United States*
HCHL	Herbert C. Hoover Presidential Library
HHP	Herbert Hoover Papers
HSTL	Harry S. Truman Presidential Library

IADB	Inter-American Defense Board
IPC	Iraq Petroleum Company
LC	Library of Congress
NA	National Archives of the United States
NRA	National Recovery Administration
OF	Official File
OPD	Plans and Operations Division, Department of War
OSS	Office of Strategic Services
PAW	Petroleum Administration for War
PD	Petroleum Division Lot File, RG 59, NA
PIWC	Petroleum Industry War Council
PRC	Petroleum Reserves Corporation
PSF	President's Secretary's File
SFRC	U.S. Congress, Senate Foreign Relations Committee
TPC	Turkish Petroleum Company
YPF	Yacimientos Petrolíferos Fiscales
YPFB	Yacimientos Petrolíferos Fiscales Bolivianos

United States Foreign Oil Policy
Since World War I

Introduction

United States domestic and foreign oil policy has received considerable scholarly and popular attention in recent years, but overwhelmingly the extant scholarship has focused on specific geographic areas and/or limited time periods.[1] Such case studies have substantially enriched our knowledge of U.S. foreign oil policy but have left unanswered some of the larger questions relating to the general place of petroleum considerations in the broader spectrum of American foreign policy. We continue to need to know more about the relative importance of petroleum in comparison with other resource industries in shaping foreign policy.[2] We also need to transcend the time, spatial, and comparative limitations of case studies to gain insight into the way in which policy has evolved over time. When were the crucial turning points? Who were the main actors in both public and private sectors? How did the institutional structure of decision making change? What role did Congress, the White House, executive agencies, and departments play in determining policy? What was the relationship between government and private enterprise in the formulation and implementation of policy, and did it change between the Wilson administration and the Cold War? How did the tensions between the major integrated international firms and the large independent companies concentrated in the domestic sector affect policy? Did the flag follow the oil rig abroad or were the companies the instruments of national policy? Why were those initiatives oriented towards achieving a higher level of state control over the foreign operations of the corporations consistently defeated during these years? This study addresses those questions from the end of World War I to the end of the Cold War and the intervention in Iraq by the Republican administration of George W. Bush. During that three-quarters of a century the Middle East progressively acquired greater importance both as an oil-producing region with global reach and as a region of growing strategic significance for the United

States. The study's thematic unity is provided by its focus on the attitudes, beliefs, and policies of those within and outside official circles of power – those who contributed to the determination of policy or offered alternatives to policy that were not followed.

Although, as the first edition of this study suggested, the fundamental features of foreign oil policy were well established by the early Cold War, the events of the post-1950 years were momentous in international oil relations; not only were the challenges that American policymakers faced more acute in terms of the nation's national security but also the international arena was far more volatile. The nationalism that policymakers and corporate leaders alike had faced prior to World War II, in much of Latin America for instance, became a more serious challenge in the post-World War II years. The fire of that nationalism was increasingly fanned by emergent religious fervour in the Middle East, where, as suggested by political scientist Samuel Huntington, among others, the West in the post-Cold War years faced a "clash of civilizations." The nationalizations that had occurred in Bolivia and Mexico before World War II found vibrant echoes in the Near and Middle East after 1950, beginning with a major crisis in Iran early in that decade. Some features nonetheless remained the same, even if the actors changed. The debate over the extent to which the state should exercise a direct role in the international petroleum industry was a constant in the course of the twentieth century, although the weight of opinion remained overwhelmingly in favour of private enterprise and the attainment of a balance between private and public interest. Certainly, with the departure of Harold Ickes from the policy scene little consideration was given again to the notion of the state playing a more direct role in international oil development. A second constant through the 1950s and 1960s was the often uneasy collaboration between the American and British governments and companies, characterized by both rivalry and recognition of the need to attain some level of common cause, especially in the Middle East.

Although some features of u.s. policy were constant after World War II, a number of other critical circumstances changed in its aftermath. The end of the twenty-year-old Red Line Agreement in 1948 marked the climax of an era of dramatic corporate and diplomatic expansion and the coming of age of United States-based corporations in the Middle East. The challenges those corporations faced and the implications of those challenges for American policymakers, however, evolved dramatically over the next half century as the region underwent significant political and economic change. Some, though by no means all, of the strategic challenges that the United States faced in the Middle East, and elsewhere in the post-1948 world, derived from the conflict occasioned by East-West tensions and in particular by specific Soviet-American jockeying for position and advantage; by 1948 the context had changed significantly. The intensity of the Soviet-American confrontation in the early Cold War years, the concentration on the European recovery program, and the gradual emergence of a greater degree of autonomy among third-world producing nations created a context in which it became increasingly difficult to separate oil-related issues from the larger questions of the Cold War.

In this work I take issue with the historical literature on oil policy that contends that the private sector directly determined the nature of United States foreign oil policy during these years. I question, as well, the historical validity of the argument – advanced by the Senate Foreign Relations Committee's 1975 subcommittee report on the multinational oil companies – that the United States did not have a foreign oil policy before World War II.[3] Rather, the evidence suggests that U.S. policy was premised on the twin objectives of strategic security and economic strength and a private-public partnership based on shared values and goals throughout the interwar and war years.[4] Policymakers consistently and often vigorously sought to achieve those ends through the maintenance of the Open Door for American investment in the international petroleum industry and to combat the threat of emergent nationalism in host nations, whether they were major producers or consumers of petroleum products. Specific tactics often changed in response to the exigencies of a particular situation, but the general thrust of overall policy objectives showed striking consistency, whether implemented by Republican administrations before 1933 or Democratic ones thereafter. What is impressive about the evidence gathered by the Senate Foreign Relations Committee in the 1970s is not the absence of pre-1950s foreign oil policy but rather that with historical hindsight those policies could be found to be seriously flawed. They failed in the long term, and occasionally in the short term, as the expropriations of the 1930s in Mexico and Bolivia or the post-World War II nationalizations throughout the Middle East indicated, because of the limited capacity of the state to control the private sector in a free-enterprise system. Foreign oil policy could be, and indeed generally was, remarkably successful as long as the strategic objectives of state planners and the profit motives of the companies coincided. Successful policy depended also on American power. As long as the United States could contain emergent nationalism, policy appeared to serve United States needs. Whether a different approach might have more effectively anticipated the rise of OPEC is another question and perhaps entirely conjectural. My own belief is that the period before 1950 represented a lost opportunity during which the United States might have moved in concert with other major producer and consumer nations towards a more rational, internationalist approach to develop a raw materials policy that would have benefited both producers and consumer societies. That American policymakers failed to achieve the internationalism implicit in the United Nations movement of that era is the real tragedy of American diplomacy. It was not that policymakers failed to anticipate host-country nationalism: the record suggests that State Department officials were even sympathetic to it by the late 1930s. The real failure was in maintaining the belief that American power would continue to be adequate to overcome any obstacle to the realization of foreign policy objectives.

One of the major dilemmas in attempting to assess and trace the evolution of American foreign oil policy is to determine the relationship of oil to other factors in foreign policy. Because, unlike Great Britain, the United States was one of the world's major oil producers, that commodity was not considered as a strategic raw material in the strict sense applied during the interwar years by such bodies as the Army-Navy Munitions Board; that is, as an essential industrial-military mineral unavailable in the United States in adequate supply for the conduct of war. Throughout these years the United States was a net exporter of oil and oil products. In 1929, for instance, the United States imported only $145 million in oil products and exported $962 million.[5] Yet that figure is itself not indicative of official attitudes toward the security of oil supply, since State Department officials, the United States Geological Survey, and the Federal Oil Conservation Board all continued to speak as though the security of supply was threatened and to recommend conservation at home and expansion abroad. Simple trade figures cannot, therefore, be used to test attitudes. The complexity of the industry also makes it difficult to assess the impact of industry spokesmen on policy formation. The major integrated firms engaged in international operations and the independents concentrated in domestic production viewed each other with considerable suspicion. The independents feared that substantial foreign production would lead to increased importation into the United States, weakening the price structure and their own competitive positions. Tensions between these two interest groups complicated the making of foreign policy and served in the long run to render it more impotent than it might otherwise have been.

How high a priority petroleum was in the hierarchy of American foreign policy objectives remains difficult to evaluate. Even when oil was not in short supply, which it was not from the late 1920s to World War II, the diplomacy surrounding it was active, vigorous, and expansionist. Oil conformed rather well to established principles in American foreign policy, in particular the Open Door assertions of equality of access and of treatment for American nationals overseas. Insofar as petroleum was an integral part of diplomatic debates surrounding United States foreign investment, direct and portfolio, oil was a major issue. World War I drastically altered the importance of oil in international relations. With three times the calorific power of coal, the greater ease with which military and commercial shipping could take on fuel oil, its growing use in aviation, and its importance to the industrial sector, oil rapidly assumed major strategic and economic significance in the industrial nations and modified the relationship between the major powers and third-world producers. United States domestic demand for all oil products during the 1920s reflected a dramatic increase, from 429 million barrels in 1920 to 888 million on the eve of the Great Depression. By 1925 the United States was consuming 70 percent of world liquid-fuel production.[6] Prices decreased markedly during these years as new fields came into production, notably those in Iraq and east Texas, and as extractive and refining technology improved.

Overseas investments in petroleum reflected the intensification of business interest in oil. By 1927 one-tenth of u.s. overseas direct investment, approximately $1.5 billion, was in petroleum operations, although less than $300 million was in fixed assets. Over the period 1918–43 u.s. crude-oil production also increased substantially, from 355.9 million barrels in the former year to 1.5 billion in the latter. In 1918 the u.s. had approximately 203,000 producing wells; by 1943 it had 405,000. In 1918 the underground proven reserves of the u.s. were calculated at 6.8 billion barrels. By 1943 that figure was in excess of 20 billion. At the same time technological improvements increased the gasoline yield of crude oil from 25 percent to over 44 percent per barrel of crude oil. The economist Mira Wilkins estimates that by 1929 u.s. direct investments in the oil industry in Europe alone were approximately $239 million, followed by Canada, Latin America, Asia, Africa, Australia, and New Zealand. To keep foreign oil investment in perspective, it should be noted that the largest single-sector u.s. investment in Latin America in 1929 was in sugar in Cuba, followed by mining and smelting in Chile and Mexico, and then oil producing, refining, and distribution in Venezuela and Mexico.[7]

United States oil companies played a major role in the general expansion of the international industry. At the turn of the century, world production was dominated by the United States, with 43 percent of total production, and Russia, with 51 percent. As the companies moved into the international arena in the early twentieth century, that pattern evolved. The Russian Revolution severely damaged oil production for a decade, and during the first two decades of the century American, Dutch, and British firms experienced considerable overseas expansion. By 1914 Russian production was down to 16.4 percent and u.s. up to 65 percent. The Royal Dutch Company, which had been formed in the

1890s to develop Sumatran oil resources, and the Shell Transport and Trading Company formed in 1897, formally united in 1906 to form the Royal Dutch Shell Company, with 60 percent Royal Dutch capital and 40 percent Shell. By 1913 Royal Dutch Shell had subsidiaries in Romania, California, Trinidad, and Venezuela. The British-owned Burmah Oil Company, which alone controlled some 1 percent of world production in 1900, gradually expanded its influence in the same years, acquiring 97 percent control of the Anglo-Persian Company in 1909; this became the Anglo-Iranian Company in the 1930s and British Petroleum in 1955. By 1914 the British government had acquired a minority interest in Anglo-Persian, and the company, under the careful guidance of Sir Charles Greenway and then Sir John Cadman in the 1920s, underwent significant expansion, with exploration activities covering the Middle East, Latin America, Africa, and Europe. Yet Standard Oil of New Jersey remained the world's marketing giant in the 1920s, although it did not show as much dramatic expansion as other United States-based oil firms, in part because of the Supreme Court dissolution of the Standard Oil Trust in 1911. Jersey had total assets in excess of $1.1 billion in 1920 and $1.4 billion in 1927; but Standard Oil of California, part of the original Standard Oil Trust, more than doubled its assets in the same period, from approximately $246 million to $579 million. Standard Oil of Indiana assets climbed from $238 million to $463 million; Standard Oil of New York increased from $300 million to $678 million; and Gulf Oil from $260 million to $553 million. The other major company, the Texas Company, actually experienced a slight decline in total assets from $333 million to $325 million. Royal Dutch Shell, in contrast, increased from $320 million to $480 million, and Anglo-Persian from $110 million to $248 million. By the late 1920s, companies controlled by United States nationals accounted for 60 percent of world production, and their exploration, development, and marketing operations spanned the globe.[8]

It is difficult to imagine, given the importance of oil to United States firms and the American political economy, that it did not have a significant impact on the geographic focus as well as on the priorities of foreign policy following World War I. Throughout these years petroleum played a significant role in American interest in Latin America, the Near East, the Dutch East Indies, and such a major East European producer as Romania. Clearly other considerations, commercial and strategic, also shaped policy toward those areas. In Latin America, the Caribbean, and the Far East, and in relations with Britain, well-established policies substantially antedated the arrival of oil on the international stage. Yet it is unimaginable that the course of American foreign policy towards those areas and nations was not altered by oil-related considerations. Latin American countries were within the American strategic perimeter, some in close proximity to the Panama Canal, making them of clear importance to the United States, whether they had rich oil resources or not; yet for anyone who has read the diplomatic records of these years, it is difficult to escape the conclusion that oil became a significant determinant of policy for those countries with such resources.

The Middle East in the 1920s and 1940s and the Netherlands East Indies in the 1920s present evidence of direct linkage with oil policy. Lying outside traditional American spheres of influence, those areas rapidly increased in significance to the United States following World War I, as American enterprise and state officials sought assured access to the oil resources of both regions. One of the major diplomatic issues of the first postwar decade revolved around an effort to establish reciprocity in access to petroleum resources among Great Britain, the United States, and the Netherlands, as well as their respective colonial areas and spheres of influence. The striking feature of this debate was that it was not a simple or classic account of the flag following trade and investment but rather of the state using private enterprise as an instrument of policy for mutual benefit, at the same time that the state refrained from direct participation in international oil operations.

There is little evidence to support the thesis that the oil industry conducted the oil diplomacy of the United States in these years. For one thing, the oil industry was often too diverse in its interests, not simply the "majors" versus the "independents," but also the differences between those concerned with sources of supply and those whose main interests were marketing. The thesis that policy derived from the private sector is based on several assumptions: that bureaucracy lacks an independent power base and must depend on the support of its most important private-sector constituents; that business is the "keystone of power which defines the essential preconditions and functions of the larger American social order"; and that foreign policy decision makers are a "highly mobile sector of the American corporate structure," often playing a direct role in high-level policy formulation.[9]

If this hypothesis is applied to 1920s petroleum policy formation, movement between government and industry employment seems to have been limited, certainly less striking than during World War II, when industry personnel comprised a significant number of active policymakers. During the latter period some individuals assumed major positions; for example, Jersey Standard's Max Thornburg and Ralph Davies of California Standard, who became State Department petroleum adviser and deputy administrator of the Petroleum Administration for War respectively. World War I played a less significant role in promoting business-government integration of personnel, although for the time the operations of such entities as the u.s. Fuel Administration and the War

Industries Board did much to fulfill the more conservative, stabilizing dimension of the progressive movement.[10] This experience of business-government cooperation during the war spilled over into the postwar era, a development encouraged by the generally pro-business sentiments of the Republican administrations of the decade.

In terms of foreign oil policy, a casual sampling of those in the State Department who had some responsibility for oil-related matters in the 1920s suggests that links with industry tended to follow government service. The pattern may have been different for other departments and agencies, but there is no evidence that other departments were more influential in shaping foreign oil policy prior to World War II, although the commerce department under the firm and creative guidance of Herbert Hoover did play an active and frequently direct role, much to the chagrin of State Department officials. The senior officials had no prior industry involvement. None of the undersecretaries of state (including Robert Fletcher, William Phillips, Joseph Grew, and Robert Olds) had formal industry ties. The chief of the Division of Near Eastern Affairs from 1922 to 1926, where much of the new interest in petroleum development concentrated, was Allen Dulles. Dulles had no industry links, and his term of office preceded the appointment of his brother, John Foster, as senior partner in the prestigious law firm of Sullivan and Cromwell. The State Department's economic adviser, Arthur Young, had no industry involvement; Stanley Hornbeck, who was technical adviser from 1921 to 1924 and subsequently chief of the Division of Far Eastern Affairs, was primarily an academic Asian specialist. Arthur C. Millspaugh, the department's petroleum adviser from 1920 to 1922, subsequently served as administrator general of finances of Persia and later Haiti before joining the Brookings Institute in 1929. Of the secretaries of state between 1919 and 1928, Charles Evans Hughes and Frank Kellogg were both products of progressive-era reform – Hughes as governor of New York and Republican presidential candidate in 1916, and Kellogg as one of the government prosecutors in the 1911 antitrust suit against Standard Oil. Although both were supportive of the major companies while in office and Hughes assumed an advisory role to the American Petroleum Institute after leaving office, neither was, in the narrow sense, part of the American corporate structure before assuming office.

Industry ties were closer in the departments of commerce and the interior before 1950 and between the departments of defense and energy in the post-1980s, especially in the Reagan, George H.W. and George W. Bush presidencies. This was not surprising given the technical requirements of those divisions. Van H. Manning, for instance, one of the most active exponents of industry-government cooperation in the early 1920s, was trained as a petroleum engineer and served with the u.s. Geological

Survey and the Bureau of Mines before becoming the director of research for the American Petroleum Institute in 1920. In 1924 Manning joined the Pan American Petroleum and Transport Company, one of the interested parties in Iraq petroleum development. Franklin K. Lane, secretary of the interior under Woodrow Wilson, was also an official with Pan American Petroleum by 1920. William B. Heroy, a geologist, served with the Geological Survey and the Fuel Administration during the war, before accepting an appointment as foreign operations manager with the Sinclair Consolidated Oil Corporation, also actively engaged in the search for foreign oil concessions. In the context of the Korean War, as chapter 10 details, Interior Secretary Oscar Chapman appointed Bruce Brown to head the Petroleum Administration for Defense. Brown had been a member of the board of Standard Oil and president of Standard subsidiary, Pan-Am Southern Corporation. There is no indication, however, that he had a significant impact on overall foreign oil policy. American governments consistently recruited individuals from industry because of their expertise, but as the Anglo-American oil discussions of the Kennedy and Johnson years suggested, American officials were cautious about their industry contacts and company officials were consistently cautious about the application of antitrust laws. There is little doubt that during the Reagan and two Bush administrations industry-government ties were very close, in particular with the linkages of Richard Cheney, Caspar Weinberger, and Donald Rumsfeld to such major global corporations as Bechtel and Halliburton, linkages detailed in chapter 12. President George H.W. Bush worked in the Texas oil industry before entering politics, as did his son and later president. Bush Sr was a co-founder of several companies in the course of the 1950s, including Zapata Petroleum Corporation and Zapata Off-Shore, which specialized in offshore drilling equipment. James A. Baker III, who served as one of Reagan's secretaries of the treasury and George H.W. Bush's first secretary of state, joined the Carlyle Group, a private global investment firm, as senior counsel in 1993 after leaving public office. Frank Carlucci, who succeeded Weinberger as Reagan's secretary of defense, also served on the Carlyle Group Advisory Board.[11]

On the whole, no common pattern emerged among officials active in shaping oil policy, at least insofar as their industry links were concerned. What they did have in common was their upper-middle-class backgrounds and similar educational experience, officials being drawn primarily from eastern ivy-league universities, some having received graduate training in Europe. Educational and even regional background became more diverse in the post-World War II era, with the increasing importance in Washington of Southern and Southwestern state politicians, especially from the Johnson administration forward, and of the

West in Richard Cheney's case. That some individuals who held major offices had oil industry links prior or subsequent to holding office does not in itself prove that they worked in the interests of the industry. Many officials did not have direct industry links, including Harold Brown, Carter's Secretary of Defense, who was a distinguished physicist and university administrator. Nonetheless, these men shared common class background and values. There is no indication that any key American political leaders in the post-1950 period questioned the need for energy security or the need for a private-public partnership in achieving that goal. Government officials predictably differed amongst themselves as well as with industry leaders over tactics, short-term objectives, and the degree of influence to be exercised by the state. For state officials, control over the access to foreign oil supplies was primarily a question of national security; for the companies it was a question of markets and profit. For state officials, security of petroleum supply increasingly took precedence over such considerations as antitrust policies, liberalization of international trade, and the strict application of the Open Door policy, theoretically committed to equality of access for all nationals, with no discrimination among American interests. The main objective of both the companies and the U.S. government prior to World War II was to break down colonial barriers and to gain access to British and Dutch spheres of influence to obtain new sources of supply, if not for immediate use, then as protection against the future. To accomplish this breakthrough, the United States had to contend not only with European rivalry but also with emergent nationalism.

At the opposite end of the interpretive spectrum from that which posits the state as the instrument of a dominant capitalist class is the statist thesis posited most recently and persuasively in the area of foreign oil policy by Stephen Krasner in his study *Defending the National Interest*. Krasner attempts to demonstrate that in oil policy the state not only has maintained a high degree of autonomy from the private sector but also has functioned essentially as an entity with entirely separate interests and objectives from those of the private sector.[12] My own reading of the evidence for the post-1919 years suggests a far higher degree of state-business harmony and cooperation than Krasner found, but his work serves as an important reminder that the state is considerably more than a neutral actor arbitrating among competing private interests in a pluralist society. We also need to recognize that foreign policy decision making is seldom if ever such a coherent, rational process as single-model explanations might lead one to conclude. Joan Hoff Wilson accurately captured the essence of that problem when she suggested that foreign policy is not "the exclusive result of rationally calculated national self-interest based on value-maximizing choices."[13]

When looking at the post-World War I years, one is struck by the high degree of concern that followed hard on the heels of war for the value of oil to American industrial and military power. Even though the initial fear of shortage proved ill founded by the late 1920s, official emphasis on the importance of overseas oil continued and served to shape oil policy throughout the postwar years. The Federal Oil Conservation Board, established by President Coolidge to investigate ways in which to preserve American oil, reported in 1926 that South American concessions were of primary importance to the United States. The United States military also adopted an increased interest in raw materials generally and in oil in particular. A 1921 report by the planning branch of the Office of the Assistant Secretary of War urged that the United States send a military mission to South America to investigate raw-material resources. Noting that the entry of the United States into the field of economic research was a departure from traditional practice, the report nonetheless cautioned: "We must guard against shortsighted military control which would neglect the economic features of modern combat."[14]

Concern with domestic oil depletion, the perceived importance of foreign oil concessions, and the thrust of American enterprise abroad sparked an extended and lively debate in official and business circles over the nature of u.s. foreign policy, the role of the state in the private sector, and the relationship among the major oil powers. Internationally a cooperative framework was fashioned among the major powers, exclusive of the Soviet Union, which remained beyond the debate in the first decade following the Bolshevik revolution. Before the 1950s that cooperative framework gave little attention to the potential role of third-world nations in the process. At the same time that the United States sought a cooperative basis for international oil development, it sought an effective working relationship with that segment of the oil industry that was active in foreign development. The government and the major companies established the basic pattern for cooperation that would be followed in the coming decades, with an emphasis on maximizing foreign holdings and sustaining the private enterprise model.

The orientation of u.s. foreign oil policy established in the pre-1950 years provided the framework, values, and to some degree the geographic focus of policy for the remainder of the twentieth century, although the Middle East had attained primacy of attention by the 1950s and 1960s. The basic principles of policy remained consistent in subsequent decades, although there were shifts in emphasis and in the intensity of concern among policymakers as global conditions evolved: a firm commitment to secure access to oil resources as vital to American national interest; antagonism to state enterprise and a preference for private-sector investment; a close working relationship between state actors and corporate officials, although this is not to imply that there was always agreement; a constant effort to reduce dependency on any single region of the world, in particular the Middle East; and an increased focus on the Western hemisphere in the aftermath of the two major oil shocks of the 1970s. Little changed in the administrative structure of decision making after the 1950s, although the tendency to concentrate power in the White House and in the hands of the president's closest advisors on the national security staff continued, as did the increasing importance of the Pentagon relative to the State Department. The one major administrative change of the post-World War II years did not come until the Carter administration and the establishment of the Department of Energy, an initiative that President Ford had also proposed. The Department of Energy absorbed the energy-related programs formerly administered by the departments of the Interior, Defense, Commerce, Housing and Urban Development, and the Interstate Commerce Commission. The National Petroleum Council, established by President Truman in 1946 under the Department of the Interior as an industry advisory council to provide guidance on technical and policy matters, was transferred to the jurisdiction of the Department of Energy in 1977. The Eisenhower administration established the Foreign Petroleum Supply Committee under the Department of the Interior in 1953. The committee, which was chaired by the assistant secretary of energy and minerals and remained in existence until the end of December 1976, consisted of representatives of twenty-two American oil companies engaged in foreign oil operations. Several ad hoc advisory committees were established from time to time in the post-World War II years to deal with emergency circumstances. These included the Emergency Petroleum Supply Committee, established by the Johnson administration to deal with the impact of the 1967 Arab-Israeli war, and the Project Independence Advisory Committee, established by the Nixon administration to address the challenges of the 1973–74 Arab oil embargo.[15]

In the post-World War II era, military and foreign policy planners shifted their position on the question of imports and domestic resources, increasingly pursuing the line of reasoning that national security required a well-developed domestic industry, with Naval Petroleum Reserves in a state of readiness and with a strategic petroleum reserve developed to meet emergency circumstances. Such thinking was naturally intensified by the Arab states–OPEC oil embargo of the 1970s, which underlined the dangers of reliance on foreign oil for any significant proportion of domestic requirements. Thus, from the 1950s on strategic planning continued to stress the need for secure access to foreign supplies, at the same time seeking to reduce dependency on such supplies.

After 1950 u.s. policymakers confronted a range of critical developments that influenced oil policy. Cold War and East-West tensions provided the larger context until the collapse of the Soviet Union in 1989. Even thereafter, Russia remained an important player in the Near and Middle East. The most significant challenge was the emergence of a stronger sense of solidarity among many of the developing nations that ranked among the leading world producers, especially in the Middle East. The institutional manifestation of that sense of solidarity was the establishment of OPEC (Organization of Petroleum Exporting Countries) in the 1960s. The capacity of OPEC members in the Middle East and Latin America to affect international price and supply significantly altered the balance of power to favour the Middle East producing countries, especially after the 1973 Arab oil embargo and the Iranian revolution that overthrew the Shah during the Carter presidency.

The Iranian revolution, the Soviet invasion of Afghanistan in 1979, the Iran-Iraq war in the 1980s, the consolidation of Saddam Hussein's power in Iraq, the increasing importance of Islamic fundamentalism, and then the al-Qaeda-inspired attack on the United States on 11 September 2001 brought the Middle East to the forefront of American policy. Since the end of the 1990s the United States has fought two major wars in the region against Iraqi forces and has established a significant military presence in Afghanistan to defeat the Taliban and to seek to destroy the supporters of al-Qaeda. Clearly not all of these developments were occasioned by the importance of oil resources in the region to the international economic world order, but it is difficult to imagine, in the post-Cold War environment, even given the traditional concern over Russian interests, that the United States would view the region as of the highest strategic interest without the oil reserves of the Middle East and Central Asia.

CHAPTER ONE

Forging Policy for the Postwar Era

In the several years that followed World War I, informed opinion in government circles and in the private sector became increasingly anxious about the security of American oil supplies and the international position of the United States in the search for resources. Although the United States remained a major producer and exporter of oil and oil products throughout these years, concern over an impending shortage for American use was an important factor in shaping United States diplomacy. There was particular concern that the United States was being outflanked by Great Britain in the international arena as the major companies extended their global reach. One consequence was what historian John DeNovo referred to as the search for an aggressive oil policy. Several individuals were especially prominent in the articulation of a harder line on international oil resources and their accessibility to American interests. Woodrow Wilson himself appears to have believed that Britain would be a major commercial competitor in the postwar era and saw the appointment of Sir Auckland Geddes, a prominent British business figure, as ambassador to the United States after the war as confirmation of his fears over British policy. Those who were leading advocates in the late Wilson administration of an aggressive United States policy included Josephus Daniels, secretary of the navy, a progressive reformer who frequently clashed with the oil companies over policy relating to naval oil reserves; Franklin K. Lane, secretary of the interior; Mark Requa, an engineer who had been director of the petroleum division of the United States Fuel Administration during the war and was by 1920 a vice-president of the Sinclair Consolidated Oil Company, one of the largest of the independents with international interests; Van H. Manning, who was postwar director of research for the American Petroleum Institute; Harry Garfield, in 1919 director of the U.S. Fuel Administration; George Otis Smith, director of

TABLE 1
United States Petroleum Production and Foreign Trade, 1920–46

| Yearly Average or Year | Quantity (thousands of barrels of 42 gallons) | | | | | |
| | Production | Imports | | Exports | | |
		Crude	Refined	Crude	Refined	Bunker oil
1921–5	647,961	94,857	12,545	13,330	76,455	36,501
1926–30	895,762	67,919	23,779	20,062	119,700	50,198
1931–5	889,311	38,395	23,901	36,413	70,896	34,868
1936–40	1,242,276	32,701	30,774	63,651	86,876	35,845
1940	1,353,214	43,085	40,528	51,495	63,960	35,037
1941	1,402,228	52,029	48,564	34,484	60,736	30,400
1942	1,386,645	13,540	25,780	35,560	71,251	25,417
1943	1,505,613	13,803	51,834	43,313	96,860	47,895
1944	1,677,904	44,846	56,663	31,802	161,854	71,815
1945	1,713,655	74,003	58,742	35,353	136,283	82,314
1946	1,733,424	89,210	57,047	42,574	90,884	62,494

Exports of refined oils include residuum prior to 1913 and natural gasoline prior to 1932, and exclude them thereafter. Exports exclude re-exported imported oil.

Source: U.S. Bureau of the Census, Statistical Abstract of the United States, 1948 (Washington 1948), 771.

the United States Geological Survey.[1] All of these men, whether they had industry ties, like Manning or Requa, or were antagonistic at times to the companies, like Daniels, concurred that the United States was compelled at that juncture to develop a vigorous overseas oil policy if American interests were not to be left behind by British and Dutch firms, whether government supported or entirely private enterprise. Daniels claimed in a diary entry early in 1920 that Great Britain was "taking over oil concessions and blowing them up and buying wells here," actions that in his opinion would provide Britain with a "great controlling influence on ... world commerce."[2]

In response to the urging of Requa, Manning, and Smith in early 1919, Garfield cautioned President Wilson that the United States should not "permit England to control supplies necessary to the maintenance of our industries ... our Navy and Merchant marine." Requa and the others emphasized the increasing consumption of petroleum products in the United States and warned that 40 percent of domestic oil had already been exhausted. Such alternative sources of petroleum as oil-shale extraction were perceived as too expensive at the time, with the result that attention shifted naturally to the development of foreign fields and the need for the United States government to provide strong support for its nationals in gaining access to and control over those reserves to offset the initiative of British and Dutch interests, whether government supported or not. Their recommendations provided the framework for debate on foreign oil policy during the coming decade and well into the 1940s. They wrote to Garfield:

This position of our country can and should be safeguarded and rendered secure by the Government giving moral support to every proper effort of American capital to make its circle of activity in oil production co-extensive with the new expansion of American shipping. This means a world-wide exploration, development, and producing company financed with American capital, guided by American engineering, and supervised in its international relations by the United States Government. In its foreign expansion, American business needs this Governmental partnership, and through it the interests of the public can best be safeguarded.[3]

Although the idea of a single American company, formally supported by the United States government, did not materialize, it is significant, especially in light of the debate in the 1940s over the Petroleum Reserves Corporation, that such an initiative should have come from individuals in the administration with close identification with the international oil industry. In the short run the recommendations had the effect of stimulating a review of oil policy in the State Department, passage in Congress of a Mineral Lands Leasing Act in 1920, and the unsuccessful effort the same year by California Senator James Phelan to create a government oil corporation.

The State Department review was a substantial one. The nineteen-page report prepared by the Subcommittee on Mineral Raw Materials, under the department's economic liaison committee, represented the work of the State Department, Fuel Administration, Geological Survey, Bureau of Mines, Shipping Board, War Trade Board, Federal Trade Commission, and the War Department. The report noted that in 1917 the U.S. produced 66.2 percent and consumed 63 percent of the world's total production, and indicated that the trend was toward increased reliance on oil products for naval and commercial shipping. Citing as evidence of impending domestic decline a paper given by the chief geologist of the Geological Survey at the 1919 annual meeting of the Society of Automotive Engineers, and a dated document submitted to the Senate in 1916 by Mark Requa, the committee concluded that the United States would find itself increasingly dependent on imported petroleum to meet its domestic industrial and military requirements.

The committee's recommendations were surprisingly vague given the level of concern expressed in its conclusions. It suggested that the government should take action to secure adequate reserves in foreign fields, especially the Gulf of Mexico and the Caribbean; government should adopt a policy of "encouraging, assisting, and protecting United States citizens in securing and developing petroleum properties in other countries"; try to prevent U.S. holders of domestic properties from transferring them to foreign nationals; cooperate with the companies to establish bunkering facilities in commercially strategic posts; and take "retaliatory measures as a final means to combat discrimination abroad." Even before the report was completed, the State Department instructed Caribbean area legations to report on oil deposits and the attitude of local governments toward the participation of foreign capital in the exploitation of those resources, and the committee recommended that U.S. consular and diplomatic officials be instructed to give particular attention to lending assistance to American firms seeking properties within their jurisdictions.[4]

During 1920 the support for a more expansive oil policy gained momentum. Former Secretary of the Interior Franklin Lane was quoted in the *Times* to the effect that the control of petroleum resources had become the most important international issue outside the League of Nations, as the United States and Britain sought to be independent in supplies. At the annual meeting of the American Petroleum Institute a few months later, Walter C. Teagle, president of Standard Oil of New Jersey, echoed Lane's concern that some foreign governments were "deliberately placing obstacles in the way of those who would like to assist in the development of new sources of supply," and stressed the need for the American petroleum industry to "look to the development of petroleum outside the country." George Otis Smith cautioned at the same time that American reserves were being exhausted. In late 1919, Secretary of State Robert Lansing informed the British ambassador that oil production in the United States would shortly peak, that its reserves faced exhaustion, and that the U.S. was especially vulnerable because of its high rates of consumption and the lack of American oil holdings abroad. Lansing's comments were prompted in part by Admiral William Benson, chief of the Office of Naval Operations, who had reported to Lansing that both his office and the Shipping Board believed that the only way for the U.S. to gain ground on British control over international oil was to insist "that the British Government concedes American nationals in British producing fields the same privileges that British nationals enjoy in American producing fields." He specifically targeted the Persian and Burmese fields as priorities.[5]

The American Petroleum Institute (API) formally urged the need for such a policy of reciprocity. At its meeting of 27 September 1919, the board of directors adopted a recommendation of its committee on foreign relations, chaired by Walter Teagle, that diplomatic negotiations be initiated with the British to establish reciprocity. The committee also drew attention to the restrictionist policies of Argentina, Japan, and the Netherlands, and cautioned against prolonging wartime controls in the United States. Bearing the vigorous title *The Menace of Foreign State Monopolies to the American Petroleum Industry*, the report was a clear indication of the direction of business sentiment at the end of the war, with its emphasis on aggressive expansion, competition with other nations, and maintenance of free enterprise.[6]

Similar views emanated from the American Institute of Mining and Metallurgical Engineering (AIMME), of which Herbert Hoover was president until he joined President Harding's cabinet as secretary of commerce. The petroleum section of the institute in early 1920 forwarded to President Wilson and Congress a resolution urging adoption of a more concrete and positive oil policy and the use of reciprocity to gain leverage for access to overseas natural resources.[7]

Congressmen began to bear some of the pressure for a change in policy and to lobby the State Department on behalf of their constituents. Pennsylvania representative Guy Campbell, for instance, informed Lansing that the president of the Transcontinental Oil Company of Pittsburgh, a Jersey subsidiary, claimed that foreign oil interests were protected from competition at home by their own governments and given active government support for acquiring "extensive holdings ... in American properties." Transcontinental's president, F.B. Parriott, urged the adoption of a "definite national policy" to enable Americans to retain control of domestic properties and compete effectively for the development of foreign fields.[8]

Department of State officials were uncertain how to proceed with the issue in the dying months of the Wilson administration. As one official observed to the secretary of the AIMME, the department did not believe it had the means to stimulate American corporate action abroad, to direct American capital to foreign petroleum development, or to challenge foreign companies. But the department's hand was forced by events at home and abroad. Internationally, American officials rapidly learned of a confidential agreement between Britain and France, the San Remo Agreement, in which they agreed to share participation in the petroleum development of Mesopotamia, North Africa, and other French colonies, as well as in Romania. Within a few days the department cabled the American ambassador in Britain instructing him to remind Britain of the U.S. position on equality of treatment in enemy territory acquired during the war, and requesting discussions on mandated territories, stressing the need for a cooperative relationship between the two countries. At the request of Congress, the department, under Acting Secretary Frank Polk, also prepared a report outlining the international restrictions on American oil operations abroad, which argued in general that although restrictions did exist, many, such as the British Defence of the Realm Act of 1915, grew out of the war and were likely temporary, and it was too early to determine either their long-term impact or how newly organized governments would deal with petroleum development. The document nonetheless provided evidence of extensive restrictionism throughout the British and Dutch empires, where prospecting licenses and concessions were often granted only to British or Dutch subjects. In the Netherlands East Indies, only residents and companies incorporated under Dutch laws with boards of directors composed of a majority of Dutch subjects were eligible to obtain concessions. At that time, Royal Dutch Shell had a complete monopoly over production in the area. Without clear evidence of a strong national oil policy, American companies were reluctant to extend their operations and thus accomplish the general objectives of that policy.[9]

There was a flurry of activity in early 1920 among government officials concerned about a potential oil shortage. The Council of National Defense, including Secretary of State Polk, Secretary of War Newton Baker, Secretary of the Navy Daniels, Van H. Manning and Wesley Frost of the Office of the Foreign Trade Adviser, drew up recommendations to forward to President Wilson. It was agreed that if an actual shortage materialized, the government would have to take up its royalty oil in leased lands, exercise its option on production in the Oklahoma Osage Reservation, try to encourage Mexican production, embargo exports of fuel oil in an effort to gain access to British empire oil, open naval oil reserves, and consider reconversion of some vessels to coal. Frost subsequently informed Polk that "in future it is going to be necessary for this Government to work with the oil men in encouraging development abroad ... The Government should take all pains to establish just and cordial relations with the oil men."[10] The State Department also vigorously objected to Britain's conclusion of the San Remo Agreement. British officials with equal vigor denied that Britain was attempting to threaten American supremacy in petroleum production or to adopt measures inconsistent with the American interpretation of most-favored-nation clauses in treaties.[11]

THE PHELAN PROPOSAL AND
THE MINERAL LEASING ACT

In May 1920, the Democratic California senator and chairman of the Senate Committee on Irrigation and Reclamation of Arid Lands James D. Phelan introduced a motion proposing the organization of a United States oil corporation along the lines of the United States Shipping

Board's Emergency Fleet Corporation to direct a general effort to acquire foreign oil concessions. Phelan had already tested his idea with
little success on Secretary of the Interior John Payne, to whom he wrote
on 21 April: "If we are not prepared to back up our nationals in the
world field ... there is but one thing to do, and that is to organize a corporation ... and properly finance it so that this Government can secure
oil properties outside the territory of the United States." The Senate
motion was referred to the Committee on Public Lands, where it died.
But its consideration underlined the depth of attachment to a free-
enterprise model in foreign oil development even at a time when there
was a perceived strong need for vigorous government support for
American nationals abroad.[12] Objections voiced to the idea were
similar to those articulated twenty years later during discussion of the
Petroleum Reserves Corporation, that foreign governments would be
unwilling to grant a government corporation access to petroleum
resources because of the threat to national security and sovereignty
such a corporation could pose. Moreover, critics remained unconvinced that a government corporation would be able to provide a
stronger guarantee than private enterprise of foreign supply, since host
nations would retain ultimate jurisdiction in either case. In a report
prepared for the API, Assistant Secretary of State Norman Davis indicated that he saw little likelihood of a government oil corporation
being established, but did anticipate the establishment of a policy that
closely linked business and government.[13]

The failure of Phelan's proposal to gain administration support did
not deter him from speaking out on the international oil issue. In
January 1921 he and Senator William McKellar, a Tennessee Democrat,
introduced bills attempting to impose penalties on the nationals of
those governments that restricted the operations of American petroleum interests.[14] The McKellar proposal would have prohibited exports
of oil products to those nations that discriminated against American nationals in the acquisition of such products. His motion also requested
the U.S. Shipping Board to report on the incidents of discrimination.
McKellar indicated that he had been prompted to act by the findings of
his investigation into British war debts that suggested that Britain had a
greater capacity to pay than was admitted and was diverting capital
into foreign oil development. As with other individuals who advocated
a harder American oil policy, McKellar was convinced that State Department policy was ineffectual in contrast to the British.

The Phelan and McKellar proposals, in spite of their failure to gain
passage, reflected a broader American effort to improve the competitive capacity of American interests abroad, a sentiment that led Congress to pass the Mineral Leasing Act in early 1920; this legislation had

the support of the departments of state and commerce, and the attorney general's office. The legislation enabled the Department of the Interior, which had jurisdiction over public lands, to refuse to grant drilling and operating permits on public lands to the nationals of those nations which did not provide reciprocal privileges to American citizens. That spring Congress also transferred control of the Naval Petroleum Reserves from the Department of the Interior to the Department of the Navy, and requested President Wilson to report on the extent of restrictions imposed on oil development in their territories by Mexico, Britain, France, Holland, and Japan.[15] The Wilson and subsequently the Harding administrations viewed such legislation as a weapon by which the British and Dutch governments would be compelled to cooperate with the United States in facilitating equality of access to oil-producing areas, possibly with more American willingness to have European participation in the western hemisphere as a trade-off for American access to the Middle East and the East Indies. Such a threat was a real one to British and Dutch interests. Royal Dutch Shell's main subsidiary in the U.S., for instance, was very active in the naval petroleum reserves, in 1919–20 taking one-third of all the crude oil produced on the reserves and two-thirds of the gasoline produced.[16] Nor was the U.S. reluctant to use the legislation: Holland was treated as a nonreciprocating nation until the end of the 1920s with the settlement of the Dutch East Indies issues; Britain was able to take advantage of the recognition of the Netherlands as a reciprocating nation at the end of the decade, but remained a nonreciprocating nation through the Hoover years. Early in the period, the Department of the Interior denied permits to Shell,[17] which in turn contended that the American policy had seriously reduced their competitiveness in U.S. territory. Shell Union Company of California was interested in Alaska properties in the mid-1920s but refrained from attempting to enter the area because of the leasing act. As California Union Oil official G. Leigh-Jones informed Deterding and Kessler in late 1925: "The position which we have to face at the moment is that we are now losing what may be good opportunities in California and Colorado and also in Alaska." At the same time, the Royal Dutch Shell Group clearly thought that the group's interests in the Far East were more important than the Shell Union's American operations, and if the company did not press vigorously for the United States to grant reciprocal status to Holland and Britain initially, it would appear to have been for that reason.[18]

The diplomatic negotiations surrounding the issue of reciprocal treatment for oil development were prolonged and arduous, and it is not the intent to trace them in detail here. What is important is the perspective of both the British and American governments. During consideration of the leasing bill in Congress, the British ambassador to the United States, Auckland Geddes, expressed the view that although British restrictions in some colonial areas were restrictive and anachronistic, the issue was not one that should hamper Anglo-American relations, since he thought that it was essentially Standard Oil interests that were anxious to have the U.S. pursue a harder line. Standard Oil should, he reported, have been placated by then-current discussions with Anglo-Persian Oil with a view to cooperation in the rich North Persian area, a project Herbert Hoover was especially anxious to bring to fruition.

Archaic as some of the British colonial restrictions may have been, there was considerable resistance in some British circles to tampering with them. The Board of Trade and the Foreign Office were initially very reluctant to alter policy because of concern over the security of foreign supply, something which was of even greater concern for Britain with its lack of domestic resources at that time. A 1920 Foreign Office memorandum reflected the degree of the concern. Citing a 1917 document produced by the Lord Balfour Committee on Commercial and Industrial Policy after the war, the memo concluded that "the experience of the war has shown that some special form of government control is necessary in respect of a certain number of commodities of vital military importance, the supply of which within the British Empire is limited." Yet the Balfour committee had also concluded that an explicit policy of excluding foreign capital in areas other than a few vital ones was unwise.

Foreign Office officials were also well aware that it was access to the British sphere of influence and territories rather than Britain itself that was sought by American oil interests, and it would consequently be of little value to reduce or eliminate restrictions in Britain. One of the crucial difficulties was how to reconcile the interests of a nation that produced nearly 70 percent of world oil output from its own territory with a nation that produced only 3 percent of its requirements from its own territories but was one of the three major consumers, importing some sixty-seven million pounds sterling worth of petroleum products in 1920, only 2 percent of which came from British territories. British officials also tended to point out that in spite of imperial restrictions, American firms were very active in petroleum development in the empire, specifically Imperial Oil in Canada and General Asphalt of Philadelphia in Trinidad, which in 1920 was one of the largest producers in the western hemisphere.[19]

Such arguments did not convince those oil companies anxious to develop in British territories. A.C. Veatch, for instance, of Sinclair Development Corporation, explained to the State Department that although

British restrictions of oil development in Canada to British or Canadian companies did not apply to private lands, much of the prospective oil development was in western Canada, where activity was almost entirely on state lands.[20]

American foreign oil policy in the 1920s consequently became wedded to attempting to accomplish equality of access for American nationals and to the maintenance of reciprocity among the major oil nations. That policy was very clear, at least in outline, before Woodrow Wilson left office. Secretary of State Bainbridge Colby observed to the British that because of the shortage of petroleum, its increasing commercial significance, and the growing importance of supplies from undeveloped regions of the world, the U.S. desired peaceful and enlightened international petroleum principles recognized by all nations.[21] By 1920 there was a ubiquitous agreement among American of-

TABLE 2
American Investments in Oil Production Abroad (in millions of dollars)

Location	1908	1914	1919	1924	1929	1935
Europe	3.5	8	7.5	12	20	20
Romania	2.5	5	7.5	12	20	20
Russia	1.0	3	–	–	–	–
Canada and Newfoundland	15	25	30	40	55	55
West Indies	2	3	5	32	52	52
Aruba	–	–	–	25	45	45
Trinidad	2	3	5	7	7	7
Mexico	50	85	200	250	206	206
Central America	–	–	3	3	3.5	3.5
South America	5	22	83	220	444.5	426
Colombia	–	2	20	55	136	126
Peru	3	15	45	65	68.5	60
Venezuela	2	5	18	100	240	240
Asia	–	–	–	15	73	110
Arabia (including Bahrein, Iraq, Palestine)	–	–	–	–	1	10
Syria, Cyprus	–	–	–	–	7	25
Netherlands East Indies	–	–	–	15	65	75
Total	75.5	143	328.5	572	854	872

Source: adapted from Cleona Lewis, America's Stake in International Investments (Washington 1938), 588.

ficials that it was, in William R. Manning's terms, "the psychological time to define the principles for which the State Department stands before the oil men," and they agreed that it would have a beneficial effect on British opinion to reassure American enterprise of official support. Among policymakers there was some difference of opinion on the geographic areas that should receive primary focus, with Wesley Frost, foreign trade adviser in the department, stressing Latin America and

TABLE 3
Foreign Investment of United States Oil Companies by Major Activities and by Hemisphere (in thousands of dollars)

| | Cumulative investment, 1918-44[1] | | | |
| | Gross assets[2] | | Net assets[3] | |
	Amount	% world total	amount	% world total
Exploration and production	1,289,550	41	851,753	40
Refining	431,526	14	255,548	12
Transportation	161,653	5	93,142	4
Marketing	819,292	25	568,889	26
All others	459,706	15	390,877	18
Total	3,161,727	100	2,160,209	100
Western Hemisphere (excluding U.S.)				
Exploration and production	1,155,508	61	761,085	61
Refining	243,529	13	130,534	10
Transportation	137,409	7	81,730	7
Marketing	184,195	10	123,156	10
All others	171,008	9	158,725	12
Total	1,891,649	100	1,255,230	100
Eastern Hemisphere				
Exploration and production	134,042	11	90,668	10
Refining	187,997	14	125,014	14
Transportation	24,244	2	11,412	1
Marketing	635,097	50	445,733	49
All others	288,698	23	232,152	26
Total	1,270,078	100	904,979	100

[1] Total amount invested at the end of 1944, plus all gross amounts written off or revalued since 1918.

[2] All assets and investments including current assets and gross fixed capital assets.

[3] All assets and investments including current and fixed capital assets at depreciated values.

Source: National Industrial Conference Board, *The Petroleum Almanac* (New York 1946), 359, based on "American Petroleum Interests in Foreign Countries," a report to the Senate Committee Investigating Petroleum Resources, 15 October 1945.

TABLE 4
American Oil Company Holdings in Foreign Countries, 1921

Country	Production (barrels daily)	Holdings (acres)
Mexico		
Atlantic Refining Co	5,000	130,500
Pan American Petroleum and Transport Co	200,000	1,500,000
General Petroleum Corporation	–	50,000
Mexican Gulf Oil Company	75,000	250,000
Sinclair Consolidated Oil Corporation	large, but no precise data	
Sun Oil Company	–	leases
Texas Company	large, but no precise data	
Tidewater Oil Company	–	leases
Union Oil Company	–	20,000
Panama		
Panama Gulf Oil Company	–	3,000
Sinclair Consolidated Oil Company	–	1,300,000
Colombia		
Union Oil Company of California	–	small
Texas Company	–	exploration
Costa Rica		
Sinclair Consolidated	–	1,000,000
Pan American Petroleum	–	concessions
Standard Oil of California	–	concessions
Venezeula		
Sun Oil Company	–	2,000,000
Texas Company	–	prospecting
Haiti		
Sinclair Consolidated	–	entire island
Trinidad		
Sinclair Consolidated	–	leases
Poland		
Vacuum Oil Company	–	concessions
Angola		
Sinclair Consolidated	–	50,000,000
Timor		
Sinclair Consolidated	–	5,000,000
Sakhalin		
Sinclair Consolidated	–	Russian half
Asia Minor		
Standard Oil Company of New York	–	1,527,244

Source: "Oil Interests in Foreign Countries," June 1921, Commerce files, OF, oil, Herbert Hoover Presidential Library.

with others increasingly turning at this early stage to the potential of the Middle East. By the close of the Wilson administration, American oil policy was firmly established on a basis of business-government cooperation, in which it was the role of the government to facilitate the competitive capabilities of the private sector abroad, and to ensure access to foreign resources as well as security of supply for the United States. The U.S. also sought a broadening of international cooperation in oil development, although it was prepared to use restrictive policies to combat what it perceived as protectionism overseas. The result was that by the beginning of the Harding administration, with Charles Evans Hughes serving as secretary of state and Herbert Hoover as secretary of commerce, the time "seemed ripe for negotiations with Great Britain regarding world petroleum questions."[22]

The Harding administration inherited not only the basic orientation of its oil policy from the Wilson administration but also its geographic focus. In a carefully prepared memorandum on oil policy drafted for the Harding administration, Arthur C. Millspaugh identified the most significant countries and areas for development as Colombia, Venezuela, Argentina, Mesopotamia, Ecuador, Bolivia, North Africa, and Japan, and placed the Arabian peninsula in a third list of remote "possibles," suggesting that even in the 1920s American officials were not endowed with total prescience. It was also significant that although Millspaugh was one of the strong advocates of an Anglo-American understanding on international oil, he approached such a position from a nationalist perspective, suggesting that if British nationals were to gain an extensive control of the fuel bunkering business in foreign ports, "such control might be used to place American ships at a disadvantage."[23]

CONSOLIDATING THE OPEN DOOR

The Harding administration's contribution to the development of a foreign oil policy was severalfold, although it departed little from the basic precepts established by its Democratic predecessor. It sought to maintain a close government / business relationship; it exercised vigorous diplomacy to move toward reciprocity with Britain and the Netherlands under the terms of the 1920 leasing act, especially with respect to the Middle East and the Dutch East Indies; and it sought to counteract, with limited success, the evolution of nationalist and confiscatory policies in the Soviet Union and in Mexico. Such efforts were neither as weak nor as ineffectual as they have been portrayed by historians, although not all the objectives were realized during the Harding years.[24]

As secretary of state, Charles Evans Hughes confronted the remnants of the public debate over a foreign oil policy, and an intensification of dissention between the major firms and the independents over oil import duties. He also faced Cabinet rivalries from Secretary of Commerce Herbert Hoover and Secretary of the Interior Albert Fall, until the latter left office as a result of the scandal that arose from his leasing of the Teapot Dome reserves to personal friends. Hughes emerged in essential control of oil policy from these interdepartmental struggles, even though Hoover continued to exercise a high degree of influence because of his close links with the private sector and his insistence that he be consulted on all matters relating to foreign economic policy.[25] Congress also played a continuing part in the debate during the Harding years. It was the essential forum for discussion of the ultimately unsuccessful effort to have a duty imposed on imported crude oil. Oil was a distinct issue during Senate discussions of the Thompson-Urrutia Treaty between Colombia and the United States, resolving the issues outstanding between the two countries since the friction created by questionable American involvement in the Panamanian independence movement during the Roosevelt administration. Although oil was not a specific component in the treaty, it was generally assumed that potential Colombian petroleum development was a factor in the Senate's willingness to compromise and offer an indemnity payment. Denying that he had been influenced by the oil lobby, Senator Henry Cabot Lodge, in part at the urging of Albert Fall, nonetheless articulated the prevailing wisdom that "the question of oil is ... vital to every great maritime nation." Lodge urged strong diplomatic support for American investors abroad and distributed a map of the world indicating the extent of Royal Dutch Shell operations. Both Lodge and Fall inaccurately portrayed Shell as a British government enterprise, an impression that British Ambassador Geddes and Shell legal adviser Avery D. Andrews promptly sought to correct.[26]

Hughes kept Congress at bay over the oil tariff, with the support of both Hoover and Fall, and with the submission to the Senate of a supplementary report outlining the restrictions on American petroleum prospectors abroad. At the same time he took the initiative in establishing policy. Before the Senate debate on the oil tariff and the Colombian treaty had concluded, Hughes approached a diverse group of public officials and the executive officers of the major petroleum companies, inviting them to suggest specific provisions that might be included in agreements on petroleum trade and develoment that could be concluded with other nations.[27] At the same time, the department established an interdepartmental committee under the chairmanship of the foreign trade adviser. This government body was intended to work closely with the American Institute of Mining and Metallurgical Engineering's committee on foreign oil policy. The latter, in the spring of 1921, included, among others, Mark Requa, David White of the U.S. Geological Survey, A.W. Ambrose of the Bureau of Mines, the noted petroleum geologist Everett DeGolyer, Van H. Manning of the API, and A. Veatch of the Sinclair companies. The institute's report was indicative of the approach of the more internationally oriented figures in the private sector. It recommended the repeal of the restrictive provisions in the 1920 leasing act and firm diplomacy to ensure equality of treatment of American nationals abroad, with no stipulation on the nationality of shareholders or management. The report also reaffirmed the opposition to direct government financial involvement in the industry.[28] Such views were similar to those expressed to Herbert Hoover when he met in early May with many of the main industry spokesmen, including William Mellon, H.F. Sinclair, J.W. Van Dyke, Manning, Doheny, and J. Howard Pew. John Barneson, president of the General Petroleum Corporation, in a premeeting letter, informed Hoover that there was a definite need for a high degree of government protection of American interests overseas, which in his view had not been forthcoming in the previous eight years. "I think," he concluded, "all that is necessary is a firm hand in dealing with foreign questions where our citizens acquire property."[29]

There was some support for the negotiation of a more general international agreement on oil, specifically with Great Britain, and much of the initiative came from Arthur Millspaugh. Millspaugh was concerned not only about British and French intent in negotiating the San Remo Agreement but also about the ability of the American government to direct U.S. companies along lines consistent with American foreign policy, and cited as an example of the problem the possibility of a restrictive agreement among the companies for the Turkish Petroleum Company concession in Mesopotamia and the recent conclusion of a monopolistic arrangement in Czechoslovakia by a French subsidiary of Jersey Standard. Although Millspaugh's idea of a formal international agreement received neither industry nor administration endorsement at the time, major industry spokesmen such as A.C. Bedford, chairman of Jersey, and E.C. Lufkin, chairman of the Texas Company, shared his suspicion of British intent, advocated the pursuit of reciprocity, and urged that attention be directed to recent developments in areas that were coming under the control of former allies, such as mandated territories, to ensure that restrictive privileges not be concluded that reduced the competitiveness of American enterprise.[30]

Hughes pursued policies that were consistent with industry objectives. In part as an effort to correct damage to Anglo-American relations committed by Albert Fall in his earlier lobbying of Senator Lodge and the Senate Foreign Relations Committee, Hughes informed the British ambassador that the U.S. objective was simply to "open avenues of legitimate enterprise for the development of natural resources, free from monopolistic concessions or privileges and from the restraint of discriminatory legislation."[31] Bedford expressed similar ideas at the first annual meeting of the international Chamber of Commerce in London, which he attended as representative of the American Petroleum Institute. Eight of the twenty-seven resolutions adopted at the meetings related directly to the production of raw materials, and the resolutions embodied nondiscriminatory regulations governing their development. Van Manning saw such developments as an indication of British willingness to cooperate with American interests, perhaps involving an amalgamation of private interests in the oil development of the Middle East. Manning thought this was the general preference of John Cadman, who was technical adviser on petroleum to the British government and shortly to become general manager of the D'Arcy Exploration Company, the subsidiary of Anglo-Persian.[32]

Manning tended to overestimate the British consensus at this stage in support of a more liberal international oil policy. Although the Foreign Office and Petroleum Department were moving in that direction, Admiralty representatives on an interdepartmental petroleum committee emphasized the need to retain at least the regulation requiring oil produced in the empire to be refined in British territory. The Foreign Office was sympathetic as well to Anglo-Persian–Jersey cooperation in northern Persia, the government because it was hoped it would promote Persian political stability, reduce competition among the companies, and reduce Anglo-American tension over oil questions. From Anglo-Persian's perspective, such cooperation was a concession to government desires, and it was prepared to cooperate as long as it retained the marketing rights for Persia. Neither the companies nor the British government were prepared to countenance the participation by American interests in activities in the Persian Gulf area. To Sir P. Lloyd-Greame of the Foreign Office, cooperation with the Americans at that stage was both good business and good policy.[33]

The Colonial Office shared the restrictionist inclinations of the Admiralty in 1921. To Colonial Office officials, the source of conflict with the United States was not general restriction on oil development in the empire but rather in isolated areas, such as Mesopotamia, where the dispute involved a specific concession. The United States already possessed a natural advantage over Britain in oil development, and to the Colonial Office, British policies needed to work to counteract that advantage, especially since American interests already had the right to participate in the exploitation of crown lands and to have access to private lands within the empire. With respect to Burma, where Standard Oil was anxious to gain a footing, the India Office was concerned that the American intent was to obtain a monopoly over the oil trade in Burma and to allow the actual development of the oil fields to stagnate rather than to upset market conditions with surplus oil in the region.[34]

Discussions with the British and French governments over the Netherlands East Indies and Mesopotamia provided the specific context for the application of more abstract policy and for the development of a more internationalist position by both the U.S. and British-Dutch interests. In the first instance, negotiations led to the admission of U.S. firms into the highly attractive and previously protected Djambi fields in the Dutch East Indies. In the second, a more formalized arrangement brought partnership for a group of American companies, incorporated as the Near East Development Corporation, in the Turkish Petroleum Company.

The Dutch East Indies

From 1920 to 1928, when the United States recognized the Netherlands as a reciprocating nation under the Leasing Act, the question of American access to the Djambi oil fields in Central Sumatra was one of the main formative issues in the development of U.S. foreign oil policy. Debate over this issue demonstrated not only a high level of continuity in American policy from the late Wilson through the Coolidge administrations, but also the geographical breadth of commitment of American power in support of U.S.-based enterprise in the effort to acquire foreign petroleum concessions. Part of this objective derived from the intent to expand the American merchant marine which, as Secretary of the Navy Edwin Denby indicated, required fueling stations on world trade routes, preferably under American control and developed by American business interests. In a period of often alleged isolationism, the United States acted in firm defense of its nationals abroad and with a clear conception of its national interest, efforts that drew the United States further into the vortex of global expansion. The debate over the East Indies suggests that the commitment had little to do with abstract, ideological considerations, but rather derived from a pragmatic perception of the American need for strategic raw materials. Throughout the debate, the United States pressed for several objectives: access to the mineral resources of the area on the basis of equality, not only with other foreign nationals but also with Dutch enterprise, private or public. It did not insist on identical but rather equivalent treatment. State Department officials were also cautious not to show favoritism for one American corporation over another, although of the two main companies actively seeking concessions, Sinclair Consolidated of New York, as an independent rather than one of the major firms, had considerable appeal to officials sensitive to criticism that they tended to act primarily in the interest of the majors. Officials also preferred a public agreement on principles between the Netherlands and the United States, even though they recognized that private negotiations would be necessary to arrange the details of any specific concession.[35]

The involvement of American firms in the development of Dutch East Indies petroleum predated World War I, when Jersey Standard obtained concessions and operating licenses through a Dutch subsidiary, Koloniale, in Java, Sumatra, and Borneo. By 1920, the Netherlands East Indies was producing over fifteen million barrels of crude oil, most of which was exported as crude oil or fuel oil, benzine, gasoline, and kerosene. The Bataafsche Petroleum Maatschappij, which was 40 percent British Shell and 60 percent Royal Dutch, was the dominant company in Borneo and Sumatra. None of the early American properties proved of commercial value by the end of the war, with the result that American interests sought access to the Djambi fields, in which Royal Dutch Shell was active,[36] and they obtained official support for their endeavor. American officials were concerned that the Dutch authorities would transfer former German properties to Royal Dutch, as well as properties which might become available. This suspicion was heightened by the passage in 1917 of a Dutch East Indies mining law requiring majority Dutch control on the boards of directors of mineral extracting firms. Early in 1920, the State Department instructed its representatives in Java and The Hague to determine whether or not oil lands were closed to American citizens, whether special status was accorded Royal Dutch Shell, and to protest against any discrimination.[37]

That fall an application of the Sinclair Consolidated Oil Corporation for the right to participate in the development of the Djambi fields was turned down by East Indies authorities at the same time that a restrictive concession was granted to Royal Dutch. The Department of State was moved to press forward in its effort to obtain a nonrestrictive policy in the area. As Secretary of State Colby informed American minister in the Netherlands William Phillips, "a measure of exclusion ... would seem to compromise in that region the principle of equal opportunity which it is hoped may be a solution for the future oil problem throughout the world." The department stressed to the Dutch foreign ministry that "the interest of the Government of the United States lies in the recognition of the principle of neutral or reciprocal access to vital natural resources by the nationals of the United States and by those of foreign countries." Phillips also cautioned that the Department of the

Interior, which had been permitting corporations to acquire mining titles in the U.S. even if a major portion of the stock was held by foreigners, would find it necessary to modify that practice unless the Netherlands granted reciprocal treatment to American nationals.[38]

Even though Charles Evans Hughes pressed the issue with equal vigor the following year, he did so to little effect. The Dutch Parliament passed legislation granting the Djambi concession to Royal Dutch in mid-1921 and took little notice of an offer from Jersey to enter into a contract to join a Dutch company in compliance with East Indies mining laws.[39] Throughout, the Dutch government maintained that the Jersey affiliate, the Koloniale, had a smaller production than other companies not because of discriminatory legislation but "exclusively because other companies ... started much earlier with the exploitation of oil fields and therefore obtained better fields." The Netherlands chargé d'affaires in Washington also expressed the hope to Hughes that the American government would not press the Djambi issue further, that the legislation was already an accomplished fact, and additional agitation would only lend strength to more restrictionist sentiment. American capital, he indicated, was welcome in the other fields.[40]

As in other areas, the British government appears to have been sympathetic to the American position, if only because it hoped that if American interests were entitled to participate in the Djambi fields, the British would be able to obtain a share in the concession for a company "more representative of British interests than the Royal Dutch." Americans also saw cooperation with the British as the most likely way to offset competition from Germany and Japan for oil development in the East Indies, as well as the restrictionism of Dutch policy in its colonies.[41]

Shell companies used the opportunity afforded by the East Indies debate to attack the British imperial restrictions and their effect on Shell operations in the United States, with the major oil development possibilities that existed there. At the same time that there was general support in the Shell group for the principle of the Open Door, however, there was no desire to see Standard Oil or other American interests acquire a competitive advantage overseas. In the case of the Netherlands East Indies, Shell officials noted that there was a danger that Standard Oil would benefit over Shell in the Netherlands' effort to gain recognition as a reciprocating nation from the U.S.[42] Shell officials in the United States also argued that no grants should be made in the East Indies to Standard Oil until the United States modified the Leasing Act and showed greater leniency in granting permits to foreign enterprise on public lands. As Shell official Avery D. Andrews in the U.S. argued to J.E.F. deKok in The Hague, in commenting on the recent recommendation of the U.S. Oil Conservation Board that American companies seek foreign oil properties, "if the United States advocates the open door abroad, it must first remove restrictions at home." Shell group officials agreed that the U.S. should modify its policies, especially toward the Shell Union Oil Company's operations in California, but it was also agreed that it was the Shell Union's responsibility in the U.S. rather than that of the group to lead the campaign, in which they anticipated the support of Jersey.[43] After the United States recognized the Netherlands in 1928 as a reciprocating nation, Andrew Agnew of Shell raised the issue of British restrictions once again with the British Petroleum Department. Agnew noted that Shell, because of its Dutch affiliation, would be able to minimize its difficulties, but that a British company without that connection would be unable to do so. "From Empire point of view," he stressed, "it is abundantly clear that these non-reciprocating laws should be abolished, especially when it is remembered that Great Britain depends almost entirely upon foreign sources of supply for its petroleum products."[44] For the moment, there was no change in the British position.

In late 1927 / early 1928 the American persistence in the East Indies bore fruit with the negotiation of a grant to the Koloniale in the Djambi fields at the same time that Royal Dutch Shell obtained additional concessions contiguous to their operating properties. Confirmation of the Koloniale contract and recognition of the principle of the Open Door resulted in extension to Holland of reciprocal status under the Leasing Act. When the Dutch minister for the colonies introduced the enabling legislation, he indicated that he regarded the American character of the company as an advantage, in that it reflected the ability of the East Indies to attract productive foreign capital. For both Koloniale and the State Department, the grant to the company capped eight years of negotiations, and added substantially to the commitment the company had already made to the area. Although Koloniale in 1924 acquired title to a former Shell concession in Telang Akar, struck oil there and began construction of a refinery, and the following year received development rights to another 600,000 acres of land, the Djambi grant had much greater symbolic value from the American point of view, reflecting a victory for Open Door diplomacy. Insofar as one of the American objectives had been to counteract Japanese interests in the area it failed, however, because shortly after the confirmation of the Djambi concession to Koloniale, the Netherlands granted a small (25,000 acres) concession to a Japanese firm, the Mitsui Bussan Kaisha, in North Borneo. But the door was now clearly open for American capital. Standard Oil of California began exploration work in the Dutch East Indies in the mid-1920s; after 1936 it joined ranks with the Texas Company. Between 1930 and the outbreak of World War II, which totally disrupted operations, the Standard-Vacuum Company expended more than $4.5 million on exploration in the area. At the beginning of the period only Standard Oil had been active in the Far East, and as State Department official Francis B. Loomis observed in 1924 to Hoover, there was a "pressing need for petroleum production in the Asiastic Tropical countries" if the United States were going to be able to ensure supplies of bunker fuel for the American navy and merchant vessels. The Netherlands East Indies was the most promising area if access could be obtained. Strategic and commercial considerations combined, therefore, to bring a concerted American effort to consolidate its position in the area during the 1920s.[45]

Mesopotamia

The American effort to gain a foothold within the British-dominated territories of the former Ottoman Empire was equally protracted and only partially successful by 1928. Company and government negotiations resulted in the incorporation into the Turkish Petroleum Company of five American firms: Jersey Standard, Standard Oil of New York, Gulf Oil, Atlantic Refining, and the Pan American Petroleum Corporation, a subsidiary of Indiana Standard. Together they formed the Near East Development Corporation to become equal partners with British and French interests in the Turkish Petroleum Company, whose claims to concessions predated World War I. As with the American-Netherlands negotiations, those over Mesopotamia began shortly after the war in a context of widespread government anxiety over potential petroleum shortages and with American firms anxious to tap Middle East resources to improve their marketing positions in Europe and the Far East. From the American perspective, the primary issue in Mesopotamia was, as in the East Indies, recognition of the principle of equality of access to international resources, a principle Britain was as reluctant to apply to its sphere of influence as the Netherlands was to its colonies in the 1920s. Although the Anglo-American modus vivendi that was achieved by 1928 gained access for the American group, it represented a victory more for American power than for the principle of the Open Door, and the agreement was of a limited nature rather than one which threw the resources of Mesopotamia open to the international petroleum industry.

In June 1922, Charles Evans Hughes authorized Jersey Standard chairman A.C. Bedford to negotiate with officials of the Anglo-Persian Oil Company a practical basis for entering Iraq. Hughes imposed two conditions: that the principle of the Open Door should be respected, and that the State Department should have the right to approve any agreement.[46] Neither Hughes nor his successor Frank Kellogg departed significantly from these conditions, but they, as well as other major officials such as Herbert Hoover, recognized the need for a higher degree of cooperation among firms active internationally than might have been acceptable under domestic antitrust laws. Indeed, Hoover early in the decade suggested that American oil firms interested in enhancing their ability to compete for foreign concessions should form a single company to do so. Although his initiative failed, he continued to work vigorously in subsequent years to encourage an effective cooperative relationship among the companies and between the public and private sectors.[47]

The Near East Development Corporation was the closest the international companies came in the 1920s to the formation of a single company for foreign development work. In 1928 several companies did cooperate to establish a Webb-Pomerene corporation, the Export Petroleum Association, Inc. The idea of a single enterprise to facilitate cooperative action in the international sector held considerable attraction for some officials and appears to have had a distinct influence during negotiations over access to the Turkish Petroleum Company. Van H. Manning of the API was one of the leading exponents of this approach early in the decade, and the concept also received attention in the Bureau of Foreign and Domestic Commerce (BFDC) on the eve of the Red Line Agreement. J.H. Nelson of the bureau suggested at that time a merger of American interests abroad under the provisions of the Webb-Pomerene Act, which some analysts believed made possible the division of foreign markets by otherwise competing American firms. Nelson was convinced that the export prices received by American corporations were adversely affected by several factors, including the perceived opposition of Royal Dutch Shell, the British and Dutch governments, artificially low-priced Soviet oil, and the tendency toward state oil monopolies abroad.[48]

The Hoover, Manning, and Nelson concept did not meet with unanimous support in government or business circles. Joseph McGrath of the BFDC's minerals division noted to director Julius Klein that a number of American producers of copper, cement, and zinc had combined under the Webb-Pomerene Act to reduce competition among American firms in foreign markets, but he queried the feasibility of accomplishing the same objective for the development of petroleum in foreign-owned fields. Nelson also underestimated industry opposition. Jersey Standard counsel, for instance, expressed concern that a purely American combination under the Webb Act would produce retaliation from other petroleum nations, would interfere with the operation of supply / demand factors, and would make it impossible to establish prices or production quotas satisfactory to all parties. Indeed, one Jersey official speculated that the major firms would not participate in such a scheme unless "obliged to do so by the Government." What the American companies appeared to prefer was an arrangement that would both strengthen their commercial position and achieve a modus vivendi with major foreign competitors, something which American group participation in the operations of the Turkish Petroleum Company might accomplish.[49]

As in the Djambi field negotiations, British government and company officials tended to support some form of accommodationist policy toward American interests in the Middle East, even though there were disagreements over the details of such cooperation. The petroleum department of the British Board of Trade, for instance, concluded that from an international point of view, general cooperation among the major powers would be preferable to the "jealousies and recriminations ... of recent years." The Treasury Department concurred, and during the years leading up to the Red Line Agreement it supported a number of joint British-American marketing ventures.[50] The British nonetheless envisaged American participation as a very junior partner in the development of Middle East resources. As one Foreign Office official commented in 1927, "in order to tranquilize the U.S. Government, we welcomed the suggestion that an American oil group should be given a participation." The secretary of state of the Foreign Office contended subsequent to the agreement that the British government had never advocated or accepted the Open Door policy for Iraq. Rather, it had "hinted that the open door principle meant that Americans should have equal rights with British subjects in British territories." Insofar as the Open Door was concerned, the British official position throughout the negotiations was that American participation in the Turkish Petroleum Company (TPC) was conditional upon State Department acknowledgment that such participation would satisfy the full American claim to United States participation in Iraq.[51]

The British companies moved toward support for the government's position early in the discussions, in part because it was believed that cooperation would serve the economic and political interests of the companies, but also, as TPC managing director H.E. Nicholls indicated, because that company wished to accommodate the British and American governments and encourage controlled, cooperative development in the Middle East fields, rather than excessive competition for concessions and the disruption of prices through unrestricted marketing of newly developed oil.[52]

Although there remained strongly protectionist sentiments, most notably in the Admiralty and the Colonial Office, the Foreign Office and more progressive business elements moved both government and industry toward compromise and cooperation with the Americans in the Middle East. Winston Churchill, then colonial secretary, informed his counterpart at the Foreign Office, Lord Curzon, in early 1922, that "so long as the Americans are excluded from participation in Iraq oil we shall never see the end of our difficulties in the Middle East ... The importance of reconciling American oil interests ... is so great that we may well pay a high price for it." Stanley Baldwin, as Chancellor of the Exchequer in 1922 and prime minister the following year, was equally supportive of accommodating the Americans. Following a visit to London by Jersey president Walter C. Teagle in 1922, Baldwin met with several British oil company officials at the Board of Trade to discuss the means to accomplish that end. That government opinion was more advanced at this stage than some elements in the private sector was reflected in the strong reticence of Shell's Sir Henri Deterding to engage in any formal combination of British interests and his sharply worded admonition to Baldwin that Shell would not be "trampled on" in the interests of Anglo-Persian or British-American relations. Yet Baldwin, Lord Cowdray, and Deterding of Shell did share the American preference for a free-enterprise initiative in oil development, reflecting the view that British government financial involvement in the Anglo-Persian Oil Company had reduced the company's effectiveness and further direct intervention in the oil industry should be avoided.[53]

The cooperative approach among American interests was equally pragmatic rather than premised upon abstract principles of international relations. As much as the Harding and Coolidge administrations sought the Open Door as a policy objective, they recognized their inability to achieve a truly Open Door structure in the Middle East. Nor was that entirely what the companies sought. As negotiations progressed in 1923, Walter Teagle assured Charles Evans Hughes that the "entire scheme" would give opportunity to "all other American oil interests to develop territory in Mesopotamia" under a subleasing system, even though only those firms associated with the Near East Development Corporation would participate in the production of the Turkish Petroleum Company. At this stage, five years before the Red Line Agreement was settled, Hughes recognized the limiting nature of the agreement, but like other officials thought the advantages of even a restricted American entry into Mesopotamia outweighed deficiencies in the agreement. He informed the president in late 1923 that the agreement was monopolistic, that it differed from "what has ordinarily been termed the Open Door," but that it was essential to proceed from a "practical rather than theoretical point of view if we are to be of any real assistance to American business interests ... In matters of this general character," he observed to President Coolidge, "I believe this Government should encourage a fair cooperation rather than competition between rival American and foreign interests." The president concurred.[54] Although Hughes's approval was premised upon the belief that the agreement between the British and American companies would open Mesopotamia to American interests, the intent of both government and industry was not to achieve unrestricted development, but rather controlled access and gradual development of Mesopotamian petroleum resources. Acting Foreign Trade adviser Wesley Frost most accurately captured the pragmatic approach of the United States at this juncture when he informed Van Manning of the American Petroleum Institute that the "open door formula does not aid very materially because in most countries the supply of petroleum is so limited that the door cannot remain open except until two or three companies have actually taken control of the resources. What we need," he asserted with splendid candor, "is to regard the open door as merely prefatory."[55]

The crucial corporate negotiations took place during 1923 and 1924, though it required another four years of discussion to bring a resolution to the outstanding points at issue. Throughout, there was close consultation between the corporate and government groups. The contention advanced by some historians that the companies demonstrated little effort to adhere to State Department guidelines is not sustained by the record of the negotiations between European and American groups. In fact, one of the main impediments from 1923 on was the nature of the Open Door provision, which was Article 34 in the 1923 draft. Nicholls cabled Teagle in late 1923 that the "impasse would disappear if we disclosed to [the] Iraq Government [the] Open Door formula."[56] Standard Oil representatives, on behalf of the American group, pressed with vigor for the inclusion of a clause providing for the right of transfer "to any person, firm, or corporation, irrespective of nationality." Standard Oil counsel Guy Wellman argued that because of State Department policy, the American group had to insist that the operations of a subleasing system would not be defeated by either British or Iraq law; that the TPC would adhere to the principle of the Open Door; that the Iraq government should be made to understand that the agreement permitted the TPC to make transfers to firms or individuals irrespective of nationality; and that the British Foreign Office and the TPC should assure the American group that these conditions did apply. Wellman observed that although the State Department was not insistent on approving the details of the agreement, it did require that the oil resources of Mesopotamia should be on a nonmonopolistic basis, and envisaged the subleasing system as a means to achieve that end. Teagle added that they wished the "privilege of having American firm(s) or individual(s) qualify to do business in Iraq on [the] same terms and conditions as British companies," and Wellman assured Allen Dulles, then chief of the Near Eastern division of the State Department, that the American group sincerely desired the implementation of the subleasing provisions in the TPC concessions. The State Department's economic adviser concluded that "in the present instance" there was justification for an agreement "granting an apparently exclusive right to the T.P.C.," but in which "there are flexible provisions for future participation on a competitive basis."[57]

Official American concern over possible restrictions in the region were heightened by the conclusion in 1924 of a British treaty of alliance with Iraq, ending the postwar mandate arrangement; but the treaty contained no guarantees of equality of economic opportunity. The following year, the Iraq government signed an agreement with the TPC giving the company a seventy-five-year oil concession to all of Iraq, including the still-disputed Mosul area. At the same time Iraq granted a concession to a subsidiary of the Anglo-Persian Company for the so-called transferred territories along the adjusted frontier between Iraq and Iran. Such developments appeared to strengthen the British position and placed greater urgency on the need for American interests to reach a satisfactory conclusion of their negotiations. As Secretary of State Frank Kellogg later observed to the secretary of the navy: "In view of the extent of our probable future dependence upon foreign reserves of petroleum, the importance of keeping the Government of the United States in a position consistently to support and assist American interests will ... be appreciated."[58]

By 1926, drafts of the group agreement stipulated that "the conditions under which the TPC should accept a concession in Iraq should be such as to give practical effect to the principle of the 'Open Door.' " Nicholls assured Teagle that there had been no intention to limit subleases to British interests and agreed to make the point explicit in the concession terms. At the same time, the agreement was equally clear that only the TPC or its designated companies had the right to negotiate for or obtain concessions in "the area bordered in red on the attached map." This self-denying provision was the essence of the Red Line Agreement and applied to Turkey, Syria, Palestine, Trans-Jordan, and all of the Arabian peninsula except Kuwait.[59] The American group sought to have the self-denying provision apply to Iraq alone, and Standard Oil of New York in particular sought the right to have absolute liberty of refining and marketing within the Red Line area, including the marketing of oil produced by them outside the area.[60] Teagle informed Deterding and Sir John Cadman in London in

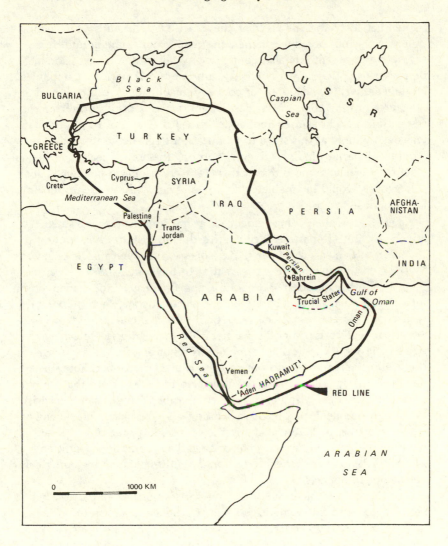

FIGURE 1
The Red Line Agreement, 1928 (source: file 36-1-30, RG 80, National Archives USA)

September 1927 that in view of the State Department's Open Door policy it was not possible for the American group to be bound by any restrictive covenant. He also contended, with an uncharacteristic lack of prescience, that it was unlikely any of the American companies would ever wish to negotiate for concessions outside Iraq. The board of TPC agreed to exempt the Near East Development Corporation from the restrictions insofar as they applied to Iraq. J.B. Lloyd of Anglo-Persian was even willing at this stage to eliminate the self-denying clauses and include a separate binding agreement among the non-American groups. Deterding was convinced that if the TPC were properly managed, outside groups would be unable to compete, even with an exemption for the American group.[61]

There is thus compelling evidence that the American group sought to adhere to State Department guidelines during negotiations leading to the 1928 settlement. Whether it did so essentially because it believed State Department support was essential to the conclusion of an agreement is another question. The State Department was not maneuvered into a position in which it had to accept with reluctance a monopolistic, restrictive agreement in order to facilitate the entrance of private American enterprise into the former Ottoman empire.[62] Rather, the agreement was the logical outcome of efforts dating from the passage of the Webb-Pomerene Act to obtain a high level of cooperation abroad among American firms and of the consistently stated policy that United States security depended upon the participation of American enterprise in the development of foreign raw materials. The accomplishment of those objectives in 1928 was the result of a high degree of cooperation between the state and private enterprise and a pragmatic recognition by government officials of the international realities confronting American petroleum companies.

The TPC arrangement did not prove satisfactory to all parties, business or government. American interests did gain access to the area under the company's concession, but depression conditions after 1929, the minority position occupied by U.S. firms in TPC, and the availability of other rich fields contributed to the tendency to restrict development in Iraq. Jersey Standard's Venezuelan subsidiary, Creole, was thus producing 450 thousand barrels a day by 1946, but its Iraq interests were producing only slightly more than 9 thousand.[63] The Red Line arrangements had also enabled Jersey's competitors to make substantial gains in the Middle East at the former's expense, with Gulf Oil withdrawing from TPC in 1934 and expanding in Kuwait, and with California Standard and the Texas Company developing Saudi Arabian resources through Aramco (the California Arabian Standard Oil Company until 1944).

The agreement did provide a favorable context for further cooperative endeavors among the major companies. In the immediate aftermath of the Red Line settlement in 1928, and with a view to dealing
with the problem of Soviet oil in the international market, the heads of
the major firms, Teagle, Deterding, and Cadman, met at Deterding's invitation in Inverness-shire, Scotland. There, at Achnacarry Castle, in
addition to indulging their interests in trout and grouse, they also
drafted what would become the "As Is" agreement, creating a cooperative structure for pricing, production, and a means to share profits from
exchanged production and reduced transportation costs. It was also in
the aftermath of the Red Line settlement and the Achnacarry Agreement that the long-discussed cooperation under the Webb-Pomerene
Act came to brief fruition. The belief among company officials that a
purely American association would not stabilize the market was
reflected in the composition of the Export Petroleum Association, Inc.,
formed in 1928. Its capital stock of 100 shares was issued to 15 American companies, including Standard Export Association (Jersey Standard), Standard Oil of New York, the Texas Company, Gulf Refining
Company, and the Vacuum Oil Company; but it also included the Shell
Union Oil Corporation, Royal Dutch Shell's main operating subsidiary
in the United States. One of the association's first actions was to adopt
U.S. Gulf of Mexico prices for four grades of gasoline and two of
kerosene, thus using the basing point pricing system adopted under the
Achnacarry Agreement. It was precisely this effort to link domestic and
international price control that led the Federal Trade Commission to
object that the Webb Act was not intended to allow U.S. exporters to
combine with foreign producers and distributors. The failure of the Export Association did not discourage further efforts to control the
market. Achnacarry was followed by several other cartel-like agreements: a 1930 Memorandum for European markets; a 1932 Heads of
Agreement for Distribution; a 1934 Draft Memorandum of Principles;
and a 1939 Draft Principles of Emergency Arrangements, occasioned by
the outbreak of war in Europe and the disruption of normal trade and
production.[64]

During the course of the 1930s there were also alterations in the composition of TPC. In 1931 Socony and Jersey acquired the interests in TPC
of Atlantic Refining and the Pan American Petroleum and Export Company, thus reducing the breadth of American participation in the company. In the same year the TPC partners eliminated the complex subleasing system, which had earlier been portrayed as the vehicle by which a
more competitive and broadly participatory situation in the region controlled by the TPC might have evolved.

After World War II, when the American companies remaining in

TPC sought to extricate themselves from the restraints of the Red Line Agreement they would do so with the assistance of the State Department and in a radically different strategic and market situation. By 1947, as we shall see in a later chapter, the American companies were able to negotiate in the Middle East from a position of enhanced power. Viewed in hindsight, the oil policies of Hughes, Hoover, and Kellogg were remarkably successful, rather than ephemeral and dominated by the private sector as they have often been portrayed. The main weakness of the policies that evolved during the decade was the failure to establish a realistic government mechanism for the exercise of government control over the international oil industry, at least of American companies operating abroad. One consequence was that the state acquired no effective means to ensure the realization of its basic objective, which remained assured access to foreign supplies of oil.

CHAPTER TWO

Containing Nationalism, 1919–1928

The effort to establish reciprocal access to petroleum resources in British and Dutch territories was the most sustained dimension of American foreign oil policy in the pre-1928 years. The emergence of nationalistic perspectives and politics in producing nations, however, also became an increasingly serious threat to American participation in natural-resource development overseas. In the long term this development would pose one of the most constant and perplexing dilemmas of American foreign policy in the modern era. Restrictionist policies became increasingly common during the 1920s and thereafter, not only in the British and Dutch areas under colonial controls, but also in both developed and developing nations, including France, Argentina, Romania, Spain, Venezuela, Colombia, Mexico, and the Soviet Union. In several countries restrictionist sentiment resulted in the formation of state oil monopolies in the development of oil resources or their marketing, creating situations that severely threatened American abilities to maintain an open door for commerce and investment. Only in the Soviet Union, however, was there expropriation, following the Bolshevik revolution. In Mexico, the threat of expropriation clouded Mexican-American relations for much of the 1920s, following acceptance of the 1917 Constitution, which embodied the potentiality of nationalization of subsoil resources in the national interest. The manner in which the United States responded to these developments served to shape foreign petroleum policy well into the post-World War II era. In general, there was a remarkable lack of empathy for foreign nationalism in American policy-making circles throughout the interwar years, remarkable for a nation that itself grew out of a revolutionary past and that had employed protectionist policies to enhance its own economic development in the nineteenth century.

THE SOVIET UNION

The Soviet situation was not only the most dramatic but also the arena in which the United States proved most ineffectual, in part because petroleum was only one facet of the broader international issues created by the Russian Revolution – issues that contributed to the American denial of recognition to the Soviet government until 1933. The absence of formal Soviet-American diplomatic relations substantially altered both government and company policy. Unlike the case of Mesopotamia, in which the state and commerce departments were extremely anxious to see American enterprise well established, in the Soviet case the companies were clearly cautioned that if they sought and obtained concessions in the Soviet Union, they did so at their own risk and could not anticipate diplomatic support.[1] From an official perspective, Soviet oil, so long as it remained under state control, provided no opportunity to reduce the American strategic dependency on foreign oil. At the same time, the Soviet Union was one of the world's major producers, and the marketing of Soviet oil in Europe and Asia threatened the market positions of American companies. Jersey Standard officials, for example, were concerned that their failure to participate in Soviet oil development would provide an opportunity for Royal Dutch Shell and other British interests to gain a commercial advantage. The Achnacarry Agreement in late 1928 would temporarily resolve company differences with a cartel-like arrangement, but during the pre-1928 years the issue was one of considerable commercial significance to American interests. As Everit Sadler explained to Arthur Millspaugh and other State Department officials, Standard Oil would comply with any request not to do business with the Soviet Union as long as the State Department could ensure that other foreign oil interests did not profit from their absence. Sadler went so far as to claim that Standard would have to "fold up its tents in the field" if the company did not obtain State Department support for its foreign operations in the Soviet Union and elsewhere.[2]

American companies did not lose as heavily from the Soviet expropriation as their European counterparts, especially Shell. Edward Prizer of the Vacuum Oil Company estimated that corporation's net loss from confiscation at $3.3 million, and was especially irritated to see the Soviet Naptha Syndicate by the early 1920s selling products manufactured in the company's former refinery. "The Soviets," Prizer remarked to Hoover, "not only take our property but trade upon our name and reputation."[3] Standard Oil of New Jersey did not lose property as a consequence of the initial confiscation, but anticipating that the Bolshevik phase of the revolution would not succeed, the company

began to invest in the Russian holdings of the Swedish Nobel enterprises and in the then independent state of Azerbaijan, which contained
the rich Baku fields. The relatively small investment there of $160,000
was lost when the Soviet Union seized control of Azerbaijan and the
Baku fields in the spring of 1920. Undaunted, Jersey made new investments of almost $9 million in the Soviet Union between 1920 and
1925 through the Nobel group. As a result Jersey acquired an equal interest in the Russian holdings of Nobel, which included companies
owning approximately one-third of Russian production, 40 percent of
Russian refining, and 60 percent of distribution.[4]

The pragmatic approach reflected in Jersey's willingness to commit
capital so shortly after the revolution was indicative of the general
orientation of American oil companies with international operations.
The Soviet Union had major resources, and U.S. firms were anxious to
participate in their development, or at least gain a share in marketing
Soviet products. Their considerations were premised on the market,
although company and government officials insisted on Soviet recognition of the principle of compensation for expropriated properties. Consequently, although Jersey was interested in the Nobel holdings, the
company rejected, in late 1920, a Soviet approach to participate in the
development of a new concession until the Soviet government recognized titles to prerevolution holdings. Pragmatic as the companies may
have been, historians have noted that both Hoover and Hughes tended
to react from more ideological premises. Hoover especially was convinced that any American investments in what he considered an un-
sound economic system were unwise, although he did move by 1922
toward recommending trade relations with the Soviets.[5] The Slavic section of the BFDC was also more supportive of U.S.-Soviet trade links during the 1920s than was the Department of State. This was reflected in
the support that the bureau lent to the Sinclair Corporation before the
Federal Oil Conservation Board in 1925 when it sought government
support for its efforts to develop a concession on Sakhalin Island.

The most sustained American attempt to participate in Soviet oil
development in the early 1920s came from Sinclair's oil interests, the
Sinclair Exploration Company. Sinclair had no compensation claims
against the Soviet government and was prepared to accept a concession on the northern part of Sakhalin, which was at that time under
Japanese occupation, and an exploration contract in the Caucasus. In
both instances, the Soviet Union appears to have been using Sinclair interests in an effort to gain recognition by the United States and to exert
pressure on Japan to withdraw from Sakhalin. Both efforts were unsuccessful. Sinclair's contract stipulated that the company had to begin exploration by March 1925. When it sent an exploration party to Port

Alexandrovski in late 1923, however, the group was denied permission by Japanese authorities to conduct exploration, and State Department officials declined to intervene on the company's behalf. By 1925, the Soviet government had cancelled the contract, and Sinclair's efforts to appeal the decision through Soviet courts proved fruitless.

The State Department's refusal to support Sinclair derived from the belief that the Soviet initiative was a thinly disguised effort to bring American business pressure on the department in favor of recognition. Clearly the Japanese occupation also complicated the picture. Given the refusal to recognize the Soviet regime, the State Department was in no position to exert diplomatic support for a contract between an American firm and the Soviet government in territory occupied by a third power, which was an ally of the U.S. The most that Hughes would concede to former Secretary of State Robert Lansing, whose law firm (Lansing and Woolsey) represented Sinclair in the dispute, was that Sinclair should be given equal opportunity by the Japanese government to obtain concessionary rights in the area, but that the department would not be compromised by the terms of contracts negotiated by American nationals with a government it did not recognize. The department took a similar position with Standard Oil of California when it requested support to explore areas covered by prerevolution patents. Standard officials indicated that the Japanese were themselves interested in oil development in Sakhalin, and without official American support no American companies were likely to gain Japanese approval to operate in the region.[6] Hughes reiterated that the department's position remained unchanged. There was no objection to American corporations doing business in Russian oil fields at their own risk and as long as such operations did "not jeopardize or infringe the vested rights of others."[7]

The BFDC was more supportive of Sinclair and looked to the newly created Federal Oil Conservation Board (FOCB) as a way to increase the sensitivity of government officials to the need for more positive controls and support for the private sector. Bureau officials hoped that FOCB would "bring about a new order of things at the state department," which they as well as army and navy officers thought was insufficiently supportive of American oil interests abroad. The bureau's view was that the Japanese refusal to allow Sinclair engineers to work in Sakhalin was contrary to Japanese pledges to the United States at the time of the joint invasion of Siberia in 1918 and later at the Washington disarmament conference that it would enforce equality of commercial opportunity in territory under its jurisdiction. When the secretary of the interior took the question to the FOCB in 1925, the committee's advisory committee recommended that the U.S. government protest

Japanese acquisition of petroleum properties in Sakhalin arising out of the opportunities afforded by its military occupation. Noting that Sakhalin oil was especially well suited for naval use, the committee thought that the Sinclair company should give assurances that other American companies would be invited to participate in its concession and that it give the American government a preferential right to a percentage of any production. Such a recommendation was entirely consistent with the board's view that the most effective way for the United States to conserve domestic reserves was to foster overseas production by American firms.[8] Logical as the position may have been, it did not sway the State Department from its course.

Failure to recognize the Soviet government seriously hampered the ability of the State Department to deal with such issues as compensation and petroleum development. At the Genoa conference in 1922 – held to consider the larger issues of Russian war debts and to which the U.S. sent only observers – the Soviet commissar for foreign trade, Leonid Borosovich Krassin, indicated that it was the intent to establish a parent trust to control the entire petroleum industry, with various fields to be operated through private subsidiaries. The Soviet Union continued to maintain that it would not recognize concessions granted by the czar, but that those who held former concessions would be granted priority in allocating participation in new development.[9] Throughout the Genoa conference, there were press reports that Royal Dutch Shell had reached an agreement with the Soviets on participation in petroleum concessions, reports that the British vigorously denied. The rumors proved false, but given the failure of the United States to participate officially in the conference, Hughes could only instruct American Ambassador to Italy Richard Washburn Child to inform the Soviets informally that the U.S. could not "countenance any arrangements to the prejudice of American interests in Russia." A.C. Bedford of Jersey Standard informed Hughes that a monopolistic agreement between Shell and a Soviet oil syndicate would deny Jersey's right under its Nobel contracts to purchase and export oil from their properties. Such a development would be, in his view, a dangerous precedent for the interests of private property. Bedford contended that when viewed in conjunction with the Anglo-French San Remo Agreement two years earlier, Royal Dutch Shell's activities in the Soviet Union severely threatened the American position.[10]

As David Lloyd George predicted at Genoa, the failure of the governments to reach agreement on Russia contributed to the need for a private arrangement among the companies. In Paris in the fall of 1922, Henri Deterding took the initiative in adopting an intercompany agreement not to enage in independent negotiations with the Soviet Union.

That agreement remained in force until 1924, when it was learned that Shell, contrary to the agreement, was purchasing Soviet kerosene for sale in the Indian market. By 1927, Standard Oil of New York and Vacuum Oil were both engaging in similar purchases and marketing.[11] Soviet oil remained the one area of production over which the majors had no effective control during the decade. The Achnacarry agreements, which established the "Gulf Plus" system of "phantom freight" charges in order to protect higher-priced American oil from competition and to enable Anglo-Persian and Shell to raise the price of more cheaply produced oil, did not solve the fundamental problems raised by Soviet autonomy from the cartel system that was emerging or the world glut of oil that developed by decade's end. As much as some oil officials, especially Deterding, may have railed early in the 1920s against the "stolen oil" being marketed by the Soviet syndicate, within a few years they were participating in its marketing for their own preservation, and American policymakers lost another potential economic weapon that could be used with the USSR to negotiate on the issue of compensation. This was a clear instance in which private economic interests were not fully compatible with the general direction of American foreign policy, and the companies were correct in their assertion that the State Department was unable or unwilling to protect their short-term commercial interests. For the industry as a whole, the question of Soviet oil was resolved by increased Soviet domestic demand for petroleum products during the 1930s as the Russian economy expanded. Until 1933, however, Jersey and the other majors sought a variety of solutions, from boycotting Soviet oil in international markets to prorating Soviet exports among the majors for sale within their own markets.[12] The question of compensation and confirmation of pre-1917 contracts that had been among the main reasons for denying recognition to the Soviet Union remained unresolved.

MEXICO

To some of the more extreme elements in the industry and official circles, Mexico in the late 1910s and early 1920s seemed to be moving in a direction equally threatening to American property and security. Although the economic, diplomatic, and political situation in Mexico in the years between the revolution and its gradual stabilization in the late 1920s was highly complex, the Mexican experience was extremely important in shaping and reflecting the general features of American foreign oil policy during the decade, most notably the response to nationalism. The complexity of the Mexican situation makes it difficult to isolate petroleum as a factor in the chemistry of Mexican-American relations at the time, but it was an important ingredient in the relationship and much of the abstract debate over the rights of private property applied precisely to the oil industry.[13]

The Mexican situation, like that in the Soviet Union, was an important index of the relationship between idealism and pragmatism in American public and private policy. Resolution of conflict revealed the ability of some segments of the business community to transcend a narrow, ideological approach in the interest of longer-term stability and development. The dispute demonstrated the often divisive opinions within the industry, especially between majors and independents, and demonstrated the emergence of a cooperative approach among the majors to international policy. What especially influenced American policy in Mexico, and this sharply distinguished it from the Soviet, Mesopotamian, and East Indian instances, was that it fell within the immediate political and strategic sphere of influence of the United States. Equally important was the high level of participation in the petroleum industry that had been attained by American interests at the outset of the crisis, again, clearly setting off the Mexican situation from the others. But the timing was similar, and the fear of domestic oil exhaustion, belief in the need for American participation in foreign oil development, and considerations of national security all emerged as factors shaping policy.

The Mexican situation also suggests that those historians who contend that after 1925 the U.S. government adopted a "more passive" approach to the oil companies are incorrect. This development did occur during the interwar years, and there were frequent examples of a hard-line policy after 1925 in Mexico as well as in Colombia, Chile, Venezuela, and Peru. What emerged in Mexico was not so much a more passive approach to the companies but a divergence between State Department and company officials over what was in the best long-run economic interests of both the companies and the United States. In many ways in the 1920s, company and government officials articulated similar viewpoints on national security, the sanctity of private property, and the need for access to foreign raw materials. What transpired between 1917 and Dwight Morrow's triumphs as American ambassador in 1927–8 was that more pragmatic and progressive elements within business and government came to the fore, with the result that although government continued to listen to the industry, it was both the more moderate voices and a more complex range of business opinion to which they were attuned.[14]

Several features shaped American oil relations with Mexico after 1917. One was the fact that U.S. enterprise there was more extensive than elsewhere in the world. In 1912, over 57 percent of Mexican production was American owned, with a total of 45,000 barrels a day. By 1922, more than 79 percent of the production of 508,000 barrels a day was American owned, in comparison with the 5 percent of Venezuelan production by American firms and the 80 percent control in Peru. In 1924, 57 percent of the total investment was American and 26 percent British.[15] Because of geographic proximity and the promising nature of Mexican reserves, a broad range of American firms was involved, the most significant of which by 1919 were Sinclair interests, Edward Doheny's Pan American Petroleum and Transport Company and its subsidiaries: Huasteca Petroleum Company, Tamiahua; Tuxpan; and Mexican Petroleum Company; Jersey Standard's Transcontinental Petroleum Company; Atlantic Refining Company; Gulf Oil; the Texas Company; and Continental Mexican Petroleum (a John Hays Hammond interest). Doheny, Jersey, Texas, and Hammond were the dominant U.S. interests. Pan American was the largest producer with 200,000 barrels a day, followed by Mexican Gulf Oil with 75,000. Atlantic was the only other producing company.[16] The main British-Dutch interests were Royal Dutch Shell, El Aguila (the Mexican Eagle Oil Company, which Shell acquired in 1918 from Weetman Pearson), and the Corona Company. What was especially significant about the corporate picture in Mexico at the outset of the controversy was the large number of companies and apparent competition among them, a situation that was similar in Venezuela at the time and in marked contrast to that in the Middle East or the East Indies. In Mexico and Venezuela the competition gave way rather quickly by the mid-1920s to the domination of two or three firms. In Mexico, Standard Oil of Indiana acquired Pan American Petroleum in 1925 and controlled 57 percent of production. In Venezuela, Jersey Standard and Gulf controlled 45 percent of production by mid-decade. Increasing concentration of control over production paralleled more competition in the retail trade. However, Doheny's Huasteca company became a major competitor in the Mexican gasoline trade, holding 30 percent to Aguila's 49 percent and Pearson's 21 percent of the market. Huasteca also held 7 percent of the kerosene trade to Aguila's 53 percent. On the west coast of Mexico, Standard Oil of California was a gasoline competitor, which Aguila attempted to meet by marketing its California production in the area to reduce shipping costs.[17] The decline in the number of companies with a major role in Mexican production was a significant factor in the stabilization of Mexican-American petrolem relations and facilitated State Department and other official efforts to realize objectives acceptable to the companies.

A second feature of the American side early in the conflict was the degree of business-government cooperation, the intensity of industry pressure, and the personnel movement between the industry and government. This movement was striking in the late 1910s and early 1920s in areas that related to Mexican policy, more so than in other areas examined in this study, and derived from the fact that there were more U.S. companies active in Mexico, many of them independents with a significant domestic political influence but a smaller role in international oil development than that of the majors. Chandler P. Anderson, for example, was one of the most important of the industry lobbyists. An international lawyer, he served as State Department counselor from 1914 to 1915. As late as 1927, by then in private practice, Anderson was the liaison for several of the majors with the State Department. Secretary of State Bainbridge Colby performed legal services for Jersey before his appointment as secretary. When Franklin Lane left his post as secretary of the interior at the end of the Wilson administration, he became a vice-president of the Doheny group's Pan American Petroleum; former secretary of the treasury and Wilson son-in-law William G. McAdoo also worked for Doheny. Such links make it tempting to draw conclusions suggesting an instrumentalist pattern of policymaking, but this does not seem to have been the case even in Mexican oil diplomacy during the 1920s. Rather, the executive, from President Wilson through Coolidge, and Secretary of State Colby through Kellogg, showed a remarkable independence from the specific objectives of many of the oil industry leaders, even though they believed they were acting in a manner that was in the long-range interests of the industry as a whole.[18]

The main issue throughout the course of events in the decade was the way in which Article 27 of the Mexican Constitution of 1917 would apply to the oil industry and to other U.S. investments. Although there were several fringe issues related to taxes on exports, interpretation of the Constitution by the Mexican courts, and often personality clashes, how and whether Article 27 would be applied remained the focus of debate. Article 27 was a complex but vital feature of the 1917 Constitution. It vested in the nation ownership of land and regulation of all natural resources, and stipulated that expropriations would only occur for reasons of public utility and with endemnification. It reserved the right to acquire mineral concessions to Mexicans or Mexican corporations. What was unclear was whether Mexico would apply these provisions retroactively. From the companies' perspective, retroactive application of a concession program in proven fields would result in further increasing competition among the companies, which they wanted to avoid. For Jersey Standard, which had held no pre-1917 titles, any application of the article was unsatisfactory, and the Department of State argued that retroactivity violated legally acquired titles.

"It becomes apparent," Hughes informed the American chargé in Mexico in 1921, "that foreign individuals may only obtain [concessions] by conforming to the obnoxious provisions of the constitution."[19]

Mexican officials over the following years gradually amended retroactivity with the principle of "positive acts," that is assurance of titles to those corporations that had, prior to 1917, demonstrated a clear commitment to develop their properties. It was assurances that the provisions would not be applied retroactively which led the United States to extend de facto recognition to the Carranza government.[20] A limited application of retroactivity and the concept of positive acts were the basis for the Mexican Supreme Court's decision in the Texas Company case in 1921 and four other accompanying decisions. They formed an integral part of the otherwise vague Bucareli understandings reached in 1923 in Mexico City between American and Mexican commissioners. As part of that agreement, the Mexican commissioners gave assurances that Article 27 would not be applied retroactively to those interests that had prior to 1917 performed some positive acts "which would manifest the intention of the owner of the surface to make use of or obtain the oil under the surface." Those who could not demonstrate that they had made such a commitment would nonetheless be granted preferential rights in seeking permits to develop the resources.[21]

Although considerable uncertainty remained, it was not until late 1925 that the Mexican Congress passed a general petroleum law implementing Article 27 and incorporating the Texas case and the general features of the Bucareli agreements. The law required foreign corporations to apply for concessions confirming titles, and provided for fifty-year concessions where positive acts predating 1917 could be demonstrated, and thirty-year concessions in other cases. At the same time, President Elias Plutarco Calles authorized the creation of a national petroleum administration to supervise the implementation of the legislation.[22] Two years of company defiance and diplomacy followed, until in early 1928, largely under the guidance of the conciliatory and popular American ambassador, Dwight Morrow, Congress enacted a new petroleum law, this one providing unlimited concessions for holdings predating 1917 where positive acts had taken place and assuring preferential consideration over third parties for thirty-year concessions where no positive development could be demonstrated.[23]

In outline, that was the legislative history of the Mexican oil situation by 1928. But the main issue is how the course of events in Mexico influenced the development of American foreign oil policy and whether policy in this instance differed from what occurred in the Middle East, the Dutch East Indies, and the Soviet Union. What was distinct in the Mexican case was not the nature of American policy but the context in which it evolved and the circumstances that shaped it. Government and industry officials portrayed the question narrowly in terms of the protection of American property. Although questions of national security and the Open Door were occasionally mentioned, they did not form the overriding focus they did in the Middle East or the East Indies. In terms of the post-1945 world, the real issue was whether the industry and American government were prepared to accept the principle of national control over resource development, but it was only the Mexican side that presented the issue in those terms. In the early years of the conflict, Mexican officials and ideas were often referred to as Bolshevik in inclination, and as late as 1927 Secretary of State Frank Kellogg, partially inspired by Ambassador Sheffield, penned a red-scare style of memorandum for the Senate entitled "Bolshevik Aims and Policies in Mexico and Latin America," although this provocative and unrealistic approach evoked broad criticism in the American press, Congress, and even business circles.[24]

Charles Evans Hughes was more measured in his response to the perceived threat to American firms in Mexico, but he as well emphasized that the "fundamental question at issue has been the safeguarding of American property rights ... against a confiscatory application of the provisions of the Mexican Constitution." In his instructions to the American delegation to the Bucareli talks, Hughes also indicated that to avoid a "serious crisis" there should be a clear understanding of General Obregón's policy prior to American recognition of his government. Referring to the Texas Company case, Hughes indicated that the judicial branch's decision did not provide "adequate protection" for American interests. The secretary of state also cautioned that although the department was not a party to negotiations then under way between the companies and the Mexican government on the issue of taxation, the commissioners should determine the state of the negotiations and take them into consideration during their own talks with Mexican authorities. Hughes expressed concern that taxation would be used as a weapon of confiscation. In this sense he was entirely consistent with the approach taken earlier by the Wilson administration. Wilson's ambassador, Henry P. Fletcher, informed the Mexican government in the spring of 1918 that the February decree establishing a tax on oil lands and contracts predating 1 May 1917 tended toward confiscation. "The United States," he warned, "cannot acquiesce in any procedure ostensibly or nominally in the form of taxation ... resulting in the confiscation of private property and arbitrary deprivation of vested rights." Reflecting the political and corporate complexity of the issue, the Independent Petroleum Producers Association of America supported the export tax, but the companies in Mexico briefly suspended exports in

July 1921, prompting the dispatch of the USS *Sacremento* to Tampico to protect American property and lives endangered, it was believed, by the discontent fostered when the curtailment of exports resulted in high unemployment.[25]

The major American companies sent two high-level missions of oil executives to Mexico to negotiate on the oil tax. The first, in the late summer of 1921, included Teagle, Doheny, J.W. Van Dyke (president of Atlantic Refining), Sinclair, and Amos Beaty (president of the Texas Company). The composition of the delegation was clear indication of the importance the companies placed on the issue. The agreement they reached provided for the monthly payment of a production tax but achieved the temporary suspension of the export tax. The second committee the following year substituted E.L. Lufkin of the Texas Company for Beaty. It proposed the formation of a Petroleum Development Company of Mexico and the transfer to it of all petroleum rights in some 700,000 hectares previously acquired by the companies and outside developed zones. At the same time, the committee insisted that the government recognize the companies' exclusive rights in any federal zones located within the boundaries of their properties. Both proposals failed to gain Mexican support.[26]

In the Mexican case, arguments of national security and commercial advantage came not so often from the State Department as from other departments and the companies hoping to gain State Department support. The U.S. Shipping Board, for instance, indicated in 1921 that 63 percent of the world's fuel-oil supply came from Mexico and California alone and that from "an oil standpoint, the importance of a stabilized Mexican Government cannot be overemphasized."[27] There was also concern in American quarters after the war to increased British activity in Mexican petroleum, concern that was a spillover from the general debate on oil shortages and foreign restrictions on American capital. There was some basis for such concerns in Mexico. For Mexican officials after the revolution, increased investment by British and Dutch interests promised to provide a counterweight to U.S. influence. British companies also showed substantial interest in Mexican production in spite of the unstable political situation. In 1918, Shell Transport and Royal Dutch obtained 1.5 million shares of El Aguila, in negotiations that were conducted with the full support of the British Petroleum executive. During the war, Lord Cowdray (Weetman Pearson) also pursued with the British Board of Trade the idea of creating a British Imperial Oil company, an all-British company that would develop foreign oil properties, a similar conception to that advanced in the United States by Mark Requa and James Phelan. Cowdray warned that the fear of U.S. oil depletion would stimulate Standard Oil activity abroad.

"Unless some counter action be taken," he wrote, "it will be found a few years hence that there are few, if any, prospective fields throughout the world not controlled by them or the Royal Dutch.[28] American concern that the British approach was a confrontational one with American interests was given further credence when El Aguila withdrew in 1921 from the oil producers' association of Mexico, which included all the U.S. companies. The rift occurred when Aguila officials refused to be bound by an association agreement to refrain from taking up additional properties under Mexican regulations until issues raised by the regulations could be resolved. The association accused Aguila not only of violating the agreement but of informing Mexican officials of association plans. General J.A. Ryan of the Texas Company was convinced that the British government was providing Aguila with strong support, and other American interests appear to have shared that view.[29]

British interests also sought to expand and consolidate their Mexican holdings during and after the war. From 1919 to 1923, Henri Deterding and Cowdray conducted protracted negotiations concerning the establishment of a worldwide pooling arrangement in which Aguila's production in Mexico would be pooled with the exports of Royal Dutch Shell. The discussions were aborted largely because Aguila's production declined by 1923.[30] This high degree of cooperation among British interests and the friction within the oil producers' association produced considerable suspicion of British intent among American interests active in Mexico, who in turn pressed the State Department for vigorous support in the area. Important as petroleum was to American policy-makers in the 1919–23 period, the range of U.S. interests in Mexico was sufficiently broad to mute the impact of the oil industry on American policy. Unlike the situation in the Dutch East Indies or Mesopotamia, where opening the door for American capital on the basis of equality with other investors was a primary objective of American policy, in Mexico there was a complex fabric of strategic and economic interests. Consequently, although arguments of national security were advanced, they were less conspicuous than in other geographic areas. This did not prevent the companies from advancing such arguments in the belief that they were more likely to gain State Department recognition. In the spring of 1918, for instance, Edward Doheny forwarded to Mark Requa a company pamphlet that he prepared on the importance of Mexican oil to the United States. The future welfare and prosperity, Doheny claimed, required the "uninterrupted operation and control of the oil fields in Mexico now operated by American companies." The strategic importance of Mexican oil had, in his view, been intensified by the British protectionism in Mesopotamia, the increased use of fuel oil for naval purposes, and the likelihood of the decline of domestic reserves in the U.S. To Doheny, Mexico was a "logical and natural source of supply."[31]

The Mexican Revolution raised with American officials the question of the reliability of those reserves. Even before the 1917 Constitution had been adopted, there was concern among some navy officials that Mexico was not secure. As Assistant Secretary of the Navy Franklin Roosevelt indicated, the development of the California naval oil fields and the commercial areas would end the usefulness to the navy of its facilities at Tampico.[32] The broader web of American interests in Mexico led the American government to transcend the narrower interests of the oil companies in an attempt to ensure a stable general environment for American investment and the protection of private capital, as well as access to Mexican oil resources. The State Department on several occasions rejected specific proposals from the companies, although it used, effectively in retrospect, the threat of nonrecognition to press its position on the oil issue with Mexican authorities. In 1921, for example, the department declined a plan in which the companies would purchase Mexican bonds on the New York Exchange and sell them at par to the Mexican government, on grounds that such action would be unfair to American bondholders. The plan was strongly opposed by the International Committee of Bankers, headed by Thomas P. Lamont of J.P. Morgan and Company. Charles Evans Hughes also dissuaded the oil companies in 1922 from granting a loan to the Obregón government because the department was determined that the Mexican government would meet American demands before steps were taken to provide American recognition and support. Several years later, Frank Kellogg sought to reduce competition between British and American companies in order to preserve a united Anglo-American front before Mexican officials and avoid "any appearance of controversy between British and American oil interests in Mexico at this time."[33] In 1925, Kellogg also indicated to his outspoken and anti-Mexican ambassador James Sheffield that the companies had not demonstrated that pending oil legislation would necessarily affect their pre-1917 rights. Kellogg insisted that he was "inclined to the view that the bill under consideration is capable of being construed in a way that would prevent it from affecting" those acquired rights, and he informed Sheffield that further opposition to the bill was "inopportune," preferring settlement through a general agreement on all outstanding issues, as in a treaty of amity and commerce. Kellogg's moderation at the time was in marked contrast to the position of the president of Jersey Standard's subsidiary, Transcontinental Oil, Everit Sadler, who was calling for military intervention to enforce American desires. Although Kellogg ultimately criticized the legislation publicly, he refused to endorse the oil embargo advocated by the American ambassador and some of the companies.[34]

The company position by 1927 was highly intransigent. In reply to a Senate request for information on those companies that had refused to comply with Mexican petroleum laws, the Department of State furnished a list of American and British companies which together controlled 90 percent of actively producing Mexican lands and 70 percent of the oil produced.[35] The American chargé in Mexico City, Arthur Schoenfeld, indicated that although the political situation was stationary, there was considerable anxiety among the companies about their future prospects. Some company officials believed, Schoenfeld reported, that the best hope was a modification of Mexican policy "under the pressure of financial necessity and ... firm resistance of the United States government to its confiscatory policy."[36]

It was into this highly charged atmosphere that Dwight Morrow moved in the fall of 1927 as American ambassador. Morrow carried with him the full prestige of his affiliation with J.P. Morgan and Company and the International Committee of Bankers, as well as the intent of the State Department and the companies to find some resolution to the ten-year-old dispute. With Morrow's corporate connections and the State Department holding the oil companies on a tight rein, Morrow managed to mold with the Mexican government and in consultation with the companies a new petroleum law under which the companies were prepared to operate, although it failed to meet their ideal objectives. The new legislation, which went into effect in January 1928, provided for the confirmation of concessions predating 1 May 1917 on which development work had taken place and imposed no time limits on titleholders. For properties on which no development had taken place, the owners would receive preferential consideration for concessions, which would be limited to thirty years in duration. The latter properties were also subject to national control. The concept of "positive acts" was again confirmed by the Mexican Supreme Court in November 1927 in a decision upholding a claim of Standard Oil of California.[37]

Like Morrow and the State Department, the British Foreign Office was unsympathetic to the more extreme views of the companies. The British ambassador to Mexico, Esmond Overy, in a thorough review of Dwight Morrow's efforts, indicated the need to urge moderation on the companies. T.M. Snow of the American department of the Foreign Office was even more direct. "Mr. Overy," he noted, "does not in the least exaggerate the unscrupulousness of the oil interests. They were prepared to go to any lengths to gain their ends – even to the extent of staging a revolution, and even though this would have completed the ruin of American and British holdings of other classes of Mexican investments."[38]

The lengthy conflict also produced some modification in the oil companies' activities in Mexico. The most striking feature was the diversion of capital to what was perceived as more promising and stable areas. The Mexican Eagle Company, for instance, in response to what it considered onerous taxation and oppressive legislation, in 1926 sought other sources of crude-oil supply, ultimately arranging with Venezuelan Oil Concessions Limited for the purchase of five million barrels of crude oil per annum from 1928 to 1935. In 1928, similar considerations led the directors of Aguila to separate the assets of the company external to Mexico from those directly necessary for its Mexican operations. It accomplished this through the formation of the Canadian Eagle Company, to which three-fifths of Aguila's assets were transferred. The two companies continued to operate along similar lines to those prior to 1928.[39] As noted earlier, Standard Oil of Indiana acquired Pan American Petroleum in 1925, giving it control as well of several Venezuelan properties, including El Lago and a refinery at La Salina. Gulf Oil's Mexican production peaked in 1922, and the subsequent decline led the company to intensify its efforts to bring in production in Venezuela, which it accomplished in 1925, and to turn its attention to the Middle East. In 1922, Standard Oil of Venezuela was incorporated, and Royal Dutch Shell shortly brought in a commercially productive well in the Lake Maracaibo district.[40] At the same time Standard Oil's Mexican operations became profitable by the end of 1928, suggesting that profits could be made even with efforts to increase national controls over resource development in a host nation. It was a lesson the companies were slow to learn, although the Soviet case demonstrated the extent to which pragmatism triumphed over ideology. For the United States government, oil policy was by 1928 clearly established on the basis of what has been described as the associational state, with the private sector playing the crucial developmental role in acquiring foreign oil resources, and the state serving to pave the way for the companies in strategic and delicate areas. There would be little change during the coming decade in the nature of American policy, although the context would change radically with the onset of depression after 1929 and with the outbreak of international conflict in 1939. The main issue that the United States faced over the next decade in shaping oil policy abroad was responding effectively to the emergence of nationalism on a major scale in the developing world, especially Latin America, where the Mexican experience between 1917 and 1928 provided a harbinger of events to come.

CHAPTER THREE

Oil Policy in Depression: The Hoover Years

In spite of the international depression that set in after 1929, accompanying domestic and international overproduction in oil and price declines, the major oil companies continued their efforts to acquire concessions overseas and to strengthen their marketing structures. American and foreign majors intensified cooperative ventures and sought to consolidate their holdings in order to minimize competition. Some fifteen United States firms formed a Webb-Pomerene export corporation during the Hoover years to reduce price competition overseas. Although it did not achieve what James Phelan, Mark Requa, and other advocates of a state-controlled oil company had long envisaged, it was indicative of the cooperative thrust within the industry. The majors also continued to expand and reaffirm the various "as is" agreements that followed the Red Line and Achnacarry agreements of 1928. There was a sustained thrust toward consolidation in areas involving overseas production and marketing.

Standard Oil of New Jersey moved steadily away from its traditional concentration on refining and marketing to become one of the world's leading producers of petroleum, ultimately surpassing Royal Dutch Shell and Anglo-Persian.[1] Under Walter Teagle's presidency, Jersey in 1931 discussed the feasibility of a merger with Standard Oil of California in order to avoid competition and duplication of facilities. California's movement into Middle East development and production promised to provide the company with substantial supplies of crude oil, which Jersey would be able to market in the Far East to meet Shell competition. Although the merger did not materialize, the initiative met with government cooperation, and in 1931 Standard Oil of New York (Socony) and the Vacuum Oil Company did realize a merger with the ultimate approval of the U.S. Supreme Court, thus reuniting two companies that had been part of Standard Oil at the time of the Supreme Court dissolution of the holding company in 1911.[2]

Paralleling efforts to regulate domestic production, major industry leaders sought international controls. Henri Deterding openly espoused the idea of global production restrictions by the companies in 1928, and J.B. Kessler, the managing director of the Royal Dutch Shell group, took up the issue publicly in 1931. Writing in the prominent industry publication *World Petroleum*, Kessler advocated a formal agreement among the world's leading producers and exporters. There were several features to Kessler's plan: He suggested that the major companies form an international finance syndicate to establish a common fund to offset losses incurred by smaller and weaker companies. Major producers in the Dutch East Indies, Persia, Colombia, and Egypt would agree to adhere to conservation guidelines. Several countries that consumed more than they produced, such as Argentina, Japan, France, Canada, and Germany, would agree not to export their domestic production. Major producers for world markets, such as the United States, Romania, and Venezuela, would need to obtain government approval to prohibit drilling until minimum production levels were reached. To Kessler, these were the major countries that would need to be involved in an international agreement. Poland, Mexico, and Peru had experienced declining production in recent years, and increased Soviet consumption had removed Soviet oil as a significant threat to stabilization.

World Petroleum editorially endorsed Kessler's appeal for international cooperation by governments and the industry as "the only effective means of bringing about the stabilization of the petroleum industry." Reflecting the view of the major companies, the journal also attacked efforts to impose crude-oil import tariffs in the United States, on the grounds that an American tariff would serve to increase competition by enabling oil supplies from other producers to displace American exports and increase unemployment in the American refining industry. American antitrust laws, as well, were identified as a factor inhibiting efforts to achieve industrial cooperation, although there was no consensus on their role within American circles. Judge C.B. Ames, for instance, vice-president of the Texas Company, contended in the same issue of *World Petroleum* that the antitrust laws had little to do with the industry's problems, and urged instead that the administrative machinery for regulating the industry in the U.S. be streamlined to facilitate industry cooperation. A large part of the problem of course were the different requirements of the independent and integrated companies. Wirt Franklin, president of the Independent Petroleum Producers Association of America, told the Rotary Club of Charleston, West Virginia, that the domestic oil industry was being destroyed to the advantage of the "great oil importing concerns," resulting in the "impoverishment" of one-third of the United States and lowering the "civilization" that had been built on oil. Walter Teagle aptly expressed the views of the majors when he wrote President Hoover in late 1929 and the large companies favored conservation, but any proposal coming from them would be subject to political attack. Teagle indicated as well that he was prepared to accept an oil import tariff if it would help to unite the industry as a whole behind the conservation program.[3]

Except for some voluntary production guidelines in the United States encouraged by the Hoover administration and congressional passage of an import tariff on petroleum, the state played an ineffective role in shaping oil policy in these years, with the result that the companies depended heavily on private-sector initiative for production and marketing restrictions. Even then, efforts were often ineffective. In June 1932, United States, British, Russian, and Dutch oil interests met in New York City in an effort to reach agreement on international production controls, but failed, largely because of Soviet refusal to participate. Some industry figures were highly critical of the administration for its lack of a clearly defined and vigorous policy. Henry L. Doherty, for example, wrote Secretary of the Interior Ray Lyman Wilbur in late 1931 that "until such time as the Federal Government takes action regarding oil, our industry will ... remain in the state of chaos." Doherty even broke with the American Petroleum Institute because he felt it was inadequately supportive of strong federal regulation.[4] Doherty's voice was not alone in urging continued government attention to the petroleum industry. Although the major oil shortage scare of the earlier 1920s had been dulled by new discoveries and production in excess of demand, the Federal Oil Conservation Board continued throughout the Hoover administration to stress the strategic and economic significance of oil. It criticized the tendency to allow extensive private holdings on the Naval Reserves, especially in California, and noted the substantial oil requirements even in peacetime of the armed services. "The wheels of 80 percent of all our horsepower, fixed and automotive," wrote the authors of the 1932 FOCB report to the president, "are turned by the consumption of a resource whose known reserves have never been many years ahead of exhaustion,"[5] a factor that was especially worrisome in light of high American consumption and export levels. Secretary of Commerce Robert Lamont stressed to the 1931 annual meeting of the American Petroleum Institute that 281 of 291 American seagoing naval vessels burned petroleum products, and all of the army and navy's airplanes.[6]

The complications of the depression substantially hampered the Hoover administration's efforts to pursue foreign policy that was consistent with domestic problems. Hoover came to the presidency with a carefully nurtured positive relationship with the business community and with a strong commitment to industrial organization with government support. Had the depression not intervened and taxed Hoover's determination to adhere to a free-enterprise model, there is every reason to assume that his accomplishment in domestic and foreign policy would have been more striking. Even with the impediment of the depression, foreign oil policy under Hoover and his secretary of state, Henry Stimson, remained consistent with principles established in the late Wilson and Harding-Coolidge years. This included the Open Door and government support for business overseas and for business co-operation. Only the conflict over an oil import duty ran against the grain of earlier policy, which was clearly designed to protect U.S. resources and maximize the exploitation of foreign resources. The focus of oil policy also continued its gradual shift toward the Middle East, with Iraq and Kuwait dominating the diplomatic scene, and with Anglo-American relations the axis on which oil diplomacy revolved. The main corporate expansion was in the Middle East, Indonesia, and Venezuela. In Latin America, the Hoover administration inherited an increasingly difficult legacy of nationalism, whipped to a new level of intensity by the dislocations of depression conditions. In both areas, the Middle East and Latin America, Hoover's policies proved successful in expanding American corporate participation and fighting a holding action against Latin American efforts to gain fuller control over their own natural resources.

EXPANSION IN THE MIDDLE EAST

The Middle East provided the most important area of diplomatic action, and the long-standing issue of British restrictionism within its sphere of influence, especially within the empire, continued to confront American efforts to realize the Open Door. British accommodation to the reality of increasing American power and American persistence paved the way for American entry into Bahrein, Kuwait, and Saudi Arabian fields in the early 1930s, although the route to Anglo-American accord was a thorny one, hampered by continued conflicts within the British government between the more restrictionist Admiralty, Colonial, and India offices, and the more accommodationist Foreign Office. What limited victory the U.S. did achieve was a more accurate reflection of the reality of American power internationally than of British liberalsim, although Foreign Office officials correctly anticipated a more pro-British approach from Hoover than from his recent predecessors. The 1929 visit to Washington by Prime Minister MacDonald was symbolic of the increased harmony. For government and the officials of some American companies, the main issue of these years in the Middle East was to circumvent the limitations of the Red Line Agreement in order to allow expansion of production and increased market control. Among the companies, Gulf Oil and Standard Oil of California were the main activists, in the case of Gulf seeking to extricate itself from the Red Line and to gain concessions in Kuwait. Standard of California, which had not been a party to the Red Line, concentrated its energies on Saudi Arabia. The expansion of both firms as well as the Texas Company in the Middle East in the 1930s threatened not only those companies that were tied to the limitations on expansion built into the Red Line but also the marketing provisions of the "As Is" arrangements, since the foreign business of Standard of California and the Texas Company was not covered by the original agreement. Consequently, there was a good deal at stake for both the companies and their respective governments during the prolonged negotiations that preceded access to both Kuwait and Saudi Arabia.[7]

Prior to 1927, the Eastern and General Syndicate of London obtained oil concessions on the island of Bahrein, the mainland of Saudi Arabia, and Kuwait. It in turn offered concessions to Burma Oil, Anglo-Persian, and other producers, none of whom were interested at that stage, and then to Gulf Oil, which in 1927 took options. Since it was outside the area covered by the Red Line Agreement, Kuwait had special appeal to the companies. In late 1928 the British government informed the Eastern and General Syndicate and the sheik of Kuwait that a British nationality clause would have to be included in any oil concessions granted by either Kuwait or Bahrein. Although Britain modified its position on Bahrein in early 1929, following an objection by the United States and representations to the Admiralty from the Colonial Office, Kuwait remained a point of friction for the remainder of the Hoover administration. As Secretary of State Henry Stimson informed the American chargé in London, Ray Atherton, in late 1931, the British "nationality clause" would effectively exclude an American company from Kuwait. The State Department was intent on maintaining the principle of equality of treatment for American commercial interests in the development of Kuwait petroleum resources and British interests. It was not prepared to support any exclusive rights for Gulf Oil or any other American firm, but it was concerned with advancing Gulf's case in this instance, especially in light of Anglo-Persian's active interest in Kuwait. As Assistant of State William Castle, Jr, informed Eastern Gulf Oil's president, the department would support the company's claims only on the understanding that it would "confine its exploitation rights in Kuwait to a reasonable area of the territory."[8]

British government circles remained as divided over the question of imperial restrictions on resource development as they had been in the earlier 1920s. By 1930, as the Bahrein decision suggests, there was a broader consensus favoring abandonment of restrictions than had been the case during the debate over the implications of the U.S. Leasing Act of 1920, but the service departments, the Colonial Office, and the India Office, under which fell much of the jurisdiction for the Persian Gulf, remained wedded to the practicality of the policy. The Foreign Office was, in the words of one official, Under Secretary of State for Foreign Affairs Sir John Simon, anxious to avoid embarking on a "fight for oil" controversy with the United States over Kuwait,[9] especially since the Hoover administration had appeared willing not to press for American access to north Persia. When the Foreign Office pressed its view with the India Office, it was informed that the application of the British control clause in concessions for the mainland territories on the Persian Gulf was a "long established principle of the policy of the India Office," and that admission of American interests into the area would create difficulties for British authorities in protecting them in the interior as well as inject American power into the region, enabling the United States to interfere in gulf affairs. Following further American protests in London, the India Office nonetheless agreed in early 1932 to recommend to the Government of India that U.S. participation in Kuwait was in the interest of "stability and world peace" as well as local prosperity and development, a judgment with which India agreed. Admiralty officials dragged their anchor, however.[10] Vice-Admiral F.C. Dreyer, deputy chief of Naval Staff, vigorously objected to dropping the British control clause on grounds that Kuwait oil production would provide an alternative to the dependence on Anglo-Persian operations in Persia at a point that was closer to the areas where oil would be required. In the event the Soviet Union occupied the Persian oil fields, Kuwait would provide a fallback position. Rather than easing restrictions, Dreyer advocated strengthening controls by requiring that the local manager of any firm operating a concession should be a British subject and that 51 percent of capital should be British. Dreyer contended that the Foreign Office unduly minimized the sheik's treaty obligations to Great Britain. "It would be intolerable," he informed Oliphant, "that we should allow this position to be compromised because the U.S. Government intervene in support of American oil combines. This country has on several occasions publicly asserted its special interests in this area and this should be well known to the U.S."[11]

Negotiations were complicated by the arrival in London in early 1932 of the newly appointed American ambassador, former Secretary of the Treasury Andrew Mellon. Mellon's family controlled Gulf Oil and in order to avoid the appearance of a conflict of interest in the discussions, it was agreed that Ray Atherton would assume responsibility for them. This did not preclude Mellon's interference, however, and on several occasions he directly pressed Gulf's case with British officials and with the State Department prior to his appointment.[12] To William Castle, the potential conflict of interest was insignificant. When he informed Atherton that he could, if Mellon requested, assume full responsibility for the Kuwait issue, he added that the department was simply protecting "the rights of American citizens" and argued that it was "merely accidental that the Mellon family has an interest in the Gulf Oil Company." The fact remains that Mellon's appointment under the circumstances, especially given the domestic political cloud under which he had resigned as secretary of the treasury, created an unnecessary opportunity for conflict of interest and left the administration highly vulnerable to criticism. At the same time, there is no indication that Mellon's appointment had any effect on the direction of American policy. Gulf Oil would have received State Department support in Kuwait whether or not Mellon had been in the Court of St James. Whether the British would have listened so attentively without Mellon's involvement is another question. In spite of his active intervention with the British government on at least three occasions during his tenure of office, the concession had not been finalized when he left London in March 1933 to be replaced under the Roosevelt administration.[13]

Following cabinet-level discussions of the American and British positions in Kuwait, the British Foreign Office in April 1932 informed the U.S. embassy that the British government was prepared not to insist that any concession in Kuwait be confined to a British corporation, if the sheik were willing to grant a concession without a restriction. John Cadman of Anglo-Persian at the same time assured the Foreign Office that it had no objection to participation by an American firm, in part because his company did not intend to compete in Kuwait. Modification of both positions proved nettlesome during the coming year, with the sheik cautious not to offend British interests, and Anglo-Persian showing revitalized interest in Kuwait petroleum development. By the end of 1932, Cadman wrote the Foreign Office that Anglo-Persian was "in full cry for the Kuwait Concession and shall press to the bitter end, unless," he added, "we are able to fix things up with the Mellon people." The Foreign Office also experienced additional obstructions from other departments. The Dominions Office, for instance, indicated that to negotiate with the U.S. as an empire was distasteful to the dominions, especially Canada, which preferred to conduct its own discussions on oil policy. The failure of the former Labour government to have a general policy statement approved by the 1930 Imperial Conference posed further difficulties, but from the point of view of the Eastern

Division of the Foreign Office, the important thing was to get policy into force; without agreement with the U.S., each case had to be settled on its merits, which meant a conflict with other departments. [14]

When no concession had been formalized by the fall of 1932, both the companies and American officials began to press for a resolution. In September the U.S. chargé protested the failure of the Colonial Office to make a ruling on the Eastern and General Syndicate's concession. He was assured that U.S. interests were not "labouring under a disadvantage." [15] Mellon spoke personally with Sir Robert Vansitartt of the Foreign Office in mid-October, and when no action ensued, he formally protested in early November against what he considered deliberate dilatoriness on the part of British authorities, an assumption he shared with Gulf officials.

Mellon's concerns were not unjustified. Foreign Office officials were displeased by tactics used by the Eastern and General Syndicate in Bahrein. After gaining its concession and before conducting any exploration work, the company sought further concessions in an effort to gain what the Foreign Office feared was full control over the region. In Kuwait, G.W. Rendel noted that many British departments preferred to see Anglo-Persian given the concession as in the best direct interest of Britain, [16] but the Foreign Office was determined to maintain an attitude of impartiality between the two companies because of its assurances to the United States. Although the India Office well into 1933 argued that with Standard Oil of California in Hasa, foreign participation in the Iraq Petroleum Company, and its likely participation in Qatar, there was considerable danger of a predominantly foreign bloc along the Arabian coast. The Foreign Office saw foreign participation as inevitable, and their main task as defending British interests in the area, which meant keeping American participation to a reasonable level. The Admiralty was also anxious to have included in any Kuwait concession the sheik's right of preemption in emergencies, a stipulation that a proportion of the oil would be refined in British territory, and that any naval base constructed at Bahrein would be specially safeguarded. [17]

The Gulf–Anglo-Persian relationship over Kuwait was indicative of the uneasy affinity of the major companies early in the depression. Although the two companies would ultimately move toward a marriage of convenience in Kuwait, their basic association was a competitive one. B.R. Jackson of Anglo-Persian informed W.T. Wallace of Gulf Oil in the fall of 1932 that his company regarded Kuwait as within its "natural and particular sphere of influence," and warned that they would not "passively look on while any other companies, with no reasonable interest whatsoever in that area, are endeavoring to secure concessions there." Some British officials were displeased with the role

Anglo-Persian had played in the Middle East. Gilbert Laithwaite of the India Office contended that Anglo-Persian had not been adequately agressive in seeking concessions in the Middle East at an earlier date when there was less competition. In the case of Kuwait, Laithwaite believed that the company may have sacrificed British political interests for its own commercial advantage.[18]

By 1933, Gulf and Anglo-Persian were moving toward accommodation. In March, shortly before his departure, Mellon met with John Cadman, and in May, Gulf Exploration Company vice-president William T. Wallace went to London to meet with Cadman and William Fraser, deputy chairman of Anglo-Persian, who indicated their willingness to have Gulf as a partner in a Kuwait concession. The India Office was concerned that such an arrangement might take any concession out of bona fide majority British control and that American personnel would predominate in the development. The actual agreement later in 1933 provided for a fifty-fifty sharing arrangement in exploitation and the financing of the concession, terms that were overly favorable to American interests in the view of the Foreign Office. For the companies, however, cooperation was clearly the preferred path. Cadman informed Mellon at their March meeting that competition between the companies would be "costly to whichever concern secured the concession." Cadman specifically suggested on that occasion that Mellon might use "his good offices" to "stimulate" agreement between the companies.[19] For Gulf Oil, the main impediment to agreement was concern that the Anglo-Persian Oil Company (APOC) would use its joint ownership to impede actual development of the concession to conserve its market position.[20] Several factors made British interests increasingly anxious to participate in the Kuwait concession. One was the cancellation of its major concession in Persia, seriously shaking the prestige of the company and Britain in the Persian Gulf;[21] another was the awarding of a concession in Saudi Arabia to Standard Oil of California.[22]

The agreement the companies concluded in December 1933 reflected the mutual anxieties of both sides. It specified that in the event the initial concession did not include all of Kuwait, the company would attempt to obtain the remainder of the territory, to which the agreement would also apply. The companies agreed not to use oil, if developed, to "upset or injure" the marketing positions of either company, and gave assurances that they would consult regularly to establish mechanisms to accomplish that end. Because APOC was anxious to protect its position in India and its sources in Burma, the agreement granted special status in those instances. Confirming Gulf's suspicion that APOC was more anxious to gain and hold a concession than to bring additional oil into a glutted market, the agreement stipulated that the British company could provide Gulf's requirements from its other fields. In further defense of British interests, the following March (1934) the India Office, acting for the British government, signed an agreement with the newly created Kuwait Oil Company that it or its subsidiaries would remain British companies, with 50 percent of the capital and voting power held by British subjects, and with employees of the company subjects of either the sheik or Britain. As well, the local representative of the company had to be approved by British authorities, be resident in Kuwait, and could only conduct political negotiations through the British political agent. As further protection for Britain, it also asserted the right to expropriate with compensation.[23]

Although confirmation of the Kuwait Oil Company's concession caused subsequent delay, by the end of 1933 American policy had succeeded in attaining Open Door objectives, though the Gulf–Anglo-Persian agreement was a restrictive one protecting British interests and not opening territory to other United States companies, similar, in other words, to the Red Line Agreement of 1928 that inaugurated American participation in an operating company in the Middle East. Limited as the accomplishment may have been, the State Department believed it had achieved an important precedent in Bahrein and Kuwait in gaining access for American companies to the Persian Gulf–Standard Oil of California to Bahrein and Gulf Oil to Kuwait.[24] United States interests were clearly on the offensive in the region, and British authorities continued to fight a retreating action, genuflecting to the Open Door but attempting to use their influence in the area to ensure that all concessions contained safeguards protecting British interests. For the United States, the objectives outlined in 1920 by the Wilson administration had been partially realized, with the major failing its inability to dissuade Britain, the companies, or Middle Eastern rulers from granting monopolistic concessions to British and American companies. Part of the problem lay in the inherent contradiction in U.S. policy and the nature of the petroleum industry. As long as it sought a high level of business cooperation and business-government harmony, that cooperation would tend to lead to oligopolistic arrangements. The same tendency was encouraged by the expense incurred by the companies in maintaining political representatives abroad, conducting extensive negotiations for concessions, and engaging in costly exploration and development work.

The United States was also confronted with a tension if not incompatibility between Open Door objectives and the desire of host nations to defend their national interests, and of Britain to defend its sphere of influence. This was apparent in the approach the State Department took to Iraq oil development during the Hoover years. In 1930 the

United States, Britain, and Iraq signed a Tripartite Convention, which was ratified the following year. Under the convention, the U.S. recognized the special relationship of Britain and Iraq under their 1924 treaty and received "all the rights and benefits" accruing to Britain and other members of the league. An accompanying protocol stipulated that in the granting of concessions, Iraq decisions could not be based on the nationality of applicants.[25] In subsequent negotiations for concessions, the Hoover administration adhered closely to the letter of the agreement. Undersecretary William R. Castle, Jr, for instance, informed the American counselor in London in late 1931 that, although the U.S. did not insist on all concessions being put up for public tender and recognized the right of Iraq to grant small concessions to natives of Iraq, major concessions should be available to foreign nationals through competitive bidding. Castle indicated that the department would interpret any practice that did not give American nationals equal opportunity to bid for concessions as a violation of the 1930 convention. British officials concurred with the general principle.[26]

DEFENDING PRIVATE
ENTERPRISE IN LATIN AMERICA

The issues that confronted both Hoover administration officials and the companies in Latin America were strikingly different from those in the Middle East. Although the need for industry cooperation in a period of overproduction remained a constant consideration, in Latin America United States companies were generally well established by 1929 and seeking both to expand their holdings and to deter mounting pressures for increased host-country controls over the industry. Closer to home, especially to the Panama Canal, Latin American oil fields in the late 1920s and early 1930s were of greater strategic significance than those of the Middle East, and the Unites States sought, as Britain did elsewhere, to retain commercial predominance in the area. United States officials kept a watchful eye on potential foreign involvement in Latin American oil, particularly by Britain, more remotely by Japan and Russia, but the main issue throughout the Hoover years was increasing nationalism and the threat it posed to the autonomy of American enterprise and the security of petroleum supply for the United States. Hoover-era oil policies in Latin America showed little modification from those of his predecessors, although the tone of diplomacy was more temperate, in keeping with the general thrust of the administration toward the Good Neighbor policy. There was no bureaucratic alteration in order to obligate specific responsibility for foreign petroleum policy, as had tended to be the case during World

War I and would be again after 1939. The result was that oil diplomacy tended to fall under the jurisdiction of the regional divisions of the State Department, with occasional involvement of the navy and the Department of the Interior. The Federal Oil Conservation Board had in 1926 identified Latin American oil resources as a primary target for United States interests, and the policies pursued by the Hoover administration reflected that perception. In Colombia, Argentina, and Mexico, the administration inherited the legacy of nationalistic in natural-resource development, and like the Wilson, Harding, and Coolidge administrations sought to cushion the impact of such legislation on United States companies. In Chile, there was a new threat of expropriation after 1930 for the administration to confront. None of those issues was fully resolved by the end of Hoover's presidency, but policy clearly reflected the developmentalist philosophy that imbued the administration's approach to the third world, with the belief that exportation of the free-enterprise model abroad was the most effective route to international prosperity.

The companies were well established in Latin America by the end of 1928. In spite of the increased interest shown by the companies in Middle East resources, Latin American fields witnessed the main growth in the late 1920s. United States oil investments in South America increased from 17 percent of total foreign oil investment in 1919 to 34 percent in 1929, and South American oil production by 1930 was 13 percent of world production, an increase of 12 percent over the previous decade.[27] Mexico lost its position during the decade to Venezuela, which by 1928 was producing 106 million barrels of crude oil, in comparison to Mexico's 50 million. There were four major firms involved in Venezuela by 1929: the largest producer was Royal Dutch Shell, followed by Gulf Oil, and Standard Oil of Indiana's El Lago company; in 1928, Jersey Standard gained control of the Creole Syndicate, which had extensive operations in Venezuela, and in 1932 acquired Pan American Petroleum and Transport from Indiana Standard.[28] In Colombia, Standard Oil's Tropical Oil Company was the major developer, but Gulf and Royal Dutch Shell were also actively seeking concessions. In Peru, which was the region's major exporter until the ascendency of Venezuela, the International Petroleum Company, a subsidiary of Standard Oil, was the leading oil interest, displacing Shell in the course of the 1920s. Although production was low, Jersey Standard was well established in Bolivia by the mid-1920s, but the diplomatic attention devoted to Bolivian expropriation of the company's properties remained a decade away. The Bolivian market was controlled by three companies by 1930: the International Petroleum Company; Richfield Oil, and Anglo-American. International Petroleum alone supplied 60 percent of the market. In Argentina, Latin America's only major petroleum-consuming nation, American firms were involved primarily in marketing. The largest producer of the private companies was Astra, in Comodoro Rivadavia, which was Argentine owned with some German capital participation, and foreign investors concentrated their attention in the early 1920s on adjoining concessions. A large proportion of Argentine petroleum was imported from Mexico and the United States rather than locally produced, and hence the marketing function of American firms was of increased importance. The formation of an Argentine state oil company, YPF (Yacimientos Petrolíferos Fiscales), and efforts under President Hipolite Yrigoyen after 1928 to form a state monopoly, threatened the American position and led to concerted lobbying efforts to alter the direction of Argentine policy, especially by Jersey Standard, which was the primary target for the rhetoric of Argentine petroleum nationalism.[29]

Developments in Colombia and Chile in the late 1920s and early 1930s effectively illustrate the main features of U.S. foreign oil policy in Latin America. That policy was firmly directed toward counteracting nationalism and ensuring a place for private American firms in the oil industry. At the same time, the state increasingly sought to ensure that the oil companies played a positive role in Latin America, that they would show some flexibility in responding to changing political exigencies in Latin America rather than adopting such an intransigent position that the security of all American interests in an area would be threatened. A secondary, and rather remote consideration was the defense of American capital against foreign competition. Both cases illustrate that any contention that the oil companies found a less sympathetic ear in Washington after the mid-1920s is ill founded as is the hypothesis that the companies did not need state assistance by that time. Rather, there was a close, if not always harmonious, working relationship between Hoover administration officials and major oil-company executives on issues relating to Latin America, and it is not too extreme a claim that in some instances, such as Colombia, the fact that U.S. enterprise was able to gain and retain certain petroleum concessions owed much to formal state intervention, as was true in Bahrein and Kuwait at the same time.

In Colombia, as in Argentina, it was Jersey Standard that was the main focus of nationalistic resource legislation. But the other major protagonist in the oil diplomacy of the period was Gulf Oil. The shift toward modified Colombian oil policy began in 1926 during the presidency of Pedro Nel Ospina, but it was left to Liberal President Enrique Olaya Herrera in Colombia and the Hoover administration after 1930 to resolve the issues that emerged. Two petroleum concessions dominated the Colombian situation in these years: the Barco concession on the Venezuelan-Colombian border southeast of Lake Maracaibo, in which Gulf Oil was principally interested, and the De Mares concession in the Magdalena River Valley, where Standard Oil's subsidiary Tropical Oil was well established.[30]

In 1926 the government of Pedro Nel Ospina revoked the title of the Colombian Petroleum Company (Gulf Oil) to the Barco concession, and in early 1928 the minister of industries implemented new petroleum regulations by decree requiring private companies to provide evidence of concession ownership. The intention here is not to detail the course of political and diplomatic events that ensued, but rather to examine the objectives of U.S. policymakers in responding to this challenge and the relationship between the state and the companies in defining policy objectives.

The Hoover administration adopted a strongly protectionist position when faced with the direction of Colombian policy, although it refrained from some of the rhetorical excesses that had characterized Frank Kellogg's term as secretary of state. His successor, Henry Stimson, was a polished professional and an efficient administrator who could delegate adequate responsibility to allow him to ride and play club tennis with his colleagues, as well as recuperate from frequent bouts of insomnia and diary writing. He was also less concerned with British competition in Latin America than had been his predecessor, reflecting in part the generally pro-British orientation of the Hoover administration. The State Department consequently modified the hard line it had taken against the efforts of the Anglo-Persian company to obtain a petroleum concession in the Colombian-Panamanian border region, which Kellogg had portrayed as threatening "to exclude American interests from reasonable opportunity to participate in the future development of petroleum resources of Colombia." Both State Department and company officials had seen the 1927–8 oil legislation as a "shield" to mask the intent to transfer large and potentially rich tracts of oil lands to British interests. Whether they were correct or not in their assessment, the British government was anxious to ensure that APOC and other British companies had access to Colombian resources.

During 1929, H. Foster Bain, a former director of the U.S. Department of Mines, and J.W. Steel of the U.S. Geological Survey, participated with other international specialists in assisting the Colombian government to draft comprehensive petroleum legislation. Bain was the major figure of the group and Americans the dominant influence, although Bain held sufficiently aloof from the companies' representatives in Bogota to receive their criticism that he was overly theoretical in his approach and ill informed on the specific problems of development that confronted the industry locally. The remark of a Texas Company vice-president that Bain was too "saturated with the U.S. Government viewpoint" was indicative of the dissatisfaction the companies felt at the lack of adequate U.S. support they had received, as well as their general antagonism toward government intervention in the private sector. The companies were caught between the international overproduction of petroleum by 1930 and the desire of the Colombian and other host governments to have actual development of any concessions granted. The local representative of Gulf Oil, for instance, indicated that his company wanted confirmation of title to the Barco concession but intended to hold it in reserve until the market improved. The comments of American officials also suggest that Gulf expected more State Department endorsement than it was likely to receive, although given the strong support for Gulf Oil's concession hunting in Kuwait at the same time, the degree of leverage exercised by the Mellons was apparent. The main, and arguably more appropriate support provided by the American government by 1930 was generally directed toward wooing incoming president Olaya Herrera, who had served as the respected Colombian minister to Washington until the election. The department encouraged the companies to be cooperative in providing financial assistance, and arranged for Olaya as president-elect to meet with George Rublee of the law firm Covington, Burling, Acheson, Schorb, and Rublee, who subsequently became Olaya's adviser on oil policy, to serve, as one State Department official described the role, as "a buffer between the companies and the Colombian Government." At the same time, Rublee saw his role as an informal State Department adviser whose task was, in the words of Undersecretary Francis White, to "keep the oil question there from becoming acrimonious." During the coming months the Olaya administration, Rublee, and the American minister, Jefferson Caffery, devoted a high proportion of their energies to resolving the outstanding oil issues, and Rublee worked closely during the process with Caffery and company officials in drafting new petroleum legislation and settling the Barco concession dispute. Rublee's efforts were not without tensions with the companies, especially Gulf Oil officials, who associated him with what they perceived as an unsatisfactory settlement of American-Mexican oil relations, where Rublee had served as Dwight Morrow's adviser. Fortunately for Gulf, both its local officials and the State Department recognized the need for compromise if the company was to avoid acrimony and possible loss of the Barco concession in Colombia, especially on the issue of production levels and the length of an exploration period. From Gulf's perspective, compromise was attractive. Colombia promised to be an important area of development if political instability in Venezuela threatened Gulf's holdings there. They consequently reached agreement in early 1931, prompting the secretary of state to cable heartiest congratulations, adding that the department did not want to pass judgment on the terms of the agreement, which the department saw as a private matter. Since Standard Oil representative H.A. Metzger suggested that the contract was the best he had seen come out of Colombia, one could conclude that American policy had been a resounding success and that the company had little reason for complaint, although the concession never yielded its anticipated levels of production. This often uneasy state / company relationship, agreeing on general objectives, often disagreeing over the details of policy, was characteristic of the Hoover years. The Hoover administration was fundamentally committed to American capital abroad, but equally concerned that the companies should behave in a way that protected the full range of American interests. Clearly petroleum was a high priority, with the result that the State Department played an unusually active and direct role in helping to create an environment abroad that was favorable to the American presence. In this sense the Hoover administration adhered to policies consistent with those of previous administrations.

The United States response to developments in Chile during the Hoover years reflected the administration's desire to balance petroleum considerations with the broader range of U.S. interests, as had been the case with Mexico earlier. Chile was outside the immediate strategic area of the United States, the industry was relatively insignificant in comparison to that of Venezuela, Mexico, or Peru, and American investment in petroleum operations was small, in contrast to the substantial commitment to mining, especially copper. As late as 1939, Standard Oil of New Jersey estimated its installations in Chile at $5–10 million, whereas Kennecott Copper was valued at $300–400 million.[31] Under the circumstances, American officials were loath to pursue a policy, or allow the oil companies to act in a manner, that would threaten the larger and more significant investments.

During the Hoover years there were four major petroleum companies active in refining and marketing petroleum products in Chile, none of which had developed oil at commercial levels within the country. The largest was Royal Dutch Shell's subsidiary, Shell-Mex, followed by Jersey Standard's West India Oil Company, the Union Oil Company of California, and the International Petroleum Company. In mid-1930 the Department of State was informed that the Chilean government had introduced legislation proposing the nationalization of the petroleum industry and the establishment of a governmental monopoly for refining and distribution, along the lines that had been discussed in Argentina in the late 1920s under Yrigoyen. The initial legislation provided for participation by foreign capital, but clearly enactment of the bill threatened the independent existence of foreign enterprise in the Chilean petroleum industry. The legislation authorized the president to establish refineries to grant concessions to national or foreign firms in partnership with the state, which would own and control the enterprise.[32]

The Department of State did not initially protest the consideration of the legislation, because in the view of department officials no American rights were immediately jeopardized. As late as November 1931, an official of the Latin American division noted that there were no grounds for formal representations by the United States government. "Our only interest," he observed, "would appear to be to make certain that such American property as may eventually be expropriated for the benefit of the monopoly, as well as such other property not expropriated as may be rendered useless by the creation of the monopoly, is indemnified on a fair basis."[33] The insistence on adequate compensation for any property expropriated remained a basic principle of U.S. policy during the dispute, but policy also came to the colored by other considerations. One was reticence to see monopolies established in the extractive industries that would exclude foreign, especially American, capital, something that Hoover had also sought to combat as secretary of commerce. The department also declined to support the granting of monopoly privileges to a single American enterprise[34] or to distinguish among competing United States firms, although it adhered less rigorously to the latter than the rhetoric would suggest. In keeping with general practice, the department insisted that it would not be a party to or pass judgment on business negotiations in the private sector. In terms of the broader place of international relations, the department sought to encourage Anglo-American solidarity, or at least a united front by British and U.S. firms against the direction of Chilean policy. It sought as well to counteract the efforts of the Soviet Union to sell large quantities of oil in Chile, in part because the issue of Soviet expropriation of foreign properties had not been resolved, but also because of a strong desire to minimize Soviet involvement in the hemisphere.[35]

Through the first two years of the discussions, State Department officials indicated that they felt the companies, especially Standard Oil of New Jersey, were taking too extreme a position. The American chargé in Santiago, R. Norweb, indicated in late 1931 that the company's local manager, G.S. Laing, had stated that Standard Oil would have to give up its business in Chile if the legislation passed. The company was not prepared to work with a government monopoly or accept the principle of 75 percent profit for the state enterprise. The president of the West India Company outlined essentially the same position as Laing in a subsequent meeting with department economic adviser Herbert Feis and chief of the Latin American Division Edwin Wilson, among others. Company officials stressed the dangers for American enterprise inherent in the Latin American trend toward state monopolies, notably in Argentina, Chile, Uruguay, and Nicaragua, and expressed concern that the Chilean and Uruguayan governments would purchase Soviet oil if credit could be established on the basis of commodity exchange. It was confirmed in November that the USSR had made a definite proposal to supply Chile with a year's supply of petroleum and kerosene in return for nitrate, but the negotiations did not reach fruition, largely because both Shell and Standard Oil of New Jersey instructed their local representatives not to handle Soviet oil. Still, the only initiative the department took was to have the ambassador in Chile, William Culbertson, stress to the Chilean foreign minister that in the event a petroleum monopoly was established, it was expected that American companies would have equal opportunity in any bidding for government contracts.[36] Not until after the legislation passed in May 1932 did Culbertson recommend that it was time to make a formal declaration of "our intention to support a claim for full and effective compensation in case American interests are forced out of business." The department did so in June, informing Standard Oil of New Jersey of its action.[37] Throughout there was close consultation between British and American interests.[38] The State Department's position remained moderate, however, in part because the legislation required executive initiative to go into effect, and there were indications that neither the Chilean president nor foreign minister supported the more nationalistic features of the act. The department was also adamant, however, that it did not intend to be drawn into the companies' assumption that their involvement in any contract with a Chilean state company should require the participation of the U.S. government. Jersey was informed categorically that such questions were of a private business nature on which the department did not need to be consulted.[39]

When a coup overthrew the Chilean government in June 1932 and installed a socialist administration headed by Carlos Davila, the United States found itself confronted with an altered situation. The likelihood of national action in the petroleum field now appeared possible in other sections of the economy, and the United States immediately warned the Davila administration that its earlier insistence on compensation in the event of expropriation of petroleum properties applied equally to all American property in Chile.[40] For the moment, American fears were not realized, and the Hoover administration ended before the Chilean petroleum legislation was put into effect. In the fall of 1934, the government created the Chilean Petroleum Company, with Chilean capital, for the purpose of distributing petroleum products,[41] but that problem was a legacy to the Roosevelt administration, which was as committed as the Hoover administration had been to combating nationalism and socialism in Latin America and defending the interests abroad of American capital.

CHAPTER FOUR

From Depression to War, 1933–1941

Oil diplomacy during Franklin Roosevelt's first two terms in the presidency reflected a high degree of continuity with that of his Republican predecessors, although there were both legislative and administrative innovations. The president's preoccupation with domestic economic crises during much of the period often forced all but the more pressing issues of foreign policy to backstage. There was, nonetheless, a broad range of foreign policy considerations in the prewar years in which oil figured prominently. These issues ranged from the continuing problem of nationalistic host-country legislation, and actual expropriation of American property in Latin America, to the defense of the Open Door against rival imperial powers such as Japan in the Far East, and the protection of strategic petroleum installations in vulnerable areas after international war erupted in 1939. There was also continuity between the conservationist and national resource-planning orientation of the Hoover administration and the accomplishments of the New Deal, especially the National Recovery Administration (NRA), and these domestic petroleum developments had clear implications for foreign oil policy. In two areas, the liberalization of American international trade and the strain of antitrust sentiment and policy that ran through the post-1935 New Deal, Roosevelt departed from his predecessors and created at least the illusion if not the reality of antagonism to big business, including the oil industry. That image was offset by both constructive cooperation between business and government in the articulation of foreign economic policy, and the prewar creation of such specific vehicles to accomplish that cooperation as the Business Advisory Council under the Department of Commerce.

The geographic focus of U.S. oil policy during the prewar New Deal underwent some modification. Although outstanding issues inherited from the Hoover administration in Kuwait and Saudi Arabia were resolved by the Roosevelt State Department, the Middle East as a whole received less attention than it had during the previous fifteen years, until American participation in the world war once again underlined the strategic and commercial significance of Middle Eastern resources. The marketing of oil to belligerents in the Italo-Ethiopian war of 1935 and the Spanish Civil War after 1936 were issues of diplomatic significance, but in final analysis bore little relevance for the development of a foreign oil policy itself, except to the extent that the crises highlighted the marginal degree of state control that could be exercised over the international marketing operations of the major companies. In the Far East, Japan continued its expansion into Manchuria, and American officials worried increasingly about the security of American petroleum interests in the East Indies in the event of conflict with Japan. In that area, as Irvine Anderson has shown in his study of the Standard-Vacuum company, the United States, Britain, and the oil industry engaged in highly collaborative consultation in an effort to protect their investments. This was also true of the response after 1934 to changes in Japanese petroleum legislation.[1]

It was Latin America, however, that received most attention and that was most significant in shaping the oil policies that characterized the peacetime Roosevelt administration. Pivotal among developments in Latin American oil were the return of Colombia, under leftist Liberal President Alfonso López Michelson, to a nationalistic oil policy from 1934 to 1938; Chile's revival of its state monopoly plan; Venezuela's movement in that direction late in the decade; and actual nationalization in Bolivia in 1937 and in Mexico the following year. The response of the Roosevelt administration to these issues reflected the same commitment to the Open Door, defense of American capital abroad, and cooperation with the industry that had characterized earlier administrations. However, there was a subtle yet important change in the tone of American oil policy, indicative of a trend that had emerged clearly in the Hoover years. Although oil continued to be viewed as an important strategic commodity, and although the State Department retained its commitment to the free-enterprise model, there was a distinct tendency in State Department policy to bring the oil companies to adapt to changing political realities abroad, especially in the third world. Consequently, companies were increasingly encouraged to show flexibility in the face of nationalistic legislation altering royalty structures, modifying exploration and development periods, stipulating the hiring of host-country nationals, and stimulating secondary industrial development linked to the extraction of oil. Some companies responded with more flexibility and foresight to these changing realities than others, but State Department officials increasingly attempted to demonstrate to the companies that American interests in general would be more secure if they could maintain a low and cooperative profile in Latin America without, of course, sacrificing the private-enterprise approach or endangering continued access to Latin American resources. Such an orientation in policy became especially acute during World War II when petroleum supplies from the East Indies and Middle East became temporarily inaccessible, but they preceded the war in origin and grew as much out of the changing realities of Latin American political developments as out of the wartime emergency.[2]

PERSONALITIES, BUREAUCRACY, AND POLICY

The relative continuity in the nature of American oil diplomacy before World War II derived in part from the rigidity of foreign policy decision-making structures, the relative lack of dramatic change in personalities, and the basic needs of the American political economy. The depression may have served to shake Americans free from a nineteenth-century belief in the inevitability of progress, and confirmed the accuracy of 1920s social critics, but it did little to alter the search for hegemony abroad, foreign markets, and sources of raw materials, all of which were linked to domestic prosperity. In terms of conducting foreign oil policy, the State Department underwent no modification before World War II. Petroleum problems as they arose were relegated to the specific geographic divisions although in the event of major crises, such as the Bolivian and Mexican expropriations late in the decade, senior officials and the White House participated not only in the broad parameters, but often in the details of policy. Foreign policy in its specifics was also the product of a remarkably small number of men. Although departments other than state, and powerful segments of the private sector, obviously contributed to the shaping of foreign policy, policy was essentially the product of a small elite: Roosevelt himself, who participated more actively and directly than any president since Wilson in decision making; Cordell Hull, the Tennessee Democrat and persistent advocate of liberalized international trade, who served as secretary of state until ill health and increasing estrangement from Roosevelt led to his retirement in 1944; William Phillips, a Republican who had supported FDR in 1932 and whom Roosevelt selected as undersecretary until 1937, when he was replaced by Sumner Welles. Welles was as close to Roosevelt as any member of the department and the clearly predominant figure in shaping Latin American policy, along with his close associate Laurence Duggan, after 1935 chief of the Latin American Division. Both were Latin American specialists of considerable ability. Another important Roosevelt appointment in the western hemisphere was Josephus Daniels, who served as ambassador to Mexico. Roosevelt's former superior as secretary of the navy under Wilson, Daniels was one of the more outspoken departmental advocates of a new approach to Latin American relations and possessed a deserved reputation for fighting pitched battles with the oil lobby in earlier years. Adolf Berle, Jr, who had the rare skill to be close to both Hull and Welles, served as an assistant secretary after 1938. By decade's end, Nelson Rockefeller's appointment as director of the Office of Inter-American Affairs, including the Inter-American Development Commission, rounded out the circle of department personalities close to the president, individuals who often circumvented Hull in shaping and implementing policy. These were the dominant figures, and it is a striking comment on the continued insularity of American foreign policy perceptions that their main focus was the western hemisphere, something which was underlined by the 1937 amalgamation of the Mexican and Latin American divisions into the Division of American Republics, reporting to Welles.[3]

Figures of secondary importance whose responsibilities lay elsewhere included several holdovers from the Hoover administration: for example, R. Walton Moore, an assistant secretary until 1937 when he was appointed department counselor as a consolation prize for failing to gain the coveted undersecretaryship. Moore's interests were European in orientation. This was true as well of George Messersmith who became an assistant secretary in 1937, even though he served as ambassador to Cuba during the war. J. Pierreport Moffat in European affairs was another legacy from Republican appointments, as was economic adviser Herbert Feis and two figures in the Far Eastern Division: Stanley Hornbeck and Joseph Grew. Grew served as ambassador to Japan from 1932 to Pearl Harbor. It is striking that not a single major figure in the department in the pre-1939 years could be considered a Middle Eastern specialist, especially remarkable given the high level of interest in the area during the decade following World War I.

Outside the State Department but within the administration, several other individuals contributed to foreign petroleum policy. Secretary of the Interior Harold Ickes, a feisty old-line progressive Republican, served as petroleum administrator under the National Recovery Administration codes, and although they applied to the domestic oil situation, they had distinct implications for foreign policy as well. The Department of Commerce lost much of the power in foreign economic policy it had possessed during the heady days of Hoover's secretaryship and presidency, but Secretary Daniel Roper continued to contribute to the general formation of policy, as did Jesse Jones of the Export-Import

Bank, Claude Swanson as navy secretary until 1940, secretaries of war George Dern (1933–6) and Harry Woodring (1936–40), and Henry Morgenthau, Jr, as treasury secretary after 1934. Each of them played a highly peripheral role, but in an area such as petroleum policy, with its strategic and overseas economic implications, it was virtually inevitable that other departments would intrude on State Department territory.

Considering the constant warnings of impending petroleum shortage in the midst of glut that came even during the Hoover administration from such agencies as the Federal Oil Conservation Board, there was a curious lack of attention to petroleum from the Department of War. The planning branch of the Office of the Assistant Secretary of War, with responsibility for planning industrial mobilization, price fixing, and procurement policies in the event of war, gave little attention to oil as a strategic raw material during the 1930s. A 1934 list of twenty-six strategic raw materials prepared by the commodities division of the office made no reference to petroleum, although it included coffee. In 1934 and 1935, when a branch of the American Petroleum Institute requested Woodring, then assistant secretary of war, to provide a speaker on oil and industrial mobilization for an API meeting, Colonel C.T. Harris, director of the planning branch, indicated that "as oil is one of those materials for which we consider the domestic supply ample, we have not prepared elaborate plans for restrictive control. Consequently, the War Department has nothing definite or complete enough on the subject of oil and mobilization to interest such a gathering."[4] By 1941, and certainly by the 1950s, such a response would have been unthinkable, and it indicated a retardation of the more advanced military-industrial planning activities that had been conducted in the 1920s. Harris's evident complacency was not shared by all of his colleagues, however. When he questioned why a commodity such as oil should receive so much attention when the army and navy in the event of war required only 25 percent of peacetime production, he was reminded that such estimates were based on the 1924 General Mobilization Plan and failed to consider the greater degree of mechanization that would characterize a future war. Although his position failed to gain official endorsement, Captain C.A. Carlson urged that it should be U.S. military policy not to use domestic U.S. resources when foreign supplies were available. In part, failure to take more decisive measures along those lines derived from the supreme confidence that in the event of a wartime oil shortage for military use, supplies from Venezuela, Colombia, and Mexico were assured.[5] In other words, the strategic defense perimeter for petroleum explicitly included Caribbean basin resources as a natural extension of U.S. domestic reserves. The Department of War did become increasingly sensitive to the issue of petroleum requirements, although the focus of department discussions with oil executives in 1935 and 1936 concerned the security of domestic resources in the event of war, rather than attempts to obtain additional foreign sources.[6] That emphasis appears to have been more characteristic of military interest in the earlier 1920s and the 1940s. The furthest the war department went in the 1930s tended to be expressions of support for the conservation attempts of the interior and navy departments on public oil lands, especially the Naval Reserves. As Secretary of War Woodring wrote Swanson in early 1938, the war department included oil as an essential material in its industrial mobilization plans and was "very much interested in adequate measures for the conservation of this natural resource." Since the war department saw petroleum as of primary interest to the navy, it was hardly surprising that war department officials constantly rebuffed suggestions to establish a military petroleum reserve. The director of the planning branch stressed that mobilization plans provided for the regulation of such commodities by civilian agencies established under presidential authority. To Harris, military administration of the industry during wartime was impractical.[7] Although the Army-Navy Munitions Board did establish in 1939 a subcommittee on petroleum, under the chairmanship of oil man Joseph E. Pogue, there was no real departure from complacency on resource supply or from dependency on private-sector initiative. As late as September 1941, Brigadier General H.K. Rutherford, chairman of the war department facilities board, stressed that U.S. reserves were adequate for "many years to come," even though from a strategic standpoint the increased use of foreign oil might be justified.[8]

Given this absence of significant army contribution to the debate on oil policy, the initiative fell to the State Department and to a lesser extent the navy, and in domestic coordination to the Department of the Interior under Harold Ickes. The domestic petroleum industry was one sector of the economy that received attention in the early New Deal, and efforts to control production levels, limit new development, and stabilize prices paralleled similar efforts among the major firms internationally and were essential to the global stabilization that the majors sought. Historians have identified two phases to Roosevelt's domestic oil policies. The first, from 1933 to 1935, concentrated on restricting production and stabilizing prices under the National Recovery Administration oil code. The second, from 1935 to Pearl Harbor, related more to institutionalizing some reforms, such as state-legislated production controls and federal regulation of interstate commerce in oil produced beyond established quotas.[9] In both phases, the underlying philosophy differed little, if at all, from that of the Hoover administration, but the programs were carried out with more vigor and success. The industry, through the API, actively participated in the drafting of a code for petroleum, and major officials such as Walter Teagle endorsed a stabilizing code. Its provisions enabled the federal government to recommend production quotas and granted presidential discretion to fix prices. Ickes's appointment as administrator carried with it, as well, the power to restrict oil imports to the level for the last half of 1932, which Ickes proceeded to do. At the same time, an import duty of twenty-one cents per barrel remained in force until modified in 1939 and 1943 as the result of reciprocal trade agreements with Venezuela and Mexico respectively, although there was opposition to import duties from the U.S. Shipping Board and the Department of Commerce, on grounds that the duty increased the cost of fuel for the merchant marine. Cordell Hull also indicated to NRA administrator General Hugh Johnson that import restrictions would reduce the production of petroleum in Latin American countries exporting to the U.S. and adversely affect relations with those countries. Johnson responded that "a planned domestic economy may at some times and places clash with international economic flows. This may be one of them."[10]

The NRA code remained in force until 1935, when the Supreme Court brought the entire structure tumbling down. But the pre-1935 actions had accomplished the objective of raising oil prices, with crude up to one dollar a barrel by the fall of 1933.[11] In 1935, in an effort to find a substitute for the NRA, the Senate passed a measure introduced by Tom Connally of Texas, the "hot oil" bill, which recognized the efforts of the Interstate Oil Compact that included all of the oil-producing states except California and Louisiana, continued import restrictions, and formalized federal control of commerce in oil produced in excess of state quotas (that is, "hot oil").[12]

Although these measures were largely cosmetic rather than structural in nature, they encouraged a high level of business-government cooperation and facilitated the domestic stabilization that was essential for efficient international expansion as well. The antitrust suits initiated in 1936 against twenty-three oil companies and their conviction of a price-fixing misdemeanor under the Sherman Anti-Trust Act two years later seriously undermined that business-government harmony. Company officials felt that the administration had let them down, having encouraged the type of cooperative activity for which they were prosecuted.[13] Coming as the lawsuits did at the same time as the first expropriations of American oil properties in Latin America and the lack, from the companies' perspective, of an adequately forceful State Department response, oil industry-government relations reached a low ebb in domestic and foreign policy, where they remained until the war revitalized cooperation and restored business confidence. Whether this brief antitrust phase was an "unrealistic" approach to the industry's problems, as has been suggested, is another question. But the effort to discourage a high level of cooperation among the integrated companies and increase competition certainly ran counter to the basic thrust of the international companies since World War I.[14]

Roosevelt himself appears to have been as sensitive as any of his predecessors to the need for oil conservation, regulation, and foreign expansion, and to have had a more pronounced dedication to general conservation. In June 1934, for example, he established the National Resources Board under NIRA (National Industrial Recovery Act) authority, the membership of which included the secretaries of interior (as chairman), war, navy, agriculture, commerce, labor, and a representative of the Federal Emergency Relief Administration. Its task was to prepare for the president a program to deal with the development of land, water, and other national resources. The board gave no significant attention to petroleum, but did examine, during the next eight years, issues ranging from the importation of strategic raw materials to the stabilization of employment.[15] Ickes, after consultation with Roosevelt, also established in early 1934 a Planning Committee for Mineral Policy, whose eleven members were drawn from a broad range of departments, including state, war, commerce, the geological survey, the Bureau of Foreign and Domestic Commerce, the chief forester, and Charles Leith of the Science Advisory Board. Herbert Feis was the State Department representative. Although these bodies discussed problems of energy resources and the competitive relationship among them, there was little progress of a concrete nature in defining priorities and establishing clear policy links between domestic and foreign oil development.[16]

New Deal regulatory agencies, and especially Ickes, did not gain unanimous endorsement from the oil industry, and some of the enmity created in these years would carry over into the war period and cloud Ickes's relations with the industry as petroleum administrator for war. Nonetheless, there was more industry support for Ickes's efforts to coordinate production and pricing than some of the more vitriolic criticism would imply. In early 1935, Warren C. Platt, editor of the *National Petroleum News*, sharply critiqued Ickes's appeal for closer government supervision. "Ickes," Platt wrote, "is evidently bound and determined to gain more control for himself over the oil industry. I would not be surprised but the man has illusions of perhaps a national dictatorship with himself as our Mussolini." *Petroleum News* called for Ickes's resignation, but other correspondence in the Ickes papers suggests that industry opinion was not so uniformly negative. E.A. Landreth, for instance, a Fort Worth independent producer and a director of the American Petroleum Institute, publicly challenged Platt's view, indicating that Ickes's approach was fair and had the support of a broad range of independent and major companies. Oscar Sutro, a vice-president of Standard Oil of California, also expressed support for Ickes's regulatory approach. In his opinion federal control could be confined to supervision of trade agreements necessary to prevent domestic waste and to keep the industry reasonably stabilized, but he strongly objected to federal antitrust laws, which he contended had "forced waste, overproduction and senseless competition on American industry."[17]

Whether or not Ickes had dictatorial ambitions, the vigorous secretary of the interior was the most outspoken advocate in the Roosevelt administration of a firm petroleum policy, and to the extent Roosevelt required persuading, Ickes carried the president along with him. In the fall of 1934, in an appearance before the House Committee on Interstate and Foreign Commerce, and the following year in the report of the petroleum administrator, Ickes stressed that United States reserves were limited and the resource irreplaceable. Since the country was using its reserves more rapidly than other nations were using theirs, the U.S. would likely be the first major power to face a shortage. The U.S. should not, he argued, be dependent on costly substitute fuels or become dependent on foreign oil supplies, since oil was "indispensable" to national defense.[18]

A year after the passage of the Connally "hot oil" legislation, regulating interstate and foreign commerce in oil, Ickes also established a petroleum conservation division in the Department of the Interior, with George Holland as director, E.B. Swanson as associate director, for production, and John Frey as associate director for refining and marketing. The new division was intended to administer the Connally Act but also had broader responsibility to discuss oil- and gas-related questions with all federal departments and agencies.[19] It was not until late 1937 that President Roosevelt requested Ickes to have a study on oil resources prepared. What prompted Roosevelt's initiative at that time is difficult to determine with any precision, but it is evident that there was a growing consensus around him that the oil issue was pressing. In January of that year, his long-time associate James A. Moffett, formerly of Jersey Standard, then chairman and president of the California Texas Oil Company, underlined Ickes's concern over oil shortages. Noting that world consumption in the previous four years had increased 40 percent, while production was up only 35 percent, Moffett cautioned that "the United States and Venezuela, plus any source of supplies which must be found and made available, will be pressed to the limit to supply the demand of the next four years." Moffett stressed that the fact that Germany, Japan, and Italy did not own any oil-producing territory "would indicate that the forward picture for future supplies may have an important political territorial effect in the future. I have particularly in mind Borneo and the Dutch East Indies."[20]

O'Shaughnessey's Oil Bulletin, published by South American Oil Reports in Connecticut, picked up the conservationist refrain in April, endorsing the recommendations of the prominent petroleum geologist Everett de Golyer. The *Oil Bulletin*, as the voice of oil interests with foreign operations, was logically especially supportive of de Golyer's suggestion that the U.S. admit foreign oil imports to the extent they did not disrupt the domestic industry and encourage American companies to secure foreign reserves. The *Bulletin* also endorsed the geologist's call for adherence to more efficient techniques in prospecting, producing, and refining petroleum.

Later in the year, E.B. Swanson, director of the Petroleum Conservation Division, expressed similar views in a statement to the National Resources Committee. Swanson indicated that high domestic consumption would ultimately render U.S. reserves inadequate, although he could not predict when the trend would lead to actual scarcity. Like de Golyer and Ickes, Swanson stressed the need for efficient techniques in exploiting oil resources to maximize recovery rates. He argued that the lighter and more valuable petroleum products could be derived primarily from domestic production, with foreign sources providing the heavier crudes.[21]

It was within this context of ongoing discussion of oil policy that Roosevelt suggested to Harold Ickes in late December 1937 that it would be useful to send a presidential message to Congress on energy resources, including oil, coal, and hydroelectric power. The draft message, which Ickes's office prepared, contained all of the ideas on oil policy advanced by the interior secretary since 1934, but the main thrust of the paper was the determination that the U.S. not risk exhaustion of its oil resources before the other major powers. The message was not delivered, in part it seems because other administration officials thought the timing inauspicious, with antitrust suits pending and with the companies' position precarious in Mexico and Bolivia.[22]

Roosevelt nevertheless requested the National Resources Committee in March 1938 to undertake a study of all energy resources. That study was undertaken by Dr Ralph Watkins of the University of Pittsburgh. As part of the project, Watkins met with State Department officials, including Frederick Livesey of the economic adviser's office, to discuss the foreign policy implications of energy control. In addition, Cordell Hull outlined for Ickes what the Department of State's objectives were in this area, especially the general desire to ensure free trade in petroleum products, which the secretary of state contended were normally complimentary to domestic products rather than in competition. Hull also stressed that the department, in his view, had taken no "unusual steps to aid the efforts of American citizens to secure the ownership of oil properties abroad." Hull failed to define "normal," but he did suggest that the department had done nothing except to express interest in such developments,[23] a rather inaccurate portrayal of the events of the previous twenty years, even if this was the role that Hull believed appropriate.

Jersey Standard took some interest in the Watkins report. On two occasions Jersey officials visited the State Department specifically to discuss the study, expressing the hope that fuel oil in competition with other energy resources would not be penalized. Jersey officials also stressed that the company was sponsoring a drive for increased government encouragement of American ownership of natural resources abroad.[24] Jersey need not have worried about the Watkins report, since no concrete measure ensued. The administration did press Congress for an oil conservation bill during 1939, and Roosevelt personally recommended it to the House Committee on Interstate and Foreign Commerce;[25] but the war intervened before policy could crystallize.

THE FAR EAST

Developments in the specific realm of foreign oil policy, as suggested earlier, reflected a high degree of continuity during the prewar Roosevelt administration. Although there was diplomatic activity in most areas in which American oil interests were active during the 1930s, developments in the Far East and Latin America had the most pronounced impact on the evolution of petroleum policy, and it is consequently on those areas that the discussion will focus.

The dilemma that Japan posed to American oil policy was not initially a new one. In July 1934 the Japanese government enacted legislation providing that importers of petroleum had to maintain stocks equal to one-half their previous year's imports. Moreover, refiners had to possess equipment capable of refining a minimum of 50,000 kiloliters per annum. The legislation was also designed to control prices. Several months later, the Japanese regime in Manchukuo approved a petroleum law establishing a state monopoly on the refining of imported oil. At the time the legislation passed, British-Dutch and American firms in the Dutch East Indies and the United States were the prime suppliers of Japanese oil requirements. Among American interests, the dominant company in the area was Standard-Vacuum (Stanvac), formed in 1933 as a result of Socony-Vacuum and Jersey Standard combining the former's Far East marketing capacity with the latter's producing capabilities in the East Indies. The Texas Company, Standard of California, and the Union Oil Company were also active.[26]

For Stanvac and Royal Dutch Shell interests, the Japanese legislation seriously threatened their marketing and refining flexibility. For the United States and Britain, the Japanese position was more threatening, indicating an effort to acquire a high degree of control over its oil industry and to ensure a high level of domestic reserve, which the British and Americans feared would be put to bellicose use. By projecting the establishment of a government monopoly, the 1934 legislation also challenged the American preference for the free-enterprise model. To the extent that the monopoly law was applicable to Manchukuo, a state the U.S. did not recognize, the initiative would also serve to tighten Japanese control in northern China, running against the grain of American policy since the 1920s. The crisis was thus more extensive than a threat to U.S. oil interests, but it was in terms of oil policy that the administration met the challenge.

There was an immediate consultative response from British and American interests, although the Foreign Office soon complained of U.S. lethargy. In August, Ickes met with Walter Teagle, Henri Deterding, and Stanley Hornbeck, all of whom agreed that a boycott of oil shipments to Japan would likely be the most effective means to alter Japanese policy, if a coordinated program could be organized.[27] In these early discussions both the companies and the British were more united on a positive course of action than was the State Department. The companies through the early fall refused to comply with Japanese marketing quotas, and the British ambassador approached the Japanese government on Shell's behalf. To this point, the State Department had taken no action, and Deterding and Frederick Godber of Shell pressed Teagle to obtain the department's cooperation. State Department preference was clearly to have the companies initiate and control any boycott, although all officials recognized that the main difficulty would be to gain the compliance of smaller firms. Not surprisingly, it was not until the end of September that Ambassador Joseph Grew was instructed to object to the legislation. By early October, Britain, the U.S., and the Netherlands were, as British Ambassador Sir R. Clive aptly suggested, "in step"; it had been agreed to protest the legislation on grounds that it made the investment climate uncertain and violated the Nine Power Treaty of the 1920s, but to allow the companies to conduct any boycott on their own.[28]

The official reluctance to participate in a formal boycott derived from several factors. One was the British concern that it could not count on full American cooperation, which was vital to the success of such an operation. More serious was the belief, especially strong in the British Board of Trade and the Admiralty, that a united effort to enforce the Open Door policy in Japan and Manchukuo would provide Japan with the excuse and occasion to seize oil properties in the Dutch East Indies. The dilemma was a Hobson's choice. To show excessive firmness might force the Japanese into more aggressive action; to show weakness on oil policy could have disastrous consequences for British interests in China and possibly India. British investment in Shanghai alone was 76 percent of the total British investment in China. The British cabinet consequently agreed that the oil companies could initiate an embargo if they desired. The United States, conversely, took no formal position, much to the chagrin of Foreign Office officials, who blamed the failure of British policy on a lack of full cooperation from the U.S. As one official observed, "The manoeuvres of the United States Government in this business make a rather unpleasant impression ... There is a mixture of obtuseness and craft in all this and an apparent desire to push us into the front line while refusing to take the one essential step which would have helped."[29]

The failure of the contemplated petroleum boycott of Japan in 1934 derived in part from a lack of commitment by the American government and willingness to use the oil companies as a weapon of diplomacy. Clearly the United States had less at stake in the region than did Britain, but as with other areas of international relations in the 1930s, a harder line against Japan in 1934 might have altered the later course of events. In final analysis, it was the lack of government support that doomed the boycott. Although several of the smaller companies in Japan, especially Standard of California and the Union Oil Company, failed to cooperate with a boycott, a direct government commitment to the plan would have placed more pressure on the companies to conform.[30] The boycott thus failed to affect Japanese policy in 1934, but it would be used again in 1940 when the strategic threat posed by Japan was much greater than the narrower corporate interests in the area. By that time, there was also a more closely integrated relationship between the companies and the government in decisions relating to Japan, for instance the refusal to sell oil-cracking processes to Japan that would enable it to manufacture high-octane aviation gasoline.[31]

The Japanese situation in 1934 served to highlight problems in Anglo-American relations in the Far East. But what was more important, in terms of oil policy abroad, the situation demonstrated the inadequate level of control the state could exercise over the private sector abroad in times of emergency. A close associational state-business relationship was adequate to meet normal requirements but provided inadequate state leverage in the event of disagreement. State reluctance to support the aborted boycott in any formal manner also underlined the extent to which defense of the Open Door policy and free enterprise abroad was less important than the more urgent need to contain Japanese expansionism. Besides, actual petroleum resources were not at stake in the Japanese situation, simply marketing rights, and it would have been foolhardy, as the British Admiralty pointed out, to force Japan into a corner that would force it to seize East Indies resources in order to obtain adequate supplies.

LATIN AMERICA

Geographic proximity, a sphere-of-influence tradition, and the threat-ened loss to American interests of actual petroleum resources provided the main factors that account for the different American reaction to the intensification of oil nationalism in Latin America in the later 1930s. Timing was also a consideration. When Bolivia expropriated Jersey Standard properties in 1937, and Mexico the following year announced the nationalization of many foreign-owned oil companies, the interna-tional situation had substantially deteriorated. Japan had invaded China and was engaged in a major war; the Spanish Civil War had for two years involved European powers in a conflict that threatened to ig-nite into an international war; Italy had invaded Ethiopia; Nazi Ger-many had concluded an alliance with Italy, remilitarized the Rhineland, and in March 1938 annexed Austria. By 1937 there was sound reason for a sense of insecurity, even in the isolationist United States, and this accounts in part for the nature of the reaction to events in Latin American oil policy.

It is possible to exaggerate the extent to which expropriation in Bolivia and nationalization in Mexico actually affected the develop-ment of U.S. foreign oil policy. The issues have received considerable and detailed attention from historians, but rarely have they been ex-amined in terms of general oil policy.[32] Clearly, the issues were highly significant in U.S.–Latin American relations, and, in conjunction with the wartime emergency that followed, did lead to a reassessment of American foreign oil policy. Nonetheless, the war itself may have been a more important catalyst in prompting the reassessment than the ex-propriations, and the settlements negotiated would certainly have been different had the war not ensued and placed additional pressure on the United States to secure its supply of foreign petroleum and other strategic raw materials available in Latin America. At the same time that the war heightened official American concern about the security of oil supply, it made officials increasingly reluctant to pursue policies that would alienate Latin American governments. This was especially applicable in the Bolivian case, where the State Department was less convinced of the strength of the company's claim than it was in Mexico. There is also a danger of linking the Bolivian and Mexican cases. The State Department did not do so at the time. Rather, officials saw them as distinct, since Bolivia did not actually nationalize Standard Oil property, but seized its holdings on the basis of alleged fraud in taxation and export of oil to Argentina during the Chaco War with Paraguay. Besides, in Bolivia, unlike in Mexico, Standard Oil did not own the land, although the dispute often focused on rights to the subsoil.[33] Consequently, efforts to obtain compensation for nationalized property were consistently advanced in conjunction with recognition of the right of host nations to nationalize in the public interest. Throughout the crises in Bolivia, Mexico, and Venezuela in the years immediately prior to the war, hemispheric solidarity, the security of oil supply through the Open Door, and liberalized trade were the first priorities, followed by efforts to discourage the creation of state enterprise abroad.

In the Bolivian case there were the additional problems of resolving issues relating to the Chaco War and general commercial relations between Bolivia and the two major regional powers, Argentina and Brazil.[34] Throughout, there was again a close but not always amicable relationship between state and company officials, many of the latter becoming increasingly convinced that a weak defense against nationalization abroad and a brief flurry of antitrust activity at home made the Roosevelt administration a less-than-trustworthy partner. A close examination of the crises, however, indicates that there was in fact a high degree of consensus between state and company officials on desired policy.

Although the U.S. had faced expropriations in the Soviet Union after 1917 and had been confronted with the possibility for the previous twenty years in various parts of Latin America, the Bolivian expropriation of March 1937 was the first concrete Latin American action along those lines. One aspect in particular made the expropriation a diplomatic issue; this was the Bolivian contention that since confiscation was the result of illegal actions by Standard Oil of Bolivia, the company was not entitled to compensation for lost property. Diplomatic intervention was complicated, however, by a number of considerations, not the least of which was the inclusion of the Calvo Clause in the original contract between Standard Oil and the Bolivian government. The Calvo Clause was a restricting agreement binding the company to resolve all disputes over its Bolivian operations without recourse to the United States government. The company claimed that neither it nor the

United States government could be bound by such a restriction. The State Department hedged on this issue throughout the negotiations without directly confronting it, but by its very participation in the negotiations over the following several years in effect circumvented or violated the clause.[35] A second consideration that muted State Department enthusiasm for a stronger stand against Bolivia was the relative unimportance of Bolivian oil in comparison with Mexican and Venezuelan oil, and the importance of other Bolivian strategic raw materials, such as tin, lead, zinc, and tungsten. Although Standard Oil had an estimated $17 million invested in Bolivian development, it had not drilled a new well in the five years prior to the confiscation and at the time was discussing a possible sale to the Bolivian state oil company, YPFB (Yacimientos Petrolíferos Fiscales Bolivianos). In 1937, production was only slightly in excess of 1000 barrels a day. Well into the crisis, Cordell Hull informed the Bolivian minister to the United States that the U.S. was concerned about potential European agression in Latin America, especially in undeveloped natural resources. "The dollars and cents," he noted, "involved in the oil seizure were small compared to the great injury that would result to Bolivia ... if that sort of an act should go unpunished."[36] A third complicating feature in the Bolivian case was the American fear of Nazi influence in Bolivia by the time war erupted in Europe. Indeed, it was not until the Bolivian coup attempt of July 1941, which implicated the German minister to Bolivia, that the United States intensified its efforts to find a solution to the oil confiscation by extending the possibility of financial assistance through Export-Import Bank credits. Although a payment to Standard Oil was not an explicit condition of the American approach, it was made clear to Bolivian officials that loans depended on an across-the-board reciprocity,[37] and Bolivia by early 1942 agreed to a $1.5 million payment to Standard Oil.

Company opinion throughout the dispute was united on the injustice of the Bolivian expropriation but less than consensual on appropriate action. General business opinion was evident in the 15 April 1937 editorial of *O'Shaughnessey's Oil Bulletin*, which labeled the Bolivian decree an "unfortunate act of violence." James D. Mooney of General Motors wrote the secretary of state that although the company had no investments in Bolivia, that government's action was "of grave moment to American industry as a whole ... throughout Latin America."[38] Thomas Anderson, a Jersey Standard vice-president, most effectively portrayed the hard-line approach, although his views were shared by Jersey President Walter Teagle and Standard Oil Counsel Thomas W. Palmer. Throughout, Armstrong emphasized the serious international implications if Bolivia succeeded in confiscating the Standard

Oil properties without compensation. He also lightly dismissed the significance of the Calvo Clause, informing the department that it had frequently ruled that a Calvo Clause in a contract was not justification for a denial of justice by a foreign nation. To Armstrong, the legal approach that the department advised throughout 1937 and 1938 was of limited value because of the doubt of gaining a fair trial in Bolivia, and he consequently urged the department to lend its support to arbitration. Armstrong pressed as well, unsuccessfully, for the State Department to support an embargo on Bolivian Oil in Argentina and on the sale of Mexico oil in the United States. By this stage, the companies were concerned that similar developments might occur elsewhere in Latin America, especially Colombia under Alfonso López Michelson.[39] By 1939, Armstrong remained adamant that the "program of confiscation and spoliation" in Bolivia and Mexico made a strong U.S. stand imperative. He stressed to Green Hockworth that the State Department should explicitly inform Bolivia that the charges against the company were unfounded, that the oil concession was not subject to cancellation, and that the company would not sell its properties under duress. Failing Bolivian compromise on these issues, Armstrong desired arbitration. Armstrong also made it clear to State Department officials that the company was contemplating withdrawing from Latin America unless the State Department proved more vigorous in the defense of American private enterprise.[40] Even after the Bolivian Supreme Court, in what was generally considered a predetermined verdict, decided in 1939 that it could not act in the company's favor, the State Department was unwilling to take concrete measures. Armstrong maintained his insistence on a hard line, although other Standard Oil officials had come to see the wisdom of a compromise. Armstrong emphasized to the department that the company would accept nothing short of admission of error by Bolivia and a restoration of its properties. In his view it was the principle rather than the value of the company's properties in Bolivia that was vital. Eugene Holman, who was generally responsible for Standard Oil of Bolivia affairs, Thomas Palmer of Jersey's legal department, and H.A. Metzger, Jersey's urbane representative in Argentina, all included toward negotiation, possible arbitration, and compensation for lost property.[41] It was increasingly this more moderate position that prevailed, gradually isolating Armstrong, but the process was a difficult one. After the meeting of 28 April 1939, several company and department officials worked together to draft an agreement that it was hoped would be acceptable to both sides. The main dimension of the proposal was the creation of a mixed board to determine compensation. That proposal went to La Paz in early July.[42] The proposal floundered over wrangling about whether rights to the subsoil would be part of compensation, as well as whether Standard's original contract was valid, even though by the end of November Standard was willing to exclude any claim to the subsoil.

With the failure of legal action, private negotiations, and proposed arbitration, the department adopted a different tack. In early 1940 the State Department handed to the Bolivian minister in Washington a memorandum indicating the possible creation of a joint board of experts to report on the mineral, agricultural, and industrial potential of Bolivia. When the report was completed, the United States government would be disposed to consider what it or private U.S. companies could do to assist in carrying out the recommendations of the committee. There were two preconditions to American assistance: one was an agreeement on American-held Bolivian bonds in default; the other was settlement of the Standard Oil claim.[43]

Armstrong, even at this stage, desired the State Department to support the company's view either that negotiations be confined to the valuation of the property and interests of the company or that it be expanded to include all the alleged denials of justice. He specifically requested, that the U.S. government be "the party plaintiff," something the State Department was determined to avoid. Increasingly, in fact, the Bolivian and Mexican cases did become linked in State Department planning. Sumner Welles clearly was of the view by early 1941 that to push for an immediate settlement of the Standard case in Bolivia would "lead to blowing up the political situation ... Settlement," he argued, "should be made a part of the whole picture, although, of course, technically not linked with measures of economic assistance. As I see it, the Bolivian situation should be handled in much the same way as we are attempting to handle the Mexican situation."[44]

The basic difference between the company and the State Department during critical phases of the negotiations was over the degree of state involvement in the settlement. Clearly the department believed and acted on the assumption that the main issue in Bolivia was a failure to pay compensation for expropriated property. It consistently brought the parties together, and sought above all to try to keep the conflict from embroiling the politics of Bolivia and the region at a very sensitive moment in international relations. For their part, company officials, including more moderate figures such as William Farish, were disappointed that the State Department would not provide official sanctioning for any agreement. This was disconcerting, Farish informed Bonsal, "in that it might indicate that a foreign government in confiscating American property does not violate international law." Bonsal, on the other hand, was concerned that further delay in reaching a settlement could result in Bolivia making the oil properties available to a third party. "The major question of the issue," he wrote Ambassador to Mexico Josephus Daniels, "is in fact the finding of an acceptable formula for the development of this oil." Bonsal also thought that the United States could ill afford the repercussions in the rest of Latin America that might result from neglecting Standard Oil's interests in Bolivia.[45]

Although the State Department did not present the extension of a $5.5 million credit to Bolivia as linked to the Standard Oil settlement, there is no escaping the causal relationship. The American chargé in La Paz, Allan Dawson, noted their connection in the official Bolivian decree in early 1942, and the agreement stipulated that the Export-Import Bank credit had to be used promptly by the Bolivian Development Corporation for developing the petroleum resources of Bolivia. When the Bolivian Congress hesitated to approve the agreement, Dawson informed the Bolivian foreign minister that he would "be glad to tell any of his colleagues or the President himself that I considered the Standard Oil Settlement a cornerstone of the economic cooperation program."[46]

American oil policy proved generally successful in Bolivia. Anticipating that actual recovery of property was unlikely, the State Department established adequate compensation, nonintervention, and political stability as its objectives. In those it succeeded. Although Standard Oil's involvement in Bolivia ended with the settlement of its claim in 1942, the United States had been able to win its point on compensation through some economic arm-twisting, to protect other American investments in Bolivia, and to retain at least the possibility that foreign capital would be welcome in continuing to develop Bolivian oil in conjunction with YPFB. That the State Department had kept Bolivia very much within the broad outlines of the American approach to oil development was also reflected in the fact that R. Townshend served as Bolivian petroleum adviser for four months in 1942 before joining the newly established petroleum adviser's office in the State Department, and that Bolivia requested the United States to provide experienced oil personnel to assist in the administrative reorganization of YPFB, a reorganization for which Nelson Rockefeller, the highly placed coordinator of Inter-American Affairs, had indicated the possibility of financial support. Successful ties reaffirmed during the war paved the way for readier access by U.S. capital during the postwar years. Yet the result was not, as some analysts have contended, a subordination of the oil companies' interests to the national interest, implying that the oil industry was not part of that national interest. Rather, resolution of the conflict was indicative of the extent to which the state and oil industry could effectively explore what was in the long-range interest of the state and industry as a whole and reach a conclusion reflecting a high degree of consensus.[47]

MEXICO, NATIONALIZATION, AND WAR

The development of American oil policy in the aftermath of the Mexican oil nationalization was equally indicative of the effort to balance state and private-sector objectives.[48] As in Bolivia, a small number of Roosevelt-administration personalities played the critical roles, including Roosevelt himself, Secretary of State Hull, Undersecretary Welles, Assistant Secretary Adolf Berle, Jr, Assistant Secretary and wartime Ambassador to Mexico George Messersmith, Laurence Duggan in the American Republics division, and Josephus Daniels as American ambassador to Mexico. The main factors distinguishing the Mexican situation from the Bolivian were geographic proximity, which made Mexico of more immediate strategic significance to the United States, and the substantial value of American and British investment in oil. By 1940, U.S. direct investment in Mexican petroleum was approximately $41.9 million,[49] substantially less than that in Venezuela. But Mexico, nonetheless, had sufficient production and refining capacity to be of interest to potential belligerent powers in Europe.

In Mexico, as in other areas of American petroleum involvement, the same difficulties arose over business-government relationships in the setting of a policy that would meet mutual needs: that is, protect private property abroad, maintain the Open Door, secure adequate petroleum supply, and ensure that the Mexican dispute did not serve to undermine more positive Latin American relations built up during the Roosevelt presidency. As in the Bolivian dispute, business relations with the State Department were close but not always harmonious. At times even the broad consensus on business-government cooperation appeared in jeopardy, suggesting a fundamental divergence between the national interest and the major oil companies. In general their differences in this instance appeared to transcend narrow profit versus security considerations to encompass attitudes toward international development, subsoil mineral ownership, and the rights of host nations to control U.S.-based multinational corporations. The oil industry emerged from the Mexican conflict, as it did from the Bolivian dispute, convinced that the American government had shown inadequate fortitude in advancing the industry's claims. The crisis also demonstrated once again to the administration how difficult it was to control corporate behavior abroad and ensure that private and public policy coincided. By the beginning of the war, the inadequacies of American foreign oil policy were so evident to both private and public sectors that a substantial reassessment of policy began.

Mexican oil nationalization came swiftly in March 1938 under executive decree by President Lázaro Cárdenas, but the conflict had been brewing for twenty years. What immediately occasioned the measure was the explosive situation that arose in the oil fields, with administration-supported oil workers attempting to gain improved wages and living conditions, and with most of the companies refusing to yield. President Cárdenas met the challenge by unilaterally ordering wage increases. The companies appealed unsuccessfully to the Mexican courts, and then turned to economic pressure and an effort to obtain diplomatic support. It was at this stage that Cárdenas struck back, expropriating most of the foreign oil holdings, of which 70 percent were British and most of the remainder American.[50]

The private and diplomatic negotiations necessitated by the expropriation lasted until 1941. Great Britain pursued from the beginning a more concrete hard-line policy, breaking diplomatic relations and imposing economic sanctions on grounds that the expropriation was illegal. Although the American companies advocated comparable measures for the United States, the State Department, while supportive, held back, divided between such old-line antibusiness progressives as Ambassador Josephus Daniels and the more professional diplomats, perhaps best represented by Sumner Welles, George Messersmith, Adolf Berle, Jr, and Laurence Duggan. The division was complicated further by Daniels's longtime association with and his direct access to the president. The recurrent conflict between Cordell Hull and Sumner Welles over the general direction of department policy, and the intervention by such other members of the Cabinet as Henry Morgenthau, Jr, at treasury, who tended to side with the moderates,[51] added to the factors that eroded the development of a clearly defined policy.

The State Department did vacillate on policy, but it is incorrect to conclude from that vacillation, as some analysts have, that this allowed the companies to determine policy from 1938 to 1941.[52] Such a thesis exaggerates the weakness of the state, implies a consensus among the companies that did not prevail, and underestimates State Department determination to maintain private American enterprise in Mexico. The thesis also rests on the erroneous assumption that oil-company expansion abroad in the previous two decades had drawn a reluctant State Department into the position in which it had to protect American interests overseas. Again, the conflictual model sheds little light on what transpired. Such expansion that occurred was a reflection of the general growth of the American political economy.

In the case of Mexico, as in Bolivia earlier, and subsequently Venezuela, the issue was not whether the state should play a role but which role would ensure the widest protection of American interests, of which oil was the most important single commodity. The administration wanted to ensure compensation was paid, if the expropriation could not be reversed, that the conflict did not adversely affect other American investments in Mexico and elsewhere in Latin America, and that any policy pursued did not drive Mexico into the arms of Germany and Italy. Had the hard-liners in the companies and administration prevailed, Mexico might have been forced for financial reasons to tie itself more closely to the Axis powers after 1938. As it was, the oil expropriation and American company retaliation served to increase that possibility. In March 1939, Mexico exported slightly less than 2 million barrels of oil, of which 1.3 million went to Germany and 186,000 went to Italy.[53]

The concern by both Britain and the United States over the security implications of the Mexican oil seizure was evident from the outset. The British ambassador, Sir Ronald Lindsay, emphasized to Cordell Hull in late March 1938 how important Mexican oil would be in the event of war. After outlining the steps the U.S. had already taken, from expressing formal objection to suspending Mexican silver purchases, Hull assured Lindsay, then and through the summer of 1938, that the United States had no intention of allowing "some hostile war-like nation to get hold of these oil resources and control of the oil situation." At the same time, the Roosevelt administration, and here there appears to have been a general consensus in the State Department, remained firm in its recognition of the right of a nation to expropriate foreign property in the national interest, as long as adequate compensation was provided. Where oil and other natural resources were concerned there were complications, however, as Herbert Feis was prompt to point out. Did the United States, he queried, want to accept expropriation of property with compensation solely on the basis of the capital investment involved, if that capital investment had led to the discovery of oil? There was the additional problem of timing. Sumner Welles emphasized that adequate compensation for expropriated property should be provided at the time of expropriation, and he warned the Mexican ambassador to the United States in June 1938 that the United States would not recognize the legality of further expropriations unless "effective compensation" was paid at the time of taking the property.[54] Even in State Department circles, divided in their opinion of the Mexican expropriation, there was marginal sympathy for the companies and more substantial anxiety about the potential international repercussions of the situation. Josephus Daniels, for instance, who persistently advocated a more compromising policy toward Mexico than did either the companies or many of his colleagues, nevertheless worried about increased ties with Germany and Japan. By September 1938 he was reporting that Mexican trade was slumping, and that Mexico was being compelled to dispose of its oil through barter arrangements because of the difficulty of selling for cash. The Mexican finance minister, Eduardo Suarez, indicated there were substantial oil sales to Germany and smaller ones to Italy and oil-hungry Japan. One of Mexico's difficulties was its inability to obtain tetraethyl from American companies in order to improve the quality of its refined products, thus forcing Mexican sales of crude oil and semirefined oil to Germany on a barter basis through the American firm W.R. Davis and Company of New York.

The *Washington Star* reported on 12 December 1938 that Davis's firm had negotiated a contract to supply $17 million in Mexican oil in return for German industrial equipment through 1939. Under a separate contract, Mexico was to supply the German Navy with oil in exchange for $8 million in cash and an additional credit for the purchase of German products. The *Star* lamented that "the establishment of vital economic ties ... inevitably link Mexican interest with the ultimate destiny of Nazi-Fascism in Europe." Daniels commented that "the oil companies seem to have no concern for the result of their refusal to confer with the Mexican Government upon our trade."[55]

The oil expropriation and increased Mexican economic ties with Germany, as Daniels recognized, not only created problems for American oil companies and for U.S. security, but also challenged other American economic interests in Mexico. In early 1939 the manager of the Mexico City branch of the National City Bank of New York informed both head office and the American embassy that such major United States firms as General Electric were losing bids on Mexican contracts to German competitors, in part because German goods were being made more readily and cheaply available in exchange for bartered oil. These reports of increased Axis economic ties paralleled unverified reports to the state and war departments from FBI director J. Edgar Hoover of increasing Nazi activity in Mexico. In late September 1939, for example, Hoover informed Adolf Berle that there were 250 German pilots in Mexico and eight German submarines operating from the port of Vera Cruz, and that Germany had promised to "give" Mexico British Honduras in return for wartime oil support.[56]

Japanese interests also threatened to gain a direct foothold while Mexican-American private negotiations floundered in the course of 1939. The American military attaché, Lieutenant-Colonel Gordon McCoy, reported in September that the Mexican government had issued its first drilling permits since the expropriations, to the Veracruzana Oil Company, which was directed by the Mexican assistant secretary of communications but controlled primarily by Japanese capital. The company's drilling permits included the Isthmus of Tehuantepec, where it was believed the company also planned to construct a pipeline.[57] Such a development posed a security threat to the

United States by facilitating Japanese access to western-hemisphere oil resources and directly establishing Japanese interests in the vital Central American area. It further threatened to frustrate the American tactic of forcing a settlement of the expropriation issue by attempting to cut Mexico off from her export markets and reduce the price Mexican oil could command in world markets. Such tactics would not succeed if Mexico were able to negotiate on a government-to-government basis with nations that were short of oil or, like Mexico, were moving in a nationalistic direction and were equally anxious to break the domination of the British–Dutch and American majors.[58]

One of the factors that accounted for the appearance of State Department lethargy on the expropriation in 1938 and 1939 was the clear preference for a private settlement between the companies and the Mexican government. Such a conclusion, it was believed, would enable the department to protect American interests, strategic and commercial, in Mexico without giving the appearance of pressuring Mexico into submission and thus compromising the Good Neighbor policy in the region. This approach depended on maintaining a firm but noninterventionist stand with Mexican authorities; but it also depended on the companies' willingness to accept the principle of compensated expropriation, to compromise on property valuation and the ownership of the subsoil. Private negotiations, actively encouraged by the department, floundered on each of these issues, much to the growing chagrin of Cordell Hull and Sumner Welles, who took a very direct role in the proceedings.

The idea advanced by the companies that the State Department, as Harold Ickes phrased it, "plucked daisies" while the industry conducted the oil negotiations does not bear up under security. Throughout, department officials encouraged private negotiation only as a means of achieving public policy. The department and President Roosevelt intervened with Mexican officials during the negotiations; they arranged to bring the parties together, encouraged fruitful liens of enquiry and discouraged others, prepared drafts of proposed agreements, and in general worked closely with the company officials directly involved. The administration also took concrete measures to discourage Mexican quiescence, including opposing American purchase of petroleum from the expropriated properties and pushing down the price of silver to undermine Mexico's international financial position.[59]

It was when publicly encouraged private negotiations appeared to have reached an impasse in mid-1939 that the department pressed for more direct official action and Roosevelt personally proposed arbitration on the oil issue to President Cárdenas. That personal appeal had little opportunity to take effect before Germany invaded Poland. Even with this request for arbitration, in his covering letter to Daniels, Sumner Welles stressed that the U.S. government did not view the dispute as one between the two nations.[60]

The oil companies chose their spokesmen carefully for the negotiations, seeking individuals who not only could command their confidence and that of the Mexican government, but would also have easy entrée to official American circles. Sinclair and the other independent companies appointed Patrick J. Hurley in late 1938. Formerly secretary of war in the Hoover administration, the Republican attorney also subsequently served with George Marshall in the Pacific theatre and as President Roosevelt's personal emissary in the Middle East during World War II. The majors, led by Jersey Standard, acquired Donald Richberg, a nationally prominent progressive lawyer who had played an important role in drafting the National Industrial Recovery Act early in the New Deal and had served as chief administrator of the NRA in 1935 until its demise that year. Both men, especially Richberg, were strong advocates of business-government cooperation. Rather than working as a singular spokesman for company policy, Richberg played an important intermediary role, helping to shape company policy along lines more in keeping with State Department policy.

Of the two, Hurley acquired the simpler assignment, finding Sinclair interests willing to reach a settlement on the basis of a valuation of the expropriated property. Richberg faced a tougher uphill fight. He consulted frequently with both Welles and Hull and refrained from pressing the companies' positions too vigorously when he wished to avoid the impression that discussions were faltering over company intransigence. For precisely this reason, there were times when he expressed the view that the companies would have to "fish or cut bait" in the negotiations. Indeed, he ultimately resigned in early 1941, frustrated with the failure of the discussions to progress. There was little doubt, however, where Richberg's basic sympathies lay. Although he expressed private and public support for Roosevelt-Hull policy, he told a meeting of the National Petroleum Association in April 1939 that Mexican reservation to the nation of its subsoil resources was unacceptable and that the companies had no intention of legalizing the expropriation by accepting the "status of creditors."

The Richberg negotiations in 1939 and 1940 faltered primarily over those two issues, but the companies' opposition to the expropriation went much deeper. By 1939, following expropriation in Bolivia two years earlier, Standard Oil officials clearly feared the rapid spread of nationalization of oil properties in Latin America unless the Roosevelt administration and the companies went to the barricades over the Mexican expropriation. Company officials also contended that although compensated expropriation in principle might be defensible, negotiation with Mexico was fruitless because of its incapacity to pay for nationalized properties. Since Mexico had nationalized, Jersey vice-president William Farish argued, knowing that it lacked the capacity to compensate, the action was illegal. The majors were also strongly opposed to a settlement that would involve their minority participation in a Mexican state oil corporation. They had experienced similar developments already in Europe and elsewhere in Latin America and found the structure unduly restrictive.[61]

When negotiations floundered on these issues in the summer of 1939, it was the Mexican chargé in Washington to whom Welles directed his irritation, however, when he cautioned that the U.S. government could "no longer stay out of the picture." Laurence Duggan also warned Ramón Beteta in even stronger terms that unless a settlement was reached the oil companies might successfully campaign to defeat Roosevelt in the 1940 elections, with the possibility that a new Republican administration less favorably disposed to Mexico would come into power. Given the predominantly Republican leanings of the majors, such a threat had little meaning, and Cárdenas had his own political obstacles in 1939.[62]

Welles's annoyance with the majors was less public but equally strong. Reporting to Hull late in the year on a conversation with Richberg, Welles critiqued the lack of sincere and active negotiation by the companies. He added that it was "impossible for the department of state to remain quiet for much longer." If Standard Oil did not intend to negotiate further on concrete proposals, the department would have to insist on arbitration. His vexation at this stage prompted the drafting of an arbitration proposal by the companies and the department, in which Britain and the Netherlands would also be represented. The draft included provision for the interim protection of the property and a specific article included by the companies designed to counteract Mexico's use of a Calvo Clause. That proposal, too, failed to break the impasse. Rather, in the fall of 1940, the State Department proposed to Mexico a general settlement of a number of outstanding issues, including agrarian claims, defaulted Mexican bonds, Mexican currency and silver, and the oil question. For oil, it posed two alternatives: the first that Mexico make an advance payment of $9 million toward final compensation, and that each government would appoint appraisers to evaluate the properties; the second was that the companies extend services, financing, and marketing facilities, and retain a percentage either of annual oil production or of net proceeds from its sale. A meeting of the Mexican ambassador and Standard officials on these alternatives also proved "unfruitful," however, and a long-desired private solution finally evaded the department.

The Mexican expropriation, more than any other foreign oil policy conflict in the interwar years, underlined some of the fundamental differences that divided the private sector from government on foreign oil issues. The Red Line negotiations in the 1920s had revealed some of the inconsistencies in the Open Door policy and the difficulty of reconciling an antitrust tradition at home with support for what increasingly amounted to an oil cartel abroad. There was no retreat from the commitment to the Open Door and the need for American holdings abroad of strategic raw materials, but there was in the 1930s a liberalization of American foreign economic policy, reflected in the Reciprocal Trade Agreements Program and in the increasing sensitivity of American officials to corporate behavior abroad that was in keeping with the image of the Good Neighbor. Only slowly awakening domestically to the realities of organized labor, the establishment of social security, and the role of the corporation in a welfare state, the oil companies had not yet effectively projected changing domestic realities into the foreign sector. That was the fundamental crisis of the Mexican expropriation and of the general response to increased oil nationalism in Latin America.

Josephus Daniels captured the dilemma effectively in commenting to Cordell Hull on a speech delivered at the University of Virginia by Thomas Armstrong of Jersey Standard. Although concluding that Cárdenas had no legal right to expropriate without agreement on the valuation of the oil properties, Daniels argued that the fundamental issue surrounding the consideration of wages and working conditions in the fields and the expropriation was national sovereignty. Cárdenas, Daniels asserted, had the right to insist that the companies obey the Mexican Supreme Court. At Virginia, Armstrong had demanded the return of the companies' properties and a return to labor agreements in force in 1927. Daniels countered that there was "no right for any other nation to intervene in what is purely a domestic concern. The increase in wage agitation is universal. No country can control the problem in a neighbor."[63]

Daniels was ahead of his time even among his more enlightened colleagues, although there were individuals in the department and in the companies who recognized the wave of the future. What was important in 1938–41 was that Daniels's empathy for Mexican aspirations would take American policy in a direction not unlike that of Welles's *realpolitik*, that is toward acceptance of the right of expropriation with compensation and a solution that would allow both Mexico to save face and the United States to protect corporate and security interests in the area. Those were the objectives throughout the private and public negotiations (which ultimately resulted in an agreement with Mexico in late 1941, only three weeks prior to Pearl Harbor) that covered both general American claims in Mexico as well as the oil controversy, and ultimately provided for a payment to the remaining companies of less than $29 million. Strikingly absent from the agreement was a reference to the issue of subsoil ownership.[64]

The timing of the agreement significantly determined its nature. Given the relative isolation of more moderate and progressive figures such as Daniels, Morgenthau, and indeed Roosevelt on the issue of expropriation, had a wartime emergency not threatened in 1939–41, there is every reason to believe that the administration would have adhered more closely to the companies' position, which was to try to recover American property. The main issue at the time, however, was to protect American security, which, from the American perspective, included the preservation of U.S. access to Mexican oil resources. In 1940 the United States wanted not only oil security but air and naval bases in Mexico, and the relationship between the issues was formally broached by army, navy, and State Department officials with the Mexican ambassador in June 1940. Formal ties were not established until early 1942 with the creation of a joint defense commission, more than a year after Manuel Avila Camacho had been elected to the presidency, but a general agreement on the use of Mexican bases for American planes in transit was reached in April 1941. Throughout, Mexican officials gave the impression that full cooperation hinged on a settlement of the oil controversy that conformed largely to its interpretation of the expropriation. That the war was a crucial factor in the nature and timing of the settlement was also evident in the State Department's determination to place the Mexican oil industry on a stable footing as quickly as possible. Hull unequivocally informed Daniels's successor as ambassador to Mexico, George Messersmith, in mid-1942 that "nothing except the exigencies of war should be permitted to interfere with the sound and orderly re-establishment of the oil industry in Mexico." Hull also cautioned that the rebuilding of the industry during the war should take place with an eye to the postwar era to avoid the "seeds of trouble which ultimately might leave both Mexico and the hemisphere ... without the advantages for which such great pains have been suffered."[65]

ACCOMMODATION IN VENEZUELA

The Roosevelt administration learned one basic lesson from the Bolivian and Mexican expropriations that it shortly applied in Venezuela: the government needed to play a more direct, public role in shaping oil relations with Latin American nations and the oil companies prior to the development of another crisis. The Venezuelan situation between

1938 and 1943 reflected the increasingly preemptive nature of foreign oil policy. Rather than remaining backstage, as it did during the Mexican expropriation, the State Department directly participated with Venezuelan and oil company officials in drafting oil legislation, resolving tax and concession disputes, and discouraging efforts to establish state oil industries. This was something the department had done earlier under the Hoover administration, in Colombia for instance, but for the Roosevelt administration it indicated a growing sophistication in approach. Department officials also played a more active role than they had at any earlier time in pressing the companies to overcome rigid and futile opposition to the milder implications of Latin American nationalism and to improve their public image. On the whole, however, these were refinements in the tactics of diplomacy rather than in the premises of policy, which remained wedded to the defense of private American property in Latin America, hemispheric solidarity, and the security of petroleum supply.

The factors that contributed to a settlement of the Mexican and Bolivian expropriations contributed as well to the growing subtlety of American policy in Venezuela. By 1939 there was a critical need for the United States to ensure the security of Venezuelan oil supplies, and American participation in that development was deemed vital to that security. By decade's end Venezuelan oil had displaced American direct oil exports to Europe. American direct investment in Venezuelan oil production had soared to approximately $375 million, exclusive of tankers and refining facilities on Aruba and Curacao, almost ten times the level of investment in Mexico at the time of the expropriation. Indeed, the Mexican and Bolivian expropriations and the decline of Mexico as a major world producer increased the importance of Venezuela in terms of corporate expansion and American security. Technical considerations also served to enhance the significance of Venezuela. As the companies – primarily Gulf, Standard Oil of New Jersey, and the Royal Dutch Shell subsidiaries – expanded into eastern Venezuela in the 1930s, they found the crude oil lighter than western crude and more suitable for the production of gasoline, which would be vital in the event of war.[66] Consequently, when the Venezuelan government set out after 1938 to gain more control over the industry and to acquire a higher percentage of the profits, there was strong incentive for both companies and the United States government to avoid a confrontation that might lead to expropriation.

The process of negotiation was a long and involved one, following the passage in 1938 of new oil legislation that the companies found unacceptable. Negotiations concluded only in early 1943 with the acceptance of legislation that increased the basis and level for royalty payments to the Venezuelan government, reduced the import exemptions for the companies, and confirmed existing concessions. It was a victory for American policy, but the magnitude of the victory should not be exaggerated. There is little evidence that the Venezuelan government seriously contemplated expropriation after 1938. The impediments to such action were simply too great. The industry was entirely foreign owned and controlled; it was primarily extractive in nature, with only limited refining capacity for domestic consumption, a factor that would make it extremely difficult for Venezuela to dispose of its production profitably in the event of seizure; and the government was dependent on oil revenues for some 90 percent of its expenditures. Although expropriation at the time may have been unlikely, the companies and the State Department did establish the basis for long-term cooperation during this period. Yet it was not so much the fear of expropriation but the coming of war that led the companies to a more compromising position under pressure from the State Department. This fact tends to be sustained by the timing of the settlement – late 1942, early 1943. By 1942, British sources in the Mediterranean were cut off by Germany, and Cordell Hull was concerned that Japan would gain control of the Indian Ocean and British oil properties in the Persian Gulf, take India, and then link up with Germany through Iran and Iraq. In that event the Allies would have been totally dependent on Venezuelan and American oil for military operations.[67]

The war had another effect on the Venezuelan situation. Although the war contributed to an increased demand for oil products, a shortage of tankers and German submarine warfare in the Atlantic and Caribbean had the effect of reducing Venezuelan production during the period before the United States entered the war. Germany even posed a threat to the local movement of oil products. Its shelling attack on Aruba refineries and the sinking of four shallow-draft tankers in February 1942, for instance, disrupted the entire system of transportation for months thereafter, and the navy was compelled to restrict tanker movement. Shell interests in Venezuela were hit hardest because of the curtailment of its European markets, and Gulf Oil's subsidiary, Mene Grande, was the least affected because of its traditional reliance on American markets, but all companies reduced production during this period, even though Venezuelan exports to the United States were facilitated by tariff reduction in the 1939 Reciprocal Trade Agreement. Production increased once again when the German threat on the Atlantic had been reduced, but the situation demonstrated the vulnerability of Venezuelan supplies, as well as their importance to the European conflict. By 1941, the United Kingdom received 70 percent of its oil requirements from Venezuela, and the British navy alone met 40 percent of its requirements from Venezuelan production.[68]

The importance of the war to the evolution of foreign oil policy is also reflected in the fact that it was not until 1940 that the administration began to take concrete steps to prevent a confrontation between the companies and the Venezuelan government. Roosevelt's ambassador to Venezuela, Frank Corrigan, who shared Josephus Daniels's sensitivity to Latin American aspirations, warned in late 1939 that there was a desperate need for a concerted policy to ensure that the profits from oil contributed to the social and economic development of Venezuela. Laurence Duggan echoed these sentiments in his recommendations to Hull and Welles the next spring. He argued that at the root of the present problem was the "lack of appreciation on the part of the companies to a rapidly changing philosophy on the part of the Government and Public." Duggan noted that there were some promising indications of a change in company attitudes, including the use of agricultural advisers, construction of roads for the Venezuelan government, and willingness to select advisers recommended by the departments of state and commerce. Yet he remained concerned over the companies' tendency to oppose Venezuelan oil legislation publicly through litigation, resulting in political debate and public acrimony, and he recommended that the department invite the heads of the companies to Washington to exchange views with the department. "The Department feels," he concluded, "that the tremendous investments ... made by them will be best protected by a sincere and intelligent effort on their part to assume the responsibilities which they cannot escape." Similar ideas had been expressed in the department in 1939, and there appeared to be a clear consensus that American national interest transcended the narrower interests of the individual companies. But it was not until 1940 that the ideas were translated into a more concrete direction of policy.[69]

In June 1940, the department arranged a meeting in Washington that Duggan had suggested with representatives of the four major companies. Led by Hull, they exchanged views. Although there is no public record of the meeting, on the basis of the department discussions that preceded it, it is fair to assume that Hull requested little more than the "sincere and intelligent effort" to which Duggan had referred and close consultation with the department in order to avoid a confrontation. The meeting did not lead to specific action, but it did provide the framework for effective consultation when the Mene Grande company found itself engaged in a dispute over back taxes the following year. Welles promptly and directly intervened with Gulf's president to arrange a settlement satisfactory to both sides, in order, as Welles noted, to avoid the "international implications" of a public controversy.[70]

The larger issue of resolving outstanding differences over the petroleum laws remained at the time the United States entered the war. As much as the basic outlines of American policy may have been firmly established by the end of 1941, the war brought reorganization of the policy-making apparatus and a new urgency to the Venezuelan situation. Without American involvement in the war, it is difficult to predict what would have transpired. Ruth Knowles, of the Office of the Petroleum Coordinator for National Defense, informed director Harold Ickes in September 1941 from Caracas that the companies had stopped exploration work and new developments because of the uncertain domestic and international context. In her view, there had been no serious effort made since 1938 to comply with the new Venezuelan legislation, except by Jersey Standard, and no progress toward hiring more Venezuelan skilled employees and managers or meeting Venezuelan demands for an expansion of domestic refining. The companies were also ill at ease, she suggested, because of what they saw as a lenient American response to the expropriations in Bolivia and Mexico. Yet, she predicted that self-interest alone should compel the companies to reach agreement with the Venezuelan government for the continued and appropriate development of Venezuelan resources.[71] Agreement remained elusive for another year, and when it came it was in a context of national security requirements.

CHAPTER FIVE

World War II and the Structure of Decision Making, 1940–1943

Wartime activity diffused the decision-making process in relation to petroleum: it introduced new personalities, ideas, and projects, and contributed to the first major reassessment of United States foreign petroleum policy since the end of World War I. Prior to the onset of World War II, the shaping of foreign petroleum policy had been fundamentally the prerogative of the State Department. Although there had been periods in the interwar years when other departments, as well as Congress, had been active and influential in foreign petroleum developments, there was little precedent for the proliferation of wartime agencies including the Petroleum Administration for War and the Foreign Economic Administration, and the increased contribution of the military to petroleum planning. Congress also reasserted itself, conducting several investigations related to foreign petroleum policy between 1943 and 1947. These included special hearings such as those of the Truman committee on the national defense program, and the O'Mahoney committee enquiry on petroleum resources in 1945–6, as well as the ongoing deliberations of standing committees of the House and Senate.

The policy that emerged by 1947 was the product of both bureaucratic conflicts over the specifics of policy formation and implementation, and more general considerations that transcended bureaucratic struggles for power and permanence. For an understanding of foreign petroleum policy it is essential to conquer the labyrinth of bureaucracy during the war. It is equally essential, however, to recognize that power struggles among individuals and agencies were neither the sole nor even the primary determinants of policy.

The long-standing objectives of petroleum policy were the maintenance of the Open Door for American enterprise abroad, active support for private enterprise in obtaining foreign concessions, and the conservation of domestic and increasingly hemispheric petroleum resources. Wartime planning resulted in little modification of these objectives, although there was clearly an intensification of government involvement in the industry's affairs and indeed in the industry's involvement in government planning and operations. The war contributed to a postwar strategic shift in geographic emphasis from the western hemisphere to the Middle East and a heightened awareness of the need for international cooperation in the development of policy. Although there was some perceived opposition to the concept of government-supported private enterprise in the foreign petroleum sector (as government agencies during the war assumed a greater degree of authority over domestic and international operations), that challenge, if real, was ephemeral and ineffectual.

BUREAUCRATIC RIVALRIES

The outbreak of war in Europe in 1939 exacerbated problems of international petroleum supply. In May 1941, President Roosevelt established the Office of Petroleum Coordinator for National Defense, later renamed first the Office of the Petroleum Coordinator for War and, in December 1942, the Petroleum Administration for War (PAW). Roosevelt named Harold Ickes petroleum coordinator. This appointment was appropriate not only because of Ickes's previous involvement in oil policy, but also since the idea of a federal petroleum coordinator originated with G.W. Holland of the petroleum conservation division of Ickes's department. Holland had proposed a national petroleum defense committee to serve as a control agency between government and industry and to cooperate with the advisory commission to the Council of National Defense. As Holland envisaged them, the committee's responsibilities would be to determine all problems relating to the use of petroleum in the nonmilitary domestic and international spheres, and to coordinate the petroleum work of the Department of the Interior with that of other federal agencies.[1] Holland's concept was, in fact, similar to but less formal than what ultimately emerged.

Under Ickes and his deputy administrator Ralph Davies, the PAW provided the main challenge to the State Department in shaping wartime petroleum policy. Ickes was combative, and his relationship with other members of the administration and with oil company officials was frequently stormy. He evinced neither respect nor liking for Secretary of State Cordell Hull, whom he considered inept, and he was repelled by the austerity of Undersecretary Sumner Welles. Ickes's short temper, his vigor, and his competence as an administrator, as well as his quest for administrative supremacy, led him into frequent jurisdictional disputes with the State Department and with other government agencies over the conduct of foreign petroleum policy, disputes in which President Roosevelt often found himself cast as a reluctant umpire. Although the statutory responsibility of the PAW was in the area of coordinating petroleum supplies for civilian and military use during the war, Ickes expanded its horizons, pressing vigorously throughout the war for more government participation in the industry's activities abroad and for more effective long-term planning. Ickes was one of those who echoed the concerns of post–World War I officials who feared and anticipated the impending depletion of United States domestic reserves and the necessity for large-scale imports to meet peacetime as well as emergency petroleum requirements. Ickes was neither unique nor prescient in anticipating the day when the U.S. would become a net importer of petroleum, but he was one of the major catalysts in focusing attention on long-range issues during the war.

Ickes shared with the State Department a concern over wartime duplication in the conduct of petroleum policy. For example, he complained vigorously to President Roosevelt in late 1941, when he discovered that the president had authorized Vice-President Henry Wallace to establish a policy subcommittee under the Board of Economic Warfare (known as the Economic Defense Board until 17 December 1941) to ensure adequate petroleum supplies outside the United States. In Ickes's opinion, Ralph Davies had already established an effective *modus operandi* with the board, and he saw no useful function for the proposed committee. Wallace nonetheless proceeded with the establishment of an interagency foreign petroleum policy committee, which remained in operation until Roosevelt established the Petroleum Administration for War. The formation of the PAW did not end the activity of the Board of Economic Warfare in the petroleum sector. Leo Crowley, as Board of Economic Warfare representative, served on the PAW petroleum board, which Davies chaired, and continued to do so after the Foreign Economic Administration was formed in 1943 under his direction.

In spite of the brief life of the foreign petroleum policy committee created by Wallace, it prompted the petroleum industry to establish yet another coordinating committee, the Foreign Petroleum Operating Board, the membership of which was drawn predominantly from the major industry firms. Its executive committee was chaired by George Walden, chairman of Standard Vacuum. B.R. Jackson represented the Anglo-Iranian and Burmah Oil companies (and in a sense the British government's interests), and H. Wilkinson represented the Royal Dutch Shell group of companies. Other members were all presidents of their respective firms: J.A. Brown (Socony-Vacuum), Robert Colley (Atlantic Refining), H.D. Collier (Standard Oil of California), F.J. Drake (Gulf Oil), W.S. Farish (Jersey Standard), H.N. Herron (Caltex), and W.S. Rodgers (the Texas Company).[2]

Ickes's concerns about the duplication of operations and jurisdiction were shared by others. C.V. Barry of the Board of Economic Warfare, for example, informed the State Department in early 1942 that government agencies, aware of the persistent jurisdictional disputes, were uncertain where to present problems for effective resolution. There was a widespread belief in government circles and in industry that the American oil companies' holdings abroad were not being effectively utilized for the Allied war effort, and Barry did not anticipate improvement in the situation until jurisdictional problems between the Office of the Petroleum Coordinator, the Operating Board, and the Foreign Petroleum Policy Committee were removed. A solution to this dilemma appeared especially necessary in the spring of 1942 because tanker sinkings and the high cost of tanker insurance, combined with financial losses resulting from the production of less motor gasoline, were severely hurting the oil companies.

Some reconciliation and streamlining, albeit tentative, was accomplished during the following several months. An agreement was reached whereby the Foreign Petroleum Policy Committee should be regarded as the coordinating body to secure effective action by the several operating agencies of government in all matters affecting the foreign petroleum situation. The only apparent concession to Ickes as petroleum coordinator was that his agency was to be viewed as the main vehicle for government-industry contacts.[3]

Ickes continued to strive for more power, however, and it was to satisfy him that Roosevelt established the PAW in late 1942. Its creation was not viewed with magnanimity by all sectors of the bureaucracy. The departments of war and navy, for example, both expressed opposition to the creation of the PAW on the grounds that it would represent additional bureaucratic obstacles to the procurement of war materials. Secretary of the Navy Frank Knox and Acting Secretary of War Robert Patterson urged that the present Office of the Petroleum Coordinator be incorporated into the War Production Board, with the board retaining general procurement powers.[4]

Although the formation of the PAW resulted in more effective coordination of petroleum operations, it did not end the jurisdictional conflict, especially when the PAW entered the foreign operations field. Here the State Department was jealous of its prerogatives and throughout the war sought to thwart Ickes's initiatives. Other agencies were also active, however. The Office of Price Control was responsible for the supervision of pricing in the petroleum industry, among others; the

War Production Board had final authority over the allocation of scarce materials, especially steel, which was essential for the construction of pipelines and the expansion of refining capacity. As a reflection of the importance of petroleum to the War Production Board's operations, its predecessor organization, the Office of Production Management, had employed an oil adviser, Robert E. Wilson, president of Pan American Oil, a subsidiary of Standard Oil of Indiana. The Department of Justice and the Federal Trade Commission claimed supervisory power over petroleum matters relating to antitrust policies; the Reconstruction Finance Corporation and the Foreign Economic Administration both had responsibility after 1943 at different times for the Petroleum Reserves Corporation, until it was dissolved in 1946. The War Shipping Administration exercised control over tanker allocation, at least until the end of 1942.

Coordinating the often divergent interests, personalities, and ambitions within these departments and agencies was a herculean task, and much to the chagrin of the State Department, it was often Ickes who was able to persuade President Roosevelt that he was the most appropriate individual for that responsibility.

HAROLD ICKES AS PETROLEUM ADMINISTRATOR

Ickes has tended to be neglected by historians of American foreign petroleum policy, in part because the direction in which he wished to take the United States during and after the war was not the road ultimately followed, but in part as well because there has been very little appreciation of the impact on foreign policy of departments other than the State Department during this period. Ickes was a major actor during the war in the foreign sector and served as an important catalyst in focusing attention on the long-range problems of supply and foreign production. On the whole he was more nationalistic and less sensitive to foreign opinion and the perspectives of the companies than was the State Department, and had he gained effective control of foreign petroleum policy by the end of the war, the shape of the postwar world insofar as it related to international oil relations would have been substantially different. During the war he was a key figure in the formation of the Petroleum Reserves Corporation in 1943 and its subsequent projects. His pressure on the Department of State was critical in initiating the negotiation of an international oil agreement with Great Britain, with the hope that it would become a multinational accord, and he assiduously urged strong diplomatic protection for American petroleum firms confronted with emergent nationalism abroad.[5]

In the war years Ickes and the PAW provided one of the most important forums for an exchange of ideas and information between government and the oil industry. Unlike a number of federal administrators who utilized "dollar-a-year" men, Ickes preferred to employ industry executives as salaried personnel, even though they often retained their industry salaries or part thereof while they served for the PAW. Those industry specialists and company officials who served in either a salaried or advisory capacity played important roles in providing a link between the public and private sectors. The structure improved the relationship that had evolved during the New Deal, encouraging the type of cooperation that had been characteristic of World War I and the Republican 1920s.

There were several key individuals whom Ickes managed to attract from the private sector during the war. The most significant in terms of his impact on policy and the position he held within the petroleum administration was Ralph Davies. As deputy director of the PAW from 1941 on, Davies was the real administrator of the agency, and his selection was a critical one. Like Ickes, Davies was an extremely able administrator, though he lacked the volatility and pugnacity of his superior. The oil industry had occupied Davies's entire professional life until he joined the PAW at the age of 45. He possessed a breadth of vision and sense of perspective on the place of the industry within a wider political and economic context that set him apart from many of his contemporaries in the industry. One consequence was that at no time that he served under Ickes did Davies speak for the narrower interests of the industry or of his own company, Standard Oil of California. Davies had earlier organized and become president of Standard Oil of British Columbia, before moving to Standard of California as a vice-president and director. His relationship with Ickes began with his appointment in 1935 to the National Marketing Committee under the National Recovery Administration's code of fair competition for the oil industry. At the same time, he created and assisted in the administration of the Pacific Coast Petroleum Agency, which was adopted by Ickes, in his capacity as petroleum administrator, to provide for joint government-industry regulation of the West Coast industry. By the time of his appointment to the PAW, Davies was considered by some to be "one of the most capable persons in the oil industry."[6]

Other appointees who served with Ickes during the war were George Walden, Everett de Golyer, James Terry Duce, William Crampton, and Roy Hawkins. Walden had been an executive with Standard of New Jersey and subsequently with Standard Vacuum, where he had been actively engaged in the foreign oil trade. During the war he worked as a special assistant to Davies and as U.S. petroleum attaché to the

American embassy in Great Britain. De Golyer was an internationally respected geologist and a noted authority on petroleum reserves who had served as a consultant to the governments of Mexico and Brazil. In 1943 he headed the Petroleum Reserve Corporation's technical mission to the Persian Gulf that emphasized the vast potential of the region and which prepared the way for diplomatic negotiations with the British. De Golyer shared with Ickes some assumptions about the nature of the oil situation that confronted the United States. In his estimation the United States did not possess adequate reserves for future emergencies or to meet civilian requirements in the postwar years. He was also highly critical of the failure, in his view, of American policymakers to articulate and enforce a consistent and satisfactory foreign oil policy. De Golyer placed more confidence than did Ickes on the potential role of Congress in defining the oil needs and policies of the nation. In an area that was as vital to the American economy and security as was oil, De Golyer urged that Congress needed to play an important role. Duce, Crampton, and Hawkins each worked as director of the foreign division of the PAW. Duce held the post from Pearl Harbor to October 1943. He was a vice-president and director of the California-Arabian Standard Oil Company (Armaco from 1944). Duce was in turn succeeded by Crampton, who had been a vice-president and director of Jersey Standard's subsidiary in France. In March 1945 Hawkins was appointed to the position. As with Duce and Crampton, Hawkins's previous experience had been with a major international firm, as managing director of Jersey Standard's subsidiaries in Italy and Latin America.[7]

The relationship between the PAW and the industry was a source of some criticism during the war. Although, as a subsequent examination of Ickes's role in the formation and operation of the Petroleum Reserves Corporation suggests, a substantial degree of the criticism emanated from the industry itself – especially from the independent firms, which feared domination by the majors – in the early stages of the war allegation of industry domination came from Ickes's colleagues as well. Leon Henderson, director of the Office of Price Control, charged in a radio address on 30 October 1943 that the oil industry controlled the petroleum administration and was using its government ties in an effort to obtain oil price increases. Ickes responded on this occasion, as he did on others, that the PAW had employed the technical and administrative expertise of oil company executives but that all basic issues of policy were determined by the administration. "We take pride in the record ... by the partnership between the oil industry and Government which has marked the course of our joint efforts." He subsequently wrote to Freda Kirchwey of *The Nation*: "We could not have done the job that we have done if we had not been able to persuade the big oil companies who alone had the technicians necessary to do the job to give us those technicians in order that they might serve the industry as a whole."[8]

Criticism came as well from those close to Ickes. Abe Fortas, undersecretary of the interior and in 1943 secretary of the Petroleum Reserves Corporation, resigned the latter post in April 1944 because he believed he was being bypassed in decision making by Ralph Davies and Ickes; he also objected in principle, however, to the selection of personnel with oil company connections for PAW work.

If Ickes perceived any conflict of interest in his staffing policies, there is no evidence that he was prepared to modify his approach. Indeed, his staffing practices appear to have been specifically designed to achieve a balance between the major and the independent companies, at least in numerical terms. Of the oil company personnel employed by the PAW in an executive capacity in 1943, twelve or 46 percent came from major companies, and fourteen or 54 percent were from either independents or other government agencies. Among PAW employees receiving $5600 or more per annum, sixty-two or 35 percent were acquired from major companies, and eighty-four or 48 percent were from the independents or other industries. The remainder were drawn from gas companies, foreign oil companies, government service, and universities.[9] If Ickes can be faulted for creating a situation in which there were possible conflicts of interest, it must be recalled that the State Department, in its selection of petroleum advisers and attachés during the war, was equally dependent on individuals drawn from the private sector who retained their industry ties during their terms of government service.

In addition to oil company personnel employed by the PAW in a technical and executive capacity, Ickes and Davies established industry committees to provide a consultative basis for the effective coordination of petroleum supplies. Such committees not only facilitated the exchange of vital information between industry and government, but also established a framework for the petroleum industry to present a more united front in business-government relations. The most important of these industry committees were the Foreign Operations Committee (FOC) and the Petroleum Industry War Council (PIWC). The FOC was composed of nine industry executives experienced in foreign operations and drawn from the major companies, as well as two British observers. John Frey and Chandler Ide, PAW's official historians, argued in 1946 that the FOC was a significant component in the drafting of PAW policies. It met regularly and worked directly with the foreign division of the PAW. The membership of the FOC also provided a source of criticism for the justice department after the war. In the context of the debate in 1952 over the degree of cartelization in the industry, a justice department memorandum prepared for Assistant Attorney General H.G. Morison emphasized that the FOC and its subcommittees included many of the officials from the major companies who had established and maintained the various "As Is" arrangements since the late 1920s. [10]

The PIWC was a larger, more amorphous entity, drawing together more than seventy industry leaders, including the presidents of each of the trade associations within the industry. Its chairman, William R. Boyd, Jr, was also president of the American Petroleum Institute. The council functioned as an important coordinating body for the office of the petroleum administrator. As the war progressed, its members also took an increasingly active and direct interest in foreign petroleum policy. [11] In fact, it was the PIWC and its subcommittee on petroleum interests in foreign countries that took the lead in promoting public support for private enterprise and in opposing, much to Ickes's chagrin, both the Petroleum Reserves Corporation and aspects of the Anglo-American oil agreement. So vigorous and effective was this opposition that it would be difficult to view the PIWC as a useful vehicle for advancing the government's perspective on oil development.

One factor that further influenced the relations between the industry and government during the war was the ability of the industry and the willingness of the Roosevelt administration to suspend antitrust activities in the interest of the war effort. The members of the PIWC were especially firm on this point, stressing that their cooperation with the administration and the coordination of industry operations should not make them or their firms vulnerable to prosecution. As early as September 1940, Assistant Attorney General Thurman Arnold and then Defense Commissioner Leon Henderson were feuding over Arnold's proposed antitrust suits against the major oil companies. Ickes himself appears to have opposed the suits, and both he and President Roosevelt wanted the suits delayed until Henderson could study their potential impact on current negotiations with those companies in defense-related matters. Although Attorney General Robert Jackson's decision to order a delay in the suits was seen as a temporary wartime expedient, it was to have serious implications for American oil policy by encouraging further cartelization within the industry. [12]

Although there were areas of conflict among departments and agencies over the conduct of petroleum policy, there were also significant areas of cooperation. One of the areas in which the PAW and the State Department achieved substantial progress early in the war was in the establishment of a petroleum attaché program. An appointment to London was a high priority because of the need to coordinate Anglo-American supplies. After this position was established in 1943, the American petroleum attaché in England was incorporated into the Mission for Economic Affairs, and the attaché himself became a member of a British War Cabinet subcommittee, the Oil Control Board. The British Petroleum Mission in Washington was also integrated into American supply deliberations.[13] Although London was the priority appointment in the program, the first attaché to leave for his post was Walter Smith, who went to Madrid in March 1942. In general the attaché program included major producing nations in Latin America and the Middle East as well as militarily strategic locations. The selection of attachés drawn from Standard Oil interests on the advice of petroleum adviser Max Thornburg was criticized by both Herbert Feis and Laurence Duggan. Thornburg's justification for his nominees was that the war had disrupted the international operations of the major companies and thus a number of officials from that small group of firms that had multinational interests were available for such positions.

Supplementing the petroleum attaché program were the series of technical missions initiated by the PAW with State Department cooperation. These missions were essentially of a fact-finding and exploratory nature, designed to consider the potential petroleum reserves of a region, the possibility of expanding production and refining in producing areas, and means to improve transportation systems. PAW sponsored missions to Mexico, Australia, South America, the Middle East, and finally China in the spring of 1945.[14]

STATE DEPARTMENT PERSPECTIVES

The State Department was understandably less concerned with problems of wartime petroleum supply than were the military divisions and the temporary agencies. Embroiled as it was with the rapidly altering political map of the world during the war, the department focused on the place of petroleum in broader foreign policy issues. It attempted to reorganize its decision-making structure with a view to achieving both a more effective response to current petroleum problems and a more coherent long-term policy to meet postwar contingencies. At the outset of the war, there was no single office within the State Department that had jurisdiction over petroleum matters. In general, each geographic division coped with petroleum questions as effectively as it could. On those occasions when issues appeared to require a broader policy statement, as had been the case with the Open Door policy in the 1920s and the response to nationalization in host countries in the late 1930s, more senior and central officials became involved. The one office that provided a moderate degree of coordination among the geographic divisions on petroleum and indeed on most aspects of economic policy in the early war years was that of the Adviser on International Economic Affairs, an office held by Herbert Feis during much of the period encompassed by this study. In mid-1941 the State Department moved to correct this situation, in part because of the need to articulate a long-range petroleum policy in response to the deterioration of oil relations with Venezuela, Mexico, and Bolivia, and in part in response to the need for a central figure to coordinate State Department activities with those of other agencies and departments. In July 1941 the department obtained the services of Max Thornburg as a special assistant to the undersecretary of state and as a consultant in Feis's office. [15]

The circumstances that gave rise to Thornburg's selection appear vague. At the time of his appointment, Thornburg was an official of the Bahrein Petroleum Company and Caltex. Herbert Feis claimed to have recommended his appointment; others in the department saw his corporation ties as potentially valuable, providing a firmer link between government and the industry, especially important at a time when the department was under fire from the industry for failing to provide adequate support in Latin America. Thornburg, however, did more to consolidate ties with the industry than Cordell Hull was prepared to tolerate. Unknown to Hull, during the two years that he served in the department, Thornburg remained on company salary. The disclosure of that information to Hull late in 1943 led to his dismissal. Given Thornburg's known ties to the industry and the fact that double salaries were not uncommon for corporate executives serving in government during the war, it is unlikely that this discovery alone would have resulted in his dismissal. Other factors included Hull's frequent unfamiliarity with operations of his department, his dislike of Summer Welles, and Thornburg's candid support of the company perspective. [16]

Despite Thornburg's dismissal, his years of service were important ones in the drafting of a crude blueprint for American oil policy. Although the structure of the decision-making process is the focus of the present discussion, it is important to note the extent to which Thornburg concerned himself with the short-range problems of oil policy. When he drafted an early statement of objectives for his office, he identified his priorities as the articulation of a postwar petroleum policy; implementation of a policy for national defense; and the assumption of administrative responsibility in such specific areas as shipping and wartime petroleum pooling among the Allied powers. "This work," he observed, "will give continuous attention to the interests of the United States in oil operations abroad." It would also, in his opinion, serve to link wartime considerations with postwar planning. [17]

It was predictable that such an ambitious program would bring Thornburg's office into conflict with the petroleum coordinator. Just as

Ickes had lashed out at Roosevelt and Henry Wallace when it appeared that the Board of Economic Warfare would usurp his prerogatives, now he resented what he believed was a further intrusion onto his territory with the appointment of Thornburg as chairman of the Foreign Petroleum Policy Committee.[18] Nevertheless, one must not confuse this conflict of personalities and bureaucratic struggles with a dispute over the fundamental elements of policy, as some analysts have done. Ickes did not resent Thornburg because of any fundamental disagreement over the objectives of a foreign petroleum policy, nor was he antagonistic because of Thornburg's ties to the industry. As his administration of the PAW indicates, Ickes had neither serious qualms about the corporate connections of his own staff nor reservations about the need for a higher degree of centralization in petroleum policy planning, which Thornburg's appointment represented. Nor did he disagree with Thornburg's basic ideas on oil policy. As he wrote Thornburg late in January 1942, "so far at least as the foreign field is concerned, you and I have been seeing eye to eye as to the imperative necessity of formulating a long range petroleum policy." Ickes, like Thornburg, believed that to be effective a foreign oil policy would need to be formulated with full "cooperation and understanding between the industry and the government." Hence, although Ickes saw his jurisdictional dispute with Thornburg, the State Department, and the Board of Economic Warfare as a "savage struggle," it is crucial to distinguish between the conflict of egos and the extent to which such conflict actually represented a fundamental difference in long-term policy objectives. Indeed, Ickes was at times more cooperative with Thornburg than was his deputy administrator, Ralph Davies, who had known Thornburg within the California Standard Oil Company empire. Davies and Thornburg remained suspicious of one another during their years in government service. Early in 1942, when Ickes had moved toward cooperation with the Foreign Petroleum Policy Committee, Thornburg continued to balk, claiming that he was "not yet completely sold on the idea," and he declined to send a representative to meetings of the committee. Given Davies's influence with the corporate sector, Thornburg believed the committee would remain impotent until Davies followed Ickes's lead and agreed to cooperate, as he ultimately did. It is significant that following Thornburg's departure from the Department of State in mid-1943, the chairmanship of the committee passed to Davies.[19]

The record suggests that the State Department very early recognized that the Foreign Petroleum Policy Committee did not represent an effective vehicle for the formulation of long-term foreign petroleum policy. Shortly after Thornburg's appointment, Walter C. Ferris was employed as his assistant to conduct an extensive study of United

States and foreign oil reserves, resources, and legislation, a project that Undersecretary of State Sumner Welles described as of "the highest importance." Thornburg saw the project as a starting point for the establishment of a long-range and global policy for "what is perhaps the most important of the strategic raw materials." Thornburg was especially concerned that the U.S. limit its wartime petroleum commitments, lest it reduce its options for the postwar period. He also thought that oil would be only one of several commodities that should be considered in the determination of U.S. economic policy. The function of the oil adviser's office was to "isolate, for study, certain politically important aspects of world oil supply and to determine cause and effect relationships which must become component in the changing body of policy that currently expresses this Government's attitude toward the rest of the world."[20]

Other divisions in the State Department responded positively to the attempt to clarify petroleum policy, although in some instances there was concern that more general principles of American foreign policy should remain predominant. For example, Harry C. Hawkins of the Division of Commercial Policy stressed the importance of integrating the petroleum study into trade-agreement negotiations, especially with oil-producing countries such as Mexico. He also emphasized the principles articulated in the Atlantic Charter of "access, on equal terms, to the trade and to the raw materials of the world which are needed for their economic prosperity." Rather than assuming, as Ferris appeared to do, a pessimistic view of a competitive postwar world with an aggressive United States foreign oil policy pitted against that of Great Britain, Hawkins urged that policies should be advocated that were "designed to bring about and maintain a better world order." Hawkins also expressed a viewpoint that was consistent with the emerging consensus on foreign oil policy, to the effect that domestic reserves should be conserved and that petroleum requirements should be met as much as possible from imports "irrespective (in peace time) of the origin of ownership of the imported oil."[21]

Ferris incorporated a number of these considerations into a memorandum on foreign petroleum policy that he completed in the spring of 1942. A draft, circulated in April, retained the notion of the possibility of postwar international conflict among the major powers over petroleum. Yet it also emphasized the equal-access ideals of the Atlantic Charter, tempered by spheres-of-interest considerations. Ferris did envisage some international agreement in petroleum matters following the war, however, and this provided the basis for the subsequent American drive toward the negotiation of an Anglo-American petroleum agreement. Ferris anticipated that any international agreements would likely have to await the end of the war and would need to be limited to pricing and marketing as opposed to ownership, although he recognized that proposals to extend access to oil resources to those nations requiring petroleum would be significant as well. A third area that he expected would be subject to international agreement was the establishment of a multinational corporation to operate some foreign concessions, with countries participating according to their petroleum needs. The model he had in mind was the Iraq Petroleum Company, in which American firms had gained a share in the 1920s. Although this was an unlikely approach to petroleum development in the stable or controlled areas such as the United States or the Soviet Union, Ferris saw some merit in its application to areas that were being developed, such as Africa, or to areas such as the Netherlands East Indies and Romania that had been occupied during the war and were the focus of considerable international competition and diplomatic controversy.

In Ferris's view, several special considerations were likely to shape the development of American oil policy. One of these was the extent to which the domestic U.S. industry had been integrated in terms of control over production levels. With oil-producing states enforcing prorationing regulations based on general demand estimates drawn up by the United States Bureau of Mines, and with the federal government preventing interstate commerce in petroleum produced in excess of state prorationing regulations, the industry had passed beyond the laissez-faire conditions of the pre–New Deal era. It was this same type of systematization that would legitimately be sought in the international sphere. A second consideration was the special status of Latin America in U.S. policy. Ferris noted that there was a trend toward nationalization of subsoil rights in Latin America; this, combined with the commitment of the U.S. not to interfere in the internal affairs of the American republics, appeared to pose some difficulties for the United States in pursuing an aggressive oil policy there. Ferris anticipated that these trends might be offset by "financial considerations," such as the extension of credits to Latin American countries. A final consideration on which Ferris placed considerable emphasis was close and effective government / industry cooperation, as a *sine qua non* for the articulation and implementation of an oil policy. "The industry alone," he contended, "is technically equipped for foreign oil operations and marketing, and only by learning how to avail itself of the industry's facilities can our Government play an effective role in foreign oil matters."[22]

Thornburg added further considerations in reporting to Sumner Welles on the state of his work. He thought that the lend-lease program placed the United States in an unusually advantageous position to influence the course of international petroleum policy following the war.

The U.S. could, for example, require lend-lease debtors to grant oil rights to oil-short nations, which would in turn expand their trade with the United States. He also reiterated a perspective that had gained increasing acceptance during the war among the major international firms and State Department officials: a concerted effort would have to be made to share the fruits of petroleum exploitation by host nations if the U.S. hoped to retain and possibly expand its world position. Earlier expropriations in Bolivia and Mexico, current difficulties in Venezuela, traditional difficulties in gaining access to petroleum concessions within the British and Dutch spheres of influence, and the general fear of expanding nationalism impressed upon company and government officials alike that they would have to offer more attractive development opportunities in order to maintain their operations abroad. As Thornburg noted, "access to raw materials by nations in need of those materials should be recognized as involving at the other end – and particularly in the case of oil – the exploitation of wasting resources in the supplying country. It is not through economic accident that the great oil bearing regions of the world are, for the greater part, backward in social and economic development." In order to rectify that situation, Thornburg argued that a larger proportion of oil capital would need to be redirected for purposes of economic development in the producing states.[23]

Like most policymakers involved with petroleum questions during the war, Thornburg was convinced that the U.S. was moving toward dependency on imported petroleum. In his view, the problems would be exacerbated unless the government adopted an oil policy that anticipated conflicts between American oil companis and foreign governments. Citing the example of Venezuela in 1942 as an instance of effective American diplomacy, he stressed the need to provide a mechanism for the United States to resolve such conflicts before they reached destructive proportions. The problem was especially acute, he believed, because the locus of petroleum wealth and power was shifting to the Middle East. "The most important single piece of equipment in existence," he concluded, "is the twelve inch valve on the Mediterranean end of the Iraq pipeline. The hand on that valve, and it is not an American hand, can head the tanker fleets of the world in almost any direction it wishes by raising or lowering the level of supply in Europe." Although the U.S. possessed superior technical knowledge and was the major supplier of essential petroleum equipment, it would be unable to determine international oil policy unless it made a concerted effort to establish a coherent policy of its own.[24]

Thornburg's work attracted considerable attention in the State Department. It is significant that with the nation at war, petroleum was considered sufficiently important to absorb a considerable proportion of government time. The Board of Economic Operations, for example, which met weekly under Assistant Secretary of State Dean Acheson's chairmanship, decided to circulate Thornburg's study and to discuss it themselves at meetings in 1942.[25]

The developments in Iran, which will be examined later in the study, coincided with the disputes late in 1941 and 1942 over administrative jurisdictions and the preparation of the Thornburg study and provided the catalyst in the congealing of State Department sentiment and priorities. As Adolf Berle observed, Iran was "the first big case to arise during the present war regarding access to raw materials."[26] From early 1942 on, the Iranian situation presented a major challenge for State Department and other officials concerned with petroleum supply.

During the ensuing two years, the bureaucracy continued to change in an effort to cope with the evolving international petroleum situation. Some segments of the armed forces believed that the Ickes group had shown inadequate initiative in the area of controlling foreign supply and had failed to gain the confidence of the industry. The Foreign Petroleum Policy Committee, which tried to coordinate those companies conducting business abroad and to have the armed forces transmit their requirements through it rather than the oil coordinator, lacked the statutory authority to function effectively. Early in 1942 the director of the Naval Transportation Service had urged the establishment of a central agency, to be composed of the best people from the petroleum coordinator's office, the Foreign Petroleum Policy Committee, and the War Shipping Administration, but Ickes's gradual consolidation of authority undermined this initiative. With centralization taking place under the petroleum coordinator, in July 1942 the armed services established an Army-Navy Petroleum Board responsible for gathering data on petroleum products of concern to the armed services and for determining overseas destinations of petroleum supplies. Because of the nature of the board's duties, it worked closely with the petroleum coordinator.[27]

Although primarily a wartime supply committee, the Army-Navy Petroleum Board at various stages of the war became involved in long-range petroleum policy planning. Part of the explanation for its influence lies in the personality of the board's director, Captain Andrew F. Carter. Prior to the war, Carter had been president of the Shell Eastern Petroleum Corporation. Consequently, he had the type of contacts in the British and American petroleum industry that gained him considerable credence in policy-making circles during the war. Carter was an ambitious and talented individual who believed that the United States needed to pursue a vigorous foreign petroleum policy with particular attention on the Middle East, and he succeeded in winning many of his wartime colleagues to his point of view.[28]

The State Department further refined its committee structure in the course of 1943 in an effort to win back some of the initiative it believed had been lost to other agencies, especially the Petroleum administration for War, and to ensure that it retained effective control over foreign policy considerations that were related to petroleum matters. A petroleum-policy study group under the direction of Herbert Feis began deliberations in January and sought the advice and cooperation of the geographic divisions of the department. At its meeting of 11 January 1943, Feis indicated the need to develop a farsighted policy on oil in order to protect American interests abroad and at the same time to provide adequate protection for the legitimate interests of other nations.[29]

Thornburg, who worked closely with Feis in the early months of 1943, anticipated that the State Department would find the companies cooperative in the development of a foreign oil policy, in spite of their traditional opposition to government controls. This was due, he contended, partly to the willingness of company officials to accept increased government involvement in wartime as a temporary measure. It might have been attributed as well, however, to new trends in the international petroleum industry that made the companies anxious to obtain additional public support. One such trend was toward increasing nationalism abroad, which company executives believed required a firm diplomatic response from the United States; a second was the realization that American petroleum exports would likely decline in proportion to the need for imports after the war. This would intensify the need for foreign concessions at a time when their stability appeared uncertain. Under the circumstances, both government and company officials appeared to recognize the need for effective cooperation in the international sphere to ensure the security of American-controlled supplies. Thornburg thought this cooperation might take several forms: the establishment of joint committees, such as those created under the PAW; an exchange of personnel; increased U.S. government participation in shaping petroleum legislation abroad, within what Thornburg vaguely defined as "proper limits"; more active diplomatic support for legitimate American interests overseas; and the negotiation of trade agreements and other intergovernmental agreements in which American companies would receive specific attention. He tentatively suggested what would become a strongly disputed issue in the late years of the war, that the government might at some stage secure its own financial or operational interest in foreign reserves, although for the moment Thornburg was silent on the specific means and area in which such activity might take place.[30]

Herbert Feis found the geographic divisions cooperative in these exploratory discussions early in 1943. James Wright of the Division of the American Republics, for example, warmly endorsed the effort to establish a "closely knit and sound United States foreign petroleum policy." Wright agreed with Thornburg that past problems had their origins in the failure of the United States to develop a coherent policy. In order to avoid such developments as those that had followed World War I, he suggested it was essential to achieve the close cooperation of other nations, whether they had petroleum resources or not, as long as their citizens were active in foreign petroleum operations, a thinly disguised reference to the British and Dutch. Wright saw the fundamental problem as the removal of suspicion and conflict between lost nations (in Latin America and elsewhere) and private American corporations, an objective he hoped to accomplish by establishing more clearly areas of mutual interest between the two than had been the case in the past. Wright empathized with the companies for the difficulties they faced in Latin America, recognizing the high-risk nature of their investments and the competitive nature of the industry. At the same time, he acknowledged their previous abuses of power, which had served to foster local hostility, conflicts with labor, and the trend toward nationalization. The gradual accomplishment of stability in government-oil-company relations in Venezuela and Colombia nevertheless convinced Wright that tensions could be reduced through firm but reasonable diplomacy and a willingness by the corporations to compromise and to give credence to the Latin American perspective. The Colombian and Venezuelan situations suggested that the petroleum operations had "come to the realization that what is best for them is not the seemingly free and easy ways of the past but rather the ability to enter an area, explore it freely, and develop good structures with a sense of security and stability." Wright's conclusion was one increasingly shared in government and corporate circles, to the effect that "without a real mutuality of interest there can be no enduring prosperity."[31]

The Feis committee, which came to be known as the Committee on International Petroleum Policy, was the crucial body in the first half of 1943 in shaping and reflecting the State Department's search for a concrete policy on petroleum. Officials recognized the urgency of crystallizing a policy if the country were to negotiate effectively with other powers, notably Britain.[32] In their early deliberations, Feis and his colleagues on the committee concentrated on four dimensions of foreign petroleum policy: the preparation of an analysis of American aims and objectives in the foreign petroleum field (done by the economic adviser's office); a study of the relationship between the U.S. government and the oil companies with a view to attempting to anticipate advisable future steps for regulation, cooperation, or unification (assigned to the Office of the Petroleum Adviser); and examination of Anglo-American petroleum relations in terms of prospective problems and solutions; and a summary of current and possible difficulties that were anticipated in petroleum relations in various parts of the world.[33]

Two fundamental developments emerged from the deliberations of the Feis committee during 1943. One was the decision to pursue negotiations with the British with a view to the stabilization of petroleum relations in the postwar period. A second was the decision to establish a petroleum reserves corporation to encourage the development of American-held concessions abroad and to provide the government with a more formal and reliable link to foreign petroleum development.

The Feis committee also spawned a further, although somewhat short-lived effort at interdepartmental petroleum policy planning. Immediately prior to the official formation of the Petroleum Reserves Corporation in June 1943, Feis was named to head a special committee on petroleum, composed of representatives from civilian and military departments and agencies. Because of its membership, the creation of this committee was a major development in the effort to articulate a formal and cohesive foreign oil policy for the United States. The State Department was represented by Feis, Alger Hiss (Office of Far Eastern Affairs), James C. Sappington (Office of the Petroleum Adviser), Paul Alling (Chief, Near Eastern division), and Howard Trueblood of Feis's office. The Department of War and had one representative, Brigadier-General Boyken Wright. The navy was vigorously represented by Andrew Carter and William C. Bullitt, who at that time was special assistant to the secretary of the navy. The PAW named three of its prominent officials: James Terry Duce, Everett De Golyer, and C.S. Snodgrass. All of these men were committed in varying degrees to close government/business cooperation. Each of them was also convinced of the need to adopt a specific and aggressive foreign petroleum policy.

Several factors coalesced at this stage to reinforce their efforts. One was the formation of the Petroleum Reserves Corporation in June 1943 under Ickes's direction, providing the secretary of the interior with a strong base from which to shape the deliberations on oil policy. A second factor was the unsettling effect of Max Thornburg's departure from the Department of State in July, and the decline of Feis's influence with the secretary of state until Feis also left the department in October of that year. With Feis's departure, the special interdepartmental committee on petroleum that he had chaired ceased to function, and it was not until December that the State Departmnt established another interdivisional petroleum committee under James Sappington of the petroleum division. At the same time it named Charles Rayner to occupy the posi-

TABLE 5
World Petroleum Reserves 1942 (in millions of barrels)

Area	Initial major production	Recoverable reserves
Foreign		
Persian Gulf		14,529 (21.0%)
Iran	1913	9,369
Saudi Arabia	1939	3,744 (5.4%)
Bahrein	1935	216
Kuwait	–	500
Qatar	–	700
Eastern Mediterranean		6,045 (9.0%)
Iraq	1934	6,000
Egypt	1918	30
Misc.		15
Far East		1,621 (2.0%)
Netherlands East Indies	1895	1,366
Burma	1900	95
Sarawak and Brunei	1920	68
Sakhalin	1929	40
India	1900	27
Japan	1901	27
Europe		9,286 (13.0%)
USSR	1876	8,543
Romania	1899	
Germany	1908	
Poland	1895	
Misc.		(743)
South America		8,378 (12.0%)
Venezuela	1921	6,155
Colombia	1928	740
Argentina	1917	304
Trinidad	1917	262
Peru	1908	165
Bolivia	–	48
Ecuador	1928	16
Mexico	1907	688
Total foreign		39,859 (57.0%)
Domestic		
United States	1861	29,589
Canada	1929	180
Total Domestic		29,769 (43.0%)
Total World		69,728

Source: Box 2, Petroleum General, PD.

tion of petroleum adviser vacated a few months earlier by Thornburg. Rayner, like Thornburg, was a career oil man, having served first in Singapore from 1909 to 1917 as Far Eastern manager for Standard Oil of New York. Until the outbreak of World War II, when he became petroleum adviser in the Board of Economic Warfare, Rayner had been an independent oil producer in Texas, and the Department of State may well have anticipated that his appointment would ease some of the tensions and criticisms that had been occasioned by Thornburg's close ties to the major international firms.[34]

Between the onset of war in Europe and the reorganization of petroleum planning personnel in the State Department at the end of 1943, U.S. foreign petroleum policy underwent several distinct developments, even though some of those developments were tentative and not destined to reach fruition in the postwar era. Both the nature of policy and the individuals who shaped it changed to some degree during this period. The locus of decision making on foreign petroleum matters was far more diverse by the end of 1943 than it had been in 1940. The State Department's traditional predominance had been successfully (though perhaps temporarily) challenged by other departments and agencies. In terms of the instruments of policy, the most significant innovation that emerged from the interdepartmental deliberations of 1940 through 1943 was the formation of the Petroleum Reserves Corporation, which is the subject of the following chapter.

CHAPTER SIX

The Petroleum Reserves Corporation

The formation of the Petroleum Reserves Corporation (PRC) resulted from an important consensus in 1943 among civilian and military policymakers and significant segments of the petroleum industry that vigorous government support for American enterprise abroad was essential for private enterprise to retain its foreign concessions and for the United States to ensure American security and economic viability in the postwar era. The formation of the PRC reflected a shift in the attention of both several major corporations and policymakers toward the Middle East – a shift that had been under way for several years but for which the war acted as an additional catalyst. The PRC was also a project for which segments of the Roosevelt administration, other than the State Department, evinced the greatest enthusiasm, notably the military and the Petroleum Administration for War, in part because the PRC and its projects were portrayed as short-term responses to meet the exigencies of the war and the temporary insecurity of concessions in Saudi Arabia.

IDENTIFYING PRC OBJECTIVES

The establishment of the corporation in June 1943 and its relatively brief activity during the subsequent year underlined some of the fundamental differences in approach to petroleum policy between the Department of State on the one hand and the military and the PAW on the other. The former identified a broader range of policy objectives, among which were the realization of the principles of the Atlantic Charter in postwar reconstruction, a general stabilization of international financial and economic relations, and the preservation of regional spheres of influence, such as the Good Neighbor in the western hemisphere. Such objectives could be compromised, it was feared, by a foreign oil policy that appeared too aggressive, that cast the United States into an openly competitive position against Britain in the Middle East, or that alarmed sensitive governments in major producing countries and contributed to retaliatory action against American corporations. Insofar as petroleum policy was concerned, both the military and the PAW had narrower conceptions of the national interest and of the main problems with which the U.S. was confronted at the time. They identified the main objective as the conservation of domestic and hemispheric reserves, with increased importation resulting from the expansion of production in the Middle East, under the auspices of private enterprise if that were possible and with direct government involvement if that proved essential to realize American objectives. Throughout the debate over the establishment and operation of the PRC, these divergent perspectives came into frequent confrontation.

In the private sector, there was a parallel lack of unanimity over the means if not the ends of policy. There was a general reticence among the companies to see government directly involved, financially or administratively, in the development and marketing of foreign petroleum. Among the major oil companies, the response to the formation of the PRC often varied according to the nature, location, and degree of security of the company's operations. Those such as Standard Oil of California, whose vast concessions in Saudi Arabia appeared insecure, were initially prepared to accept U.S. government participation in their operations. Those such as Standard Oil of New Jersey, which found themselves restricted in production and marketing by such limiting agreements as the Red Line of 1928, sought both liberation from those limitations and restraints on potential marketing competitors recently arrived in the Middle East fields. It was the domestic independents, however, which articulated the strongest and most sustained criticism of the PRC and expanded foreign production, on the grounds that expansion abroad restricted domestic employment, exploration, and development within the U.S. The policies that ultimately emerged and the fate of the PRC were the product of debates among these often divergent interest groups.

The PRC emerged not only from the general debate over foreign petroleum policy, but also from the specific dilemma of how to sustain the financial weakened government of King Ibn Saud of Saudi Arabia. The latter aspect of the problem had existed for two years prior to the creation of the PRC. American petroleum interests in Saudi Arabia, specifically Standard Oil of California and the Texas Company's subsidiary, Caltex (subsequently Aramco), which held sole concessionary rights in Saudi Arabia, early in 1941 urged President Roosevelt to provide financial support for King Ibn Saud in order to prevent his collapse and that of "the entire Arab world." James A. Moffett, chairman of the board of Caltex, was the main protagonist in this early initiative. Interestingly, he was also one of the main critics of Harold Ickes and the PAW.[1]

What Moffett proposed in 1941 was that the United States purchase from Saudi Arabia finished petroleum products with a value of $6 million per annum for the next five years. In return, the king would waive royalty payments of an equal amount for that period. California Arabian Standard had already advanced the king $6.8 million against future royalties, but was evidently reluctant to extend further credits at that time. Moffett also urged that the Department of State suggest to the British government that it increase financial assistance, on a purely political and military basis, not, Moffett stressed, in a manner that would enable the British to gain petroleum concessions in the country. Moffett's objectives were clearly protectionist of the company's position. Not only did he not wish British firms to gain access to Saudi Arabia, but the oil he proposed to sell to the U.S. government was King Ibn Saud's royalty oil rather than that which the company would normally market. Moreover, in order to maintain existing marketing patterns, Moffett indicated that any excess oil would have to be marketed outside the Pacific area.

Moffett's initiative met with an unreceptive response in government circles. No one questioned the long-range strategic value of Saudi petroleum, but the navy had tested Saudi production and found it of low quality for navy use. Gasoline produced from Saudi crude was second grade, unsuitable for high-octane aviation fuels, it was believed, and it was thought that the high sulfur levels of the diesel fuel would contribute to the corrosion of diesel engines. To the navy, the petroleum was not of sufficient value in 1941 to justify a more formal commitment to Saudi Arabia. Secretary of Commerce and head of the Reconstruction Finance Corporation Jesse Jones concurred entirely with the navy assessment. As much as Ibn Saud had demonstrated his anti-Nazi sympathies, was admittedly financially embarrassed, and was an important figure in the Arab world, Jones thought it was the responsibility of the British to provide assistance, perhaps by redirecting American lend-lease funds.[2] Even with the U.S. at war, and recognizing the significance of Middle Eastern petroleum, American policymakers in 1941, including President Roosevelt, were reticent to become further involved either politically or financially in the affairs of the area, viewing it largely as within the British sphere of influence. A year later, when the American legation in Iraq urged the protection of oil installations in Bahrein and Saudi Arabia, the war department still perceived the problem as one within the British theater of operations and its responsibility.[3] At the same time, Britain and the Soviet Union were occupying Iran, holding the line against an Axis advance into the area, but also consolidating their own positions and complicating great-power influence in the region for the postwar period. American caution in 1941 was to be displaced by a willingness two years later to assume more direct responsibility for the region. An acute shortage of aviation gasoline by 1943 and concern that a tightening of British political controls in Saudi Arabia would undermine the security of the American concession served to make the Roosevelt administration more receptive to overtures from those who sought an expansion of the American presence in the Middle East. It was not solely the interests of the oil companies that drew the United States into greater involvement, but rather the way in which the interests of the companies were tied to the broader definition of American strategic concerns. The loss of Burma and the East Indies to Japan made especially acute the need for the Allies to expand Middle East production.[4]

The U.S. government examined the possibility of establishing refineries to produce aviation gasoline in several areas of the Middle East in 1942 and 1943. They were substantially restricted by the necessity to work within a British sphere of influence. The construction of a 100-octane aviation fuel plant at Bahrein was dependent on adequate military protection, which would have to come from the British and which was viewed as inadequate for that purpose in 1942. In addition, State Department negotiations to permit American forces to enter Saudi Arabia proved to be lengthy, and until agreement was reached it was not strategically sound to commence an expansion of facilities in the area.[5]

The establishment of such oil facilities abroad at government expense also posed problems for their control and operation at the end of the war. State Department officials were aware that installations ranging from pipelines and storage tanks to refineries would affect the postwar development of commercial airlines, sea routes for the merchant marine, army and navy activities, and the general marketing of petroleum products. With the exception of French Equatorial Africa and the Belgian Congo, in early 1943 the United States had no agreements with foreign powers concerning these installations. What was desired were assurances that the United States would have equality of access in the postwar period, or preferably ownership.[6]

The expansion of refinery capacity abroad remained more urgent in the spring of 1943 than the question of control over such installations after the war, and the initiative came largely from the PAW. Ickes pressed petroleum adviser Max Thornburg to agree to the formation of a high-level Cabinet committee to discuss oil questions and to make recommendations directly to the president, an approach Thornburg favored. Consequently, although the executive order establishing the PAW had carefully circumscribed its powers, making the PAW subject to control by the chairman of the War Production Board for the allocation of scarce resources, of the State Department in the area of foreign relations, and of the departments of war and navy in military matters, it was Ralph Davies who chaired the first meeting at the Department of the Interior in late February of an interdepartmental foreign petroleum committee.[7] Not the Cabinet-level committee Ickes envisaged, it functioned as a subcommittee of the petroleum board. Composed of representatives of state, war, navy, the Board of Economic Warfare, the Lend-Lease Administration, the Office of the Coordinator of Inter-American Affairs, and the War Shipping Administration, this committee concentrated on the refinery question; it also provided much of the momentum for the expansion of petroleum operations in the Middle East. The main function of the committee was "to coordinate all matters related to foreign petroleum, including the screening of requisitions for materials requested for oil fields and refinery operations in foreign countries. It would also determine the essential requirements of foreign countries which could be supplied from the continental United States or the Caribbean."[8] By late April, the committee had reported to the petroleum board on the proposed Saudi Arabian refinery. There was general agreement that the refinery should go ahead, but there was a difference of opinion over location, one group preferring the eastern edge of the Mediterranean, with a pipeline from the producing fields, and another faction preferring construction on the mainland of Saudi Arabia in order to shorten the shipping distance to military operations in the Far East.[9] The Petroleum Reserves Corporation, once established, took up this question.

Coincident with the increased government deliberation over the most appropriate means by which the U.S. could expand its influence in the Middle East and increase aviation fuel availability, business leaders were pressing for closer cooperation between government and business. Joseph Pogue, vice-president of Chase National Bank, a frequent State Department correspondent on business-government relations, urged Herbert Feis to recognize that "the future of the post-war world is dependent upon the disposition made of petroleum as an economic and social force." Lamenting that there had been undue emphasis on the areas of conflict between government and business, Pogue stressed the need for both government and private enterprise to accept the presence of industry in the "formative period of thinking and planning." Pogue did not, however, support increased government intervention in the industry. Rather, as he indicated to Far Eastern specialist Stanley Hornbeck, the foundation of U.S. policy should be "a maximum of liberty and a minimum of regulation" in which the government should refrain from "any form of participation ... in foreign developments."[10]

Others were prepared to go further, at least for the moment. The Texas Company, for example, chose this occasion to return to its previous efforts to protect its Saudi Arabian holdings. The company president, W.S. Rodgers, in February 1943 circulated a memorandum among the departments of state, war, navy, and interior, reminding officials that in spite of the fact that the company's Saudi Arabian concession was significant to American security, the country was the only major neutral in the area that was not receiving lend-lease funding. Rodgers specifically proposed what he anticipated would be attractive to the American military given the shortage of aviation fuel. Rodger's plan involved the establishment of a separate reserve in Saudi Arabia to supply the U.S. military at preferential prices. Although at this stage there appear to have been no assurances that such a procedure would have been acceptable to Ibn Saud, clearly the Roosevelt administration found it sufficiently attractive to authorize lend-lease assistance the same month. The presence of major petroleum deposits under American control in Saudi Arabia was clearly the decisive factor in this decision. Neither Saudi neutrality nor its financial difficulties during the war had been sufficient incentive to attract official American support until it appeared that American oil interests were in jeopardy. The petroleum shortage and the evident threat to private enterprise turned the tide in official opinion, and the United States was drawn further into the affairs of the Middle East.[11]

By 1943, with one-quarter of Iraq production, all of that in Bahrein, and that in Saudi Arabian fields under American control, the importance of the Middle East to American petroleum security was evident, and the administration was now prepared to move aggressively and in rather new directions in petroleum policy. The State Department's Foreign Petroleum Policy Committee now gave sympathetic consideration to the possibility of the government taking options on foreign reserves, and it was in the belief that a single American body should have jurisdiction over such operations that the administration moved toward the creation of a reserves corporation. As initially envisaged within the Department of State, such a corporation would be government controlled but would not itself seek to exploit or own foreign petroleum reserves. Rather, it would contract for foreign reserves with a single industry company consisting of a board of directors representative of all interested companies and perhaps with a government representative. Although the government would have some influence over the industry in contracting for the reserves of such countries as Saudi Arabia, Colombia, Iraq, and Venezuela, the degree of government participation was expected to be minimal, and there was to be no financial participation at the operating level. Although the comparison appears not to have explicitly been made at the time, the concept of a single industry company with government representation was not unlike the structure the State Department had attempted to erect in Iraq in the 1920s with the Eastern Development Corporation, although that had lacked entirely the direct participation of the government. The proposed corporation appeared to be a middle way between the traditional reliance on the private sector and the example provided by the British government's participation in the Anglo-Iranian Petroleum Company.[12]

Some State Department officials had serious reservations about such a project. The division of commercial policy, for example, was anxious that government involvement in the acquisition of foreign reserves would be contrary to the principles of the trade liberalization program. Those in the Division of American Republics were especially concerned that such a policy would be misinterpreted in Latin America. Philip Bonsal, who participated in much of the departmental deliberations on petroleum in 1943, informed both Feis and Thornburg that government acquisition of reserves in the less-advanced countries would conflict with the principles of the Atlantic Charter. "I am frankly not convinced of the desirability of this Government's obtaining foreign oil reserves, particularly in Venezuela and Colombia," he wrote in late February. Herbert Feis, concerned as he was that a new American imperialism "was raising its ugly head," appears not to have supported Bonsal on this occasion, although there was a discernible effort to keep petroleum policy within the lines established by the Atlantic Charter.

Others in the State Department, however, did share Bonsal's concerns. Assistant Secretary Adolf Berle later expressed to Cordell Hull strong reservations about the direction of the petroleum discussions. Clearly influenced, as was Bonsal, by his familiarity with the Latin American situation, where the trend had been toward the development of state enterprise, Berle warned that any corporation similar to that proposed "would be considered at once as a nationalistic concession-hunting group and would immediately call forth action by other governments." Berle's reservations about the reserves corporation were tempered by his support for an international agreement on oil. "If such a corporation," he suggested to Hull, "could work by agreement with the British and, if possible, the Russians and Chinese ... under some arrangement by which the oil rights it bought were shared on appropriate terms with other United Nations, I believe something could be done."[13] Berle and other officials found themselves caught between a fear of provoking a nationalistic backlash abroad and the evident necessity for a "stand-still" agreement in international petroleum affairs.

By the end of March 1943 the State Department Committee on International Petroleum Policy was prepared to make a recommendation to the secretary. Eschewing direct government financial participation in private enterprise abroad, the committee recommended the establishment of a petroleum reserves corporation under the supervision of the Department of State "to operate in the foreign petroleum field with the immediate task of obtaining the contemplated options, first in Saudi Arabia and then elsewhere." The department viewed the reserves corporation as a long-range instrument of policy designed to protect American security rather than one only for the immediate exigencies of the war. Over the long term, the corporation would provide focus and control to United States foreign petroleum policy. It was anticipated that the corporation, if established, would also facilitate cooperation among the companies for the acquisition, development, and conservation of foreign reserves. As Thornburg explained to Hull, "the establishment of a Petroleum Reserves Corporation would provide at once an agency in which many related functions could be centered and through which much might be accomplished in furthering international stability insofar as oil is a factor." The recommendation was firmly premised on the conviction that the rapid depletion of U.S. reserves for the war effort threatened postwar American security. "Unless," the authors of the report admonished, in terms that were prescient of the postwar course of events, "our ability to derive required supplies from abroad at all times ... is safeguarded, the United States will be in hazard a) of having to pay an economic or political toll to secure the oil, or b) actually fail to secure it." The international supply of petroleum, it was believed, would be adequate for the needs of all nations; the problem was to find a mechanism by which to ensure access to reserves and to exercise some control over supply, a dilemma that was at the root of U.S. foreign petroleum policy in the twentieth century.[14] The solution to the problem that the Feis committee offered addressed itself to both the issue of access to supplies and control over marketing, although the U.S. would go further along the lines of advocating production and marketing controls when it pursued an international agreement on oil during the next few years. In this area the members of the Feis committee anticipated that an oil agreement would depend on the prior establishment of a world security system and would itself create a "worldwide system of actual administrative control of the world's petroleum resources." The precise nature of such an agreement was still embryonic in 1943, but officials were clearly moving in the direction of attempting to realize the principles of the Atlantic Charter providing for the equality of access to raw materials, but with major power influence over the subsequent allocation of those materials. It was also anticipated that an international agreement would instill more stability into the relationship between host countries and the international corporations. Although a broad international agreement was not expected until the end of the war, the committee suggested that in the interim the government study the potential of more limited, possibly regional, agreements.[15]

The main question confronting the government, in Thornburg's opinion, was whether or not it should undertake "to remove or lessen part of the risks to private enterprise of great national importance abroad." More generally, the problem of how to determine the desirable relationship between the government and private enterprise continued to plague the department. Thornburg noted that in Venezuela in 1942 the department had collaborated "unofficially" with the private sector in order to obtain a settlement. In Mexico and Argentina there had been direct diplomatic participation in support of American enterprise; in Saudi Arabia the outlines of policy remained to be completed. Nevertheless, Thornburg argued persuasively that it was not advisable to leave policy to private enterprise, "particularly with the prospect of circumstances in the future even more difficult than those which the private companies have failed to cope with in the past," a significant statement from a man whom Hull would shortly dismiss for excessively close ties with his former employer.[16]

The Feis committee report met with immediate approval from the State Department, whatever the reservations may have been at the divisional level, and was promptly dispatched for consideration by the departments of war, navy, and interior. At the same time, Hull recommended to the president that the status of the American representative at Jidda, Saudi Arabia, should be raised from chargé ad interim to minister resident in recognition of the significance to the United States of Saudi Arabian petroleum, as well as the desire of the war department to obtain landing rights for American aircraft.[17] If anything, the other departments were more advanced, and perhaps less cautious, in their approaches to the petroleum question.

The main concern of the military was understandably the wartime supply problem, although they were equally cognizant of the need for long-term planning. In May, the Army-Navy Petroleum Board, which since January had been an agency of the Joint Chiefs of Staff, reported that projections for 1944 indicated that the total production of crude oil in the western hemisphere would fall 700 thousand barrels below requirements. Among the areas from which additional petroleum could be derived, Saudi Arabia was the only producer where a substantial refinery, with a 100–200 thousand barrel-a-day capacity, appeared feasible, although smaller ones could be brought into production at Cartagena, Colombia, and in Panama.[18] The State Department's proposal for a reserves corporation thus fell on fertile soil in the military branches, although there were some reservations about the degree of the crisis. Secretary of War Henry Stimson, for example, noted that there was a general anxiety among officials that the U.S. was faced with imminent oil scarcity. While recognizing the seriousness of such a shortage, and although prepared to support the navy's desire to consolidate the American-held concession in Saudi Arabia, Stimson had his private reservation that the danger of domestic resources exhaustion was exaggerated. When he and Secretary of the Navy Frank Knox discussed with Ickes the acquisition of Saudi Arabian reserves by the proposed reserves corporation, Ickes was, unlike Stimson, "heart and soul in favor of that program."[19] The consequence of Knox's and Ickes's enthusiasm and Stimson's willingness to acquiesce was a prompt recommendation from the joint chiefs to the president that the Reconstruction Finance Corporation be authorized to organize a corporation specifically to obtain foreign reserves.[20]

The apparent consensus among the departments tended to mask some fundamental differences of view over the nature and the functions of the projected reserves corporation. The main factor that appears to have determined the position of the Joint Chiefs of Staff was the fear that Britain would gain the upper hand in Saudi Arabia and possibly elsewhere in the Middle East where the United States had made gains since World War I. Although the record is now generally well established that Britain did not intend and did not attempt to exclude the Americans from petroleum development within its sphere of influence after the war,[21] the perception of policymakers in the United States at the time was different, and it was, after all, on their perception that decisions were reached. Admiral Horne, for example, who was vice-chief of Naval Operations, utilized the anti-British argument effectively at the crucial meeting of the joint chiefs, in suggesting that the British had already approached King Ibn Saud. Horne and Admiral William Leahy informed General Marshall that in fact there was adequate petroleum in the United States to meet the immediate requirements of the war, but that the reserves corporation was being established with a view to the oil reserves of the future and to enable the U.S. to "build in." Marshall was reluctant to alienate the British on the eve of postwar negotiations and indicated his preference to inform the British of American intentions in order to avoid repercussions.[22]

There were similar concerns with British sensibilities elsewhere in the administration, although there were those like Marshall who preferred to mute any anti-British dimension to the petroleum reserves initiative. Henry Stimson, for example, was concerned that Knox had been "egged on by Bill Bullitt," who was "chuckful of anti-British feeling." Stimson himself tended to prefer the approach of Herbert Feis, with whom he had become increasingly close over the years. Feis and Stimson had personal reservations about the government acquiring ownership of foreign concessions and urged that control be established on a contractual basis as originally envisaged.[23]

By this juncture, however, the momentum had shifted to Ickes and the Petroleum Administration for War, and it was clear that he had gained Roosevelt's agreement to have the proposed corporation establish financial control over the Arabian American Oil Company. Not only did it appear that Ickes had successfully circumvented the Department of State in shifting the nature of the corporation, but he also sought to eliminate its control over the operation of the corporation itself. The compromise among the four departments (state, war, navy, interior) that evolved during this period was essentially a tactical victory for Ickes. Although the agreement stipulated that the Department of State would have final approval over all petroleum negotiations with foreign governments and the power to approve all major projects, it accepted the intent to enable the corporation to acquire stock control over California Arabian, a position with which the department was not in full agreement, largely because it feared that such an approach would alienate Ibn Saud. A stronger secretary of state than the aging Cordell Hull might well have effected a distinctly different course of action. Indeed, by failing to make his department's position clear in June 1943 at the time of the Petroleum Reserve Corporation's establishment, Hull created the impression of support for a course of action that he subsequently worked to defeat, in the process seriously weakening a major initiative in foreign petroleum policy. Hull himself effectively captured the tragedy of his position: "In the present critical stage of our international relations, and bearing in mind the extreme importance of petroleum relations in the whole of our foreign relations, the Secretary of State is unwilling to get into controversy with other branches of Government as to the course to pursue in regard to the Saudi Arabian situation."[24] Having said this, Hull's department spent the remainder of 1943 attempting to undermine Ickes's labors.

Hull appeared more concerned with the issue of which department would have ultimate control over the corporation. Others in his department expressed reservations about the possible reaction from the business community to the government financially participating in one or two American firms abroad. Paul Alling of the Near Eastern division, for example, thought that opposition from those firms that might be excluded from the initial reserves corporation projects might be reduced if the department could aid in the formation of a consortium of American firms to pool American-held concessions, although he did advocate government control of such a consortium in order to facilitate the creation of a uniform and global oil policy.[25]

If there were reservations in other areas of the administration, Harold Ickes appears not to have been influenced by them. In his letter to the president supporting the formation of the reserves corporation, he presented a situation that exaggerated the degree of the crisis, one in which there would by the end of 1944 be inadequate petroleum resources for the armed services as well as the industrial sector of the United States, a prediction that the joint chiefs did not share. Nonetheless, the basic thrust of Ickes's analysis was one that approximated the emerging government and industry consensus: the situation was critical; the United States needed to take immediate action to augment its present and long-term supplies of crude petroleum, and the most effective means by which this could be accomplished was through assuming a managerial and proprietary interest in foreign petroleum concessions. Ickes clearly believed that an unqualified free-enterprise approach to foreign oil development had been ineffective in securing American state interests. "Private entrepreneurs," he noted, "have been in competition not only with themselves but also with foreign companies in which foreign governments have exercised direct and participating controls ... Any realistic appraisal of the problem of acquiring foreign petroleum reserves for the benefit of the United States, compels the conclusion that American participation must be of a sovereign character compatible with the strength of the competitive forces encountered in any such undertaking." The first objective of the corporation under his direction would be "the acquisition of a participating and managerial interest" in the Saudi Arabian concession of Caltex, in order, Ickes argued, "to counteract certain known activities of a foreign power which are presently jeopardizing American interests in Arabian oil reserves." Ickes's phrasing was unambiguous, and there can be little doubt that President Roosevelt fully understood Ickes's intent when he signed the order creating the Petroleum Reserves Corporation.[26]

THE PRC IN THE MIDDLE EAST

The PRC in its short lifetime spawned three major projects: the purchase of a stock interest in California-Arabian Standard (Aramco after January 1944); the construction of a Saudi Arabian refinery; and the completion of a trans-Arabian pipeline to the eastern Mediterranean. None of these projects was completed under the auspices of PRC, but the initiative was critical in providing subsequent government support for private-sector expansion at the end of the war. The failure of the PRC under Ickes to realize its potential has generally been explained in terms of business opposition to state intervention in the industry, opposition that came in particular from the independent companies. Petroleum industry opposition to the PRC was indeed substantial, but to explain the failure of the policy initiative solely in terms of the private sector is to obscure both the nature and significance of the objections that emerged from other sources.

The Texas Company and Socal did prove intransigent to Ickes's overtures on Saudi Arabia, and Gulf Oil declined to pursue an offer to purchase an interest in its Kuwait operations. Yet, government ranks were also strongly divided, a division that in itself made it possible for the companies to procrastinate. The military representatives on the board of the PRC remained firmly committed to the initial effort to obtain at least 51 percent government ownership in the corporation. Secretary of the Navy Frank Knox, however, and Ickes himself had by November 1943 shifted from the stock purchase option to an effort to gain oil by contract.[27] Ickes was evidently persuaded by arguments from within the administration that direct government involvement in foreign oil would have a disturbing effect on United States relations with foreign oil producers, especially in Latin America. Undersecretary of the Interior Abe Fortas also feared that the government's involvement with the companies abroad would be criticized by the "New Republic crowd," on grounds that the PRC was functioning in support of an international cartel.[28]

Opposition to the PRC projects came as well from the Foreign Economic Administration (FEA) and from within the Department of State. Charles Rayner, for example, who was the highest-ranking petroleum official in the FEA and subsequently State Department petroleum adviser, expected the companies would cooperate with a firm oil policy under Department of State auspices but that the government should not participate in foreign reserves abroad; Oscar Cox, general counsel of the FEA, was of like mind.[29] John Loftus, of the Department of State Office of International Trade Policy, held even stronger views. He cautioned against a "facile acceptance of a scarcity theory," to which Ickes adhered, and identified as "imperialistic" American intentions to gain preferential access to foreign resources.[30] The State Department was clearly prepared to press American interests in the Middle East and elsewhere but through the private sector. Cordell Hull stressed to Admiral William Leahy and Ickes that "to the fullest possible extent consistent with military requirements, determination as to any future new refinery facilities or expansion of such facilities in the Middle Eastern area should be based on whether they a) would be controlled by American interests, b) would utilize American held oil, and c) would result in operation in direct benefit to the country in which the oil is produced."[31]

Fearful that Ickes's activities would injure American interests abroad at a time when the United States was seeking to improve its business image overseas and concerned that the proposed negotiations with the British would be hampered, Hull in early 1944 requested Ickes not to engage in further discussions with the oil companies concerning the Middle East without State Department approval. Department officials emphasized the need for a policy that would assure American nationals of government support, an approach that Ickes assessed as a "reversal," "suicidal," and a return to "dollar diplomacy." Dissatisfied as he was with the State Department, Ickes placed the primary blame on the industry. In his opinion, American companies in the Middle East were "lined up with the British and did not really want to see any independent American development in foreign fields."[32]

Business opposition to the PRC was by no means monolithic and it was of a different nature than that which emanated from government circles. Concern centered on the possibility that wartime emergency measures would provide a mechanism for the expansion of government control over the industry at home and abroad in the postwar years. As much as the industry sought to improve the consultative relationship between government and business and recommended that the "petroleum industry should be admitted more freely into the policy councils of the Government of the United States," it opposed a more direct government role. The Foreign Operations Committee of the PAW expressed accurately the industry viewpoint when it recommended that "as a general rule, the Government should not become financially interested in any foreign oil operations, either through purchase of stock in companies operating in foreign countries or by acquisition of concessions in foreign countries." The Petroleum Industry War Council endorsed the recommendation of the committee and passed an unequivocal resolution in December 1943 to the effect that "under no circumstances should the United States Government ... engage in foreign oil exploration, development or operation." The Standard Oil of New Jersey publication, *The Lamp*, struck a similar note in a December 1943 assessment of world oil policy. It accepted the thesis of domestic exhaustion and the need for a new and comprehensive petroleum policy to stimulate the search for and development of new petroleum resources, but in a "free international economy," with "demand determining distributions," and without the restrictions of "state monopolies" and "discriminatory" legislation.[33]

Industry opposition combined with substantial reservations within the administration to defeat the first initiative of the PRC, and a brief hiatus in its activities followed. Ickes regained the offensive when he announced, in early February 1944, tentative agreement with Socal and Texaco to construct a government-owned pipeline from the Persian Gulf to the eastern Mediterranean to facilitate the marketing of American-developed petroleum in Saudi Arabia and Kuwait.[34] He and the military presented the measure as one of major strategic importance.

Even among his close associates, there was concern that the pipeline project violated the principle of free enterprise. Ralph Davies, for instance, suggested that the project would give industry the impression that he had gone back on his word to keep the PRC out of direct petroleum operations. Ickes rejected the charge. Writing in the *American Magazine* in January 1944, he commented that any foreign oil policy should be consistent with American democratic principles. The PRC would "attempt to explore and encourage the national interests of the United States in the petroleum fields ... where private industry is prepared to go." He argued as well that the pipeline, like those constructed domestically during the war, was merely "supplying a utility which makes it possible for private industry to do business." Nonetheless, Ickes did anticipate that he would be criticized by both liberals, who feared the proposal would overcommit the United States abroad, and conservatives, who were antagonistic to direct government participation in the private sector. It is also evident that Ickes believed the U.S. was out of step with other major powers in its approach to resource development. He noted in his *Diary* that he did not expect that the United States alone would "be able to adhere to the system of private enterprise that has been characteristic of the United States but which is not in effect in any other country ... Even Germany ... has gone in for a type of State Socialism which, in my opinion, all other countries, even the United States, will have to adopt ... in the end."[35]

The initial public response to the project was by no means unfavorable, even though the honeymoon was brief. The *Washington Post* immediately endorsed the pipeline; the *Chicago Sun* called the approach "sound, enlightened, and in the national interest"; the *New York Times* expressed support; and *Time* magazine was enthusiastic, contending that for the first time the United States had a world oil policy, a policy that was based on effective cooperation between industry and government.[36]

The reception within the administration was less enthusiastic, even though there was little in Ickes's basic approach to oil policy at this stage that differed from State Department thinking. Undersecretary Edward Stettinius evinced some support, but on the whole the response to the announced pipeline accord was lukewarm. Hull himself agreed ultimately to government participation in the project only as a temporary measure, the status of the pipeline facility to be reexamined at the end of the war.[37] There was particular concern in the department that the pipeline would alienate the British and abort pending oil talks, although Ickes countered with the contention that the pipeline was a bargaining weapon to draw the British into negotiations.

The State Department had little to offer as an alternative. In fact, in spite of the extensive consideration that had been given to oil policy by the department, its approach had shown relatively marginal evolution since the beginning of the war. The departure of Feis and Thornburg and the appointment of Charles Rayner as petroleum adviser reflected a change in personalities rather than policies. A draft policy statement on oil of 5 February 1944 was basically a reiteration of long-standing principles. It included the recommendation that the equal-access clause of the Atlantic Charter must be implemented in respect of petroleum and that there be recognition of the principle of equal opportunity for American enterprise in exploration and development. In this sense the document could have been prepared by any Department of State from the time of the Wilson administration. The document also reflected, however, the growing protectionist attitude toward western-hemisphere resources "in the interest of national security," and recommended that petroleum exports from the western hemisphere to Europe and Asia be reduced and demand for those areas met by expanded production in eastern-hemisphere producing nations.[38] Both recommendations were consistent with Ickes's approach.

The State Department was more sensitive than the other departments involved with the PRC to the question of the national interests of producing countries in which American enterprise operated. It consequently succeeded in adding a paragraph to the proposed pipeline agreement that it was the "desire and intention of the parties not only to promote and assist in the development of petroleum in the areas affected by the agreement, but also to promote the interests of the governments of such areas, and to respect their sovereignty and protect their rights." The tentative agreement also provided that it was "the desire of the United States that American nationals that enjoy privileges with respect to petroleum in countries under foreign governments shall have an active concern for the peace and prosperity of such countries and shall exercise their rights with due regard to the rights ... of the governments of such countries."[39] The American experience with Latin American nationalism had clearly had an affect on the general thrust of policy.

Reservations within the administration to the pipeline project went further than concern about the reaction from producing nations. The research and analysis branch of the Office of Strategic Services (OSS) noted that this was the first occasion on which the United States government had entered into a limited partnership with private enterprise in an undertaking that related to foreign policy. Authors of the OSS report contended that the proposal would confront "vested British interests at both ends of the pipeline" and that it would involve a major security problem in attempting to defend United States interests in a region that was "inaccessible and desolate" and peopled by "fanatical, distrustful, and restless tribes."[40] Although the OSS was concerned about the diplomatic and strategic factors surrounding the pipeline, it was less sensitive to local sovereignty. "The principle of equitable distribution and exploitation overrides to some extent," the authors argued, "the sovereign rights of the oil producing countries and presupposes a kind of trusteeship of the big Powers over the world's oil resources."

The report explicitly opposed direct government participation in the international oil business. "The important national aims," it was argued, "can best be obtained by formulating an international oil policy and by securing the adherence of the companies to that policy ... The position of these groups and the public responsibilities connected with international oil development make it imperative to establish a close relationship between industry and government with the government formulating and supervising policy and the industry as the operating organ." The report concluded that the political power inherent in the control of oil should reside "exclusively" with government not industry; yet, prisoners of their own ideological adherence to unfettered free enterprise, the authors could offer no mechanism by which that control might be accomplished.[41]

Opinion within the Foreign Economic Administration was divided. There was a general apprehension that Ickes had not thought through the proposal with adequate care and had endangered the creation of a military commitment in the Middle East that the United States could not readily discharge. Some officials saw merit in the project from both the companies' and the government's perspective. There was recognition that the United States had to obtain secure resources outside the country because of its own limited supplies. It was also noted that marketing agreements among the companies provided little latitude for the development of Saudi resources at that time, and that without their development there was a danger that the concessions would be cancelled. In the opinion of Sumner Pike, the pipeline provided a means by which that eventuality could be avoided. The pipeline, he concluded, was a "rather grubby, down-to-earth piece of business in aid of American interests. It is a job which probably could not be done at all by the companies unaided by governments and could probably be done with government aid only in wartime when we are in a position to put on some pressure."[42]

The industry response was complex but predominantly opposed. The main factor that determined opposition or support was primarily the extent to which it was believed the pipeline would materially affect a corporation's position, although there was considerable opposition on principle to the proposed government role. Socal, Gulf, and the Texas company, the direct beneficiaries of the project, were supportive, in part because they anticipated commercial advantages over their main international rivals, but also because they believed that diplomatic support for a pipeline that would cross international boundaries was an essential prerequisite for its success. H.D. Collier, president of California Standard, defended the pipeline agreement to company stockholders on several grounds. The pipeline promised to bring Arabian oil some 3000 miles closer to the United States than the current tanker route; future oil discoveries were uncertain, and it was essential to take advantage of major ones when they became known; and California-Arabian Standard's concession was the only wholly owned American concession in the Middle East, and hence more secure than those jointly held with British-Dutch firms.[43] When the Petroleum Industry War Council (PIWC) moved to confront the project and proposed the liquidation of the PRC, Collier, along with the presidents of Gulf and Texaco, did not vote for the resolution and indeed publicly supported the pipeline.[44]

Among the major American corporations, Jersey Standard and Socony-Vacuum led the opposition. Constrained as they were by the exploitation, production, and marketing restrictions of the Red Line Agreement, both companies appear to have viewed the proposed pipeline as a commercial threat. Certainly Ickes viewed these companies as his major opponents within the industry, and his opinion was shared by Abe Fortas. Ickes noted in his *diaries* that Colonel Drake, Gulf president, had informed him that some oilmen were attempting to turn New York newspapers against the pipeline.[45] Influential as the opposition of Jersey Standard and Socony-Vacuum may have been, oil-industry antagonism to the direction of government policy was more broadly based. The independents, concerned that any expansion of Middle East production would lead to increased importation into the United States as well as lower prices, were more united than the majors in their opposition and perhaps more directly influential in congressional circles. They couched their argument, however, largely in free-enterprise rhetoric, contending, as did the president of the Independent Petroleum Association, Ralph Zook, that the PRC was an entering wedge into the private sector. In a delicate piece of political gymnastics, the industry also expressed opposition to the pipeline on the grounds that it would injure Anglo-American relations in an area recognized as a British sphere of influence.[46] Having for a generation sought United States diplomatic support to gain a foothold in British territory, the companies had now acquired solicitude for British sensitivity.

Even the oil trade journals were outspoken in their criticism. The *Oil and Gas Journal* editorialized on 10 February 1944 that the present shortages of petroleum had been artificially created by government restrictions during the war and that the return to peace would mean a return to hemispheric self-sufficiency. Andrew Carter of the Army-Navy Petroleum Board, who had inspired Ickes on the plan and who had been a long-time Shell employee, lamented to the chairman of the PIWC, William Boyd, Jr, that a large sector of the industry had misinterpreted government policy and threatened "great and irreparable injury to the welfare of the nation" if the agitation against American government assistance to companies in the Persian Gulf area persisted. Supporting the scarcity thesis, Carter observed that new discoveries had not exceeded production. "More than any other nation the United States is dependent on crude oil," he cautioned, and urged that Americans learn from past experience with rubber and tin to ensure an adequate supply of petroleum. To Carter, industry concern about government intervention in commercial activities was "a fanciful apprehension ... it is not intended that PRC shall become owner or part owner in any oil property or engage in business in competition with private industry."[47]

The national oil policy committee of the PIWC countered with policy recommendations of its own, although they were primarily of a negative nature. The committee warned against government interference in "this most individualistic of all economic activities"; it opposed the closing of public lands to exploitation or an increase in public lands set aside as naval reserves; and it opposed above-ground stockpiling for national security. It did recognize the need for limited government involvement, to reduce the financial risk of exploration in remote or uncertain areas, for example, and to provide an "international instrument of consultation and collaboration ... in which there is joint government-industry representation."[48] In this sense the report reflected a broad consensus. John M. Lovejoy, president of Seaboard Oil, for example, also urged that the principle of industry representation that had been effectively applied in the PAW should be implemented by both the PRC and the State Department in all matters relating to foreign petroleum. Like other industry commentators, Lovejoy expressed concern that the PRC represented a trend toward the socialization of American activities in foreign mineral development and urged that it be limited to the wartime emergency.[49]

J.A. Brown, president of Socony-Vacuum, challenged the contention that the company was for commercial reasons opposed to the pipeline. Brown asserted that the company rejected the project for reasons similar to those articulated by the PIWC. "We believe," he informed Secretary of War Henry Stimson, "that this project is an unnecessary and dangerous venture in imperialism, likely to provoke rather than prevent war ... If we had no investment in the Middle East whatever, we would be as vigorously opposed to the project as we are now ... and as are the purely domestic American oil companies." Were the project of value to the United States, he contended, the company would be prepared to support it regardless of its commercial implications.[50]

This cumulative criticism of the proposed pipeline from business circles took its toll, but it was the absence of a cohesive administrative position as well as the emergence of congressional opposition that most significantly contributed to the ultimate failure of the project. Roosevelt could console Ickes with claims that the project had been his as well from its inception, but he provided little leadership for the pipeline's supporters once opposition began to form and clearly saw a petroleum accord with Great Britain as a more desirable objective on which to expend his energies. Indeed, Roosevelt informed the irritated petroleum administrator in June 1944 that he had given assurances to Congress that while conversations with the British were under way, the United States would not proceed with the pipeline and would in any event give Congress thirty days' notice.[51] It also became increasingly difficult to justify either a pipeline or refinery as necessary to the war effort.[52]

Historians have tended to neglect the contribution of Congress to the wartime debate on petroleum policy. Two Senate committees in particular served to retard Ickes's momentum in Saudi Arabia. The first was the extremely important special committee investigating the national defense program, chaired by Harry Truman until he became vice-president.[53] The second was a special committee investigating petroleum resources, and chaired by Francis Maloney of Connecticut.[54] The activities of both committees restrained the administration in the development and application of petroleum policy in the Middle East, even though the members of both committees tended to share the broader objectives that Ickes brought to bear on oil policy: the need for conservation at home, substitute fuel programs, a vigorous foreign policy in support of American enterprise abroad. They did not, however, accept the tactics he attempted to follow with the Petroleum Reserves Corporation.

The Truman committee was especially forceful in its critique of previous petroleum policy and in its recommendation for positive, centralized effort in future. As Senator Owen Brewster of Maine observed, "before another generation comes on stage, America will be a mendicant for petroleum at the council tables of the world. This generation must then bear the responsibility for dissipating this most precious heritage."[55] The committee observed that a policy of leaving private companies in foreign fields free to take whatever action they desired with little more than diplomatic guidance and assistance might well prove inadequate, especially given the degree of support offered private enterprise by other governments. Although it did not endorse the pipeline project, the committee went further than Ickes or the State Department in urging compensation to the United States from its allies for the domestic oil exhausted in the war effort, specifically through a transfer to the United States of a "compensating volume of proven reserves."[56] Such a recommendation may have been, as some administration officials suggested, ill timed, and the report itself inaccurate,[57] but it effectively captured the increasingly aggressive national mood concerning foreign oil reserves and American access to them in the closing stages of the war. The failure to endorse the activities of the PRC, however, at the same time bore witness to the strength of the continuing commitment to private-sector initiative.

Such a commitment also characterized the position of the Maloney committee.[58] Although its first full report was not submitted to Senate until April 1945, after the PRC and the pipeline project had become moribund, the thrust of the committee's deliberations on the pipeline and the Anglo-American oil agreement was clear throughout 1944. The effect of the committee's establishment in March was to add a further obstacle to the project and to enable its opponents and lukewarm supporters to bury it in the general Anglo-American talks then under way. The committee specifically opposed the pipeline in free-enterprise terms. Such a project, it was argued, would have removed the "line of demarcation between the industrial and economic function of the people as individual private citizens, and the political function of the Government as agent of all the people." Moreover, it would have taken the government into "direct development" and ownership of foreign natural resources in areas of the world over which the United States had no political jurisdiction. In addition, the committee early established its position that the statutory powers of the PRC did not specifically include the right to engage in such projects as the Saudi Arabian pipeline.[59]

Although the administration invested another year negotiating an Anglo–American oil agreement as the first phase of a multilateral accord, that too would ultimately fail to be implemented, and the United States moved into the Cold War era "denuded of any institutional capability to formulate a policy of its own or to oversee the operations of the American petroleum industry abroad." Industry, freed from government intervention and uncertain of effective government-induced stability internationally, moved ahead on its own, beginning construction of the pipeline and reorganizing the corporate structure of American participation in the Arabian peninsula to ensure access for all of the majors. May 1947 found Ickes, now out of office, still lamenting to Congress that the United States had no oil policy.[60]

The evidence suggests several conclusions concerning the formulation of United States petroleum policy during World War II. The first relates to the decision-making process. Wartime bureaucracies played a major part in defining the resource problems that confronted the nation. Concern for the security of petroleum was ubiquitous within the administration, yet the main efforts to establish long-range foreign petroleum policies were concentrated primarily in the Petroleum Administration for War, the military, and the Department of State. These were the initiating bodies; the others responded to the proposals that emanated from those sectors, and their contributions were more limiting than positive. Several factors within government circles hindered the creation of a successful and uniform policy. They included personality conflicts, not the least of which was the almost constant Ickes-Hull feuding, struggles for bureaucratic power and permanence, the frequent refusal of Roosevelt to exercise decisive leadership and control over his subordinates, congressional jealousy of its foreign policy prerogatives, substantial differences of opinion among policy-makers over means, and a pervasive consensus in support of free enterprise.

Indeed, the issue that proved most divisive within the administration was the degree of direct government participation in the petroleum industry abroad that was necessary to achieve foreign policy objectives. Ickes and the military services were least concerned with this dilemma. They were clearly prepared to recommend a substantial degree of government control over some foreign reserves in the interest of national security, possible along the lines established by the British with the Anglo-Persian Oil Company. Roosevelt and some members of Congress were sympathetic to this approach but not enthusiastic, perceiving such participation in the private sector as a departure from tradition. The State Department, beleaguered by bureaucratic challenges during the war and confronted with other pressing issues, was the least enthusiastic supporter of the initiatives in which Ickes functioned as the main catalyst. It was also, in the final analysis, the most successful in quelling those initiatives and moving policy along lines it found more palatable. That policy remained remarkably consistent with what had preceded the war, a policy that has been referred to variously as private initiative with state management and "public cooperation, private salvation."[61] Of the two, the latter more accurately reflects the minimal degree of state management that was effected in the area of foreign resource control.

Secondly, there is the question of the role of the oil companies in shaping or obstructing policy. The evidence suggests that analysts have distorted not so much the nature and existence of company opposition to the Petroleum Reserves Corporation, but rather the extent to which that opposition was instrumental in determining the final outcome of policy deliberations. Had there been a clear division between corporate and noncorporate opinion, that interpretation would be more persuasive. All contributors to the debate, however, in varying degrees utilized the appeal of free-enterprise ideology, whether for rhetorical purposes or from conviction remains to be seen. The basic disagreement was over tactics rather than ends. Ickes and the military in particular were prepared to engage in institutional experimentation as one of the few instruments of policy available to them in a political economy wedded to the operation of market forces.[62]

Nor was industry opinion monolithic, reflecting a consensus on end objectives but disagreement over means. There was a fundamental rift between the majors and the independents, between those with and those without substantial foreign marketing operations. On a different plane, there was disagreement among the majors, between those that appeared to be most likely to realize economic gain from PRC projects and those whose marketing positions seemed to be threatened. The industry as a whole was prepared to countenance state intervention when such assistance was deemed necessary for economic gain. When stability and commercial advantage appeared to be attainable goals without government assistance, industry preferred to rely on private initiative. With the end of wartime conditions, the industry interpreted private initiative as adequate for the exigencies of the international marketplace.

Among those oil company officials who served in the wartime administration one can identify a similar conflict over the means by which to accomplish the long-term American objective in foreign petroleum policy – security of supply – which was believed to require unrestricted access and control for American enterprise abroad. Such officials as Andrew Carter, who had urged the PRC objects on Ickes, perceived no basic contradiction between the thrust of this institution and the maintenance of free enterprise; nor did Ickes. He and others who sought to expand the government contribution did so because they believed there were compelling reasons of national interest. They sought not to challenge private enterprise but to preserve basic capitalist structures.

Ickes's main failure was his inability to convince other policymakers of the urgency of resource control, of the need to transcend traditional liberal strategies, and to persuade industry spokesmen that his projects were in their long-term interests.

CHAPTER SEVEN

The Preservation of Domestic and Offshore Resources

The formation of the Petroleum Reserves Corporation was one manifestation of the initiatives stimulated by World War II to identify and gain control over foreign petroleum reserves of recent significance. The war also occasioned more energetic efforts in other areas, some traditional and others new. Those aspects in which there were significant developments were in the consolidation and expansion of the Naval Reserves, the development of Alaska and the Canadian northwest, and the identification of tideland and offshore resources as of substantial future importance for United States petroleum security. The debates that took place in these areas underlined the continued commitment of policymakers to the associational state in which private enterprise provided the capital and expertise and the state provided political, diplomatic, and military support. During the war, the heightened commitment to national security and the need for increased petroleum supplies intensified the degree of government participation in what might be viewed as traditional private-sector responsibilities.

NAVAL RESERVES

The naval petroleum reserves had emerged from the first period of major concern over petroleum security prior to World War I, but it was not until World War II that the navy directly produced petroleum from one of the four reserves established in 1912, in this case Reserve No. 1 at Elk Hills, California. The war created new pressures for a reconsideration of the place of the Naval Reserves within the broader parameters of oil policy. Although the commitment to the retention of the reserves for exclusive military use remained, the greatly expanded dependency on petroleum products since the creation of the reserves emphasized to planners that the reserves were inadequate themselves for the conduct of a sustained conflict. In 1943 the naval oil reserves constituted only 0.9 percent of known domestic reserves, a minor holding given the rapid mechanization of army transportation and artillery, and the major use of aircraft.[1] Consequently, there were efforts during the war to expand the reserves, most notably in Alaska, to protect existing reserves against drainage into privately operated pools, and to involve the army as well as the navy in their management. Such expansion was hindered by steel shortages that contributed to a reduction in drilling activities from 30,000 wells in 1941 to 16,000 in 1943. Although expansion and potential utilization of reserves was desired, the main objective was to keep the oil in the ground for national emergency, and this objective ran counter to those of private enterprise and frequently the state governments. At the same time, there was no fundamental disagreement between the navy and private enterprise on the desirability of a free-market economy. Although the navy was prepared to cooperate with and even initiate experiments in synthetic fuels, there remained a basic commitment to an oil-fired navy as less expensive than existing alternatives. As Chief of Naval Operations William Leahy suggested on the eve of the war, at some future time coal might once again become the basic fuel; but "from the standpoint of social benefit it would be better to defer reverting to coal until forced to do so by natural causes."[2] Such attitudes hampered the ability of planners to achieve a more comprehensive Naval Reserves policy, as they hindered the effective implementation of the Petroleum Reserves Corporation, with the result that the commitment to protect the Naval Reserves was overshadowed by their basic inadequacy for national defense.[3]

Government and business did conflict over the question of private corporate access to reserve oil and over the possible extension of federal reserves, most notably in California. Here the navy provided much of the initiative, submitting legislative proposals to Congress in 1939 requesting that petroleum deposits adjacent to and along the coast of California be conserved as essential to the national defense. The navy simultaneously urged the president to create an office of petroleum conservation. Such initiatives contributed to the subsequent appointment of Harold Ickes as Petroleum Coordinator for National Defense and led to an extended debate over the Naval Reserves and the status of mineral resources of California and other tidelands. That debate had two dimensions: the first centered on the effort during the war to treat the Elk Hills Naval Reserve as a single pool of crude oil, that is to establish the principle of unit operation; the second concerned the broader issue of federal versus state, and state versus private-enterprise development of offshore resources. The latter was a major political issue of the period, not politically resolved until the 1950s, and had substantial significance for the United States in maintaining effective control over petroleum supplies for national security.[4]

During the war the navy encouraged the participation of private enterprise in exploiting the reserves. In November 1942, the navy negotiated a contract with Standard Oil of California granting the corporation a monopoly on the right to develop and market the oil in the Elk Hills reserves, which were estimated to hold 350 million barrels of crude petroleum, for a five-year period or for the duration of the war. The navy and Standard Oil shared the cost of development. The contract brought strong objections from several sources. Representative Jerry Voorhis of California expressed opposition in Congress to a private corporation having control of a military reserve; Voorhis feared that such participation by Standard Oil in the Elk Hills reserve would increase monopolistic controls over natural resources. Harold Ickes also objected to the contract, urging the alternative approach that the Department of the Interior operate the fields for the navy. Ickes was not, however, opposed to exploiting the reserve. He saw Elk Hills as essential for the relief of the crude-oil supply problem in the Pacific coast area. The only alternative was increased importation of crude petroleum from the Caribbean, which would involve drilling additional wells in Venezuela and readjusting the tanker allocations established by the Army-Navy Petroleum Board and the War Shipping Administration.[5] More significant was the opinion of Attorney General Francis Biddle, who advised the secretary of the navy that the 1942 contract went beyond the force of existing law. Political considerations supplemented the legal and bureaucratic ones to contribute to a revision of the contract. Josephus Daniels advised the president, who agreed with the assessment, that it was an inopportune moment for Standard Oil to appear to gain control of the Elk Hills reserve. "If the Standard should get that reserve now, I fear it will give the opposition an issue in 1944, reminiscent of the Teapot Dome. I am sure you will not permit this."[6]

In addition to dissatisfaction with the Standard Oil–navy contract, there was strong sentiment in the departments of war, navy, and interior supporting the creation of an army-navy reserve to be constituted from present navy reserves and such future reserves as could be acquired, a program that would complement efforts to acquire major reserves outside the U.S. Domestic reserves should be adequate to meet army and navy requirements and would be utilized only in extreme circumstances.[7] Hence, the opposition to the Elk Hills contract was not so much the result of antagonism to Standard Oil as it was a reflection of the view that too-rapid exploitation of the naval reserves would seriously endanger national security.

In a speech draft prepared in January 1944, Ickes indicated that he proposed to recommend to Congress the creation of a domestic oil commission composed of the secretaries of war, navy, and interior to determine the necessity for and the acquisition of oil reserves. Ickes envisaged that the armed forces would be in a position to direct policy; the Department of the Interior would be charged with administering the reserves. Ickes saw no reason why private industry should oppose a policy that would give government the right, on the discovery of a new pool, to purchase the pool at market value and to hold it as an army-navy oil reserve for national defense. He was clearly confident that the war had persuaded some "practical and influential oil men that it is actually a responsibility of the Government to acquire petroleum reserves and thus be ready for an emergency." In Ickes's plan, domestic reserves would be an integral part of a broader system in which the U.S. would hold petroleum underground or in above-ground storage in ample quantities, at such strategic points as the Philippines, Alaska, Puerto Rico, Guam, Hawaii, and the Canal Zone, where the United States and the "peaceful nations of the world" could have ready access. The domestic and international reserve policy would need to be supplemented by government-supported research in hydrogenation and the development of oil shale and gas. At that time the Department of the Interior was seeking a congressional appropriation to provide $30 million for the Bureau of Mines to construct three experimental commercial plants to explore synthetic fuel development. Until more progress was made along those lines, however, Ickes urged the stockpiling of two-to-three years' supply of petroleum products for national security.[8] Ickes's ideas, which he formalized in a March proposal to President Roosevelt for the creation of a federal petroleum reserves board, were not adopted, but they reflected the growing awareness in the administration of the need for a concerted federal policy.[9] Part of the explanation for Ickes's failure in this area lies in interdepartmental rivalries, but more important was the concern that Ickes was overextending government involvement in the private sector.

There was sufficient consensus in late 1943 and early 1944, nonetheless, to lead to a new contract with Standard Oil on the Elk Hills reserve. The departments of justice, navy, and interior negotiated a temporary operating agreement in September 1943, thus avoiding litigation and a possible interruption of petroleum supplies for the Pacific war. The temporary agreement provided a mechanism by which Standard Oil would compensate the navy for oil withdrawn from the reserve; it maintained the unit plan of reserve operation in order to protect the reserve against drainage into private fields; and the provision in the old contract, which had given Standard Oil a preferential right to purchase the navy's share of oil produced, was deleted, thus removing one of the more contentious features.[10] The initiative did not go far enough to satisfy Josephus Daniels, who remained critical of the associational arrangment between state and private enterprise. "I would feel much better," he wrote the president in February 1944, "if the Navy itself were operating the reserves ... than to make any sort of arrangement with the Standard Oil. I know too much about those birds to trust them."[11] Daniels, however, was representative of an older and more anachronistic dimension of the progressive tradition, in which business was perceived as the opponent rather than the partner, and his complaints fell on unsympathetic ears.

The temporary contract was followed by congressional legislation as well as a new contract in the spring of 1944, through the initiative of the navy and the PAW. The legislation, which President Roosevelt signed on 17 June, preserved unit production, provided Congress with power to determine the amount of oil to be produced from the reserve, and stipulated that the secretary of the navy could not condemn lands or enter into joint contracts without prior consultation with the Naval Affairs committees of both houses of Congress. In the contract subsequently concluded with Standard Oil, there was an obligation not only to maintain the reserve in a state of readiness, "but also to conduct operations in such manner as will insure the greatest ultimate recovery of oil and associated hydrocarbons from the Reserve." In the president's view, the contract and the legislation together provided "every reasonable protection. We get what we have always sought – control of all Standard's oil in the Reserve as well as our own – and none of the oil can be produced without Congressional authority by joint resolution." Privately, Roosevelt was more concerned that congressional authority over the reserve was excessively executive in nature, but his reservation was not sufficiently strong to cancel the more attractive features of the legislation.[12]

Elk Hills was the most important of the navy petroleum reserves for the war effort. The wells in Teapot Dome had been capped since 1927, and oil executives were of the view that the Alaskan reserve would not be of use in the war, given problems of development and transportation. Conversely, by 1945 the navy's 100-octane plant at Richmond, California, which was being operated by Standard Oil of California for the navy, was producing 10 percent of the world's high-octane gasoline.[13] By the end of the war, the basic principles of the navy reserve policy were well established. There remained the commitment, made with their establishment in 1912, to conserve petroleum for military use in a national emergency. At the same time, there was a distinct shift toward a fuller acceptance of a government–private enterprise cooperative approach to their development, based on the assumption that the companies possessed the expertise and could most rapidly and efficiently put the reserves into operation when confronted with the military necessity.

THE CANOL PROJECT

Military and civilian interest in developing an effective policy for the naval petroleum reserves paralleled a growing American interest in the strategic potentiality of petroleum resources in Alaska and the Canadian northwest. Although as a specific project it ultimately proved of little long-term significance, the most important manifestation of wartime interest in the area was the United States Army's Canol project. Initiated in 1942 with the precise objective of supplying petroleum products along the route of the Alaska highway and for Alaska-based aircraft, the Canol project involved the exploitation and expansion of current production at Norman Wells in the Northwest Territories, the construction of a pipeline to Whitehorse in the Yukon, and the installation of a refinery at Whitehorse. The Canol project has traditionally been examined in terms either of Canadian-American relations or of American military mismanagement, as identified by the Truman committee on the national defense program.[14] Such approaches are certainly valid; but the objective here is to consider the way in which Canol highlighted the military's heightened involvement during the war in petroleum policy planning at home and abroad and the utilization of private enterprise as an instrument of government policy.

In the months following the Japanese attack on Pearl Harbor, the U.S. Army Air Force Air Transport Command experienced difficulties transporting aircraft from the United States to the Soviet Union via the Canadian northwest and Alaska. One of the main difficulties, given what the army believed was inadequate control of the Pacific coastal waters, was the provision of high-octane gasoline for the movement of aircraft in the region. The army consequently seized on the idea both of constructing a land route (the Alaska highway) and of further developing existing petroleum facilities at Norman Wells. With Lieutenant-General Brehon Somervell, commanding general of the Army Service Forces, providing the initiative, the $130 million project was pressed through the bureaucracy. There was minimal consultation with other agencies and military departments, and Canadian approval of the project was little more than a formality of the joint defense program. In the agreement reached between the Department of State and the Canadian government, the pipeline and Whitehorse refinery were to remain the property of the United States and would be operated under U.S. authority during the war; at the end of the war the Canadian government was to be given the first option to purchase the facilities. It was also stipulated that the petroleum produced would be utilized solely for military defense and that any commercial production would be under Canadian control. [15]

Pessimists at the time, the companies (including Imperial Oil and Standard Oil of California) contracted to perform the work were proved correct by the subsequent failure of Canol to produce 100-octane gasoline until the end of 1944. It was subsequently estimated that the entire output of the Canol project could have been supplied by one tanker in a three-month period at a cost considerably lower than that allocated to the development of Norman Wells and the associated pipelines and refinery. Certainly there were major miscalculations of cost and a lack of familiarity with the topography and climatic conditions in the region that contributed to delays and escalating costs. Yet, it is overly simplistic to identify Somervell as the villain in the piece, as the Truman committee did in 1944. [16] The military continued to endorse the project against the criticism of the PAW and the Truman committee in 1943 and 1944 on the grounds of military necessity, an argument similar to that which was advanced in support of the Petroleum Reserves Corporation's projects in Saudi Arabia during the same period. The initial decision to proceed with the project was made not by Somervell alone but at a meeting of civilian and military officials that included Brigadier-General Andrew F. Carter and General Walter B. Pyron, both former oil executives with extensive experience, and both active in wartime petroleum planning. Also present were representatives of Standard Oil of California and Imperial Oil. [17] When the Joint Chiefs of Staff reviewed the project in October 1943 with the guidance of the Army-Navy Petroleum Board and the Joint Production Survey Committee, they determined that the completion of Canol was still "necessary to the war effort." There were certainly reservations within the war department. Following a cabinet discussion of Canol at the end of September, Henry Stimson was sufficiently concerned about the criticisms of Canol raised by Ickes and echoed by the president that he had Julius Amberg of his office review the project. Amberg reported that the situation was not as serious as had been feared, that the pipeline was expected to be operable by January. Although Stimson's main concerns had been alleviated by the end of 1943, his undersecretary continued to hold some reservations, especially with respect to the long-range development of Canol petroleum and the role of the private companies. "Imperial should not profit unduly," Patterson wrote later in the year, "from exploration done at our expense outside the field of its original discovery and development. Retention of the installations and the right to obtain oil should be assured for a longer period. If the resources are sufficient, a military reserve for the defense of both countries should be established." Admiral Leahy shared Patterson's concern with the long-range implications of the project. To Leahy, Canol continued to seem worthwhile, not only because it would provide high-octane gasoline for local military use, but also because expansion of the facility would be possible to meet increasing worldwide shortages.

Although there may have been major lingering reservations within the war department over the utility and viability of Canol, the department presented a united front in its defense against both the Truman committee and Harold Ickes, who was the main critic within the administration. When the Truman committee criticized the department and Somervell for inadequate study prior to launching the project and for failing to gain an agreement with the Canadian government that would provide the United States with postwar participation or control in the fields, the departments announced its intention to complete the project. Part of the explanation for this decision may lie in bureaucratic self-preservation, but one cannot discount the importance that the military placed on the fact that army specialists and Imperial Oil estimated the reserves in the area of Norman Wells to be between 35 and 100 million barrels of crude at a time when there was concern in the U.S. for the security of short- as well as long-term petroleum supplies. Indeed, it is a reasonable assumption that the military perceived a similar opportunity to establish American interests in the Canadian northwest to that which was present in Saudi Arabia. Certainly the U.S. gave indication of desiring to expand the project by requesting and obtaining Canadian consent in 1943 to prospect for oil in the region, with the understanding that the United States could make use of any discoveries.[18]

Although there were long-range strategic considerations that were involved in the initiation and perpetuation of the project, the main impetus was short term and military rather than commercial in nature. As Somervell contended to the chief of staff in July 1943, "The abandonment of the Canol Project at a time when the United States is prepared to support other developments in areas which it does not control would appear inconsistent and unwise"; and Robert Patterson, as acting secretary of war, argued at the same time that "military necessity requires that the Canol Project be completed as rapidly as possible ... The success of the Canol Project may well be the determining factor which will control the size and extent of an air offensive aimed at the heart of the Japanese empire through Alaska and Siberia."[19]

Critics of the project concentrated on several features: the doubt that the refinery would produce adequate supplies of high-octane gasoline before war's end; the excessive cost of the project when compared with that of tanker transport; the lack of army consultation with other departments; and the perception that the agreement was unduly favorable to Canada. Harold Ickes was especially concerned with the lack of consultation and the failure, in his view, to provide adequate safeguards for American interests in the area. He believed the refinery should have been, as a principle of national security, outside Canada, preferably at Fairbanks, Alaska, where it would have remained useful to the United States after the war. In addition, although Canol was in essence consistent with Ickes's support for the acquisition of foreign petroleum reserves, he thought it was financially impractical.[20] Ickes did express support for Canol No. 2, which involved the construction of a pipeline from Skagway to Whitehorse, thus providing the means to move petroleum into U.S. territory. Ickes also envisaged the Canol project as a way to encourage interest in northern petroleum development and specifically to press for exploratory drilling in Alaska. Although he viewed the "huge expenditures of steel, equipment and skilled labor" for Canol as "a serious drain on the national resources," he believed the exploitation of Alaskan reserves might provide a mechanism to conserve critical raw materials and ships. Such developments were also ones over which Ickes wished to retain jurisdiction, objecting to what he perceived was navy encroachment on PAW and Department of the Interior territory both in the development of oil resources in Alaska and in research into synthetic fuels.[21] Consequently, the initiative to revise the terms of the Canol agreement with Canada took place simultaneously with the American effort to advance Alaskan oil development. Secretary of the Navy Frank Knox indicated to the president that a comprehensive program for the development of its petroleum reserves included the development of the 35,000-square-mile Reserve No. 4 (Point Barrow in Alaska) as a high priority and dispatched a reconnaissance party that spring in cooperation with the army and the interior department. Knox presented such an approach in 1944 as "an initial step to implement an integrated program for exploration in Alaska."[22] By the following year, Knox's successor, James Forrestal, advised the president that preliminary investigations in Alaska by the firm of De Golyer and MacNaughton, which was contracted as special adviser on petroleum matters, indicated that drilling should be undertaken at Umiat Mountain on the Colville River, and Forrestal had accordingly authorized a long-range exploratory program designed to determine the quantity of oil in Reserve No. 4.[23]

As the United States turned more aggressively toward Alaskan petroleum development, it also renegotiated the Canol agreement in the spring of 1944. The potential development in Alaska clearly placed the army and the American government in a position where it could afford to ease itself out of the Canol agreement, which had become a substantial embarrassment to the army. Nonetheless, it was significant that the army wished to have continued development in the area, and the new contract that was negotiated between the war department and Imperial Oil, and which was to come into effect at the end of the war, gave Imperial Oil title to all of the U.S. facilities associated with the Canol project in order to enable Imperial Oil to continue activities in the area. The Canadian government provided further incentive to Imperial to remain active in the area by reducing royalty payments. In part to meet criticism by the Truman committee that the original agreement had been excessively favorable to Canada, the revised agreement reduced the cost to the U.S. of Canol crude oil from $1.25 a barrel, plus production costs, to 20¢ a barrel, plus production costs. At the same time it provided for future deliveries to the U.S. of up to 60 million barrels of petroleum for military purposes. Nevertheless, the principle of American participation had been altered, from one of ownership of the petroleum during the war, to one in which it had the option to purchase Imperial Oil petroleum, a situation not unlike that which the State Department had preferred for the Petroleum Reserves Corporation in Saudi Arabia. The Canadian government provided, as well, a stronger measure of sovereignty in the revised agreement, in part in consideration of Imperial Oil's subsidiary status to Standard Oil of New Jersey, to the effect that Canada could at any time take possession of the "areas held under lease or permit."[24]

The declining interest in the potentialities of Canol was given a further *coup de grâce* in the following years by several factors. The first was the clear Canadian opposition to the American postwar controls and American reluctance to be involved in a development over which they did not exercise adequate jurisdiction. A second was the relative lack of interest in the Canol area on the part of Imperial Oil, which redirected its attention to Alberta, in 1947 bringing in the major Leduc fields. The only aspect of Canol that continued to appeal to Imperial Oil was the Whitehorse refinery, which it purchased shortly after the Leduc breakthrough.[25] By that time the war department's operations at Norman Wells had been inactive for two years and its attention had sharply shifted to Alaska.

The end of the war and the mustering out of naval pesonnel made it necessary for the navy to depend increasingly on private enterprise in its Alaskan developments. The Naval Affairs committees of both House and Senate concurred with the assessment that the Alaskan fields were of special promise and supported the decision to proceed on a civilian contract basis after the war.[26] This was an approach with which Harold Ickes was not in agreement during his final months in office.

Continuing to object to navy's exclusive jurisdiction over the petroleum reserves, Ickes wrote President Truman in early 1946: "I have felt for some time that the reserves should be administered by a board composed of the Secretaries of War, Navy, and Interior and that the latter, by reason of the special skills and experience provided in the Bureaus and agencies of his department, should be chairman." Ickes clearly desired that exploration work should be the responsibility of the United States Geological Survey rather than contracted out to private firms. "I am convinced," he informed the president, "that the attainment of a national plan and policy for petroleum security requires the establishment of the board which I have recommended." Confronted with a hostile presidential response, Ickes left the Truman administration to be replaced by Julius Krug, and the president approved the continuation of exploration for oil in the Alaskan reserve under civil contract.[27] The adherence to the associational state had once again triumphed. At the same time, the claim of the military to a major role in formulating a national oil policy had been clearly established.

OFFSHORE RESOURCES

Harold Ickes was as aggressive in support of establishing clear United States jurisdiction over offshore mineral resources as he had been in critiquing the Canol project. His opposition to Canol, as noted earlier, derived not from any reluctance to expand U.S. operations in foreign countries but rather from his firm conviction that the Canol project provided an inadequate degree of U.S. control and required excessive investment for a limited and uncertain return at a time when funds could, he believed, have been more profitably employed in developing Alaskan reserves. Although, as in the case of the PRC, other agencies and departments were active in the debate over offshore resources, it was Ickes who acted as the main catalyst in stimulating decisive action.

As early as 1937, Ickes had the legal department in interior examine the question of jurisdiction over offshore resources.[28] Then and subsequently there were two dimensions to the issue, federal versus state jurisdiction over the tidelands, and United States control over resources beyond the three-mile limit. By 1943, with the scarcity of petroleum products coming closer to reality and with the PRC still in embryo, Ickes urged President Roosevelt to consider ways to expand the supply of natural resources and draw to his attention the potential of the continental shelf. The secretary of the interior argued that it was imperative, owing to the complex international dilemmas involved, for the United States to "lay the groundwork" for American control over the riches of the submerged lands.

The president's sympathies were clearly supportive of Ickes's position. In 1939 he had requested the attorney general to draft an executive order asserting the right of the federal government to create naval petroleum reserves within the three-mile limit below low-water marks. With respect to resources located beyond the three-mile limit, Roosevelt indicated that "the sovereignty of the United States is actually exercised in similar cases beyond the three-mile limit and relating to the conservation of natural resources. It is my belief that the 'rule of reason' would be applied in such cases." In reference to the petroleum resources of the Gulf of Mexico, the president added: "I cannot imagine allowing foreign oil companies to take this oil within actual sight of our own coast because under 'a rule of reason' it is part of the contiguous waters and hundreds of miles from the nearest foreign land."[29]

On Roosevelt's initiative, an interdepartmental committee was established in August 1939 to study the question of title to submerged oil lands.[30] That committee's report to the president the following March stressed the acute need for a coherent policy in light of the extensive operations that were being carried out off the coast of southern California. Since 1897, some 100 wells had been drilled off the coast of California. This enquiry and much of the congressional debate at the time concerned the tidelands and was of primary significance for domestic rather than international relations. However, the ability of the federal government to establish jurisdiction in such areas was of considerable importance to the ability of the United States to develop a national petroleum policy that effectively coordinated domestic and overseas petroleum operations. Nonetheless, although Congress debated several bills on the question in the four years following the establishment of an interdepartmental committee of inquiry, there had been no concrete action as the war drew to a close.

It was the executive, especially Ickes and the Department of the Navy, rather than Congress that demonstrated the keenest desire to resolve the question and to establish clear federal controls in the interest of effective development and national security. Several bills and joint resolutions relevant to the question were introduced in Congress between 1937 and 1939, but these led to no concrete action, even though extensive hearings were held in 1938 before the House Judiciary Committee on a bill asserting federal title over the tidelands. The president's advisory committee concluded that the federal government should use court action to determine jurisdiction, a point of view shared by Harold Ickes.[31]

In 1939 the navy attempted once again to achieve congressional action on the tidelands by requesting the consideration of legislation establishing a naval problem reserve in the submerged lands along the coast of California in the interest of national security. Ickes and the navy wanted closer federal control over California petroleum development in order to restrict petroleum sales to Japan in 1939, and they seized on the national-security aspect of the tidelands issue in order to advance the federal cause.

The Senate Committee on Public Lands and Surveys and the judiciary committee conducted several days of hearings on the legislation in March of 1939 during which the navy forcefully attempted to advance the national security thesis. It was argued that the "serious depletion of the oil" that was taking place required prompt federal action within the three-mile limit; the navy was of the view that the effectiveness of an executive order "would seem to depend upon the acquiescence of other nations or upon the physical capacity of the United States to enforce it against any and all nations that may contest it." Roosevelt himself was convinced that federal jurisdiction could be exercised as far out "as it is mechanically possible to drill wells, either from permanent structures or floating equipment."[32] Captain Stuart argued persuasively before the House Judiciary Committee that "crude petroleum in natural reservoirs is the only raw material in the United States from which it is commercially feasible and physically practical to manufacture the products needed at the present time. Insurance of a competent supply of crude petroleum to meet anticipated extraordinary demands for the national defense is, therefore, essential and imperative." It was argued that California's resources would be essential in the event of any prolonged conflict in the Pacific area, especially given the absence of pipelines connecting the Pacific coast to mid-continent producing fields. Stuart was especially pessimistic that exports to "potential enemies" would be terminated "so long as law and profits permit."[33] Leslie McNemar, senior attorney in the Office of the Judge Advocate General (navy), stressed that the United States Navy would not be able to compete with Britain or Japan if it had to convert from oil to coal in its naval vessels, and observed that such conversion was not possible in any event for its submarines.[34]

Persuasive as the navy's argument may have been, it failed to sway Congress to its point of view. The entire California delegation in the House opposed more direct federal controls over California's natural resources. Even progressive members of the Committee on Public Lands, who might have been expected to support conservationist and centralist legislation, were antagonistic. Hiram Johnson of California, for example, found spurious the navy contention that California resources were in danger of exhaustion and was especially opposed to any legislation that might apply solely to California's resources. Other progressives on the committee, William Borah of Idaho and Gerald P. Nye of North Dakota, did not speak with any enthusiasm in defense of the measure, although Nye had previously introduced a resolution in Senate that would have strengthened federal jurisdiction.[35]

The failure of Congress to lend support to the executive initiative relating to offshore resources strengthened the resolve to utilize the courts, an approach that Harold Ickes especially favored. The war, however, tended to divert attention from the issue until 1944, when petroleum shortages once again lent a sense of urgency to the question. Ickes urged a test suit to determine federal authority over submerged oil lands, a position that Attorney General Francis Biddle opposed without prior passage of a statute indicative of federal policy, and for the moment the president supported Biddle. Ickes lamented the lack of initiative and foresight. "At a time," he wrote, "when the Government is under the necessity of developing some kind of petroleum reserves policy to ensure the national safety, I think it is important that we know who is the owner of what may be one of the greatest potential oil reserves in the world."[36]

With constant pressure from Ickes, and increasing interest by the State Department in the international implications of offshore resources, the administration moved in late 1944 to support a test suit. On 29 May 1945, with Harry Truman in the presidency, the justice department announced the filing in the United States District Court at Los Angeles of a suit against the Pacific Western Corporation. The suit would enjoin operations of the company, which was extracting oil under California lease in the Elwood oil field off the coast near Santa Barbara.[37] The decision to file the suit at the district level rather than with the Supreme Court displeased Ickes especially, and the case was dropped that autumn to be replaced by an original action against the State of California in the Supreme Court.[38]

In June 1947 the Supreme Court rules in *U.S. v. California* that the United States had "paramount rights and national dominion" in the area of submerged lands. It did not, however, explicitly rule that the United Sates possessed title or proprietary rights to such lands and any natural resources they might contain,[39] even though Truman administration officials appear to have construed the decision in that manner. The month following the Supreme Court decision, Attorney General Thomas Clark and Secretary of the Interior Julius Krug entered into an agreement with California, setting aside a tract of the submerged lands near Long Beach for the use of California. For the remainder of the Truman administration the principle of federal jurisdiction and development was maintained against congressional efforts to shift the jurisdiction and leasing powers to the states. In 1952, Truman vetoed such a measure, but on the whole he was less aggressive than the Roosevelt administration had been late in the war.[40]

As president, Truman had a stronger commitment to private-sector initiative, and hence was unsupportive of Ickes's recommendations for the development of national oil reserves for the use of the armed forces. Ickes lamented that had Roosevelt and former Secretary of the Navy Frank Knox lived, there would have been positive action on Ickes's request for a national petroleum commission to supervise petroleum development for national security. With Ickes's departure from the cabinet in 1946, much of the momentum for effective petroleum planning that had been built up during the war returned to the private sector, even though the Korean War would restore some of the balance. Such developments in the Truman administration had their element of irony. As committed as Truman was to national security at home and abroad during the crucial early years of the Cold War, his administration seemed prepared to entrust an aspect of such vital strategic importance as petroleum almost solely to the private sector. This was apparent not only in his response to the efforts of Ickes and others to maintain federal and government initiative, but also in his failure to pursue with any vigor an international agreement on petroleum development.

It was the Eisenhower administration after 1952 that truly turned the clock back on Ickes's initiatives by supporting the 1953 Submerged Lands Act, which established state title and ownership to resources within the three-mile limit. The states in turn confirmed leases with private companies.[41] Not only had the principle of federal control over strategic natural resources been seriously weakened against state claims, but the ability of the federal government to determine which enterprises should exploit the resources had been defeated. On the latter point there appears to have been little difference between Democrats and Republicans.

Federal authorities were less reluctant to assert jurisdiction over the continental shelf beyond the three-mile limit, the area that had clearer relevance to foreign policy considerations. Shortly before Roosevelt's death, Ickes stressed to Secretary of State Edward Stettinius that the need for clearly establishing U.S. jurisidiction was "urgent," and recommended that the president's approval of the joint memorandum on the resources of the continental shelf and coastal fisheries be obtained "as expeditiously as possible."[42] The joint departmental recommendation was that the president issue a proclamation declaring "the natural resources of the subsoil and sea bed of the continental shelf beneath the high seas but contiguous to the coasts of the United States" as subject to U.S. jurisdiction and control. Roosevelt received the memorandum on 28 March 1945 just prior to departing on his final trip to Warm Springs. He signed it three days later,[43] and although his death briefly interrupted the initiative, Ickes and the Department of State perceived the issue as one of sufficient importance to bring it to President Truman's attention only a short time after he assumed office.[44] At the cabinet meeting of 4 May Truman gave his approval to take possession in the name of the United States of the continental shelf in areas contiguous to the United States and to continue discussions with Canada, Great Britain, Cuba, Mexico, and the Soviet Union.

Truman did not, however, issue the proclamation on the continental shelf until late September 1945. The delay was occasioned in part by the lack of official response from the foreign governments approached on the issue. The British, when they did apply, expressed preference for an international agreement on continental resource policy. Failing a comprehensive international agreement, the British asserted the reciprocal rights to jurisdiction over oil exploration and exploitation in drillable areas "beyond and adjacent to the territorial waters of the Bahamas, and of the Turks and Cacios Islands which are dependencies of Jamaica." The Department of State, for its part, was determined that the U.S. should first unilaterally declare its position and then attempt to support it through the negotiation of bilateral agreements.[45]

Such a policy was not explicitly intended to limit the exploitation of continental shelf resources of American nationals any more than had been the case with the access of foreign enterprise to United States domestic resources previously. The primary objective of the proclamation was to assert United States jurisdiction in order, in the words of one official, to "guard against the depletion of our mineral resources and to regulate ... the activities of foreigners in proximity to our coast." The intent was clearly to establish United States jurisdiction in advance of the technological capabilities to exploit the resources.[46] For the moment the proclamation had little direct applicability, but stimulated by the petroleum demands of the Korean War and improved technology for offshore drilling, Congress in August 1953 passed the Outer Continental Shelf Act, which reaffirmed federal jurisdiction and authorized the secretary of the interior to issue leases to private enterprise.[47]

World War II provided the opportunity to reexamine petroleum policy relevant to domestic reserves and their significance for national security. As was the case with the PRC, it was the military and Harold Ickes who were most committed to positive state control over petroleum supplies for national defense. Accordingly, Ickes supported the consolidation and expansion of naval reserves, the establishment of a more broadly based national petroleum reserves board, which would include the army, government direction over new exploration in Alaska and elsewhere, and a firm assertion of federal jurisdiction over the tidelands and of United States jurisdiction over the outer continental shelf. Ickes did clash with the military, specifically over the Canol project, not because of any fundamental difference of view over the importance of government predominance in areas of national security, but rather because of his belief that the returns on the project were inadequate. Throughout the debates on these developments there was little inclination in the Roosevelt administration, and less in the Truman administration, to challenge the need for close cooperation between government and business. The difference between Ickes and his opponents was very much what the difference had been earlier in the century between left-wing progressives and business progressives; that is, it was over the balance of power in the business-government partnership. To Ickes, power should reside with the state, with private enterprise the secondary partner, providing technology and business expertise. That objective was most fully realized in the Canol project and the Naval Reserves, in part because the principle had already been well established prior to the war and in part because of the general consensus that existed during the wartime emergency. The objective of state primacy failed in the development of policy toward the tidelands and the outer continental shelf, where the state did little more than provide the diplomatic offensive behind which the forces of private enterprise could muster.

CHAPTER EIGHT

The Failure of Internationalism, 1943–1947

By 1943, with the creation of the Petroleum Reserves Corporation, and the continuing debates over Saudi Arabia and Iran, the Middle East had clearly displaced other geographic areas as a determinant in United States foreign petroleum policy. The desire for security of supply for both companies and nation appeared to make essential a consolidation and expansion of U.S. petroleum interests and influence in the region, at the same time that domestic and offshore resources were explored and preserved for American development. The United States adopted an aggressive position with respect to Middle Eastern oil after 1943, but that aggressiveness was tempered by the reality of traditional British predominance in the area and the threat of expanding Soviet interests. The result was that the United States pursued a multilateral approach to petroleum policy, attempting to achieve an Anglo-American accord that would minimize the ability of British firms to exclude American interests from the area and bring an end to the restrictive provisions of the Red Line Agreement of 1928. This effort to conclude an Anglo-American petroleum agreement has been viewed as a decisive turning point in U.S. oil policy, a movement toward an acceptance of international cooperation. It could be argued that effective cooperation among major petroleum-producing-and-consuming nations would have significantly altered the nature of postwar international relations, but the evidence does not suggest that the United States was renouncing an aggressively nationalistic position in seeking the accord.[1] Rather, during 1943–5, American government and company officials gave the impression they were negotiating from a position of weakness in the region and hence were prepared to accept international cooperation in order to stabilize the marketplace, an approach that had been effectively utilized in the 1920s. As United States strength and British weakness became more transparent with the end of the war, and as the oil companies demonstrated their capacity to achieve the type of controls and stability that had been the objective of diplomacy, an agreement between the nations lost much of its meaning and urgency. The result was that after 1947 the power to determine short- and long-range factors relevant to U.S. petroleum policy continued to reside more in the private than in the public sector.

This chapter examines the objectives of U.S. planners in attempting to conclude an Anglo-American agreement on petroleum, as part of the reconsideration of petroleum policy that took place during World War II, the response of the business community to the negotiations, and its role in shaping the agreements that emerged. It is not an attempt to chronicle the lengthy and complex diplomatic negotiations leading to the agreements. The evidence suggests that American planners were less committed to internationalism in petroleum relations than to the protection and consolidation of American interests in the Middle East; that it was not business opposition to the agreement that resulted in the ultimate Senate failure to ratify, but rather a lack of commitment by public officials to centralized public controls over the international oil business and the perception that the companies were more capable of achieving stability through private means with public support. As with other developments in petroleum policy examined in this study, the conclusion of planners was that the associational state was the most effective means of advancing American interests abroad.

The history of efforts to conclude and implement an accord on petroleum between the United States and Great Britain spanned nine years, from initial consideration in 1943 until the treaty was ultimately withdrawn from the Senate by President Truman in 1952. The agreement appeared to hold much promise for international petroleum cooperation when it came before the Senate Foreign Relations Committee in 1947. By 1947, the agreement had undergone several modifications. Originally negotiated in Washington in 1944 and sent to the Senate for ratification, the accord was withdrawn, renegotiated, and substantially revised by new delegates in London in September 1945 and submitted as a treaty for Senate ratification. The details of those negotiations lie outside the scope of this study. What is of concern are the objectives of United States and British policymakers, the nature of the agreements, and the factors accounting for the failure of its implementation, particularly the role of the petroleum industry and of Congress.

TOWARD COOPERATIVE DEVELOPMENT

The initiative leading to the negotiation of an Anglo–American petroleum agreement derived from several sources in the course of 1943. One was the petroleum industry itself, which sought the means to rationalize the exploitation and marketing of petroleum products, especially those derived from Middle Eastern sources. A second was the Department of State, which perceived a general agreement with Great Britain as a more effective device to reduce international conflict and defend United States security than the Petroleum Reserves Corporation over which Harold Ickes assumed command during 1943. Nonetheless, the support for an international agreement was very strong in the State Department prior to Ickes's maneuvering, and it is difficult to accept an interpretation that the agreement was essentially a means by which to circumvent and collapse the PRC. Indeed, the basic leadership in the negotiations, especially after Herbert Feis's departure from the State Department in 1943, and Cordell Hull's illness and then retirement in November 1944, was provided by Harold Ickes, who was strongly committed to the principle of an international agreement and continued to lobby on its behalf after he left the cabinet in February 1946. The composition of the force supporting the agreement was similar to that which supported the PRC at its inception. It included President Roosevelt, the military, key State Department officials, Harold Ickes and Ralph Davies of the PAW, those major companies that anticipated commercial advantage from a protective agreement, and more internationally inclined Congressmen such as Henry Cabot Lodge. Independent domestic producers were divided in their response, as were congressmen from oil-producing states. The defeat of the agreement cannot thus be interpreted as a triumph of conservative isolationists over internationalists or of that nonmonolithic entity, the petroleum industry, over the administration. Nor was this conflict so clearly one of privatism versus public control, although many of the opponents of the agreement cast the contest in that light. In essence the agreement was, in Herbert Feis's words, "a tardy and groping expression of the wish of the American government to assure the adequacy of our future oil supplies."[2]

By 1943 both United States and British officials were moving toward a consensus on the need for some form of international agreement on petroleum development in order to avoid undue competition between American and British companies. The situation was similar to that which had prevailed at the end of World War I in the sense that the Middle East promised to be the focus of either conflict or cooperation. The situation was dissimilar in the sense that the United States was no longer bargaining from a position of weakness, and American companies were now well established in the region, either on a shared basis with British-Dutch companies, as in the Iraq Petroleum Company (IPC) or the Gulf–Anglo-Iranian cooperation in Kuwait, or autonomously as with Aramco in Saudi Arabia. Moreover, the 1943–7 period presented Britain and the United States with a markedly altered diplomatic and economic context. American officials had become acutely aware of the need to conserve domestic and western-hemisphere resources once the war was over and of the immense potentiality of the Middle East. In this, government and major company officials concurred. Although the Middle East was somewhat remote to be a secure reserve in the event of war, it nonetheless offered a substitute to supply European and eastern markets, given the temporary loss to Japan of production facilities in the East Indies. There is no reason to assume, however, that American corporations did not anticipate the full recovery of those facilities at the end of the war, with the result that their attempts to consolidate and expand in the Middle East need to be viewed as efforts to gain a more complete control over international petroleum supplies and markets. In fact, a group was appointed in 1943 by the PAW at the request of the military to study a few selected areas in which wartime rehabilitation of petroleum facilities might advantageously be begun. That group included representatives of the major oil companies active in enemy-occupied territories prior to the war. Coordination with the industry was the responsibility of James Terry Duce of the PAW, as well as Sir Frederick Godber of Shell and F.C. Starling of the British Ministry of Fuel and Power. The only dimension of disagreement between the joint chiefs and the companies was over the rate of rehabilitation, with the companies anxious to employ conservationist measures that would ensure long-range production. There was agreement that no settlement should be arranged with the Dutch government concerning the postwar disposition of oil properties in Dutch possessions until the rehabilitation work was complete.[3]

The situation in 1943 was also distinct from that of the early 1920s insofar as American corporations enjoyed considerably less freedom of action in Latin America and Eastern Europe. Nations in Latin America had clearly moved toward a higher acceptance of state involvement in the petroleum industry and central Eastern Europe was threatened by either German or Soviet expansionism. The same was true of Iran, where the threat of Soviet participation in petroleum production, breaking the Anglo-Iranian monopoly, appeared imminent in 1943.

Of the factors contributing to the decision to pursue an international agreement on petroleum, the situation that prevailed in Iran in 1942–3 was a more important catalyst than the Saudi Arabian developments that led to the formation of the PRC. The two were closely related, but the evidence suggests that without the conflict with the USSR over Iran, the conclusion of a petroleum agreement would have had much less immediacy. The three-way struggle among the Americans, British, and

Russians for Iranian oil concessions was of long standing, but it reached crisis proportions between 1942 and 1944. Iran was the first important oil-producing nation that occasioned a formal discussion in the Department of State in relation to raw materials and the principles of the Atlantic Charter. It was also the first nation that concluded a treaty affecting postwar relations in which the basic principles of the Atlantic Charter were invoked, when it entered into the Anglo-Soviet-Iranian Treaty of Alliance in January 1942.[4] There were a number of factors that concerned American officials at the time the treaty was negotiated, ranging from such specific considerations as its implications for the postwar use of lend-lease-supplied facilities, to the more abstract but significant considerations of Iranian political and territorial integrity and the protection against exploitation of what was then still referred to as "backward" nations.

When in early 1943 Herbert Feis's Committee on Foreign Petroleum Policy began the deliberations that led to the recommendation that a petroleum reserves corporation be formed and that the United States pursue an international agreement on petroleum, there was no overt and specific conflict in Iran over petroleum concessions. Nonetheless, the basic framework for that conflict was clearly in place as long as the United States remained incapable of reconciling the equality-of-access principles of the Atlantic Charter with hostility to the granting of concessions to the Soviet Union. The United States had by 1943 clearly designated Iran an area in which it sought enhanced influence and had accordingly established American advisers across a broad spectrum of domestic Iranian economic activities, ranging from the opium trade to finance.[5]

Historians who have detected a contradiction in American–Iranian policy between the adherence to the internationalism embodied in the Atlantic Charter and the effort to obtain a petroleum concession for American companies in 1943–4[6] have failed to understand the nature of U.S. objectives in the Atlantic Charter, which was little more than an amalgam of traditional Open Door goals with the Wilsonian principles of self-determination embodied in the Fourteen Points. Indeed, the quest for an American concession in Iran grew out of a traditional and ongoing American effort in the Middle East and was fully consistent with the equality-of-access concept of the Open Door. If there was a contradiction, it was in the effort to prevent the Soviet Union from making similar gains in Iran and in the ill-disguised attempt to displace Britain from an area of traditional hegemony. In the case of Iran, private American companies served as a convenient instrument by which the United States might accomplish its objective of counterbalancing Soviet and British influence.

The anxiety of American officials that the United States needed to take concerted action to deflect Soviet and British influence was very much alive at the time articulation of a more general oil policy was under consideration. Paul Atkins, a member of the Millspaugh mission to Iran, observed in April 1943 that the British and Americans were being completely outmaneuvered by the Russians and expressed the view that Iran was "going to fall into their hands like a ripe apple one of these days."[7] Equally pessimistic was Wallace Murray, the State Department adviser on political relations, who informed Adolf Berle and Cordell Hull during the summer of 1943 that the Soviet Union appeared to be taking "aggressive steps" to annex Iran after the war. "Even in Teheran and the English-occupied area," he commented, "the Soviet expansionist aim is carried out with vigorous and subtle propaganda ... The Soviet armed forces in Teheran and the country have maintained wonderful discipline, and the contrast to the Americans and British is carefully pointed out ... In the South they are active in organizing the 'Party of the Masses' and through it fomenting strikes." The State Department was pleased, consequently, when Iranian officials approached Standard-Vacuum, the Jersey Standard and Socony-Vacuum subsidiary, in February of 1943, concerning a possible concession, but appear to have played no active part in the process until later in the year.[8]

If the Iranian situation was fraught with potential international strife, the one in Latin America provided an additional significant context within which the discussions leading to an international agreement on oil took place. Although the focus of excitement and indeed the main determinant of policy may have shifted to the more exotic Near Eastern fields, the western hemisphere was supplying the petroleum that enabled the Allied powers to maintain the war effort. In August 1943, for example, the PAW was importing into the United States for refining approximately 100,000 barrels a day of Venezuelan and Colombian crude oil alone. Although the Office of War Mobilization recommended that to relieve pressure on U.S. stocks of crude oil, production in the Middle East and the Caribbean should be increased to capacity and new refining facilities developed in the Middle East, Andrew Carter of the ANPB (Army-Navy Petroleum Board) informed James Byrnes that it was more practical to obtain the crude oil to bring British refining production up to full capacity from the Caribbean than from the Middle East.[9] Hence Latin America continued to hold a position of major significance in wartime petroleum policy, a fact that has been obscured by recent publications on Middle East oil.

Indeed, from the time of Max Thornburg's appointment as petroleum adviser in the Department of State, he had been insistent on the need for a carefully coordinated policy for the Americans and effective company cooperation in all fields of endeavor. At that time, he observed, no common pattern had emerged in the national oil policies of the American republics. Thornburg thought that war measures ought to be carefully adopted with a view to the postwar situation to ensure the continuation of cooperative efforts, such as that reflected in the development of the Latin American wartime petroleum supplies pool.[10]

He subsequently stressed the need for a common American viewpoint among American corporations operating abroad "instead of quarreling with each other or part of them combining with the British against the interest of the others." Thornburg also found himself entirely in sympathy with the principles of the Atlantic Charter, and advocated the scrapping of such restrictive agreements as the Red Line and "As Is" arrangements of 1928, and the breakdown of spheres of influence. To Thornburg, the Red Line was "an obsolete relic of a secret society which never had any purpose than to tie the hands of its minority members."[11] Efforts to implement such principles in the Latin American context were consistent with Thornburg's orientation. The Final Act of the Rio Conference in 1942, for example, included both a general provision expressing approval of the Atlantic Charter and a specific reference, Article XXV, which was a declaration of adherence to liberal economic principles in postwar planning. It also included a recommendation to the effect "that all nations of this continent have ... access to inter-American commerce and to the raw materials they require for the satisfactory and prosperous development of their respective economies." To Walter C. Ferris of the petroleum adviser's office, it was within the framework of the Atlantic Charter and the Final Act of the Rio Conference that a general petroleum policy for the United States would need to be developed. At the same time, Ferris recognized that the principles of the Atlantic Charter were too general in nature to be applied uniformly; the evolution of an effective policy would require consideration of special regional circumstances.[12]

Thornburg's ambition to institute a comprehensive Latin American petroleum policy was not to be realized during the last years of the Roosevelt administration. The one direct consequence for U.S. petroleum policy in the region was the decision to lend clear and definitive support to American corporations in seeking concessions and that such corporations, in adhering to Atlantic Charter / Open Door principles, should neither seek nor accept monopolistic or discriminatory concessions. On 17 February 1944, the State Department issued a policy statement to the heads of mission in all Latin American countries informing them that it was department policy for American companies to take their problems to local officials. The instructions indicated that the

United States, because of the wartime and long-range significance of petroleum, favored the development of foreign oil resources and welcomed the participation of American firms in their development. This policy statement might appear to have been little more than consistent with established practice, but the increased Latin American sensitivity to interference in local affairs had made American field officers reticent to appear unduly supportive of concession hunters. Moreover, dissatisfaction on the part of company officials with the State Department's performance in the Bolivian and Mexican nationalizations had inclined them toward less frequent dependence on American legations. Certainly in the specific case that triggered the department's policy statement, one corporation seeking a concession in Peru had opened contacts with the Peruvian government through the Lima office of National City Bank of New York rather than through diplomatic channels.[13] The Atlantic Charter was thus perceived by American officials not as an inflexible iron rule, but as a guideline, and officials identified no contradiction between the advocacy of host-country interests, attempts to assist American companies with their interests abroad, and protecting what were seen as U.S. strategic concerns against foreign encroachment.

Such considerations were reflected in the recommendations that came before the Feis committee. One of the most perceptive and influential of the background documents prepared for the committee was presented by James Wright of the Division of American Republics. Wright wrote essentially of Latin America, but it was apparent that he believed his analysis to have much broader applicability. "Any workable policy," he observed, "presupposes a vast amount of collaboration and understanding with other Governments, not only in respect of Governments whose citizens are active in petroleum exploitation both at home and abroad, but also in respect of countries which have developed or undeveloped petroleum resources, but which have not been active in the actual exploration and exploitation thereof." Thus the essential germ of an international petroleum agreement would be its intergovernmental rather than private nature. Wright also identified as a priority the improvement of the relationship between American companies and host governments. He detected improvement in this area, with a gradual abandonment of what he referred to as the "dogmatic position that they [the companies] can by power politics or by any other hook or crook run roughshod over everyone concerned." As a short-term problem Wright identified the war-induced "radical dislocation of markets." One of the objectives of U.S. policy, in his view, ought to be to ensure that inequities of supply be minimized in order to avoid political and economic repercussions that could spill over into the postwar period. In summarizing the Latin American situation, Wright suggested that the petroleum atmosphere in Colombia was now entirely satisfactory (in terms of both intercompany and government business relations), following the conflict of the Olaya and López presidencies. In Venezuela, it was anticipated that solutions to problems were well advanced and would likely be settled by pending legislation. Wright correctly identified as a major area for improvement the creation of a more balanced Venezuelan economy, which would relieve the petroleum industry from "constant future milkings to sustain the lopsided economy the country now has." Mexico, however, presented a different and more complex situation. Although the basis for a full understanding on the expropriation question existed in the November 1941 agreement, there remained the question of the status of two Standard Oil of New Jersey concessions, and until those issues were resolved it was unlikely Mexico would cooperate fully in petroleum talks or permit participation by foreign capital. There was also the question of the impact Mexican oil production would have on world markets. With current Mexican reserves estimated at 700 million barrels, the supply would be adequate for only eighteen years. One possible scenario that would affect world prices, however, was if Pemex were to dump cheap oil on the market in order to satisfy Mexican foreign-exchange requirements. Wright did not anticipate that this represented an insurmountable difficulty.[14]

Wright's support for a comprehensive policy on oil was echoed by R.L. Smyth of the Division of Far Eastern Affairs. Smyth urged the Feis committee to recommend positive policy initiatives. "Unless," he wrote, "effective measures are taken to establish a regional or a world oil policy, there will be revived problems arising out of the competition between British, Dutch and American oil interests in the Netherlands East Indies and in other areas of the Far East."[15] Smyth touched on one of the main dilemmas that confronted State Department and other officials, that is, whether to propose limited and regional agreements in an effort to achieve stability or to strive for a truly international agreement. When the Feis committee reported to the secretary of state at the end of March 1943, it recommended that negotiations begin with a more limited bilateral agreement, possibly as a preamble to a more comprehensive accord, with the first phase in the process to be an agreement with Britain on Middle Eastern oil. Feis subsequently explained the rationale of their approach in a statement remarkable for its faith in the oil companies: "There was a genuine risk in inviting undisciplined national governments to intervene in this vast international activity. If they were unscrupulous and at odds with one another, they might chain or smash it. They were, on the whole, more likely to quar-

rel than the oil companies and less likely to compromise. What was
wanted of national governments was a firm promise that they would
behave reasonably and decently if the oil companies did."[16] Feis knew
his history well, and it is likely he had a vivid recollection of the complex company and government maneuvers that had colored the 1920s.
Feis himself later reflected that it might have been a mistake to begin
with a bilateral agreement between the United States and Britain, but
the pressures within his committee and the administration more generally for the avoidance of conflict in the Middle East were very strong.

The negotiation of a bilateral and possibly multilateral petroleum
agreement was only one of the areas into which the Roosevelt administration ventured early in 1943, and even these negotiations were
delayed while the administration explored other avenues. The Feis
study group itself evolved into a special committee on postwar petroleum problems, which began its deliberations in June. That committee,
as we noted in an earlier chapter, was interdepartmental in nature. Its
key members were Feis, William Bullitt, special assistant to the
secretary of the navy, Brigadier General Boyken Wright, James Terry
Duce and Everett De Golyer of the PAW, Andrew Carter of the Army-
Navy Petroleum Board, and Paul Alling of the Near Eastern division of
the State Department, lending a distinctly Middle East orientation to
the considerations of the committee. The main function of the committee was to examine issues not directly related to the war, and at its first
meeting the committee gave special attention to identifying those areas
of the world that were oil bearing but not yet concessioned, such as
northern Iran, Afghanistan, Baluchistan, Ethiopia, and China. It was
also suggested that the committee undertake a broad factual survey of
the existing petroleum legislation throughout the world, and explore
the most effective means by which the United States might best protect
its interests in the Middle East to safeguard and develop the reserves on
a basis that would ensure their availability to all nations. The question
of an Anglo-American petroleum agreement, although raised at the
meeting, received less immediate endorsement than the urgency of dealing with Saudi Arabia, a perspective that Bullitt voiced most strongly.[17]
Frank Knox, with whom Bullitt was very influential, earlier expressed
to Cordell Hull the view that the negotiation of an international agreement did not obviate the necessity for the United States government to
seize the initiative from private enterprise in the interest of foreign oil
security. "Our government," he asserted, "must assume responsibility
for our foreign petroleum position."[18] An international agreement
among governments appeared to be one way of achieving that end. A
variation of that device was the possible creation of a joint Anglo-
American petroleum board for the Middle East, the objective of which

would be to minimize and possibly eliminate competition and ensure the development of the resources in a way that would benefit all parties, although the Soviet Union was not identified as a possible beneficiary. Such a board would have control over production, the development or acquisition of new properties, and the construction of additional plant facilities. The proposal provided only a modest role for the host nations, which would be invited to form advisory and consultative committees. The board would in turn report to an as yet unspecified United Nations body. In keeping with the generally international thrust of the concept, the principles of equality of treatment of foreign nationals and the protection of existing concessions were reaffirmed.[19] In essence, the plan embodied shared great-power predominance over natural-resource development in the third world, a substantially less enlightened approach than a broadly conceived international body in which major producing and consuming nations could function on a basis of greater equality.

The British were relatively slow to respond to American overtures to open discussions on a broad range of issues related to international petroleum policy. Although the United States did not extend a formal invitation to negotiate a petroleum agreement until December 1943, there had been informal approaches earlier in the year, and the tardiness of British action has led some to the conclusion that the British were opposed to negotiations.[20] It has also been argued that it was essentially the formation of the PRC and its threatened incursion into the Middle East that spurred the British to accept the American initiative, albeit belatedly. In these terms the PRC takes on the properties of little more than a blunt instrument designed to bring the British to the conference table. Such arguments are seriously flawed. Ickes and the PAW invested too much energy in the PRC in 1943 and 1944 in their efforts to bring Socal and the Texas Company and then Gulf Oil to terms of cooperation in the Middle East for Ickes to have viewed such efforts as mere grandstanding before the British lion. Indeed, the idea that the PRC had been influential in bringing a reluctant Britain to negotiations was in part an Ickes invention, designed to save face when the fate of the PRC was clearly in jeopardy.[21] There is also an implication in this interpretation that both the tactics and the objectives of the PRC were incompatible with a bilateral petroleum agreement with Britain. Rather, the PRC was little more than a mechanism by which the United States government might exercise some controls over the acquisition of foreign reserves within the framework of the equality-of-access principle of the Atlantic Charter. The PRC posed more of a long-range threat to host countries than it did to Great Britain.

The question of timing also raises doubts about the extent to which the formation of the PRC contributed to bringing about an Anglo-American accord. Had the British been concerned about the PRC in the summer of 1943, they would have had considerably less reason for alarm by the end of the year when the U.S. issued the invitation for talks, because by late 1943 it was clear to anyone close to the oil business that by that time Ickes's talks with the oil companies were in serious difficulty. Indeed, the evidence suggests that there was considerable support in British government and business circles for negotiations with the United States throughout 1943. What the British government opposed were the type of piecemeal discussions on such issues as the development of subsoil resources in enemy territory and the postwar use of lend-lease facilities that the Americans had suggested earlier in the year. There were British hesitations over timing and the specifics of American proposals. In the summer of 1943, the British Petroleum Department appeared to prefer to delay talks until the moment was more propitious, although that was not defined. In general, the department agreed with the suggestions advanced by American officials for the treatment of the development of enemy territory, but it did have some reservations. The British thought that further consideration ought to be given to the machinery whereby approved development work should be undertaken in liberated areas. The Americans had organized military oil units in association with the companies, and there was some British concern that since there were no corresponding units in the British forces, the latter's interests would be disadvantaged. Nevile M. Butler of the American department in the Foreign Office concurred with the Petroleum Department's assessment that the British government should allow the United States to take the initiative if it desired negotiations concerning the Middle East where, as Butler observed, Britain was "the beati possidentes."[22] Nonetheless, there was a general recognition of the imminent need for Anglo-American petroleum discussions to establish broad principles of international cooperation. The main dilemma was one of timing. Ministry of Fuel and Power officials believed, in concert with Britain's petroleum representative in Washington, Harold Wilkinson, that the United States was becoming anxious to strengthen its international position and that Britain should seize a "favourable opportunity" to open discussions. "The question of who should take the initiative," Sir William Brown commented, "is one on which we have not reached a conclusion. But we recognize that unless talks of a general character are opened, we may get a series of separate questions raised ... The question of who should take the initiative is an important one. Our experience in the past few years has indicated that if we open up the State Department may think that we are disturbed about our situation and are asking for favours. We are not inclined to think that the present instance is a suitable one on which to suggest wider discussions," but he anticipated that current negotiations between Gulf Oil and Anglo-Iranian over Kuwait or the issue of rehabilitation of Burma and the Netherlands East Indies might provide a mechanism for opening the way "to joint discussions on other oil policy questions."[23]

For the moment, then, more general issues were delayed, while the two governments attempted to establish policies for the rehabilitation of prewar concessions, consultation with governments possessing contingents of occupying forces, such as Canada, and oil-company versus military oil units as operating agencies in occupied areas. Both American and British officials agreed at this stage that no concession or right of development should be given during the period of military occupation, although they recognized that civilian or military needs might make necessary the temporary emergency development of such resources. The British also remained determined that rehabilitation and development work be undertaken by private oil companies acting as agents for the governments concerned, rather than by military units. In essence, Anglo-American agreement in these areas was a self-denying one for Britain and the United States and not binding on other members of the United Nations; it covered a broad range of territories, including enemy countries, former Italian territories in Africa and Ethiopia, as well as any enemy-occupied territories as of 1 September 1939.[24]

The British official who appeared most concerned with the PRC was Harold Wilkinson, but his views were more extreme than those of his superiors. Possibly Wilkinson consciously attempted to exaggerate the dangers of the PRC in order to stimulate Whitehall to action. Wilkinson's "Cassandra-like groanings," as he styled his lamentations, were nonetheless premised on the same views current in official London and Washington circles that the United States and Britain needed a joint petroleum policy. "If," he wrote, "we can get the United States Government to 'stop, look, and listen' at this stage and not to proceed on further ventures, then it might be possible for the ... adventure in Arabia to be nearly enough handled on the same basis as the Anglo-Iranian ... Matters are capable of developing at a much faster pace and on a much more diversified geographical scale which would spell disaster for the British Empire petroleum resources, not to mention the present oil interests of American nationals." One has little sense of such a mood of urgency prevailing in either the Foreign Office or the Ministry of Fuel and Power.

Wilkinson's assessment was nevertheless an important one, especially his identification of those American figures most prominent in moving U.S. petroleum policy along more aggressive lines. The main villain in the piece, in Wilkinson's opinion, was President Roosevelt. Ralph Davies he portrayed as a restraining force, and Ickes as strongly supportive of Anglo-American cooperation, once he could be disabused of the conviction that the British government determined the operating policies of the Anglo-Iranian Petroleum Company. Wilkinson assured Ickes that the British favored "leaving the seeking and exploitation of oil to legitimate and reputable private interests, with the Government confining itself to such encouragement and sponsorship as was necessary to assist its nationals in maintaining security of tenure of contracts." He contended that the PRC would seriously "rock the boat" of Anglo-American relations and "jeopardize, if not completely sabotage, the British oil position." There is little evidence it would have done so or that British officials shared Wilkinson's views. Indeed, Wilkinson hypothesized that producing countries, as they became more nationalistic, would provide the main obstacle to the PRC, which Wilkinson portrayed as "the rather alarming figure of Uncle Sam with the alleged taint of economic imperialism strong upon him." It appears that private producers were more anxious about the effects of U.S. government participation in the world oil market than was the British government. The point was that both sides desired negotiations and an accord but were jockeying for position as the moment for decision approached.

Wilkinson, like Ickes, was convinced that "sane cooperation between reputable oil interests of the United Nations in the foreign markets must provide the only solid basis to a real and lasting ... oil policy." Wilkinson, however, was viewed by important British officials as more an oil man than a government official, and caution is needed in identifying his reaction to the PRC with that of the British government.[26]

If there were doubts concerning Wilkinson's perspective, there was less uncertainty in identifying the interests for whom Basil R. Jackson spoke. As Anglo-Iranian representative in the United States, Jackson pressed vigorously during the summer and fall of 1943 for Anglo-American discussions on petroleum. Jackson advanced several arguments in support of his position. He contended that Anglo-Iranian would be unable to continue to occupy a relatively minor position in the international export market in the postwar period and that "some arrangements would have to be made between the U.S. government and the British government" with respect to production and distribution levels in the Middle East. Jackson also played on corporate and political anxiety over U.S. antitrust regulations to suggest that the old Red Line Agreement might be illegal under the Sherman Anti-Trust Act, a point that Gulf Oil had also offered in connection with discussions of its Kuwait arrangements with Anglo-Iranian.[27] Jackson vigorously advanced the thesis that government action had to precede corporate cooperation in the Middle East and elsewhere. Although there was a "widespread desire amongst businessmen generally to expedite discussions and settlement ... the initiated realize that until Washington has clarified its attitude on cartels and the interpretation of the Anti-Trust laws, as they affect the foreign field, it is difficult for industrial concerns ... to make cooperative plans." Jackson informed the chairman of Anglo-Iranian that such older commercial statesmen as Owen Young had "privately advised that ... there would be Congressional support for collaboration by the industries of both countries,"[28] although he failed to identify the sources of such congressional support.

In Jackson's opinion there were several factors influencing United States considerations and its support for an agreement with Britain. One was the belief that British oil interests had superior holdings to those of American nationals in key areas of the world; a second was the concern over the postwar disposition of lend-lease-financed petroleum facilities; a third was the U.S. government realization that American nationals needed to expand their social services to host countries in the Middle East; and fourth was that the U.S. wished to avoid the destructive features of unrestricted competition. Finally, Jackson identified American uncertainty over Soviet intentions, especially in Iran, as a force pushing the United States toward a cooperative posture with Britain.

To Jackson, intergovernmental cooperation was an essential prerequisite for private collaboration. Although some company officials, he argued, such as Collier of Socal, were prepared to cooperate, Jackson argued that such cooperation would need to be accomplished while men like Collier remained at the head of the firms and before control passed to what Jackson identified as "younger men untrained in what might be termed the cooperative school." An intergovernmental agreement would offset such trends by establishing "certain broad principles within which the commercial interests can get together and work out their own salvation." Jackson carefully identified the divisions within the industry. Three groups of interests, with differing backgrounds, had to be reconciled: "first, the old international cooperating companies; second, those who are partially in and partially out, such as Standard of California and the Texas Company; and finally, those who have never collaborated, such as Gulf and probably Sinclair," which had become an important factor in the Caribbean. The other issue that remained a potential obstacle for both countries and companies was what petroleum rights other countries could and should acquire given the stated equality-of-access aims of the Atlantic Charter.[29]

Jackson advanced his arguments persuasively enough to convince the British chargé in Washington, Sir R.I. Campbell, of the need for a government agreement as a precondition for corporate collaboration; but historians have tended to exaggerate the extent to which Jackson's views and Campbell's subsequent representations on his behalf pushed a reluctant British government toward negotiations. Nor, as Jackson appeared to want government officials to believe, were the companies unprepared to collaborate in the absence of a government accord, and they continued to do so in such projects as the Haifa refinery, which involved Anglo-Iranian, Shell, and Socony-Vacuum.[30] In any case, Jackson had identified a vital feature of a potentially divisive nature in postwar petroleum relations: how to reconcile the differing interests of various segments of the international petroleum community. Whether that objective could be accomplished through public or private means remained a crucial and undetermined issue during the transition from war to peace.

By mid-October 1943, some months before the United States issued a formal invitation to talks, the Foreign Office informed the British Embassy in Washington that the situation was under serious consideration at a high level, and the government desired no premature negotiations. Part of the reason for British caution stemmed from some feeling in the Foreign Office that private interests were attempting to overplay the American challenge. J. Foster, for example, observed that it was "not clear why Mr. Wilkinson assumes that the entry of the U.S. government into the oil business would be disastrous for British interests," although he interpreted the concern as deriving from the same arguments made by U.S. firms, that is, that unlimited government funds would result in wasted exploration, excessive local wages, and disruption in international markets. In other words, private concern was premised on opposition to a major entry into international oil operations that might place other priorities above that of profit.[31]

The Foreign Office was very positive about potential discussions with the United States in the late fall of 1943 and prepared a ministerial minute recommending that Churchill personally approach Roosevelt. If the response was positive, the departments concerned could then commence general deliberations. R. Law was of the opinion that unless the United States and Britain could reach some agreement on oil, "all other schemes for postwar Anglo-American economic collaboration would be doomed to failure."[32]

Although such Foreign Office officials as Nevile Butler, head of the American department and assistant undersecretary of state, remained unconvinced by Wilkinson's concern over the PRC and U.S. initiative, he was inclined to press the British position more quickly toward negotiations because of Royal Dutch Shell's desire to gain a new concession in

Persia to counteract American and Soviet activity. Butler contended that the British government was confronted with the choice of supporting Shell and risking conflict with the Americans or of moving swiftly to negotiations and constructing a standstill arrangement until talks were complete, unless a standstill arrangement would favor the American companies. Butler also sought to be cautious in dealing with American oil interests so as not to jeopardize the position of the Mexican Eagle Oil Co. (a Shell subsidiary) in its efforts to regain its concessions in the Poza Rica field in Mexico, and to provide no excuse for "the U.S. Navy or War Department or other interests a reason for bringing pressure on the State Department to play a dirty game in Mexico."[33] It was clear who Butler thought were Britain's friends in the United States.

In response to a direct query from the Foreign Office as to whether or not he recommended Anglo-American talks,[34] British Ambassador Lord Halifax responded in the affirmative, that talks should be held and that the prime minister should make a personal approach to the president. R.I. Campbell commented on the concern in the United States with the domestic reserve situation, the trend toward mixed enterprise, and the fact that elsewhere than in the Middle East the United States showed signs of favoring a general Open Door policy and had encouraged Shell developments in Colombia and Ecuador. Campbell did feel that U.S. officials had an inaccurate appreciation of their interests in the Middle East and recommended that Shell be permitted to proceed with an application to Persia for a concession, even though he anticipated there would be some public reaction in the United States. He also presumed that one of the objectives of agreement would be to promote continued cooperation among the companies, "bearing in mind the strong feeling in the United States against cartels."[35] Butler, on the whole, strongly agreed, observing, with respect to the Iranian situation, "if we decide that we do want Shell alone or in concert to go after this concession, would it not be well for them to do so at once? By the end of the war might there not be in Teheran a Persian Government under strong Russian influence which might be thrown against us?" It was agreed to let Shell proceed but to inform the Americans informally, through Wilkinson to Ickes. It was also agreed not to include in Churchill's proposed message to Roosevelt a reference to Middle East talks, "as it was felt that we should do nothing to encourage the Americans in their present tendency to regard the Middle East as the most important source of supply rather than South America or other parts of the world."[36]

Although Churchill did not take the advice of his ministers to approach Roosevelt informally, preferring to await an American initiative, it was clear by the end of 1943, when the State Department finally issued a formal invitation, that British officials were well advanced along these lines.[37] It was also evident that the PRC alone had not altered British thinking; rather, the desire for agreement arose from a complex combination of factors that ranged from the sensitivity of Shell interests in Mexico and the Shell desire to apply for a Persian concession, to obviously increasing American ambitions where Middle East resources were concerned. British delays in coming to terms with the issues, however, resulted in their failure to have the talks on a general basis rather than limited to the Middle East, as they had attempted in suggesting to Edward Stettinius that Britain was prepared to have "exploratory" talks on "general principles" concerning oil resources in all parts of the world.[38]

The end of 1943 had brought some small triumph for American policy. Although the PRC appeared to be faltering, the idea of Anglo-American cooperation advanced by both American and British officials, public and private, had reached fruition. Wilkinson was now convinced that the Americans were prepared to seek "joint salvation" rather than attempting to play a "lone hand."[39] What the British had not shaken was the American resolve to expand their holdings in the Middle East and to divert discussions from the domestic oil industry and the western hemisphere, a focus that was reconfirmed by the report of the State Department's postwar advisory committee that eastern-hemisphere sources should in future supply European, Asian, and African markets.[40]

BRITISH-AMERICAN ACCORD

An Anglo-American agreement on petroleum was both hampered and its urgency underlined by the Soviet-Anglo-American conflict in 1944 over Iranian oil concessions and the United States pipeline initiative in Saudi Arabia. Of the two, the Iranian situation was more volatile because it threatened the wartime alliance, heralded postwar rivalries in the Middle East, and threatened Iranian sovereignty. Perhaps wisely, Iranian authorities had by the fall of 1944, much to the chagrin of both Russians and Americans, cancelled any concession discussions until the close of the war.[41]

The Iranian conflict and the clear shift of U.S. attention to the Middle East provided the main context in which the first Anglo-American oil agreement was negotiated in the summer of 1944. The period in which the negotiations took place in 1944–5 also formed a significant transitional period in United States foreign petroleum policy, during which the De Golyer mission noted the future oil potential of the Middle East. These developments dramatically brought the Middle East to the forefront. The coordinating committee of the departments of state, war, and navy had by 1946 designated Iran as "an area of major strategic concern to the United States."[42]

It was in this context in April 1944 that technical, preliminary discussions with the British got under way, following several anxious months during which British political circles reacted nervously to new American initiatives in Saudi Arabia and Iran, compelling Churchill to request assurances of American fidelity.[43] The *Financial Times* portrayed the projected Arabian pipeline as a distinct addition to United States strength in the region, especially when coupled with the overwhelming superiority of U.S. domestic and American-controlled Latin American production. The *Manchester Guardian* warned that the construction of an American-owned pipeline in the Arabian peninsula would provide the United States with a "direct interest in the defense of the Mediterranean and in the Indian Ocean."[44] Indeed, contrary to what has been suggested by some authors, the PRC and the pipeline project not only did not bring Britain to the bargaining table, they almost contributed to the destruction of the mutual confidence that was a prerequisite for an effective bilateral accord.

The Americans entered the Washington technical discussions in April, and the Cabinet-level negotiations the following summer divided over methods as well as objectives. The rift between Cordell Hull and Harold Ickes had widened as Ickes's Saudi Arabian plans were delayed while the Anglo-American talks were given priority. For the moment at least, the leadership had returned to the State Department, with Charles Rayner leading the American negotiators in April.[45] But the uncertainties over policy were broader than the PAW–State Department split. Secretary of the Navy Frank Knox indicated to Hull that Andrew Carter was firmly convinced that the United States needed an "ace up our sleeves" in the form of American-owned concessions in the Middle East; otherwise the United States would be at a disadvantage in the negotiations. Ickes contended that the United States already had the British "over a barrel" because of the lend-lease debt and the projected Arabian pipeline.[46] John Loftus observed that the discussions required agreement on the application of Atlantic Charter principles. If the United States were not prepared to approve the preservation of privileged marketing arrangements in spheres of influence, it would need to insist on the cancellation of such arrangements as the Kuwait marketing clause, as well as suggest that Britain divest itself of its stock interest in Anglo-Iranian and Royal Dutch Shell. In return, the United States would pledge not to enter comparable arrangements. Loftus warned that if the opposite decision were reached, some form of private marketing cartel appeared inevitable.[47]

The petroleum industry, although by no means united, tended to be supportive in principle of the negotiations with Britain, in part because of industry desire to find ways to defeat the PRC. The State Department appointed a pre-conference panel of industry advisers, broadly representative of major and independent companies. The advisory panel was selected directly by the department because of concern that industry initiative would violate antitrust laws. Dean Acheson accordingly advised Rayner not to give responsibility for establishing the panel to William Boyd, Jr, of the API, as he had originally intended,[48] although the panel would have differed little in composition or intent had the original approach been utilized. In addition to the advisory panel, oil men then in government service, such as George Walden and Ralph Davies, were important contributors to the draft agreement and the negotiations at various stages. Such participation did not, however, create a supportive consensus within the industry once the agreement became public.

American officials were not only divided among themselves but found major impediments to smooth negotiations with the British. British negotiators insisted on recognition of Britain as an importer rather than a major producer of petroleum products, since its main supplies were drawn from outside British territory. This was a seemingly reasonable position, and the American refusal to recognize its validity lends support to the contention that American officials were determined to undermine British spheres of influence in the postwar era. A second area of disagreement was the relative influence that would be accorded to the private sector in the operation of the agreement. These issues were temporarily smoothed over in the April technical discussions but returned to plague the negotiators during the formal talks that summer.

The principal subject that absorbed the attention of the joint subcommittee at its Washington meetings in July and August 1944 was the British proposal that each country reserve the right to draw its consumption requirements from its own territories or from those in which its nationals held rights. The British perception was that after the war they would be faced with a serious foreign-exchange difficulty. The war had undermined Britain's export trade, and import needs had been met through lend-lease and increased indebtedness, resulting in overseas liabilities of some $12 billion. Were Britain not to exercise controls over oil imports, it would have to find approximately $100 million a year in foreign exchange. One alternative was to increase production of petroleum in sterling areas, and an international petroleum agreement that precluded this possibility would have seriously damaged the British position. Closely tied to the issue of sterling-area petroleum production was that of oil company autonomy under the agreement. In order to ensure oil company support, the American delegation had insisted that any international petroleum commission established under the agreement would provide a consultative and advisory mechanism entirely on a voluntary basis insofar as the oil companies were concerned. It was unlikely that the British import objectives would be attained by voluntary means, when their import controls would have virtually excluded American companies from participation in British markets. It was clear that the British were not prepared to delegate to a petroleum commission authority over one of their major strategic imports.

The American delegation thought the agreement was sufficiently flexible to accommodate the British position. Recommendations of the proposed commission were not binding on participating nations, and second, it was anticipated that the commission would give full consideration to Britain's exchange difficulties. What the Americans explicitly approved was an official U.S. endorsement of the UK right to exclude United States oil from the British market. To do so would be contrary to the Atlantic Charter principles that were embodied in the agreement and would adversely affect relations with such major Latin American producers as Venezuela, which provided the bulk of American-produced oil imported into the United Kingdom. American experts calculated that if dollar oil were excluded from the British market, approximately 35 million barrels of dollar oil annually would be seeking a market elsewhere. Such a situation would not only create a "disorderly and perhaps chaotic market" for international petroleum, but would also serve to further weaken the British foreign-exchange situation. So strongly did the American delegates feel about their position that it was asserted in the final stages of deliberation that if the British insisted on a market-restricting reservation in the petroleum agreement, any adoption of that reservation would lead the United States to drop the entire agreement.[49] The consequence was that no provision of the 1944 agreement reflected this dimension of British concerns.

The 1944 agreement reflected the basic application of the Open Door and Atlantic Charter principles to international petroleum relations. It was premised on several assumptions concerning the nature of the international petroleum situation and United States requirements, assumptions that had formed a less formalized dimension of United States foreign oil policy since World War I. They were as follows: 1) that ample supplies of petroleum were essential for the security and economic well-being of nations; 2) that world petroleum resources were for the "foreseeable future" adequate to meet current demands; 3) that the prosperity and security of all nations required the efficient and orderly development of the international petroleum trade; 4) that such orderly and efficient development could best be promoted by an international agreement among producers and consumers.

These premises were applied in eight specific articles, all of which appeared consistent with the theory and practice of previous United States foreign oil policy. Article I provided that the agreement would give due regard to consideration of military security and affirmed two general principles: first, that all countries should have nondiscriminatory but competitive access to the world's petroleum resources, and second, that the interests of producing countries should be safeguarded. Article II assured the protection of existing valid contracts and lawfully acquired rights and reiterated the principle of equality of opportunity for exploration and development. Article III provided for an international conference for the purpose of negotiating a more general agreement. Article IV required the signatories to establish an international petroleum commission. These were the main articles. Others clarified that the commission's function was advisory alone, that the agreement did not apply to the domestic petroleum industry or the importation of petroleum products in either country.[50]

The agreement fell short of the more specific goals Charles Rayner had earlier outlined to Cordell Hull as those which should be incorporated in a successful agreement. "The objectives," he suggested in March, "are to arrive at agreement on broad principles which will govern the operation of the nationals of both countries in the conduct of petroleum activities in the Middle East and elsewhere. It is hoped that the agreement will include for both peacetime and security purposes such principles as conservation of resources, orderly development, adequate participation by the producing countries, an orderly and adequate flow of petroleum products into consuming markets at fair prices, and equality of opportunity for petroleum development."[51] Nothing in the 1944 agreement would have "governed the operations" of American or British nationals. Rather it provided voluntary guidelines, with the result that there were no guarantees that any of the general principles of conservation, orderly development, and participation by producing countries would be implemented. Even the equality-of-access principle could be applied only to the United Kingdom, the United States, and their respective territorial possessions. Although the proposed international commission might have provided a satisfactory forum for an airing and resolution of corporate and government views, there was nothing save self-interest that would bind the parties either to the agreement itself or to the recommendations of the proposed commission. John Loftus echoed Charles Rayner's earlier pessimism in suggesting that the agreement was an "unsatisfactory compromise." He added: "In view of our own domestic history of unscientific and wasteful exploitation of petroleum pools, it would be a gratuitous insult for this country to propose to the rest of the world the adoption of the criterion of 'sound engineering practices' which is ... a governing principle for petroleum operations everywhere except in the continental United States."[52]

The 1944 agreement and its negotiation manifest some differences of approach between the British and the Americans over the role to be played by the private sector, although there were inconsistencies by both parties. Oil company officials formed an official component of the British negotiating team in April, including the two major figures of the Anglo-Dutch petroleum industry, Sir Frederick Godber of Shell and Sir William Fraser of Anglo-Iranian. Indeed, Fraser was also a War Cabinet invitee to serve on the official July delegation, but declined.[53] On the American side, as noted earlier, oil company officials served in a consultative capacity only, although government officials were highly sensitive to company opinion. A similar situation prevailed in defining the composition of the proposed commission. In the initial round of discussions, the British suggested a three-to-one predominance of oil company personnel over government representatives in order to emphasize the private nature of the commission. There was little unanimity on this dimension in the Department of State, with Rayner suggesting that two of five U.S. representatives should be from the industry, one of which would represent the majors. B.F. Haley, of the commodities division, however, argued that government policy to be effectively implemented by the commission would require a majority of government officials. Haley warned that an industry-dominated committee, or even one on which the industry was well represented, would "fail to be guided by the principles of a wise national policy, but may instead become, in effect, an international cartel." Rayner raised equally serious reservations concerning company representation if the agreement became a multilateral one, noting that countries such as Iraq, Venezuela, and Colombia, where the industry was entirely foreign dominated, would have to appoint foreign nationals if the principle of a mixed industry-government commission was to be maintained.[54]

The issue of the relative degree of government involvement in international petroleum operations remained unresolved during the 1944 discussions, and ambiguity in that area contributed in large part to the failure to implement the agreement that year. The publication of Herbert Feis's small volume *Petroleum and American Foreign Policy* in the midst of the negotiations elicited administration comments that even in military circles, where support for an agreement and for a strong and concerted oil policy was vigorous, there was reluctance to see a major injection of government into the private sector. Brigadier General H.L. Peckham, for example, director of the fuels and lubricants division of the Quartermaster Corps, commented to the secretary of war that the department's view had supported a "frank discussion" on areas of potential Anglo-American friction and the conclusion of a bilateral agreement as a necessary prerequisite to a broader one as well as "the establishment of a long range foreign oil policy for the United States." General Walter Pyron concurred with Peckham and with Feis's general conclusions, specifically, that the welfare and security of the United States depended on adequate control of foreign petroleum resources, that the government should lend full support to legitimate ventures abroad by American nationals, but that the petroleum industry was one where commercial decisions needed to be made quickly, and hence government should restrict its involvement to matters of general policy, such as conservation and other regulations designed to protect the public.[55]

Segments of the petroleum industry clearly believed the Anglo-American agreement and other wartime policies were invasions of the private sector. The line of division within the industry was essentially one between the majors and independents, although the majors were also more sensitive to the 1944 agreement than they were a year later. The basic independents-majors distinction was reflected at the stage of the technical discussions in April in the contrast between a Jersey Standard pamphlet entitled "Oil for the World" and statements by the president of Hogan Petroleum Company of California to the secretary of the interior and the Department of State. The authors of "Oil for the World" articulated the views ultimately contained in the Anglo-American agreement: that it was essential to find more oil and permit no waste, and that a "comprehensive and enlightened world oil policy," which stimulated exploration and provided for equal access to and a fair distribution of world petroleum products, was necessary to accomplish those ends. To Dana Hogan, in contrast, the primary objective of the majors was "to hold back the development of any reserves after they suspect the existence of such reserve"[56] in order to control supply, markets, and prices. Hogan's interpretation was a variation on the view advanced by other independents. The majors were depicted as either planning to flood the domestic market with imported oil to lower prices and drive the independents out of business, or else plotting to restrict international supply to maintain scarcity and high prices. This view was not unlike that of Abe Fortas, who in April resigned as secretary of the PRC, in part because he objected to the role Ickes had permitted Walden and Davies to play in the Saudi and British discussions. Fortas suggested to Ickes that "the interest of the oil companies with which your representatives are now or have been affiliated is not the same as the interest of the people of the United States." The draft Anglo-American agreement, which had been prepared by Davies, in Fortas's opinion provided for worldwide allocations of oil production that would have the effect of restricting production and maintaining high prices.[57]

The major companies were more concerned, both during and after the initial discussions, with both defending their positions abroad and ensuring protection against antitrust action on cooperative endeavors. J.A. Brown, for example, of Socony-Vacuum, suggested that the memorandum of understanding agreed to at the technical level should be revised to make the term "equal opportunity" more explicitly "open door," fearing that ambiguity might lead other nations, such as Mexico, to conclude that the policy had been abandoned. That conclusion could contribute to further restrictions on the foreign operations of American nationals, a concern that was echoed by George Hill, Jr, president of the Houston Oil Company. Brown also urged that the agreement should contain a clause exempting the companies from antitrust action "whenever the Government ... approves any recommendation or suggestion by the commission."[58]

Company officials clearly sensed the ambiguity and contradictions in government antitrust policies and their implications for international petroleum operations. In the case of the 1944 agreement, antitrust issues spilled over from the Stettinius mission to London that spring, when Stettinius reported that British thinking was "still far behind ours on the subject," with few British officials willing to recognize the "evils" of cartelization, and with some believing that cartels were necessary to protect investment as well as such commitments to labor as stabilized wages and pensions. The British, Stettinius noted to Hull, feel "that we in the United States will have to accept cartels after our economy ceases to expand at such a swift rate."[59] Given Stettinius's views and stature, it was hardly surprising that the companies should have sought further guarantees against antitrust action. Concern with the antitrust implications of the agreement proved an impediment to corporate and congressional acceptance of the 1944 and 1945 versions of the agreement.

The State Department rejected industry criticism of the Open Door aspects of the agreement, portraying the Open Door and equality of access as identical concepts insofar as a raw material such as petroleum was concerned. To Charles Rayner, the United States had "never taken and does not now take the position that an independent foreign country is under any obligation to open its minerals or other subsoil resources for exploitation by nationals of another country, or for that matter even by nationals of the country itself."[60] Rayner might have added, however, that the United States had traditionally sought to encourage such an orientation.

Although not unanimous, the domestic oil industry provided the most sustained opposition, and J. Howard Pew, president of Sun Oil, and George Hill, a prominent Texas producer, were among the more insistent of the domestic critics. The nature of Pew's opposition to the agreement is important because it reflected many of the considerations already expressed within government and business circles during the negotiations and in the context of the Stettinius mission to London. Pew focused on what he identified as the cartel features of the agreement and especially of the proposed international commission. Pew appealed to Hull as a long-time "ardent opponent of cartels, monopolies and all other devices for freezing the initiative and opportunities of men" and contended to the chairman of the Senate Foreign Relations Committee, Tom Connally, that the agreement embodied the "possibility of a first step in what might be a carefully laid plan for a super-state control covering the petroleum industry in all parts of the world." Pew thought analogies between the interstate oil compact and the Anglo-American agreement were spurious, since the former explicitly prohibited price fixing and had as its declared objective the conservation of oil and gas by the prevention of physical waste. Pew was pleased that the Roosevelt administration had decided to submit the agreement to the Senate for ratification, anticipating, as it turned out correctly, that its chances of acceptance were marginal.[61] Rayner accurately calculated that what was most to be feared from the active and continuous participation of private industry in policy formulation was that the private sector would exert pressures on Congress to oppose disadvantageous administrative initiatives.[62]

There was also in the fall of 1944 a cooling of previously supportive industry sources. Max Thornburg and the Cal-Tex group, for which he worked after leaving the State Department's petroleum office, was a case in point. In September, Thornburg expressed reservations concerning the commission, opposition that John Loftus interpreted as deriving from anxiety about "the possibilities implicit in a planned allocation of production quotas." In Loftus's view, the industry was inclined to rely "much more heavily upon the competitive cost advantages which they believe themselves to possess." Thornburg was also concerned that the agreement would have the effect of determining not only levels, but also the destination of production. The latter was an aspect equally troubling to Jersey Standard. Jersey vice-president Orville Harden suggested that the agreement was too vague concerning the distinction between reserves and marketing, which was Jersey's main concern abroad. Harden observed that Jersey's main profits were derived from marketing foreign-produced oil and oil products.[63] Jersey also supported the efforts to undermine antitrust restrictions and to exclude them from the operation of an international agreement. Milo Perkins, for instance, formerly executive director of the Board of Economic Warfare and in the fall of 1944 a consultant to Jersey, argued in *Harper's Magazine* in November that completely open competition in international trade was dead. Perkins supported the Anglo-American agreement as a recognition of that fact. "American business," he suggested, in a direct refutation of Stettinius's position, "even at its strongest is relatively helpless against the competition of well-organized foreign businesses *supported by the power of their governments. It's the entry of foreign governments into the picture that makes the difference.*"[64]

More general industry opinion, as reflected in such administrative bodies as the National Oil Policy Committee of PAW, was that the agreement was beyond the constitutional capability of the federal government, and that it extended federal regulatory powers over the domestic industry. John Loftus accurately summarized industry opposition in late October when he observed that what the large companies had intended as a national foreign oil policy was one of "indiscriminate commercial imperialism." In his view, the majors did not think the financial advantages of the agreement were sufficient to justify a confict with the independents, or that the proposed commission would be useful unless it was industry dominated; that the failure to modify antitrust laws made the agreement of limited use; and that the companies did not evaluate the situation as so urgent as it was a year earlier.[65]

Although Rayner tended to minimize industry opposition, James Sappington more accurately recognized the strength of the industry's position, reflected in the effort of Ralph Zook, president of the Independent Petroleum Association of America, to have the PIWC openly oppose the agreement, and in the indictment of the agreement by Glenn McCarthy, the head of an ad hoc association of independent Texas operators formed with the express purpose of defeating the agreement. McCarthy told an East Texas chapter of the API that the agreement pledged the United States industry to "the principles of international control," which would "drive independent oil operators from the industry." McCarthy contended that the agreement was unduly favorable to Britain, "giving the nation producing one percent of the oil an equal say with one producing sixty-seven percent, in determining production, marketing, distribution and price." Late in 1944 the Oil Conservation Board of Montana passed a resolution that echoed most of the industry's reservations, and added an expression of concern that the agreement would be resented abroad and its enf cement would require a major military commitment.[66]

Under pressure from Ickes, the PIWC prepared specific recommendations for revision of the agreement along lines satisfactory to the industry, the basic trust of which were to exclude U.S. import policy from the agreement, to safeguard domestic oil operations against federal controls, and to reserve the right of a signatory not to act on any recommendation of the international commission.[67]

John Frey and Chandler Ide suggested in their history of PAW that the "controversy over the first Agreement ... provided the occasion for a thorough airing of views by both industry and Government spokesmen" that led to the withdrawal of the agreement from the Senate and its renegotiation.[68] The agreement did much more than that; it provided a graphic illustration of the political capacity of the domestic petroleum industry to paralyze a government initiative that had broad support in administrative circles and among the major companies. What was decisive, however, was the failure or refusal of the major companies to provide the sustained support in the fall of 1944 when confronted with opposition that they had provided in initiating international discussions in oil. It might be argued that had the majors provided consistent support and had Roosevelt been prepared to take political risks in an election year by implementing the agreement as an executive agreement rather than a treaty, a first and important step toward more effective government / business and Anglo-American cooperation might have been implemented for postwar petroleum relations. The fact was, however, that the majors appeared willing to use the opposition of domestic oil producers to attempt to make additional gains in a new agreement. The irony of the outcome was that in making a substantial contribution to the defeat of what they perceived as an effort at government intervention and an alliance between the state and major companies, domestic producers and their political allies in fact enhanced the autonomy of the majors. The defeat of the agreement increased the likelihood that the majors would seek cartelization as the means to achieve the international coordination they had anticipated as the primary benefit of a multinational accord.

Ickes's success in having the PIWC revise the agreement rather than scuttle it was a hard-gained victory. Both he and Ralph Davies faced vigorous opposition by the foreign policy committee of the council, which was chaired by Albert Mattei, a California petroleum geologist and official of the Honolulu Oil Corporation. Mattei forcefully articulated his position when he warned Davies at a meeting of 25 November: "We are going to come in with constructive suggestions, and if you [Davies] don't accept our suggestions, we are going to tear your playhouse down." Mattei was prepared to consider revisions. So was A. Jacobsen of Amerada who urged support for a satisfactory agreement. J. Edgar Pew, in contrast, depicted the possible acceptance of the treaty as "the beginning of the end of everything in America that we hold dear. Certainly, under a system of national socialization, which this presupposes, life to me in America simply would not be worth living." Pew also preferred to draft suggested revisions of the agreement for the direct consideration of the Senate Foreign Relations Committee. Others were hesitant that a revision of the agreement by the council would constitute a violation of the antitrust laws, but such concerns were allayed by the justice department.[69]

Davies worked patiently but persistently to win industry cooperation and to refute allegations that the agreement embodied federal control of the oil industry and extended excessive powers to the international commission. Such contentions, Davies informed the PIWC, were no more than individual opinions that had no factual basis. At his request, Houston lawyer and PAW chief counsel Robert Hardwicke prepared a detailed response to such charges. Hardwicke concluded that there was no basis for the charge that the international commission was empowered to or intended to involve itself in domestic petroleum operations. If it did so attempt, the agreement provided no obligation by the United States to accept the commission's recommendations. Hardwicke concluded that the evidence was unambiguous that the two governments entered into the agreement to solve problems relating to international trade in petroleum, not domestic issues, even though Hardwicke and others would have been hard pressed to explain how control of international markets could be effective without some direction over the world's major producers. Hardwicke further emphasized that the commission itself was of a fact-finding and recommendatory nature, possessing no enforcement powers. The agreement stated simply that the two governments would "endeavor, in accordance with their respective constitutional procedures, to give effect to such approved recommendations."[70]

Davies's persistence gradually won the PIWC to a partial acceptance of his position. At the recommendation of George Hill, Jr, a member of the National Oil Policy Committee and of the technical advisory panel in the spring of 1944, the council approved a Hill motion early in December that the suggested revision of the oil agreement prepared by the committee be substituted for the original agreement then pending before the Senate Foreign Relations Committee. Such a course of action held some disadvantages. It made likely the withdrawal of the pending agreement from an already cool reception in the Foreign Relations

Committee and its renegotiation with Great Britain. Howard Pew contended that a more serious reservations was that the treaty would then become one "conceived by the oil interests and might as well have been proposed and negotiated by those interests in the first instance. It does not necessarily follow that such treaty would not be for the public welfare," he warned the council, "but it would be subject of severe criticism and attack as an instrument designed for such interests."[71]

STALEMATE IN WASHINGTON

In January 1945, following discussions between Dean Acheson, Charles Rayner, and Tom Connally, it was agreed to withdraw the treaty from the Senate, and President Roosevelt formally did so on 10 January. It was evident from Connally's view at that time that he believed no treaty of that nature was necessary and that even a renegotiated agreement that had the strong support of the major companies would be unlikely to gain his approval.[72] When Rayner and Breckinridge Long had appeared on behalf of the State Department before the committee the previous August, Connally was only one of several members to raise serious doubts about the treaty. Senator E.H. Moore of Oklahoma contended that the United States was already dominant in foreign petroleum operations, and Britain would be the main beneficiary. Senator Theodore Green of Rhode Island expressed reservations over who would determine what were valid concession rights, which were protected by the agreement. Arthur Vandenberg of Michigan was of the opinion that the British were undermining American interests in the Middle East and questioned whether it was not possible that the agreement would provide a means by which Britain was seeking American assistance against the Soviet Union in Iran. Senator Elbert Thomas of Utah, although he was pro-British and had been a firm New Deal supporter, expressed the oft-heard reservation that the agreement might serve to regulate domestic American production.[73] Under the circumstances it was unlikely the unrevised agreement would have gained a favorable committee report, and its withdrawal by the administration appeared the only mechanism by which the project could be salvaged. It would be a year before President Truman submitted a revised version.

After January 1945, Harold Ickes and the PAW became the main advocates of the agreement within the administration. As Ralph Davies informed a meeting of the National Oil Policy Committee in April, "the treaty is not being sponsored by the State Department. Sponsorship is elsewhere. If you do nothing about it – if you don't want it just relax, and you will hear nothing further about it. It is very dear to the heart of

Secretary Ickes ... and I would think would be pretty highly valued by the oil industry."[74]

Davies's contention that there was little administration support for the agreement outside the PAW was not entirely accurate. Some of the friction resulted from a desire to remove Ickes as the main motivating force. C.F. Darlington of the State Department, for example, urged that the responsibility for revisions be taken out of Ickes's and Davies's control and brought into the State Department where, he believed, the agreement could be considered in a broader political and economic context. In his view, Rayner was "subordinating himself entirely to the views of Ickes and Davies and was prepared to accept the proposal of the companies" to gain antitrust exemption.[75] Strong support for the agreement also came from Undersecretary of the Navy Ralph Bard in a statement before the Senate Foreign Relations Committee early in 1945. Reiterating many of the arguments advanced during the war in relation to oil policy, Bard contended that "without oil ... the role and the abiding purpose of our Naval establishment are brought to nothing." He observed that the navy had a major role to play in planning for future supplies by cooperating in research on synthetic fuels, exploring the Alaskan naval reserve, and assisting in the development of foreign sources outside the western hemisphere. To accomplish such developments in the foreign area, it was necessary to have "an atmosphere free from international friction and misunderstanding," to which he believed the Anglo-American agreement would be a major contribution, "an essential first step toward the larger understanding with other nations." Bard contended that international conflict could be avoided by "broad agreement in advance upon general principles" and by providing a forum for the resolution of routine problems. The navy, he concluded, "would like nothing better" than to have as many nations as possible bound by pledges of equality of access and the security of concessions.[76]

During the process of revision, in 1945, the oil industry sought several modifications in the agreement, including a clarification of the relationship of the agreement and proposed commission to the domestic oil industry. But the most important feature sought by the industry, especially the majors, was an immunity from antitrust prosecution for actions conducted with the approval of the commission. This objective provided a considerable obstacle to a consensus, with the State Department especially insistent that there be no explicit protection of the industry.[77] Even in the State Department, however, it was difficult to achieve a consensus on the issue. Charles Rayner, for example, thought the antitrust provision on which the industry had been insisting was relatively innocuous. "The point raised by industry," Rayner observed, "in connection with our anti-trust laws as they will affect industry-government collaboration in building up our foreign trade post-war is an important one and will require clarification if the desired results are to be secured. It goes beyond the field of action and applies equally to all our foreign trade activities in which such collaboration is sought." Even so, the department as a whole continued to oppose the inclusion of an antitrust exclusion provision, even when confronted by a united front in such government-industry bodies as the PIWC in January and February 1945. Although Ickes himself expressed reservations to Acheson, on the whole he thought some action essential to set at rest the fears of the business section. He argued to President Roosevelt shortly before the president's death that the proposed antitrust immunity clause was not self-executing; rather, it required legislation by Congress that would designate the government official or agency that would be authorized to approve recommendations of the international commission and to establish the standards under which immunity might be given. Ickes reminded Roosevelt that such immunity was not unusual and had been provided for under such legislation as the 1916 Shipping Act, the 1938 Aeronautics Act, and the Small Business Mobilization Act.[78]

Roosevelt was concurrently receiving conflicting views from the State Department. Undersecretary Joseph Grew informed him that Stettinius was especially concerned that the antitrust exemption would have a far-reaching effect on the entire antitrust and anticartel policy of the United States. "Despite," Grew wrote, "Mr. Ickes ... opinion ..., the clause will be regarded as an attempt to amend the Sherman Act by treaty." Grew rejected Ickes's contention that such an exemption was not an unusual procedure. Those that had been granted, such as under NRA, had been part of legislation under which the government exercised some ongoing control over the industry, a situation that would not apply under the proposed treaty. Roosevelt, as was his custom, urged consultation among the departments concerned and requested that he be kept informed.[79]

The antitrust exemption clause in the Anglo-American treaty was part of a larger industry campaign, associated especially with Jersey Standard, to simplify the legal context within which it operated, especially in the aftermath of the embarrassing I.G. Farben case of 1943, which implicated Jersey Standard in controlling international patents to the detriment of national security. R.W. Gallagher, Jersey's chairman, had written the president on the subject of international cartels in the fall of 1944 and had given a statement before the O'Mahony subcommittee of the Senate Judiciary Committee on 23 May 1944. Gallagher stressed that most of Jersey's foreign business involved

oil that was produced and sold outside the U.S. and that the often conflicting laws under which the company operated created substantial
confusion. "We do not," Gallagher testified, "believe in agreements
which fix prices, allocate resources, or restrict production – except
where production is controlled to conserve natural resources." Gallagher suggested that one means by which possible disparities between
United States and foreign laws could be resolved was through a provision that no criminal action, based on foreign activities, could be taken
under the antitrust acts except "a) in respect of foreign agreements
which should have been but were not filed with the department of commerce, or in respect of acts done in furtherance of a foreign agreement
which had been disapproved by the department of commerce."[80]
Eugene Holman, Jersey vice-president, expressed his company's perspective as well as industry sentiment when he observed at a meeting of
the National Oil Policy Committee that the "anti-trust law is as fickle as
public opinion. Some of these things you are talking about today can be
stretched to where some wild-eyed person can claim any form of cooperation – and most of these things require cooperation on the part of
the industry – is in violation of the anti-trust law."

There was considerable uncertainty, however, whether it would be
preferable for Congress to write a new antitrust law at that juncture or
to gain actual experience under the international commission, a course
that William Boyd preferred. Boyd clearly believed that Congress
would be unlikely to accept any treaty that granted antitrust immunity
to the industry. J.F. Drake of Gulf Oil thought that the industry would
be "far better off" with the treaty than without it, regardless of the antitrust clause. Holman's view was striking in that he clearly believed that
the government had a long-standing commitment to perform many of
the protective functions contained in the treaty but had failed to do so,
an obvious reference to the Bolivian and Mexican expropriations.[81] The
State Department continued without success in late 1944 and early 1945
to reach a general agreement on antitrust policy, and an interdepartmental cartel committee prepared that fall a tenative program for dealing with international cartels.[82] Its actions paralleled efforts in the
private sector. In early 1945, for example, the National Foreign Trade
Council endorsed a resolution requesting Congress to permit American
citizens to enter into agreements valid under foreign laws if such
agreements did not represent an unreasonable restraint of trade in the
United States. The *Wall Street Journal* was skeptical of the appro-
priateness of such a recommendation. It doubted that it was possible
for an international cartel not to affect domestic commerce; it also objected to the council's proposal that the Department of State supervise
the process, on grounds that it would involve a "high degree of govern-

ment supervision." Most telling was the observation that "production for home and for foreign markets cannot be segregated in watertight compartments, with free competition in one and cartelized monopoly in the other."[83] Although petroleum was unlike many of the strategic raw materials that were produced abroad only, the fact that much of the production and marketing of petroleum by American companies took place entirely outside the United States meant that with petroleum as well, the operations were often beyond the reach of the antitrust laws. As Walter Hamilton of the justice department's antitrust division emphasized, the "great task is to discover ... effective techniques of control." This was especially important in the context of the approaching end to the formalized wartime government / industry cooperation. Unless answers could be found to the dilemma, Hamilton predicted that the political state was "likely to become vassal to a feudal international economy."[84]

Standard Oil officials rather successfully created the impression that they were driven into cooperative arrangements by the behavior of the British companies. Ralph Gallagher and Orville Harden had informed Henry Wallace in the fall of 1943, following Wallace's cartel speech in Chicago, that Standard Oil had suffered more than it had gained from cartels in the foreign field, and that they were reluctant to expend the estimated $750 million to one billion dollars that would be required to rehabilitate the company's foreign operations if they were going to face similar behavior from British oil cartels.[85] The American petroleum attaché in Cairo, Colonel John Leavell, expressed a similar interpretation of the position in which the companies found themselves in 1945 in the Near East, unless the government enabled them to operate under a cartel system or made it practical for them to work within the sterling-block areas without discrimination. "From the oil companies' standpoint," Leavell observed, "in the Near and Far East, it is much simpler, easier and more profitable per dollar invested for the next decade for the oil companies to operate under a cartel system as junior partners with the British. They will be assured of some share of the market ... at prices sufficiently high to be profitable." In the long term, however, Leavell anticipated that it would be more satisfactory for the American companies to operate on a competitive basis, since they were more efficient operators and distributors. A more competitive system would also be more likely to result in higher production levels. To Leavell, "the question of whether cartels are ethical or not ... is a matter of relatively small importance to the United States." Roosevelt as well appears to have thought the dangers of cartels had been exaggerated and wished another, less pejorative, term could be found. President Truman was to carry further this low-key approach to the cartel question with his appointment of Thomas C. Clark, a Texas Democrat, as Biddle's replacement as attorney general. Clark openly preferred a mild antitrust policy, and Biddle opposed the appointment.[86]

The transition to Truman's presidency, preparations for the Potsdam meeting in the summer of 1945, and a British general election in July that turned out Winston Churchill and the Conservatives and brought a Labour government to power under Clement Atlee served to delay a formal renegotiation of the agreement in London until that September. In the interim, however, a recognition in the petroleum industry that some treaty was preferable to none had brought at least temporary support for the agreement from the industry. As A. Jacobsen, president of Shell subsidiary Amerada Petroleum Corporation, noted at a PIWC meeting of 19 April: "If we didn't get this thing followed up now, there would be a distinct possibility that after San Francisco would come a hodge-podge we wouldn't like at all. Instead of having a special oil agreement ... we will find ourselves faced with a ... master agreement made in San Francisco that proposes to cover all sorts of commodities with all sorts of countries. Here ... we have something we have had a hand in making."[87]

Stettinius, on returning from the founding meeting of the United Nations, identified the treaty as one of his priorities.[88] Simultaneously, the department continued to advance American interests in the Middle East. In the late spring, James Sappington of the Office of Economic Affairs was appointed second secretary of the American Embassy in London with specific responsibility for the long-range political implications of international petroleum production and supply. Since the embassy already had a petroleum attaché, Sappington's appointment underlined the importance the U.S. placed at this time on petroleum policy planning. The petroleum agreement fell within Sappington's jurisdiction, and his observations on British opinion reflected some reticence in British industry circles, especially toward continued government involvement in international operations in the postwar period. Both Sir Frederick Godber and Kessler of Royal Dutch Shell were opposed to the multilateral conception of the agreement, arguing that the main issue was for the United States and Britain to reach accord. Both men were especially opposed to the concept of incorporating less-developed producing countries into the agreement; rather, they argued, the interests of such producing countries should be of secondary concern to those of such major nations as Britain and the United States. Viscount Bearsted, presiding at Shell's annual general meeting in July, echoed those sentiments, supporting the "orderly development" objectives of the agreement but anticipating that private industry would take the lead once government had assisted in establishing the broad framework of cooperation for which the agreement was intended.[89]

There were important differences in the redrafted agreement that Harold Ickes and the other members of the American delegation took to London in September 1945. Ickes was also careful to maintain closer industry consultation than had prevailed in 1944, with the result that six company representatives accompanied the American delegation: William Boyd, George Hill, W. Alton Jones (president of Cities Service), Joseph E. Pogue (vice-president, Chase National Bank), A. Jacobsen, and Ralph Zook.[90] Both the revisions in the agreement and the industry representation reflected the industry's contribution. Although the majors had failed to achieve the inclusion of an antitrust exemption clause, they had accomplished what amounted to the emasculation of any potential power the international petroleum commission might have possessed. The drafters of the agreement explicitly stated that the stipulation that the commission had no power to compel acceptance of its recommendations was included to avoid defeat in the Senate. They might have added that it was essential for industry support as well. The same applied to the clarification that the agreement granted to the federal government no new powers over the domestic petroleum industry. The revised agreement also made provision for adherence by other countries, indeed stipulated that the signatory powers would initiate the calling of an international conference, but the intention here was not as it had been initially to make the agreement ultimately one broadly representative of producing and consuming countries, but rather to emphasize to the international community that the British and Americans were not attempting a "freeze-out" of other countries in the development of petroleum resources. Nonetheless, the *Petroleum Times* of London identified this international commitment as one of the most important features of the agreement.[91] The revision also deleted the list of factors that had earlier been established as guides to production, specifically "available reserves, sound engineering practices, relevant economic factors, and the interests of producing and consuming countries." The first two were removed because the domestic petroleum industry opposed any interference in domestic operations by the international commission. Significantly, in the article defining the term "countries," the specific areas were listed. For the United Kingdom, the list included those areas under direct British administration as colonies, protectorates, or mandated territories.[92]

The *London Times* observed pessimistically on 25 September, the day following the conclusion of the second agreement, that it would accomplish little of consequence without the participation of the Soviet Union. The *Times* also did not believe that one of the basic issues had been resolved to the mutual satisfaction of both parties, namely, American unwillingness to accept any international regulation of the domestic industry and British belief that such regulation was important for the effective operation of an international agreement. That dilemma clearly remained.

COMPLICATIONS OF DOMESTIC POLITICS

The other dilemma that remained was to gain final domestic political approval of the agreement. To do so required further pacification of the oil industry, even though a reasonable crosssection of industry leaders had participated in the drafting and final negotiation of the agreement in London.[93] By the fall of 1945, other problems confronted the American majors. Standard Oil of New Jersey, for example, which had earlier expressed concern with the implication of British exchange controls for its international operations, returned to the issue before negotiations had been completed in London. Recognizing that the issue had been avoided in the agreement, Eugene Holman outlined for the State Department the global difficulties Jersey was experiencing because of the trend toward payments for imports in sterling and the British stipulation that various materials should be drawn from sterling areas. The value of Jersey's annual sales to sterling areas was $100 million, exclusive of the business of Standard-Vacuum, which operated in the East and Far East. Much of Jersey's oil was derived from Venezuelan sources. Orville Harden, Jersey's vice-president, pursued the question further with Assistant Secretary of State William Clayton in urging that the United States make any postwar financial assistance conditional on a relaxation of British exchange controls. Jersey representatives in London had already received instructions from the British Ministry of Fuel and Power stipulating that material supplies for the sterling area had to be drawn to the maximum from sterling sources.[94] Harden was already concerned that Jersey would be unable to obtain adequate supplies from sterling areas and would lose markets it could only with difficulty regain. Harden warned Clayton that American-held concessions abroad were "extremely valuable to the security of our own country, and any shutback would not only seriously affect the economies of the countries involved, but would likely also result in real difficulty in connection with the maintenance of American-owned concessions."[95] State Department officials were already vigorously pursuing the general implications of the question and late in the year reached agreement with Britain on postwar exchange controls. Once those negotiations were concluded, American officials concluded they could do nothing further for Standard Oil.[96]

It has been suggested that by the time the oil agreement received consideration by the Senate Foreign Relations Committee it was no longer relevant to the international situation, that the "world had passed it by," and that the companies had fallen back on their own cooperative resources.[97] Although the major companies did devise their own solutions, the agreement was as relevant in 1947 as it had been at its inception three years earlier, as a means by which to initiate effective intergovernmental cooperation in international petroleum relations. By 1947 there was more general support for the agreement than in 1945, when industry pressure had contributed to a renegotiation of the document. Politically there was bipartisan support for the agreement. The Senate Foreign Relations Committee produced a favorable recommendation in 1947 with only one dissenting voice (that of Tom Connally, who had been replaced as chairman by Arthur Vandenberg), unlike the situation that had prevailed two years earlier. The British government also remained committed to the agreement in the lengthy period that followed signature in the fall of 1945, inviting the United States to send representatives to London in September 1946 to develop plans for the implementation of the agreement and to consider matters that might be brought to the early attention of the international commission.[98] Although no concrete steps were taken in this direction, American officials did explore the alternative possibility of developing an international petroleum agency under the jurisdiction of the United Nations. Again, discussions proved sporadic and inconclusive.[99]

Participation by the oil industry in the renegotiation of the agreement had reduced most opposition, but reservations remained and would continue to be an irritant during the lengthy delay between signature of the agreement and Senate consideration. In November 1946, the board of the American Petroleum Institute adopted a resolution supporting the agreement conditional on assurances that the commission would not have power or jurisdiction over the domestic industry, that it could not revise the status of existing concessions, and that it did not add to the jurisdiction of Congress in petroleum operations. When those assurances were forthcoming, the API endorsed without qualification Senate ratification of the treaty.[100] The opposition of the domestic petroleum industry to the agreement has been exaggerated. Support came from critical elements in the industry at important junctures, and had the Truman administration effectively channeled that support, there is no reason to assume the agreement might not have been ratified. Industry opposition was isolated and appears to have been prompted considerably by the efforts of the Sinclair Oil Corporation. In 1946, Sinclair had production in only one foreign country, Venezuela, where its subsidiary produced some 28,000 barrels a day. Its own production and crude oil it purchased in Venezuela were refined in the United States.[101] The Sinclair resistance to the agreement was premised on the company's concern that it would be frozen out of Middle East concessions. Hence, in late January 1946, the company's assistant general counsel, P.C. Spencer, prepared for distribution to the Senate and other interested parties an extensive memorandum in opposition to the agreement. Spencer claimed the traditional weaknesses in the treaty: that it would require Congress to legislate control of the domestic oil industry; that it provided for a "super world petroleum cartel"; that executive and congressional involvement in the industry would be greatly expanded; and that the treaty was unduly ambiguous in its wording.[102] Sinclair was also credited with inspiring opposition to the agreement that was expressed at the August 1946 meeting of the Interstate Oil Compact Commission by Dan Hovey of the Houston-based Hovey Petroleum Company, Elmer Patman of the Superior Oil Company, and Ghent Sanderford of Austin. Spencer also attended the sessions. Robert Hardwicke, former PAW chief counsel, reported to Davies that he and Everett De Golyer had been hard pressed to overcome the negative impression created by the opponents, even though supportive communications from Ralph Zook and Joseph Pogue were read to the commission. The effort was sufficiently successful, however, to prevent the commission from openly opposing the agreement.[103]

Davies and his colleagues took tentative measures to counteract the arguments advanced by Sinclair interests. In March, Hardwicke prepared an extensive memorandum refuting the Sinclair critique of the agreement. He did so in consultation with Victor Butler, the British petroleum attaché in Washington. Hardwicke emphasized that the general purpose of the agreement was to facilitate the orderly development of the international petroleum trade, that it was interim in nature and contained no design for extensive governmental supervision. Indeed, he argued, the agreement did not provide for "regulation, enforcement, or compulsion."[104]

Although Hardwicke's and Davies's efforts did not silence the Sinclair-Texas opposition, they did contribute to a reduction in such opposition. Wallace Hawkins of the Magnolia Petroleum Company's legal department, a Socony-Vacuum subsidiary in Dallas, commented on the calming of tempers in a note to Hardwicke. "I am sure that at the time Spencer wrote his article … there was an intense feeling resentful of obscure actions and designs to deprive the American state of their constitutional power. We were all really witch-hunting, seeing in every move on the part of the administration an effort to gain more national powers and to increase indirectly the power of the federal government." Hawkins concluded: "One can defend the treaty now as containing no lurking provisions intended to increase federal power."[105]

Ralph Zook, formerly president of the Independent Petroleum

Association and member of the PIWC at the time the first agreement was signed, was another independent to move clearly into the supporters' camp. Writing to the chairman of the Oklahoma Interstate Oil Compact Commission in early August, Zook noted the efforts that had been made by Ickes and others to meet his objections to the first agreement. Zook argued that his main reasons for supporting the agreement were to avoid an international conflict over world markets and to prevent Middle Eastern production from undermining the export markets of United States–produced petroleum. Zook observed that the expansion of Middle East production was imminent; the first shipment from Kuwait had only recently reached the United States. "Unless," he cautioned, "oil from this and other large potential producing areas is brought into the world market in an orderly manner, it can result in the importation of large amounts of cheap foreign oil which will eliminate all but the flush oil producers in the United States." Zook had identified the precise basis for commonality of interest between the domestic and international producers: market and price controls. It was these considerations that, in Zook's opinion, accounted for the support from the main oil trade associations as well as numerous local trade organizations throughout the United States.[106] But the same argument was employed to divide the groups. The *Texas Oil Journal* warned in 1946 that the agreement was an effort by the British oil cartel to control the world oil market, to eliminate free enterprise and control prices and production.

In spite of efforts to counteract opposition, Davies believed it was gaining ground in 1946 while the Senate delayed a formal hearing. The State Department was in large part responsible for the failure to press the initiative with the Senate Foreign Relations Committee, with both Dean Acheson and William Clayton identifying the pending British loan issue as a matter of first priority.[107] In anticipation of hearings that year, however, PAW officials pressed on both with consideration of Senate testimony and also with advance planning for the implementation of the agreement. In the draft speech prepared for Secretary Julius Krug, several features were emphasized. One was that the United States had known reserves of some 20 billion barrels and expected demand for the next twenty years of 36 billion barrels, recognizing that new discoveries, new extraction technology, and synthetic fuel developments might well revolutionize the American situation. At the same time that it urged the necessity of an agreement to safeguard American security, the document reiterated the soporifics that the agreement was not intended to encourage formation of an international cartel, that in spite of the absence of an antitrust exclusion provision, the issue would be treated following implementation of the agreement. The draft was even less precise at this stage in addressing the issue of what government agency should be responsible for responding to the recommendations of the international commission, and outlined the factors supporting an interdepartmental committee of state, justice, and interior. Most important, the document concluded, the failure of ratification would be "a body blow to the cause of international cooperation on oil."[108]

PAW officials remained equally unclear on the precise jurisdiction over and composition of the international commission. They were uncertain whether United States appointees should be ex officio, like the secretary of state, or individuals selected because of particular expertise, although it was assumed that all would be full-time employees of the government. It was further assumed that although formal recommendations of the commission would have to go through government channels, the commission would be free to consult directly with industry. To facilitate such consultation, consideration was given to the creation or continuation of an industry body such as the Foreign Operations Committee of the PAW.[109] Although nothing was firmly established at this time, such efforts reflected a firm commitment to an ongoing consultative mechanism between government and industry in the postwar period.

One of the major obstacles to ratification in 1946 was the change in personnel that accompanied the entrenchment of Truman's power. Harold Ickes's resignation in early 1946 brought Julius Krug to head the interior department and left Davies as a considerably less influential advocate of the agreement. Within interior there were reservations about the agreement in key positions. The department's solicitor, for example, Warren Gardner, was prepared to lend "unenthusiastic support"; but Gardner, like some of the domestic oil producer critics, thought the agreement contained the possibility of promoting the growth of international petroleum cartels. Gardner could not envisage how practical advantages could be attained in such areas as conservation and the avoidance of hemisphere cross-hauling without substantially reducing the free play of competitive forces. He also anticipated that the domestic market would increasingly be affected by the international market. The one advantage he did envisage was that a cartel-like arrangement under government supervision would be more desirable than an informal, private cartel. Gardner, like others before him, also anticipated that the agreement would be provocative in Soviet-American relations unless it were promptly expanded beyond the bilateral stage.[110]

Gardner's arguments reflected a growing consensus in government and industry circles prior to the hearings before the Senate Foreign Relations Committee. The agreement was potentially of some value;

there was some danger of cartelization; government might attain greater control over the international industry; a bilateral agreement was inadequate to achieve the broader international objectives of the agreement. Eugene Holman, Jersey vice-president, observed this broad area of industry-government consensus when he commented on a speech John Loftus, chief of the State Department petroleum division, had given at the University of Pittsburgh. "It became plain to me," Holman wrote, "as I read your statements, that you and the petroleum industry see the same general objective, namely the development of an international economic and political climate which will permit private capital ... to be invested abroad on a competitive and non-discriminatory basis and with a minimum of political risk." Holman thought this end would be attained through the Anglo-American agreement, but reminded Loftus that fear of an overly powerful international commission had been instrumental in mobilizing the industry against the first agreement.[111]

Even industry support began to fragment before the Senate hearings began. In late 1946 the Independent Petroleum Association of America, meeting in Fort Worth, reversed its previous endorsement of the treaty, allegedly in response to an August radio broadcast in which Rayner and Loftus had called for an international trade organization to control world oil production. Although such influential members of the association as Ralph Zook, its former president, and Alfred Jacobsen publicly disassociated themselves from the decision, the damage had been done. Joseph Pogue wrote association president Major B.A. Hardy that he regretted that such an influential organization should have openly opposed the agreement. Ralph Davies remained optimistic that the treaty could be implemented "unless it is allowed to go by default,"[112] but Texas groups remained in the forefront of the opposition. On the eve of the hearings, the Texas Senate adopted a resolution condemning the agreement as a possible "disruption of the entire economic structure of our state."[113]

In order to maintain government momentum as the hearings approached, in early 1947 Davies employed Gordon Sessions as a special consultant and adviser. Sessions was a former secretary of the PRC, later press relations adviser to Ickes, and an advisory member of the American negotiators who concluded the 1945 agreement. At the same time the interior department employed former PAW counsel Robert Hardwicke as a consultant to Secretary Krug and Max Ball, then director of the newly created Oil and Gas Division.[114]

When the Senate Foreign Relations Committee finally conducted hearings on the treaty for ten days in June 1947, there remained considerable uncertainty on the agreement's fate. Ralph Davies concluded that the long delay had "given rise to a good deal of misunderstanding and opposition born of narrow self-interests."[115] Changes in the composition and chairmanship of the Senate committee provided also little source of optimism. The conservative Michigan Republican Arthur Vandenberg, who had replaced Tom Connally as chairman following Republican victories in the 1946 congressional elections, was unlikely to lend vigorous support to an agreement that critics charged reduced United States power. Other members of the committee included Arthur Copper, Kansas; Wallace White, Jr, Maine; Alexander Wiley, Wisconsin; H. Alexander Smith, New Jersey; Bourne Hickenlooper, Iowa; Henry Cabot Lodge, Jr, Massachusetts; Walter George, Georgia; Robert Wagner, New York; Elbert Thomas, Utah; Alben Barkely, Kentucky; and Carl Hatch, New Mexico. In addition to the Republican majority, some of the Democratic members, such as Hatch and George, were conservative anti-New Dealers, although they were more likely to follow the administration's lead in foreign than in domestic policy. One administration advantage was the shift of Arthur Vandenberg away from his prewar isolationism toward bipartisan internationalism. A second advantage was the closeness of Lodge and Vandenberg. Together they played a considerable role in gaining liberal Republican support for military preparedness, for the Truman Doctrine and the Marshall Plan. Nonetheless, their support for the treaty was uncertain, since the previous year they had voted against a strategic raw-materials stockpiling measure.[116] Both Hatch and Hickenlooper could be expected to question any treaty that did not hold clear advantages for the United States. However, Elbert Thomas had been consistently pro-New Deal and supportive of Roosevelt's foreign policy. Whether he would remain loyal to Truman remained to be seen. Robert Wagner was an open exponent of collective security.[117]

The administration successfully presented its case for ratification of the agreement before the Senate Foreign Relations Committee, but the victory was a narrow one, and there was an impression that administrative support for the treaty was less than concerted. Administrative spokesmen included Will Clayton, undersecretary of state for economic affairs; Dean Acheson, undersecretary of state; and Charles Rayner, petroleum adviser. Acting Secretary of the Interior Oscar Chapman, who had had very limited contact with the long negotiations preceding the agreement, testified for interior, as did Ralph Davies, who remained the most articulate and consistent advocate. The military evinced less involvement than in other wartime and postwar petroleum planning endeavors, with Colonel G.H. Vogel, executive officer of the Army-Navy Petroleum Board, advancing the military argument. Among industry spokesmen who testified, prominent figures were individuals who had been active participants in previous discussions: William Boyd, Jr, George Hill, Eugene Holman, Henry Fraser and P.C. Spencer of Sinclair Oil Corporation, and Glenn H. McCarthy, president of McCarthy Oil and Gas Corporation of Texas and a director of the Independent Producers Association. Another prominent spokesman to testify on behalf of the agreement was Manley O. Hudson, the distinguished international lawyer who had guided revision of the 1944 agreement by the National Oil Policy Committee.

The hearings suggest that support for the agreement divided clearly between the administration, spokesmen for the majors, and select advocates among the independents on the one hand, and, on the other, a very narrowly based segment of the independents whose opposition had been virtually untempered during the previous three years of discussion. There was no clear division along liberal / conservative, or nationalist / internationalist lines, although such anti-New Dealers on the committee as Walter George were opposed.

The hearings produced few, if any, new agreements for or against the treaty with Britain, but they did reflect the remarkable persistence of those opponents who feared possible government involvement in the industry, the enhancement of the major companies' predominance, and the erosion of the position of domestic producers. The failure of all but a few of the companies to recognize the long-term significance of effective international cooperation was one of the outstanding features of the entire debate. The complex and significant aspects of the effort to achieve postwar international order were too frequently reduced to the simplification of unfettered free enterprise versus state control. Even those who supported the agreement expressed reservations about compromising free enterprise. Senator E.H. Moore of Oklahoma, who in general endorsed ratification, expressed sympathy for industry fears that the agreement would lead to treatment of American foreign oil operations as a public interest and therefore subject to public control. He was equally troubled by the State Department's official policy of recognizing the right of foreign governments to nationalize private property with appropriate compensation. Glenn McCarthy expressed similar sentiments but with even more vigor. The agreement, he contended, was "contrary to all we understand as clearly American ... a direct, studied attempt to place the control of the oil industry under Federal or international regulation." William Boyd, in defending the agreement, indicated that for twenty-seven years he had "fought Federal control from every conceivable point of view," but was convinced by State Department assurances that enhanced federal controls were not embodied in the treaty. George Hill shared Boyd's confidence that the treaty protected constitutional procedures in each of the signatory nations.[118] The most significant industry statement of support for government / business policy coordination and cooperation was that of Eugene Holman. "We believe," he informed the committee, "that we can effectively cooperate with government and at the same time maintain our independence."

Expressions of concern among senators focused on several aspects of the agreement. Connally, who was the most pressing interrogator, gave the impression that he thought the treaty was overly ambiguous and would accomplish little for United States interests abroad. The Texas Democrat also used the occasion to identify Ickes with the agreement in a transparent attempt to associate the treaty with an administration official who had clashed with industry interests. Connally and others sought explicitly to exploit the potential vulnerability of the domestic industry to inexpensive imported oil and to assert the noncompetitive features of the agreement. Senator Smith found it curious that an agreement between two nations that controlled 90 percent of foreign petroleum concessions could encourage free competition. Lodge pursued a similar line of questioning, speculating whether, if the real issue was the potential exhaustion of domestic resources, the appropriate policy ought to be conservation at home and increased importation. Senators Robertson of Wyoming and Hatch carried this point further, suggesting that neither the agreement nor United States import regulations prevented foreign oil dumping in the American market. "Why," Robertson queried, "sign a treaty which throws our great market open to the world without any restrictions ... when there is no need for the treaty?" Davies had to concede that tariff barriers would indeed be contrary to the principles of the agreement. "It is to promote the American idea of free enterprise, free and open markets, equal opportunity in the exploration and the development of concessions abroad."[119]

Administration spokesmen presented no new supporting arguments for the agreement. Rather, the arguments, though sound, had become increasingly worn by 1947, confirming Davies's assessment that the lengthy delays had harmed the cause. They argued persuasively that the United States faced future petroleum shortages; that the pact was consistent with the principles of U.S. foreign oil policy during the previous twenty-five years; that the State Department had no policy that "contemplates the creation of a petroleum body of a regulatory or of an executive character"; that it provided a mechanism for international consultation, and, in Dean Acheson's phrasing, recognized "the greatly increased importance that the whole problem of international oil has assumed in our economic welfare and in our national security."[120] Such arguments proved adequate to win the committee's approval but not that of the Senate, where the agreement died of old age and neglect five years later.

The failure of the United States Senate to ratify the Anglo–American Petroleum Treaty casts serious doubt on the degree of American commitment to such international solutions to world resource management in the postwar era. The agreement itself had been far from an ideal document: a likely ineffectual international commission; little more than the promise of multilateralism and no substantial evidence that either the Soviet Union or undeveloped producing nations would be incorporated in a meaningful way; a refusal to accept the need to link international and domestic production and marketing controls; and an ambiguous (at best) commitment to government supervision. It may well be that those critics were correct who charged that the agreement involved the formation of a government-sponsored international cartel that would be dominated by a few of the majors and the great powers. There were certainly weaknesses and objections to the agreement. Yet the fact remains that it held a more satisfactory promise for the future than did the course that resulted from its rejection. In the absence of the agreement, the majors moved ahead on their own, as the following chapter details, to create the production and marketing controls that might have been achieved under the agreement. Such private-sector dominance produced a situation that could only be considered satisfactory as long as the companies and the major powers were able to control, politically and economically, the producing areas. By failing to incorporate those areas fully into production and marketing decisions from the outset, the companies created a potential adversarial situation that produced a crisis of uncertainty with which the world has had to contend for the past twenty years. The United States must bear a major share of the responsibility for failing to achieve the type of international cooperative community after 1945 that the rhetoric of its officials appeared to herald. The tragedy is that there were numerous officials in the private and public sector who recognized the need for effective international cooperation, the more prominent of whom were Roosevelt, Ickes, Hull, Feis, Stettinius, and Acheson. Yet none of them seemed prepared to invade the sphere of the private sector in order to accomplish their ends. When they did propose such half-measures as the Anglo-American agreement, they found themselves confronted by the narrow, self-interested spokesmen of an anachronistic laissez-faire philosophy in Congress and among many of the domestic oil producers.

CHAPTER NINE

American Enterprise Denied and Resurgent, 1945–1948

The negotiation of an ultimately aborted Anglo-American petroleum agreement and debates over American involvement in Iran and Saudi Arabia absorbed much of the attention of those officials who sought to treat oil development within the larger framework of United States foreign policy. As the war in Europe drew to a close and the uneasy wartime alliance began to unravel, both company and government officials focused their attention on questions of postwar reconstruction, on regaining control of properties under enemy control during the war, and on attempting to reverse the losses to prewar nationalism. These efforts concentrated on several areas and developments. One was the fate of American oil enterprise in Eastern Europe. A second was the continuing effort to regain a place in Mexico and to prevent other producing nations in Latin America from following the Mexican example to nationalization. A third pivoted on Middle Eastern developments, including an East-West crisis over Iran in 1945–6, debate over the restructuring of the long-standing Red Line Agreement, the status of Palestine, and debate over the construction of a trans-Arabian pipeline. In each instance, the onset of Cold War and the need for European economic recovery provided the context in which policy evolved.

SETBACK IN EASTERN EUROPE

The situation confronting American interests in Eastern Europe was especially accute as the Soviet Union consolidated its hegemony in the area. Although the fate of American enterprise was by no means the sole consideration in United States policy toward the region, petroleum interests occupied an important and indeed symbolic place in the American effort to maintain the principles of the Atlantic Charter in the postwar world. The wartime situation in Iran tested American willingness to honor fully the equality-of-access principle. Mexican nationalization had earlier tested American willingness to accept the compensated expropriation of U.S. enterprise abroad. Potential Soviet domination of Eastern Europe after 1945 presented the most comprehensive challenge yet encountered by American enterprise in general, and the oil companies in particular. The possible loss of Romanian petroleum posed a strategic threat to American interests as well as the likelihood of economic loss.

Both Standard Oil of New Jersey and Socony-Vacuum had been active in Romania in the interwar years, the former as a major producer and refiner and the latter primarily in marketing. In 1938 American oil interests controlled 12.8 percent of domestic distribution in Romania, 28 percent in Hungary, 21 percent in Austria, 42 percent in Czechoslovakia, and 42 percent in Yugoslavia. In 1944, United States nationals still controlled 10.5 percent of Romanian production, 100 percent of Hungarian, and slightly less than 16 percent of Austrian. These were the only countries in east-central Europe where American affiliates had production as opposed to marketing operations.[1]

The war had several effects on American operations in the area. One was to alter marketing patterns. By 1938 Germany had become the leading consumer of Romanian oil products, representing 15 percent of the country's exports. The war and German occupation escalated that figure to 80 percent by 1943, thus requiring the companies to fill traditional markets in Western Europe and the Mediterranean with Venezuelan and Middle Eastern oil. A second consequence of the war was to reduce the relative importance of Romanian oil in world production. Although the military campaigns resulted in little damage to the oil fields, Allied bombing seriously devastated Romanian refineries. More important, the curtailment of supplies for non-Axis countries had required increased production elsewhere, and by the end of the war, Romanian production had declined from 2.3 percent of the world total in 1938 to 1.1 percent in 1946, compared with the increase of Middle Eastern production from 6.03 percent to 9.23 percent in the same period.[2]

The Romanian situation was especially complex because Romanian nationalism in the late 1930s and 1940s mixed with German and then Soviet occupation to produce a major threat to foreign enterprise, the most important of which was the Shell affiliate Astra Română and the Jersey affiliate Romano-Americană. Maurice Pearton has effectively documented the interweaving of these forces. Germany assumed control of the Royal Dutch Shell affiliate shortly after the defeat of Belgium in 1939, and Romanian officials used the opportunity afforded by the isolation from the West to assert more direct national controls. The

1942 Romanian Mining Law, for example, established the constitutional basis for state control over the oil industry. Although it did not explicitly prohibit foreign investment, the law did imply that such investment would assume a less significant role relative to state enterprise than it had played in the prewar years. It was thus hardly surprising, as Pearton contends, that the Allies placed considerable importance on repeal of the 1942 law as part of a peace settlement with Romania,[3] which was not negotiated until 1947.

Before war's end, there was consequently substantial cause for concern in official and corporate circles that American investment in the area was in serious jeopardy. Leo Crowley of the Foreign Economic Administration, for example, noted to the secretary of state in 1944 that the Soviet Union appeared to expect to be able to extract all Romanian production for Soviet use during the immediate postwar period. Crowley noted that the question of whether or not American companies would be reinstated in possession of their prewar properties remained unresolved, and he queried what measures might be taken to alleviate the situation. Crowley urged that official United States protection should be provided in all the countries concerned, specifically Austria, Hungary, and Romania, in part to alleviate the drain on American resources and funds that would be required to supply those markets deprived by Soviet diversion of oil stocks and equipment. Anxious as he may have been over the threat to private enterprise, Crowley's basic premise was a pragmatic one. Soviet extraction of East European oil placed an additional wartime strain on United Nations resources. In terms of Soviet withdrawals of American-claimed property, such concerns were not without foundation. It was estimated that between September and December 1944, the first few months of Soviet occupation during which German control of the industry passed to the USSR, Soviet officials removed 50,000 tons of oil equipment and 65 percent of the oil stocks of Romano-Americanà, bearing an approximate market value of $900,000.[4]

United States officials raised the issue repeatedly with the Soviet representative on the Allied Control Commission. The reply received, when there was a reply, indicated that Soviet officials perceived the equipment and stocks removed as German and hence legitimate war booty. General Schuyler, chief U.S. representative on the Control Commission for Romania, persisted in his efforts to curtail Soviet measures. At the end of 1944 he appointed Lieutenant Colonel Case Wilcox as a staff oil specialist to serve as liaison officer with the Russian economic section of the commission.[5] The State Department concurrently placed considerable priority on the issue, first attempting to make satisfactory arrangements through the representations of Ambassador Averell Harriman in Moscow, and failing that, contemplating a direct approach to Stalin from President Roosevelt.[6]

The situation further deteriorated in 1945. Although American oil company officials were granted permission by the control commission to return to Romania in March 1945, the same month brought the installation of a government under Petru Groza, a regime that the United States did not regard as a broadly representative government within the meaning of the Crimean Declaration on Liberated Europe.[7] Subsequent months witnessed additional tightening of Soviet controls. In May, the USSR and Romania concluded a protocol for economic cooperation, one dimension of which involved the formation of a joint company for the exploration and exploitation of petroleum. The protocol provided that private Romanian companies and individuals could participate as minor shareholders in the enterprise. The response of American corporate interests was predictable. L.T. McCollum of Jersey Standard informed Charles Darlington, chief of the State Department petroleum division, that unless the department was able to defend the Open Door principle for American interests in Romania, the protocol would mean the end of American oil operations in that country.

Darlington's reply provided little basis for optimism, even though in the interim the question had been raised at the Potsdam meetings. He indicated that the department was equally concerned by the protocol, that it had heard rumors of a similar agreement with Hungary and feared that these developments represented a trend in Soviet policy in Eastern Europe. Darlington could offer no concrete report of progress, save to note that the United States was attempting to establish "a policy at the highest level."[8]

Research and Analysis Branch studies of the protocol earlier indicated that although the agreement did not explicitly exclude commercial and financial arrangements between Romania and the West, the quantities of oil to be exported to the USSR under the agreement, as reparations, would be too large to leave a surplus for export elsewhere. The study confirmed the intention of the industry that the formation of a Soviet-Romanian company would result not only in ending American oil operations but also private Romanian petroleum operations.[9]

American officials sought in vain to reverse the tide. Even before the official company under the agreement came into being in July 1945, Acting Secretary of State Joseph Grew had to conclude, in requesting the American ambassador in Moscow to object to Soviet withdrawals of company equipment, that "it is becoming evident that the USSR seeks to obtain a predominant, if not exclusive, control of petroleum industry and trading position in Rumania." To Grew, Soviet isolation from American petroleum technology and equipment would be to the long-term disadvantage of the USSR, citing as evidence the six high-octane refineries provided by the U.S. during the war, but concluded that the Soviet Union appeared willing to pay the price.[10] The State Department was especially insistent that compensation for the loss of property by American nationals should be given equal importance to the payment of reparations. "Wholly-owned subsidiaries," he added, "of American enterprises ... should have their property rights and interests protected to a much greater degree than holdings acquired through cartel agreements involving ex-enemy firms."[11]

As strongly as American officials may have felt about the protection of American property in Romania, it was recognized that the United States was in an unenviable position to affect change. "Rumania," Roosevelt wrote Churchill shortly before the president's death, "is not a good place for a test case. The Russians have been in undisputed control from the beginning and with Rumania lying athwart the Russian lines of communications it is difficult to contest the plea of military necessity which they are using to justify their action."[12] The State Department briefing paper on Romania for the Potsdam meeting expressed the problem in equally precise terms on the eve of Potsdam. "The fundamental problem is the degree to which the United States will acquiesce in the exercise by the Soviet Union of a dominant or exclusive political and economic influence in Rumania. It poses," the paper contended, "the need for reconciling ... our policy of cooperation with the U.S.S.R. for the preservation of peace with our principles and commitments embodied in the Atlantic Charter, in the Yalta agreements, and in many general statements of policy." Harriman suggested that Soviet oil policy in Romania ought to be evaluated in relation to an anticipated decline in Soviet production of crude oil, a development that would make the USSR more anxious to control production in its sphere of influence.[13]

The desire to maintain the Open Door in Eastern Europe for American enterprise and the urgent need for petroleum supplies to prosecute the war against Japan combined to produce a vigorous State Department position on Romanian oil. Acting Secretary Joseph Grew cabled George Kennan, then chargé in Moscow, in mid-July that there should be no delay in objecting to the Soviet-Romanian economic pact and the withdrawal of oil supplies. "With specific reference to petroleum," Kennan was instructed, "point out sacrifices accepted by American people in restricting their military, industrial, and civilian consumption ... You should point out that oil picture in Rumania is only one aspect of a world-wide problem and that conclusion of treaties granting exclusive rights and of monopolistic corporate arrangements ... may force the United States to reconsider its policies ... with respect to supplying petroleum, technical data, equipment and products."[14] At the same time, Edwin Pauley, American representative on the Reparations Commission, warned the secretary of state that if additional oil supplies were not forthcoming from Europe, it would be a "limiting factor in the military might which can be thrown against Japan." It was clear that the Department of State and Petroleum Administration for War officials concurred with that assessment.[15]

As important as the petroleum situation in Eastern Europe may have been to American officials, it was clear that the United States was not prepared to risk a formal rift with the Soviet Union in order to resolve it. The Potsdam meetings resulted in no concrete progress. Stalin declined to give it prominence; the issue was discussed by the respective foreign ministers and referred for further negotiations to bilateral commissions. In less than two years the Soviet-American commission, having failed to reach any agreement, was terminated.[16]

The Soviet-Romanian company provided for in the May 1945 protocol was formed that July. For the next two years, the constituent companies, which included Romano-Americanà and Astra-Românà, were operated by Soviet technicians under Soviet-Romanian direction, even though in principle the companies retained their separate corporate identities. Under the agreement, the Jersey affiliate supplied one-seventh of required petroleum shipments to the Soviet Union, at a price that company officials considered inadequate to cover costs. United States-based companies held 13.8 percent of Sovrompetrol's assets, compared to 23.9 percent for Royal Dutch Shell and 8.8 percent for Romanian interests. Jersey involvement progressively declined as a result of Soviet intervention. Company officials in New York and London were reluctant to advance dollars to enable equipment purchases outside Romania, and labor problems from what the company perceived as Soviet army-supported unions continued to escalate, until by mid-1947 all English-speaking employees of Romano-Americanà had been removed.[17]

By late 1946, Department of State officials held no optimism for a reversal of Soviet dominance. C.M. Piggott, U.S. petroleum attaché in Bucharest, observed that his office had become virtually a "branch office of the Romano-Americanà," whose morale was very low. "I do not know," he wrote, "how the companies at home may feel, but unless they have written off their investment in Rumania, I frankly think they are hiding their heads in the sand."[18] Piggott's foresight was confirmed the following year when the company's properties in Romania were nationalized.

American policy was no more successful in defending American oil companies elsewhere in Eastern Europe. In Czechoslovakia, Standard Oil simply dissolved its affiliate, which was engaged in marketing, on the grounds that government controls made satisfactory operations impossible.[19] In Hungary, petroleum represented the largest American investment in the country. Following the end of war in 1945, officials of MAORT (Magyar Amerikai Olajipari, R.T.), the Jersey affiliate, were allowed to return by local authorities, but before effective operations could be resumed, the Soviet army seized direct control.

One of the main areas of dispute between Soviet officials in Hungary and company officers, other than the main question of autonomy, was the level of production that Soviet officials sought to impose. The company was willing to produce its properties at the levels stipulated by Soviet engineers, but only as a temporary measure in order to alleviate the economic situation in Hungary. Company officials expressed concern that sustained high levels of extraction would be seriously damaging to the oil fields.

When John Loftus met with oil company officials in early 1946, he concluded that the situation was critical and that further negotiation through the control commission was likely to prove futile without diplomatic agreement in Moscow and a specific provision in the Hungarian peace treaty stipulating that the properties would be returned to company management and effective control. When George Kennan raised the issue in Moscow, he was informed by Vice-Commissar Vyshinsky that the Soviet Union rejected the company's contention that Soviet operation of the fields wold be detrimental to the American owners. Vyshinsky also informed Kennan that the Soviet Union had financed part of the restoration of the oil fields and that the properties contained some German investments, which had been transferred to the Soviet Union.[20] Here, as in Romania, the Soviet position was firm, but differing domestic political circumstances as well as geographic location made possible a brief respite from Soviet direction of the company in 1947. This lasted for less than a year, however, before labor difficulties disrupted operations. The result was that in May 1948, the Hungarian government appointed a state official company controller. A few months later, company president Paul Ruedemann was arrested, briefly imprisoned, and then deported. The company's properties were then nationalized.[21] In effect, the United States had failed to sustain Soviet adherence to the principles of the Atlantic Charter, and the demise of American oil interests in Eastern Europe was both symbolic and tangible evidence of that failure.

COLD WAR AND LATIN AMERICAN OIL

American oil companies also found themselves increasingly on the defensive in such key areas of Latin American petroleum development as Mexico, Venezula, and Colombia. The need for wartime collaboration had contributed to a stabilization of inter-American relations during the war, and was reflected in such developments as the 100-octane program and the financial resolution of the prewar nationalization drive in Mexico, as well as the curtailment of nationalistic oil legislation in Venezuela. Optimism that wartime collaboration would lead to continued stability in the postwar era or that private enterprise could recapture the Mexican fields was ill founded, however. Indeed, in the postwar years, the companies and American policymakers found themselves confronted with renewed labor problems, a perceived threat from the communist left, and a continued trend toward nationalization.

In Colombia, for example, the substantial progress American interests had made in 1938–42 toward neutralizing the more nationalistic features of Colombian petroleum legislation did not prevent the important DeMares concession and refineries, operated by Jersey Standard's affiliate, Tropical Oil, from reverting to the state according to the original terms of the concession. Although the formation of Ecopetrol, Colombia's state oil enterprise, was not accompanied by the comprehensive national controls of Mexico, and although the transferral of the DeMares operations to effective state control required several years, the message was clear. The Colombian government did not intend to return to the laissez-faire policies of the earlier years.[22]

In Mexico, it was not until the fall of 1947 that specific terms of settlement were established for the outstanding oil claims, in which the Mexican government agreed to pay $81.25 million with interest over a fifteen-year period. At the same time, the larger issue of Mexico's willingness to accept a return of private capital to the oil industry remained a divisive issue in Mexican-American relations in the early postwar years.[23] As in earlier negotiations involving strategic petroleum supplies, the Mexican situation revealed divergent approaches within the Truman administration as well as among industrial spokesmen.

The position of the State Department under Byrnes, Stettinius, and Acheson was the most consistent in its approach to the Mexican question. State Department policy was based on several premises. It was agreed that foreign petroleum sources were of strategic importance to the United States, and the security of that supply was identified as the first priority. Its preference was to have production under the control of American firms, but if that could not be obtained, the department was not prepared to risk alienation of Mexico or, more important, Venezuela, through rash action in Mexico. Further, the department's perception of corporate behavior in Mexico was that it had not been entirely benign, that the companies had been unreasonable on occasions, exploitative on others, and needed to rebuild the reputation of private

American capital and entrepreneurs in Mexico specifically and Latin America in general. At the same time, department officials remained firm in their commitment to accept the principle of compensated nationalization of subsoil natural resources, an issue on which they diverged most sharply from corporate officials. The department was also unambiguous in stressing that although the United States government wished to see a settlement of outstanding questions between the companies and the Mexican government and would indeed assist in bringing the parties together and offering advice, it would not contemplate an intergovernmental agreement. Any settlement, the department emphasized, would be by agreement between Mexican authorities and private enterprise, a position to which the department had publicly adhered in petroleum relations with Iran and Venezuela during the war. Finally, there was no deviation from the decision made in 1945 by the department and President Truman that the United States would not extend credit to Mexico for the development of its petroleum resources under Mexican state control.[24]

The State Department articulated these positions consistently during the immediate postwar years, perhaps most cohesively in a department memorandum of 23 August 1946 outlining the policy of the United States government toward Mexican petroleum. The document was drafted a few days after meeting with officials of the major companies, and the hand of Assistant Secretary of State for American Republic Affairs Spruille Braden was very evident in the document, which was forwarded to American Ambassador Walter Thurston in Mexico City. The document was premised not only on the general principles outlined above, but also on an assumption most closely identified with former Ambassador George Messersmith that Pemex was not capable of developing Mexican petroleum resources in an efficient and profitable manner. Time would disprove that paternalistic assumption. The document also asserted, in contradiction of the general acceptance of compensated nationalization, that the Mexican policy of nationalization was inconsistent with articles 2 and 6 of the Economic Charter of the Americas signed on 4 March 1945 at the Chapultepec meeting of the American states.

The American government was clearly not prepared, however, to pursue Mexico on the right of nationalization. Indeed, as the August 1946 policy statement indicated, the department appeared favorable to the idea of the negotiation of a contract between Mexico and the companies that would permit the companies to operate on a management and participation basis without formally holding oil concessions in Mexico. Department officials identified such an approach as a means by which the more unpopular concession device could be avoided and yet which would provide adequate security for American interests. A similar contract had been concluded in 1944 between Union Oil Company of California and the Paraguayan government.[25]

The basis on which the companies were prepared to return to Mexico at that stage varied, with Standard Oil of New Jersey the most persistent in its insistence of a modification of Mexican petroleum laws as the essential prerequisite. More generally, however, the companies were prepared to offer minimal concessions, in part because they did not think there was a practical basis for a return to Mexico at that time. They insisted on the security of any titles, on an opportunity to make profit with no restriction on their ability to remit profits to their home offices, on the provision of a reasonable period of time in which to conduct exploration and to exploit discoveries. In return, the companies gave the department assurances that they would employ and train more Mexican workers.[26] Although the department eschewed any formal association with negotiations leading to the companies' return to Mexico, such positions were the result of extended consultation between the companies and the department; and as in earlier years, former State Department officials also found themselves employed as negotiators by the companies.[27]

There was a brief period of renewed optimism among government and company officials in late 1946 and early 1947 as President Miguel Alemán appeared to be prepared to move toward rapprochement with the companies. One such promising sign was his appointment in December 1946 of Antonio J. Bermúdez as director general of Pemex. Walter Thurston expressed confidence and admiration for Bermúdez's ability to deal with Mexican oil workers and urged that the time was auspicious for a more formal overture to Mexico for oil negotiations. That optimism was short-lived, however. Within a few weeks, Thurston was required to report to the department that Alemán was still pressing for an American loan and that both he and Bermúdez had stressed that only Mexican companies would be permitted to participate in Mexican oil development. At the same time, Everett De Golyer's work for Pemex promised to place its operations on a more efficient basis,[28] thus weakening the need for American assistance.

Pessimism aside, the department instructed Thurston that fall to open negotiations at the earliest convenient moment, taking advantage of Mexico's continued need for foreign capital and exchange and the vital role petroleum could play in generating those funds. As earlier, the department stressed that the United States did not seek any preferential rights for American over other foreign nationals, or favor one American firm over another. At the same time, Thurston was informed that the United States was not interested in developing a joint U.S.-

Mexican military petroleum reserve, an idea with which Harold Ickes had earlier been associated. Thurston's conversations with President Alemán produced results similar to previous ones: Mexico was not prepared to alter its approach, and Thurston anticipated that until Mexican laws were modified it would only be the smaller firms, such as Phillips Petroleum, Cities Service, Signal Oil, and Trumbull Asphalt, which would be prepared to conclude contracts with Pemex. Indeed, Standard Oil officials explicitly informed him they would not do so.[29]

Thurston expressed some concern that there had been a failure to achieve adequate high-level coordination of oil policy toward Mexico, and cited the activity of New York businessman Paul Shields, who, on behalf of the navy department, had held discussions with the Mexican finance minister and the head of the Bank of Mexico, thus lending credence to the Mexican belief that American funding might result from Mexican cooperation.[30]

The continued efforts to reach agreement appeared to produce results in early 1948, very much along the lines of the mid-1946 State Department policy statement, that is, on a contractual rather than concession basis. In February, the Mexican minister for foreign relations provided Thurston with a memorandum outlining such a proposal, and Thurston observed that there appeared to be "no reason to doubt that the Mexican Government has opened the door for foreign capital and enterprise ... under certain conditions and controls," which involved financial rather than operating participation with Pemex. Pemex had already obtained funds and material from Cities Service and was in the process of concluding an agreement with the Texas Company for development work conducted by Pemex itself. In return for its investments, the American firms would receive oil. Although it was a conciliatory and promising move, Thurston did not anticipate that many companies would participate until Pemex was prepared to grant "genuine operating contracts," a development Thurston thought likely.[31]

There were some congressional pressures to reach an agreement during 1948. Those pressures came from two sources: the House Committee on Interstate and Foreign Commerce and a Special Senate Committee to Study the Problems of American Small Business. Of the two, the former was distinctly more important. In June 1948, Bermúdez invited members of the House of Representatives committee, chaired by Charles Wolverton, to visit Mexico, which it did in August. Thurston believed the invitation had been extended in an effort to demonstrate to congressmen and other U.S. officials that the development work of Pemex was the appropriate course for Mexico to follow and that it was in the best interests of both countries for the United States to provide funds and materials for the exploitation of Mexican oil. The American delegation, which included representatives of the Department of State and the Department of National Defense, visited Venezuela as well as Mexico that year, but failed to produce the results Bermúdez had desired, for several reasons. For one, Wolverton was replaced as chairman of the committee in the new Congress by Robert Crosser, an Ohio Democrat who opposed the extension of an American loan to Mexico. Secondly, as State Department counselor Charles Bohlen informed Senator Kenneth Wherry of the small-business committee, although the department was favorably disposed to United States private participation in Pemex on a contract basis, there was a world shortage of oil-well supplies, the export of which was controlled by the Department of Commerce. In view of that shortage, the department believed that the supplies should be made available where they would have the strongest likelihood of producing results.[32]

By the end of 1948 it was evident to any objective observer that Pemex was well established and that Mexico was prepared to dictate the terms for the operation of foreign capital in the Mexican petroleum industry. Secondly, American policy was clearly oriented toward the avoidance of any action in Mexico that would jeopardize American petroleum operations in Venezuela. Representatives of Gulf, Standard Oil of New Jersey, and the Texas Company indicated to Assistant Secretary of the Navy Mark Andrews in late 1948 that their respective positions had undergone little modification in the past two years. Jersey officials continued to be more concerned with the nature of Mexican petroleum laws than with the terms of contracts with Pemex. Gulf officials saw the main question to be the means by which profits could be divided between the Mexican government and the companies. Gulf was prepared to operate only on the basis of paying a specific royalty and having the remainder of the oil and associated revenues accrue to the company, a situation that would have been similar to the pre-1938 pattern and one clearly unacceptable to Mexico. The Texas Company had hoped that its offer of a $30 million loan to Pemex would lead to operating contracts, but that had not happened. Rodgers and Ogarrio of the Texas Company argued that Pemex had intentionally offered contracts that would be unacceptable to American firms in order to enhance the political fortunes of Bermúdez.[33] The companies and the American government had failed to reverse the pattern of Mexican petroleum policy by the early Cold War years. In 1948 Pemex also gained control of 40 percent of Gulf's operations in Mexico, and two years later acquired the remainder. The relative unwillingness of American officials to pursue a hard line in Mexico derived in part from a sense of greater security that accompanied the development of Middle East oil, from a genuine desire to improve the corporate and diplomatic image of the United States in Latin America, and from a highly volatile political situation in Venezuela after 1945.

DEFLECTING VENEZUELAN NATIONALISM

United States petroleum interests appeared especially vulnerable in Venezuela in the immediate postwar years, and there, where the strategic and economic stakes were so high for the United States, American officials were more vigorous than in Mexico in attempting to preserve private American enterprise. Although there were at times differences of approach within both the bureaucracy and the industry, there was little disagreement over the significance of Venezuelan oil for American security. The shift of wartime attention to the Middle East had not altered the basic facts of geography or of investment. Venezuala and Mexico remained close to the United States, more readily defensible in the event of war and with transportation less complex, and hence control of, or assured access to, Venezuelan petroleum reserves remained a major determinant of U.S. policy in the postwar period.

Even during the war, the Venezuelan government had made it clear to American and other foreign oil interests that the companies would be required in future to contribute more significantly to Venezuelan development. In 1943, with the passage of petroleum legislation that February, the Venezuelan government concluded contracts with Shell and with Jersey's affiliate, Creole, that required the companies to construct additional facilities on Venezuelan soil within five years after the conclusion of the war. The contracts also stipulated that 10 percent of the oil produced in new concessions would have to be refined in Venezuela, and that all oil from such concessions that was not so refined would have to be marketed outside the Caribbean area, a clear effort to diversify Venezuelan commercial ties.[34]

With the rise of Acción Democrática (AD) under Rómulo Betancourt and the 1945 revolution, which brought to power an uneasy alliance between AD and the military, the situation in Venezuela became more acute. The companies were now confronted with a more active and complex labor movement as well as a threatened expansion of government controls, and the United States was confronted with what was perceived as a communist threat to American security in the oil industry. Although the Acción Democrática government lent early support to the idea of nationalizing the petroleum industry and gave strong endorsement to the formation in early 1946 of the National Federation of Petroleum Workers, it was either unwilling or politically incapable of pursuing an extreme position on either aspect, gradually moving toward a more moderate position prior to the military coup of November 1948 that drove the party from power for the time being.

In early 1946 the companies were confronted with increased labor militancy and a tightening of government controls. A December 1945 decree, which came into effect early the next year, increased excess-profits taxes, and the Venezuelan government evinced little sign of weakening when the State Department made representations to the effect that such actions would "cause loss of confidence and ... have a definite effect on the influx of new development capital."[35] In fact, the American chargé in Venezuela expressed the view that the Venezuelan decision to increase taxation was premised on an accurate assessment of the very high profits earned in 1945 by both Shell and Jersey Standard affiliates, as well as Venezuelan concern that with the possible diversion of foreign capital and interest to Middle East developments, it was important that Venezuela act promptly to acquire more of the profits accruing at that juncture to foreign enterprise.[36]

The advent of Acción Democrática and the increased militancy of Venezuelan labor compelled a modification in company labor policies. Although Creole continued to refuse to consider worker participation in management decisions or the implementation of the closed shop, it did consent to a collective agreement in mid-1946 following extended negotiations and impending violence. The Venezuelan labor minister, Raúl Leoni, was instrumental in these developments, calling in the oil company officials, having them agree to negotiate and to conclude an eighteen-month collective agreement in June.[37] The government gave the industry little option in accepting a wage increase as part of the settlement. Creole and Shell executives were informed that they would either voluntarily agree to pay Bs 2.00 per day as an integral rather than extra part of salary, as it had been since November 1944, or the settlement would be imposed by decree. These negotiations were important in establishing a *modus vivendi* between the industry and the government and in moving the industry toward a modification of its traditional hard line against Venezuelan labor. Betancourt was able to persuade Creole and Shell officials to convince other foreign companies of the need to accept the settlement. Creole thus moved toward a more cooperative stance with respect to the other companies, having previously tended to attempt to stand alone, and the example of conciliation it now established was effective in moderating those companies that had desired from the outset to bring the conflict to a showdown.[38]

The American government and company officials were nervous over perceived increased communist and Soviet activities in 1946. At the time of the labor crisis in May, the American Embassy in Caracas informed the State Department that a Soviet Embassy officer had been attempting to undermine the position of the United States by making public allegations that American petroleum technology was considerably inferior to that utilized in the Soviet Union.[39] The same month President Truman requested congressional legislation establishing military collaboration with Latin American nations and providing for the training, organization, and equipping of their armed forces.[40]

American military officials were more sensitive to the increased communist activity in Venezuela than was the Department of State. Following consultation among the departments of war, navy, and state in the midst of the spring 1946 labor dispute, the petroleum board hastily drafted a report on the Venezuelan situation in an effort to alert the State Department to the gravity of the situation. Colonel Robert Strong, chief of the western-hemisphere division of the war department, informed the assistant chief of staff that it was believed the oil workers' federation, with a membership of one million, was "falling under the influence of the Russians." Strong urged that the United States dispatch a military mission to Venezuela, an action that had previously been proposed to the secretary of state, that the Department of State should appoint an experienced oil man to the Caracas embassy, and that it should "take steps to counteract Soviet propaganda." Secretary of War Robert Patterson also expressed concern to the State Department that it was not sufficiently alert to the communist threat in Venezuela. The more cautious and conciliatory approach of the State Department was clear at this stage; it was also an important ingredient in facilitating a nonviolent resolution of the companies' negotiations with labor and the Venezuelan government in the spring of 1946. Implying that the war department was unduly concerned, the secretary of state urged that the current situation was not "alarming," that the United States military attaché in Caracas had failed to consult with either the American ambassador or the petroleum attaché prior to alerting the war department. Nonetheless, Byrnes informed the secretary of war, "the present situation ... is one which must be followed carefully and alertly in order that the long range interests of our government and the American petroleum operators may be safeguarded."[41] The dispute was temporarily resolved, but the American military remained unconvinced that the State Department was sufficiently sensitive to the issue. A Joint Chiefs of Staff memorandum for the record indicated that further difficulties could be anticipated, even though it was unlikely that Venezuelan oil would become unavailable to the United States in the near future.[42]

Creole production remained relatively unaffected by increased taxation and labor militancy. The company was the largest oil producer of all Standard Oil of New Jersey affiliates in 1946, with daily production in excess of 450,000 barrels of crude oil and earnings for the year in the vicinity of $100 million. Nonetheless, the company did move with some vigor to establish and expand its social programs in the area of education, housing, and health, and to implement the provisions of the spring 1946 agreement.[43] Such actions did not inhibit the Venezuelan government from initiating further tax increases at the end of the year. Although Creole president Arthur T. Proudfit informed production minister Juan Pablo Pérez Alfonso that such measures would further erode an already-damaged international credit and possibly compel the company to reduce its budget for the year, thus reducing production as well as government revenues, the government was not dissuaded. On 27 December the producers were informed that a new tax law was being submitted to the Constituent Assembly for approval.

An uneasy calm prevailed during the early months of 1947. President Betancourt expressed concerns over the potential revolutionary activity of Venezuelan exiles in the Caribbean, but the State Department continued to extend assurances of good will, and Byrnes expressed the view that the United States had "demonstrated our desire to cooperate in every appropriate manner."[44] Although department officials were not confident of the ability of Acción Democrática to survive, they were more concerned that any revolutionary attempt against the government would result in a protracted civil war that would directly threaten the security of Venezuelan oil.[45] Given the posssible alternatives, increased taxation appeared a relatively minor inconvenience, and the three major companies, Creole, Mene Grande, and Shell, together responsible for some 94 percent of Venezuelan production, proceeded with exploration programs in new areas and efforts to increase production in proven areas. Relations between the Venezuelan government and the companies appeared to have stabilized by late 1947 / early 1948. The violence that ignited more than a decade of civil war in Colombia, beginning with the assassination of Colombian Liberal Jorge Eliecjr Gaitán during the meeting of inter-American states in Bogotá, renewed American anxiety over the vulnerability of Venezuelan petroleum to subversive activity.

In spite of the United States identification of petroleum as an important issue in inter-American relations, it did not propose formal discussions on petroleum for the Bogotá meetings in March 1948. Rather, Secretary of State George Marshall informed American delegates and diplomatic representatives in Latin America that the United States recognized the need for a prompt increase in hemispheric petroleum supplies and requested American officials informally to take appropriate measures to attain that goal.[46] The department informed its representatives that the importance of the question had already been stressed to the Inter-American Defense Board (IADB) and the joint Brazilian-U.S. Defense Commission and that it would be brought shortly to the attention of the comparable Canadian and Mexican commissions. Consistent with American policy, the emphasis remained on the encouragement of private petroleum development, especially in Venezuela, but it was hoped that the possibility remained of returning other nations to that pattern as well.

The policy objective of increasing western-hemisphere production and supply derived explicitly from the concerns expressed by Harold Ickes and others during the war that the United States had borne a disproportionate share of the burden of petroleum supply during the hostilities and that this had contributed to a major drain on American domestic reserves, a drain estimated by the American delegation to the Inter-American Defense Board at one million barrels a day of reserve productive capacity. The delegation noted as well that the United States was still producing 62 percent of current world demand of 9 million barrels a day. American officials argued that the United States continued to expend its nonrenewable petroleum resources at a higher rate than did any other oil-producing nation in the world, a situation it sought to alter for clear security reasons. The United States representatives on the IADB argued that military petroleum requirements in the event of war would be substantially increased beyond the needs of World War II, especially in the area of air power, where requirements for fighter planes and bombers could in themselves equal allocations made to the entire military establishment during World War II. In conclusion the United States urged that "every American nation take those measures necessary to bring about a development of its petroleum resources so that each can assume its full share of responsibility."[47]

Accordingly, at the plenary session of the IADB on 16 March 1948, the chairman, Lieutenant General Matthew B. Ridgway, introduced a resolution that reiterated the concerns of the United States and recommended that the governments of Latin America take prompt measures to increase production, encourage exploration, improve transportation systems, practice conservation measures, and consider inter-American agreements for the cooperative development of petroleum supplies.[48]

In practical terms, American officials in the spring of 1948 remained absorbed with the issue of potential sabotage of Venezuelan petroleum facilities. Department of State officials met in late April with representatives of American oil companies operating in Venezuela, a member of the petroleum board, and Colonel P.L. Freeman, of the Intelligence Division, General Staff. The impression was given at that meeting that the Department of State would actively assist the companies by providing counter-sabotage experts and technicians, but military officials subsequently learned to their chagrin that no action had been taken. The Department of State raised the question with the FBI only to be informed that the agency no longer operated outside the United States, although it had been in the Venezuelan fields during World War II, and the CIA evidently proved uncooperative. Colonel Freeman suggested to the director of plans and operations, General Staff, that the director of intelligence should confer with the CIA to determine the most effective means of cooperation between the agency and the companies. Except for ensuring cooperation, Freeman concluded that there was little the military could do short of direct intervention in the oil fields in the event they were endangered.[49] American officials expressed relief when May day passed without incident in Venezuela, but the American Embassy continued to encourage the use of counter-sabotage experts, and the Latin American branch of the operations and plans division noted that the plans for U.S. intervention prepared by the Caribbean command had been submitted to the joint chief "with a recommendation that they be approved for emergency use with proper authority."[50] Secretary of Defense James Forrestal indicated to the secretary of state that the military establishment did not believe Venezuela capable of defending the petroleum installations against communist activity. "The effective protection of this oil resource," Forrestal added, "is so vital to the defense of the Western Hemisphere and to the United States in any possible future effort that the Military Establishment considers that the United States must be prepared to defend these installations at any time such action appears necessary."[51]

The United States also approached the Netherlands government in an effort to ensure the security of refining facilities and harbors at Aruba and Curaçao, which American military officials identified as especially vulnerable to attack. The Netherlands government proved unreceptive to an American proposal to negotiate a formal agreement for U.S. military participation in the defense of the islands but did consent to permit the United States to station a liaison officer from the Caribbean command in Curaçao. The Venezuelan government proved equally opposed to a military assistance agreement with the United States.[52]

Failing substantial bilateral cooperation, American officials continued to pursue measures designed to protect strategic resources. In early October, President Truman approved National Security Council document 29, which empowered the secretary of state to request the CIA to make surveys of the security of specific industrial operations in foreign countries that furnished materials of strategic importance to the United States. The CIA would also be authorized to devise plans for the protection of such industrial operations and to keep them under surveillance. It was clear by the fall of 1948 that the United States was prepared to take firm and decisive action to secure the strategic resources of the western hemisphere. Although Middle Eastern petroleum was beginning to make its presence felt in the United States in 1948, production in Venezuela remained of paramount importance for American petroleum security, since it was the only Latin American producer with substantial excess production available for export.

The policies of Acción Democrática only moderately threatened that security of supply. By 1948 the Venezuelan government had abandoned the intention to nationalize petroleum resources, even though such action continued to hold popular appeal. Venezuela's decision to market its royalty oil independent of foreign enterprise was disruptive of marketing patterns but posed no threat to the United States. Nor did the application of the so-called 50/50 principle to the allocation of petroleum revenues between the government and the companies, a measure that was implemented as an amendment to the income tax act of 1948. Even with this substantial increase in taxation, Creole, for example, continued to expand production and remained internationally competitive.[53]

After November 1948 and the military coup that swept Acción Democrática from power, such issues became largely academic. One of the first acts of the new military junta was to dissolve the Venezuelan labor federation and then the oil workers' union.[54] Although such measures were not in the long term successful, Venezuela by early 1949 appeared to have been stabilized and the security of petroleum supplies at least temporarily assured. Although there is no evidence of American complicity in the defeat of AD, it is also clear that there was little mourning over the smoothness of the transition to military control.

THE MIDDLE EAST, 1945–1948

Several developments of critical significance occurred in this period to shape oil policy. Among the most important was the end of the Red Line Agreement in its original form, involving a corporate restructuring in the region; the emergence of Cold War-charged issues, notably in Iran; difficulties over the monetary and commercial relations of Britain and the U.S.; and a lengthy emotional and sharply political debate over the fate of Palestine, a debate that was intertwined with continued consideration of pipeline development in the area to provide readier access to the Mediterranean from the Arabian peninsula.

Cold War considerations had by 1945 added a new and vital dimension to the evolution of U.S. foreign oil policy in the region. The end of the war presented American policymakers with the need to develop mechanisms to ensure the security of supply from the oil-rich region, although there were differences of opinion over how that security might best be attained. For the companies, the main issues remained the rationalization of production, price controls, and marketing arrangements to avoid excessive competition. With the end of the war, production capacity was in excess of peacetime markets held by the producing companies. In the view of John Loftus, this situation was favorable for the encouragement of increased competition among Gulf, Anglo-Iranian, and Arabian-American on the one hand and Shell, Jersey, and Socony on the other.[55] Loftus's evident preference for expanded competition was frustrated, however, both by the realities of U.S. strategic interests in the Middle East and by the companies, which succeeded in maintaining a cartel-like structure for pricing and marketing, with Anglo-Iranian, Gulf, and Aramco aligning themselves with the three large marketing companies. The tension between those who saw the continued consolidation of American corporate power as an instrument of American diplomacy in the Middle East and those, like Loftus, who believed that American adherence to an Open Door world with a competitive structure was more in keeping with the rhetoric of postwar economic liberalization provided one of the important themes in postwar planning.

One of the factors that led the U.S. to support a strong corporate structure in the region was the desire to contain the Soviet Union. That objective was evident in relations with Iran in the 1944-6 years. As in other areas, the Iranian situation demonstrated the importance of strategic rather than purely commercial hegemony as the objective of policy. Here as elsewhere, the flag did not simply follow the advance of American corporate power; but there was a critical juncture of interests between the companies and the Roosevelt and Truman administrations that served to produce a more cohesive policy. Under a 1942 agreement, Soviet, British, and American troops occupied Iran during the war in order to protect the region from the German advance. As the war drew to a close, American companies and Soviet interests jockeyed for oil concessions. Secretary of State James Byrnes accurately captured the prevailing State Department view when he observed in 1945 that Iran was a key to the "development of American commercial, petroleum, and aviation interests in the Middle East."[56]

The crisis that emerged in Iran in 1944-6 was only in part over oil concessions; it must, as well, be viewed in the context of the larger deterioration of Soviet-American relations over Greece, Turkey, Eastern Europe, and the decline of British power in the Mediterranean. These developments contributed directly to the articulation of the Truman Doctrine in March 1947, and the implementation of the policy of containment and of Marshall Plan aid to Europe.[57]

During the war, the Iranian government managed to defuse some of

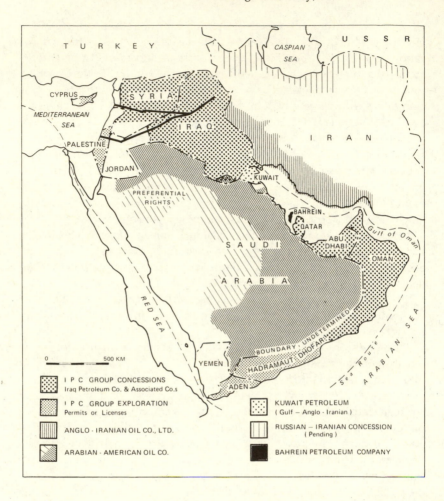

FIGURE 2
Oil concessions in the Near and Middle East, 1945 (source: file 36-1-30, RG 80, National
Archives USA)

the tensions over the postwar petroleum industry in the country by postponing the granting of any concessions until after the defeat of Germany. When the debate resumed in 1945–6, the issues for all parties in the dispute were much broader than simply the control of oil. For the Soviet Union, Iran's proximity to its own borders, the contiguous nature of oil resources between Iran and the USSR, and a larger spectrum of disagreements with the U.S. made the Iranian situation attain significant proportions. As historian Thomas Paterson argued a decade ago, the Soviet Union found itself in 1945 confronted by British dominance of the oil industry (with the likelihood of American participation), the presence of British and American military forces on the southern borders of the USSR (where they might threaten Soviet installations), and a pro-Western Iranian government. In a typically penetrating assessment of the political realties of the situation, U.S. attaché in Moscow George Kennan reported in 1944 that Soviet activity in northern Iran was prompted by concern over strategic security rather than over oil.[58] Regardless of who was the aggressor, the chemistry in 1945 provided for an explosive mixture. In northern Iran, in Azerbaijan, the Soviet-backed revolutionary Tudeh party in mid-1945 revolted against Iranian authority in an effort to gain autonomy. Soviet forces interfered with Iranian attempts to restore control, and in December Azerbaijan declared its independence. During the following year, British and U.S. troops withdrew from Iran in accordance with the 1942 treaty, as well as in an effort to compel the Soviet Union to honor its treaty obligations. In addition, the Iranian government, with Washington's support, took the question of Soviet interference to the United Nations Security Council in early 1946. Although this had no conclusive result, the Soviets did agree to attempt to settle the dispute through bilateral negotiations. The USSR made withdrawal conditional on the granting of an oil concession to Soviet interests. They reached agreement in April 1946 on essentially those terms: Soviet troop withdrawal in return for the establishment of an Iranian-Soviet oil company.[59]

Although such a development might have been consistent with the anticipated liberalization of commerce after the war, the possibility of the Soviet Union gaining a substantial foothold in Iranian petroleum resources was perceived as a direct threat to American security. The Joint Chiefs of Staff identified the oil fields of Iran, Iraq, and Saudi Arabia as "absolutely vital to the security of the U.S." Working within those guidelines, the American ambassador to Iran, George Allen, sought vigorously and successfully to undermine any pro-Soviet inclinations on the part of the Iranian prime minister, Admad Qavam, in part by cultivating the anti-Soviet shah and also by providing several millions of dollars in United States military aid to assist in the pacification of Azerbaijan.[60]

The result of relentless U.S. pressure and diplomacy was the gradual reversal of the initial direction of Iranian policy toward Soviet participation in the oil industry, with the denouement coming in the fall of 1947, when the Iranian Parliament failed to ratify the proposed Iranian-Soviet oil company. As well, Anglo-Iranian in late 1946 reached agreement with American oil companies to participate in the marketing of Iranian oil, in part satisfying American corporate and diplomatic objectives.[61]

When a new oil consortium was later formed in Iran in 1954, American companies held a 40 percent interest. Clearly Loftus's desire to attain a higher level of private-sector competition was not consistent with the general direction of policy, in which a strong corporate presence was considered coincident with American security. This preference for development to be under American corporate control was evident in the early 1947 discussions between Anglo-Iranian and Jersey Standard over the development of a pipeline. State Department officials indicated at that stage that the desire was for any pipeline company to be an American corporation in order to "enhance U.S. prestige in the Middle East"; such an arrangement, it was explained, would free the company from any difficulties it might face as a British company, including the availability of scarce steel supplies for construction that would have to come from the United States; it was also contended that American security in the region would be more effectively protected with a company that was subject to U.S. government direction in the event of an emergency.[62] It is striking that the same argument was employed against the Petroleum Reserve Corporation's proposed pipeline during the war, and under the PRC scheme, the American government would have been a more direct participant.

In the Iranian crisis that emerged in 1945–6, it is difficult to distinguish between oil itself as a determinant of policy and the larger considerations of Cold War politics. There does appear to be convincing evidence that the Iranian developments contributed significantly to the general evolution of Soviet-American relations, the place of the United States in the Middle East, and the broad issue of European recovery. Historian Thomas Paterson has noted, for instance, that American policy toward Iran was incorporated, along with the response to developments in Greece and Turkey, into drafts of the Truman Doctrine speech in early 1947.[63] Equally significant is the fact that as planners outlined the basic features of postwar policy between 1945 and 1948, oil was a vital component of what one historian has referred to as the search for a "creative peace," involving resource management and joint international programs to promote productivity and abundance through European recovery.[64] The United States sought in these years not only to contain Soviet expansion into Iran through the Iranian extension of oil concessions in the country, but also to use Middle East oil as a component of the effort to rebuild the European economy for economic and strategic reasons. In 1946 less than 25 percent of European petroleum requirements was met from Middle Eastern production; the remainder was imported from the western hemisphere. If the pattern could be reversed, it would provide a source closer to Europe as well as fulfill one objective of American policy, which was to conserve hemisphere resources. Thus it is not surprising that oil should have become an important feature in the Marshall Plan, although those developments lie outside the chronological scope of this study.[65]

It was important to the oil companies that the European Recovery Program expand the capacity of European countries to import oil products. United States-owned companies operating abroad were major suppliers of European demand, and European nations clearly required American dollars to meet their obligations. Marshall Plan agencies, including the Economic Cooperation Administration and the Mutual Security Agency, played a critical role in providing that exchange.[66] The exchange shortage as well as the capacity of American firms to market in Europe and within the British sphere was further exacerbated by British sterling-bloc policies. During the war Britain had frozen all non-sterling currencies deposited in London from sterling-area countries, which included Australia, Burma, Egypt, Erie, India, Iraq, Iceland, New Zealand, South Africa, the United Kingdom, and British colonies and mandates. At the end of the war, those non-sterling deposits remained blocked, thus, in the view of American commercial and diplomatic interests, hampering both American trade and the European recovery objectives. It was not until the end of 1945 that British-American negotiations led to the conclusion of the Anglo-American Financial Agreement, which would allow the sterling bloc to convert its sterling to dollars, and the provision was not implemented until mid-1947. Even then problems remained. Britain allowed British-owned oil companies to market products outside the sterling bloc, but U.S. companies were required to accept sterling remittances within the sterling area. In addition, bilateral sterling arrangements between producing countries and Britain on oil sales sometimes threatened the markets of U.S.-owned oil companies, as was the case with Argentina and the Scandinavian countries by early 1949.[67]

Equally significant in shaping the development of oil policy in the Middle East were the postwar debates over the status of Palestine and the development of a trans-Arabian pipeline to link the Arabian fields with the eastern Mediterranean.[68] The failure of the wartime initiative by Harold Ickes and the Petroleum Reserves Corporation to bring an

Arabian pipeline project to fruition under government auspices shifted much of the momentum to the private sector. Yet a strong coincidence of interest between the private sector and the state continued to operate in shaping policy. The objectives of American policy remained the security, development, and improved availability of Middle Eastern oil for both military ends and to aid in the economic reconstruction of Europe. The same developments would clearly enhance the commercial interests of American companies in the region. Thus corporate expansion and consolidation in the area during the Truman administration occurred with strong state encouragement.

The debate over the policy to be followed toward Palestine and the Tapline (Trans-Arabian Pipeline) project demonstrated the extent to which the close working relationship that had evolved during the preceding years, especially during the war, continued to affect postwar planning. The debates also underlined the preference of policymakers that state involvement should not include the operational and commercial levels of the foreign oil industry. The war and immediate prewar years had also, however, added a greater sense of strategic urgency and recognition of the need to demonstrate American willingness to share the wealth of third-world oil development. This view was embodied in general in an "Instruction on Petroleum Reporting" (prepared by the head of the petroleum division in the State Department in 1946, John Loftus), which was sent to all appropriate U.S. missions abroad and to thirteen major oil companies. In that communication, Loftus reiterated the adherence of the United States not only to traditional Open Door principles of equality of commercial opportunity, but also to the special considerations that pertained to oil. Oil, he noted, was not, because of its strategic importance in national defense, simply an ordinary commodity in international trade, and the United States would need to ensure that valid concession contracts and exploration and development rights were protected. At the same time, the instruction indicated that the "interests of producing countries should be safeguarded with a view to their economic advancement." This general principle was applied during consideration of the efforts to obtain transit rights for pipeline companies in the Middle East. As negotiations progressed over the Transjordan, the State Department emphasized that "whatever the historical precedents, Transjordan is entitled to receive proportionate compensation." The department further stressed that Truman administration policy was that "future pipeline and refining concessions in Near and Middle Eastern countries should reflect full recognition of [the] principle that countries that contribute ... to development of petroleum resources should receive fair and reasonable compensation."[70]

The completion of a pipeline from the Arabian oil fields to the eastern Mediterranean was viewed as strategically and commercially valuable at the end of the war. It would reduce the dependency on tankers in the Persian Gulf in the event of war, as well as facilitate the movement of Middle Eastern oil to Europe to aid in the European recovery program. At the same time, from Aramco's perspective, it would enhance its marketing capabilities. Consequently, from 1946 on, Aramco worked vigorously to obtain the necessary transit rights in the region and the required diplomatic and materials support for the Trans-Arabian Pipeline Company. Between 1946 and the final completion of the pipeline in 1950, the success of the project was in frequent jeopardy because of shifting American priorities, shortages of such critical materials as steel, and the complications infused into the debate by the conflict over the partition of Palestine, the recognition of Israel, and the first Arab-Israeli war.[71]

The larger story of the dramatic events that surrounded the creation of Israel has been told elsewhere, and the concern here is with the way in which that debate affected oil policy. In 1947 Britain announced its intent to terminate its control over the Palestine mandate and the following year withdrew, leaving behind an explosive Arab-Jewish relationship in Palestine and the region as a whole. The Truman administration, in spite of reservations held by the departments of state and defense, immediately recognized the newly created state of Israel. The essential consideration that motivated reservations in defense and state was the fear that such recognition would threaten relations with the Arab states, weaken the ability to contain the spread of communism, and endanger the security of American oil installations in the region. Loy Henderson, director of the Office of Near Eastern and African Affairs, specifically argued that American interests in the region depended on harmonious relations with the Arab states, and his views were reinforced by military planners, who saw Saudi Arabian oil as a vital component of American defense against the Soviet Union.[72] Nevertheless, what is critical for an understanding of the American decision to recognize Israel, as historian Irvine Anderson has persuasively argued in recent years, is that the Truman administration appeared to be willing to risk harmonious relations with the Arab oil-producing states by recognizing Israel as a Jewish homeland. It was a calculated risk, and clearly the administration hoped that it would be able to weather the storm that might ensue.

Aramco's efforts to complete the pipeline project thus transpired within a highly volatile international context in the region. By the time that the U.S. recognized Israel in 1948, Tapline already had agreement for transit rights with Lebanon and Saudi Arabia and an agreement with Syria was pending Syrian ratification. That ratification and the entire project were delayed by recognition of Israel and the outbreak of war. Delays notwithstanding, State Department officials remained convinced that the completion of the pipeline was important not only to American petroleum security and the containment of the Soviet Union, but also, with the recognition of Israel, as a way in which the U.S. could demonstrate good faith to Saudi Arabia. To such officials as Loy Henderson, completion of the pipeline was made even more diplomatically urgent by the dispute over the status of Israel. Henderson's views were clearly shared at the time by Secretary of State George Marshall, who during the course of the year resisted opposition from the Department of Commerce because of steel shortages, and from the domestic independent petroleum producers, and continued to emphasize the important place of the project in American Cold War strategy. Even with that support, it was not until 1949 that additional steel exports were authorized to advance the project and the transit-rights agreement ratified by Syria. Early the following year, Tapline pumped its first oil from Saudi Arabia to its Mediterranean terminal in Lebanon,[74] and the Truman administration was vindicated in its belief that it could achieve that objective in spite of its policy toward Israel. That the project was brought to successful completion demonstrated once again, however, the coincidence of public and private commercial and strategic interests.

THE END OF THE RED LINE

Simultaneous with the vital debate over Palestine and the Arabian pipeline, a major corporate restructuring occurred in the Middle East. In 1948, following two years of intricate corporate and diplomatic maneuvers and threatened litigation, the 1928 Red Line Agreement was dissolved and the companies involved entered into a new agreement. From the ashes of the earlier arrangement for the operation of the Iraq Petroleum Company (IPC) emerged a reorganized company for Iraq and an expanded Arabian American Oil Company for Saudi Arabia, combining Jersey Standard, Caltex (Standard of California and the Texas Company), and Socony-Vacuum. That dissolution and corporate restructuring marked the climax of thirty years of oil development and diplomacy in the Middle East since World War I, and epitomized the triumph of private initiative and control over American oil operations in the region. In terms of American foreign policy, the modification of the old Red Line arrangements signaled the end of the fruitful initiatives taken during World War II, to establish foreign oil policy on the basis of a firmer relationship with the companies in an effort to link the latter more effectively to government policy objectives. That the American companies were able to extricate themselves from the twenty-year-old arrangement of the Iraq Petroleum Company and the American corporate monopoly in Saudi Arabian oil development was clear indication of the altered power balance in the region, with the expansion of the American business and diplomatic presence in the area and the decline of British power. The end of the old Red Line Agreement and the apparent willingness to support further cartelization of the industry also reflected waning enthusiasm in official circles for a truly international approach to petroleum resource development.[75]

American efforts to restructure the Red Line Agreement to reduce or remove the restrictive conditions of the original document derived largely from the private sector and were closely related to investment and marketing considerations. Nonetheless, for both political and strategic reasons, that initiative was firmly endorsed and actively supported through diplomacy by the Department of State, even though some officials would have preferred to have avoided the cartel-oriented nature of the final agreement. These developments did not indicate a significant shift in post-1945 policy that some historians, such as Irvine Anderson in his study of Aramco, have identified, but rather the failure of the statist initiative of Harold Ickes and others to gain adequate support for implementation. Extricating American enterprise from the Red Line Agreement was entirely consistent with the basic trend of U.S. foreign oil policy since 1919, with its emphasis on security of petroleum supply through officially supported private development of oveseas resources. Anderson's analysis does tend, however, to confirm my own findings that the basic initiative came from the companies in 1946, and that they had sustained diplomatic support in dealing with the initially reluctant British and the more serious French opposition to the termination of the 1928 accord.

For both Jersey Standard and Socony, the Red Line Agreement had by 1945 become a commercial encumbrance. Jersey found itself especially vulnerable to the marketing implications of substantially increased production, over which it did not exercise control, in the Middle East. Jersey officials believed that the Red Line arrangement was largely responsible for the fact that it was short of crude oil supplies at the end of the war. Although its Venezuelan subsidiary, Creole, was the world's largest producing company in 1946, its Iraq subsidiary produced only 9300 barrels a day. Jersey officials anticipated that the situation in the Middle East could be alleviated if they were able to extricate the company from the restrictions of 1928 and make arrangements with Caltex for the supply of additional crude oil. The situation was compounded by the fact that Gulf Oil was able to bring in its first wells in

Kuwait in 1946 and in the following year to conclude a twelve-year contract with Shell to supply the latter with Kuwait production. Shell required that oil to meet its own commitments in Europe and Africa, as well as to maintain its position under the "As Is" agreements that had been negotiated since 1928. The Gulf-Shell contract prohibited Gulf from disturbing Shell and Anglo-Iranian markets in which Gulf itself was not established. Shell also agreed to supply to Anglo-Iranian markets some of the oil acquired from Gulf. Some years later, by 1950, Gulf's Kuwait production was sufficiently in excess of Shell requirements that Gulf had to import its crude oil into the U.S., because the western hemisphere was the only area in which Anglo-Iranian did not operate. Anglo-Iranian signed similar purchase and marketing agreements with Jersey Standard and Socony-Vacuum in 1947 as the old Red Line broke down. In the Jersey contract Anglo-Iranian agreed to sell to Jersey 800 million barrels of crude oil over a twenty-year period, in return for which Jersey would provide financing and become part owner of an Iraq-to-Mediterranean pipeline, as well as agree not to market that oil in territories east of Suez. From Jersey's perspective, the Red Line prohibition on its participation in the development of new oil resources within the area defined by the Red Line was no longer acceptable. Jersey officials were especially anxious to participate in Saudi Arabian development, and with the objective opened negotiations with Caltex in May 1946. For Caltex, Jersey and possibly Socony-Vacuum participation in Arabian development would reduce their own financial risks and investments and would also provide them with access for Saudi oil to Jersey and Socony marketing areas.[76]

During 1945 Jersey and Socony sought ways to circumvent the 1928 agreement. B.R. Jackson, the New York representative for Anglo-Iranian, informed J.E. Taylor of Anglo-Iranian in London that Socony officials were convinced on the basis of legal advice that the Red Line did not prevent them from purchasing oil products, as distinct from crude oil, from non-IPC companies within the Red Line area. The Anglo-Saxon Petroleum Company received a similar legal opinion from Patrick Devlin, KC, in early December 1945. This view, which would have extended the sources of supply for Jersey and Socony, was one of the factors that weakened the resolve of the British companies to insist on the maintenance of the Red Line Agreement, even though they opposed the American interpretation at the group meeting in London the following May. In October, at the conclusion of further group meetings, Harold Sheets, acting for the Near East Development Corporation and Socony, and Orville Harden, acting for Jersey Standard, officially informed the Anglo-Saxon Petroleum Company that they were treating the 1928 agreement as dissolved and that they were interested in negotiating a new agreement. Both the American and British companies by this stage appear to have felt secure in the view that the agreement would have to be renegotiated because of the legal opinion advanced that Nazi occupation in France, which brought CFP (Compagnie Française des Pétroles) under German control in principle, voided the 1928 agreement. By 1947, the American firms were able to appease Anglo-Iranian with offers to purchase large volumes of crude oil from Iran and Kuwait.[77]

Before the fall meetings of the IPC group, Sheets had raised the subject of the companies' intentions with Charles Rayner in New York. Sheets indicated that he urged Rayner to "get Byrnes' and Acheson's support to request the British Government to join with U.S.A. in bringing about the elimination of the Red Line restrictions and Kuwait restrictions as soon as possible." In Sheets's opinion, the State Department petroleum adviser agreed with this approach.[78]

News that the American companies were seeking an agreement of Saudi Arabia reached the press in December 1946. The French group issued a writ on the other members of the group and later on IPC, seeking a declaration by the English courts that the 1928 agreement continued to have force, and an injunction against Jersey and Socony to prevent them from joining in Aramco. At the same time, the French desired some revisions in the 1928 arrangements and made it clear that a basic feature of any new agreement would be provision for more rapid development of the jointly owned Iraq properties than had prevailed earlier. The French also insisted in early 1947 that the 1928 agreement had been one among governments, not simply private enterprise, and interpreted the Open Door principle as providing equal participation in development, rather than the American preference for equal opportunity. Although the State Department was prompt to deny formal U.S. participation in the 1928 agreement, the French interpretation accurately depicted the spirit in which the Coolidge administration had endorsed the entry of the Near East Development Corporation into Iraq.[79]

The State Department had been anxious for some time to end the Red Line restrictions, in part to ensure adequate American participation in Saudi Arabian development to protect the concession, but also because production restrictions created frictions with host nations, as well as with other members of the Iraq Petroleum Company. In early 1944, during consideration of the Anglo-American petroleum agreement, John Loftus wrote to Ralph Davies that the U.S. government could make a good case that the Red Line was inconsistent with the stated objectives of the proposed agreement. He also recognized that they would be in a weak position to request the abrogation of a private agreement that had already accomplished its purposes. Most of the old Ottoman empire had been mapped under IPC and Caltex concessions. There was also the problem of whether a marketing arrangement of a cartel character was inconsistent with the purposes of the intended Anglo-American agreement.[80]

By 1946, however, that agreement was lifeless, and the State Department was compelled to find other means to achieve American regional goals. When the department in late 1946 contemplated the implications of a proposed crude-oil contract between Jersey and Socony on the one hand and Anglo-Iranian on the other, another contract between Gulf Oil and Shell, and the proposed acquisition by Jersey and Socony of a substantial stock share in Aramco, John Loftus initially indicated that there should be no objections to the transactions. At the same time, Loftus had some reservations about the implications of both Jersey and Socony entering Aramco. He recognized that with the end of the war, production capacity was in excess of peacetime markets held by the producing companies, and increased competition could be expected between Gulf, Anglo-Iranian, and Arabian American on the one hand, and the established, principal marketing firms, Jersey, Shell, and Socony. The deals evolving in the Middle East promised to alter the situation and reduce competition, and Loftus queried whether another arrangement might not be more in the public interest and more consistent with present American foreign economic policy. "It is believed," he noted, that "the case is strong for discouraging ... the further development of joint operations and joint interests between and among the large international oil companies."[81]

In late 1946 and early 1947, company and government officials consulted formally on the negotiations, with departments of state, navy, war, the attorney general, and the Oil and Gas Division of the Department of the Interior contributing to discussions. Support for the Aramco project from these departments was extensive, because it promised to provide some reasonable security of oil supply, end the limitations of the Red Line Agreement, and allow the United States government to maintain the appearance of nondirect involvement. There remained Loftus's concerns with the cartelization features of the agreement and the implications of the French protest. At a meeting in early January 1947 involving Loftus, William Clayton (assistant secretary of state for economic affairs), other department officials, and Orville Harden, Jersey vice-president, Harold Sheets, Socony chairman, and Brewster Jennings, Socony president, the companies argued that they were on sound territory in spite of the French claim. They recognized the seriousness of the French claim, but contended that it could be overcome, and argued that the Aramco deal was in the best interest of the

United States. The State Department agreed to make an effort to explain to France the political impossibility of its participation in the Saudi Arabian concession, and it was stressed that the U.S. government did not desire the companies to withdraw from the project or reaffirm the restrictive clauses of 1928. There was no uncertainty in the department on the desirability of keeping Britain and France out of Saudi Arabia and consolidating American control, but the department shared Loftus's individual concern about the antitrust implications of the Aramco stock purchase plans. In a draft letter to each of the four companies in February, the department expressed reservations that the arrangement might conflict with U.S. trade policites embodied in proposals for the expansion of world trade and employment in the charter of the International Trade Organization as well as with domestic laws pertaining to the restraint of trade.[82]

The justice department held even stronger views on the antitrust implications of the agreement. In 1946-8, department officials conducted an investigation of cartel operations that involved a file search of the foreign records of Jersey Standard and Socony-Vacuum; at the same time it studied the general relationship among the seven main international oil firms active in the Middle East, paying particular attention to the Red Line agreements of 1928 and the 1948 reorganization and to the Aramco agreement of 1947.[83]

In early March 1947, Jersey and Socony officials met again with Department of State officials, including Paul Nitze, deputy director of the Office of International Trade Policy; George McGhee, special assistant to Clayton and his representative at the meeting, and John Loftus. Socony's understanding of the conclusions reached at the meeting was that the department wished a settlement that would minimize friction with France and avoid charges that the United States government had endorsed a monopolistic corporate arrangement in the Middle East.[84]

The U.S. did not formally reply to the French protest until early April. When it did, it stressed that in its view the restrictive features of the original 1928 agreement were incompatible with U.S. international economic policy. Unable to gain support or even a sympathetic hearing in the United States or Britain, French interests backed away from a confrontation, settling for improved production arrangements in a reorganized IPC. Calouste Gulbenkian as well agreed to terms on the eve of court consideration in Great Britain of the French grievance, with the result that the companies were saved a likely lengthy and certainly awkward public investigation into their operations in the Middle East. The 1948 agreement canceled that of 1928, but the new arrangement was similar except for the one main provision that allowed the Near East Development Corporation to become a stockholder in Aramco without accounting to the other parties involved in IPC for the proportion of Aramco's production that was marketed by Jersey Standard and Socony. This arrangement significantly strengthened the positions of both companies. Jersey, Texaco, and Standard of California emerged as equal partners in Aramco with 30 percent stock control for each firm, with Socony holding 10 percent. The agreement in general expanded American corporate dominance over the area, which gave every indication at the time of becoming the major oil field in the world, where twenty-five years earlier the United States had possessed neither diplomatic nor corporate presence of any significance.[85]

The Senate Foreign Relations Subcommittee on Multinational Corporations concluded in its 1975 report that the corporate ability to "straddle IPC and Aramco ... was an important part of the allocation

TABLE 6
Control of World Oil by Major Oil Companies, 1951

Country	Percent of world reserves	Companies							
		Standard Oil (NJ)	Socony	Gulf	Standard Oil (Cal.)	Texas	Shell	Anglo-Iranian	Group control
United States	35.75	x	x	x	x	x	x		33.6
Canada	0.64	x	x	x	x	x	x		75.0
Venezuela	11.49	x		x			x		100.0
Colombia	0.38	x	x			x	x		100.0
Argentina	0.32						x		10.0
Trinidad	0.32						x		10.0
Peru	0.21	x					x		98.0
Europe*	0.24	x					x	x	10.0
Africa	0.16						x		10.0
Kuwait	13.98			x				x	100.0
Saudi Arabia	11.49	x	x		x	x			100.0
Iran	8.94							x	100.0
Iraq	6.39	x	x				x	x	100.0
Qatar	0.64	x	x				x	x	100.0
Bahrein	0.08				x	x			100.0
Indonesia	1.28	x	x		x	x	x		100.0
Borneo	0.19						x		100.0
Burma	0.06						x		100.0
New Guinea	0.06	x	x		x	x	x		100.0
All Others	7.38								
Total world	100								66.75

x Indicates corporate presence.
* Outside the Soviet Union and the Soviet bloc.

Sources: Department of Justice memorandum, 14 January 1952, file 60-57-140, and U.S. Federal Trade Commission report, 1951.

system run by the American multinational petroleum corporations during the 1950s and 1960s." The committee also concluded, accurately in
my view, that the continued presence of Jersey and Socony in IPC contributed to what the French and Iraq had feared – the uneven production performance from Iraqi fields – and helped to create what in 1960
led to the Iraqi nationalization of the properties.[86] At the same time, the
Aramco merger, combined with the reorganization of IPC with government endorsement, contradicted the rhetoric of economic liberalization
in postwar American foreign policy. The transaction confirmed that the
United States was concerned less with the freedom of competition than
with the fact that the old Red Line had hampered American economic
strength in a major oil-producing region of the world. In 1947, as in
1928, American officials assumed that United States strategic influence
in the region depended on the strength of the private sector, but
American policy failed to provide the means to ensure control over the
companies; yet, it was assumed that the companies provided a vehicle
for the attainment of larger strategic and diplomatic objectives. Such
policy could be successful only if the companies shared the basic objectives of the state or if the state had the means to compel corporate compliance with government decisions. In the decades prior to 1948, company and state often differed over short-term objectives and policy, and
a series of administrations failed to create any mechanism of enforcement.

CHAPTER TEN

From Korea to OPEC

The 1950s and early 1960s witnessed dramatic developments in international relations in which the exploitation of oil resources and the security of supply played a significant role in foreign policy as well as in industrial development. The global reach of the United States – indeed of all the major military and industrial nations – and the increasingly high levels of consumerism in the United States, especially the love affair with the automobile, exacted ever heavier demands on oil production for military and civilian use. Rising demand provided significant commercial opportunities for both domestic producers and the multinational oil companies, but increasing expansion of overseas production of comparatively inexpensive supplies, particularly in the Near and Middle East, also exacerbated some of the traditional tensions between those domestic producers and importers, tensions which to some extent came to a head during the Eisenhower administration and the debate over oil import quotas.

The Cold War and East-West tensions provided both cause and context in which U.S. foreign oil policy evolved in the post-1950 years. Oil was certainly not the only factor that determined the areas of the world where U.S. policymakers focused their energies. Nonetheless, in countries and regions where oil resources were already well developed or held massive potential and where Soviet interests rubbed against American interests or those of its major allies, such as Great Britain, U.S. policymakers in the Truman, Eisenhower, and Kennedy administrations sought to take actions that would advance political and economic stability and protect U.S. national security. Venezuela and Mexico retained their importance as oil producers in this period, and Canada, following the discoveries in the Leduc fields in 1947, gradually gained recognition for its potential. Nonetheless, it was the Near and Middle East that increasingly absorbed U.S. attention, especially with the declining capacity of Great Britain to control this region where it had long held hegemony. The United States was confronted not only with the declining capacity of Great Britain but also with the looming shadow of the Soviet Union over the area and an increasing sense of nationalism in many of the area's countries. Maintaining governments supportive of Western interests in the Near and Middle East thus became a challenge as well as a priority, and that challenge became especially acute in Iran in the course of the decade. Tensions and open conflicts over the establishment of the state of Israel further complicated both regional and global politics. In the case of Egypt and the Suez Canal in the mid-1950s, Cold War rivalries, Egyptian nationalism, and anti-Israel sentiments converged to create a particularly volatile chemistry.

THE KOREAN WAR

Before the Iranian and Egyptian situations reached crisis levels, world attention shifted to the Korean peninsula. The massive invasion of North Korean forces across the 38th parallel in June 1950 turned the Cold War into active military engagement for the following four years. The swiftness of the Truman administration's response and its capacity to mobilize the UN and its Western allies reflected the U.S. commitment to a policy of containment in East Asia, especially an area so close to Japan and on China's borders. The outbreak of war in Korea in June 1950 came hard on the heels of World War II, in the context of an already unstable Cold War world order characterized by intense jockeying for global influence between the Soviet Union and the United States and its allies. In mobilizing industry and natural resources for war, American officials logically looked to the recent experience of World War II. In energy, mobilization required a close working relationship between government and the private sector, and that in turn necessitated once again facilitating cooperation among the companies in the oil industry and suppressing antitrust considerations. President Truman was decisive in preventing the publication of a Federal Trade Commission report in 1952 on the oil cartels specifically because such a report could be detrimental to U.S. foreign policy and national security. Paul Nitze, then Director of the Policy Planning Staff at the Department of State, reported on a meeting he and Dean Acheson held in September 1952 with Terry Duce and Fred Davies of Aramco concerning the challenges of American oil companies operating abroad. At the meeting Duce demonstrated that the oil reserves of the Middle East were at least three times those of the United States and would be a serious loss to Western nations were they to fall under communist control. Although Acheson in particular was concerned with any action that seemed to bypass the antitrust laws, especially so close to a presidential election, there was general agreement that the challenges in the oil sector were of sufficient national interest to the United States and other nations that "international arrangements rather than purely national ones might be required."[1]

Perceptions remained constant on this issue in the transition from the Truman to the Eisenhower administrations. A joint report of the Departments of State, Defense, and Interior in early 1953 stressed that the indictment and trial of the major American international oil companies would be "harmful to critical American foreign policy objectives."[2] Security of oil supplies was considerably less of a challenge during the Korean War than it had been during World War II, given the localized nature of the Korean conflict. The United States and its UN allies engaged in Korea did not have to worry about security of international shipping, or the German submarines that during World War II had prowled the Atlantic, Mediterranean, and Caribbean preying on allied vessels. Nonetheless, by the early 1950s other security challenges had emerged to contribute to anxiety in Washington. Although Middle East resources had yet to be fully developed, they were still highly important, even though Venezuelan and Mexican resources, if needed, were securely located. Approximately 40 percent of oil production in the Middle East at the outbreak of the Korean War came from Iran, and the refineries of Anglo-Iranian Oil were an important source of aviation fuel. Iran's oil production, its conflictual border relations with the Soviet Union and potentially delicate internal politics made it a high security priority for the United States and Great Britain. The Iranian situation was complicated further by the increasing muscle flexing of oil-producing countries, not only in the Middle East. The major companies were under increasing pressure by producing countries to improve the state's "take" in the revenues generated by their rich natural resource. Even before the outbreak of the Korean War, the Venezuelan government established 50 percent as the government share, a proportion that went much further than that of any other producing country at the time. The Venezuelan success in 1949 did not go unnoticed, with the result that Middle East countries brought increasing pressure on the companies to follow the Venezuelan example. Saudi Arabia was the first to accomplish its goals in negotiations with Aramco; Iraq established the same standard in 1952; and Kuwait pressed its advantage with its two major operators, Gulf Oil and Anglo-Iranian. Throughout the state–corporate negotiations U.S. government officials provided advice and encouragement, the primary objective being appeasement of the oil-producing countries, to avoid the possibility of expropriation, to maintain security of supply, and to encourage a pro-Western attitude on the part of the regimes in power.[3]

Although the Korean War was not the only catalyst, 1950 witnessed an intensified debate over the security of oil supplies and the establishment of institutions both to promote the security of supply and to facilitate the fighting of the war in Korea. The Truman administration, through an act of Congress, the Defense Production Act of 1950, established the Petroleum Administration for Defense (PAD), which was largely a successor to the Petroleum Administration for War established during World War II. PAD's specific mandate included the "development and execution of policies and programs for meeting military, governmental, industrial and civilian requirements for petroleum and gas."[4] Interdepartmental discussions on the challenges of oil security were held from the outset of the war, and the focus of policy development was on the long-term rather than the short-term issues occasioned by the war. Discussions involved PAD as well as the Departments of State, Defense, and Commerce. The objective of the interdepartmental committee discussions was the traditional one: "to assure adequate supplies of oil in the event of a major war." "It is generally agreed," the Assistant Secretary of State for Economic Affairs informed the Secretary of State, Dean Acheson, in early 1951, "that the problem would be acute if Middle East oil supplies should be lost."[5] The main focus of this national security discussion was on improving the readiness of U.S. domestic resources for military/industrial use in the event of an emergency, thus bringing the Elk Hills Naval Reserve into a state of "instant readiness" and developing a program of full-scale production and development of the tidelands oil fields of California, Louisiana, and Texas.[6]

In late 1950 the National Security Council produced NSC 97, "A National Petroleum Program." Assistant Secretary of State for Economic Affairs Willard Thorpe noted in a memorandum to Dean Acheson in early 1951 that "previous suggestions of the Defense Department for a national petroleum program" had led to interdepartmental discussions and general consensus but not to a policy that was sufficiently specific to deal with the exigencies of the "present international situation." Thorpe indicated that what was needed "and overdue" was to assign PAD the responsibility to develop, in cooperation with the other appropriate agencies, "the specific programs necessary to insure adequate supplies of petroleum for the Western powers in the event of a major war in the near future." The result of Thorpe's and others' recommendations was the establishment of the interdepartmental Foreign Petroleum Committee to advise PAD on problems affecting foreign supply. The committee, which included representatives from State, Defense, Commerce, Interior, the Economic Cooperation Administration, the Office of Defense Mobilization, the Defense Production Administration, and the National Production Authority, began to meet in April 1951. Bruce Brown was appointed to head PAD by Secretary of the Interior Oscar Chapman. Brown had extensive experience in the private sector as a member of the board of Standard Oil of Indiana and had served as Assistant Deputy Director of the Petroleum Administration for War during World War II. Immediately following World War II and the demobilization of that administration, Brown was appointed to chair the Military Petroleum Advisory Committee. In 1949, prior to his appointment to head PAD, he resigned as a member of the board of Standard Oil to become President of its subsidiary, Pan-Am Southern Corporation. One of Brown's first initiatives with the outbreak of war in Korea was to establish a Foreign Oil Branch to coordinate mobilization of the American companies involved in overseas operations, a measure that was of acute importance when workers at the Abadan, Iran, oil refinery went on strike. The Abadan refinery was the largest single refiner of aviation gasoline in the world outside the continental United States.[7]

Even at this relatively early stage in the development of a global oil policy, a desire to enhance hemispheric supplies was critical, with particular focus on increasing Canadian and Venezuelan crude oil production and "resolving problems" pertaining to the exploitation of U.S. off-shore resources.[8] Nonetheless, the main focus of concern in all government studies of this period was the security of the Middle East. PAD produced several studies in the course of 1951, including "World Wide Demand and Supply of Petroleum in Event of a Major War," and "Tanker Transportation Supplement." U.S. officials expressed concern about the capacity of the United States to ensure security of supply from the Middle East, specifically the Bahrein-Qatar-Saudi Arabia area. As one State Department representative on the senior staff of the National Security Council observed: "the impracticality of calculating and comparing the military cost in blood and treasure and the financial and economic cost of replacing Middle East production and refining facilities has only just now been recognized."[9] Willard Thorpe informed the Acting Secretary of State, James E. Webb, at the end of 1951 that a range of initiatives would have to be undertaken in the event of a major war, especially during the first six months of war, which the administration anticipated would constitute the period of most acute potential energy shortages. PAD estimated that in the first six months of a war industry would require an additional twenty-five million and the military an additional twenty million barrels of oil. Measures included the following, which were not mutually exclusive: expanding refining capacity; significantly increasing tanker (especially smaller and fast tankers able to travel without convoy support) and pipeline capacity; holding Saudi Arabia, Bahrein, Qatar, and Indonesia; stockpiling; expanding domestic production; rationing domestic consumption; and working with the CIA to deal with sabotage of oil installations abroad. Authorities also recognized that it would take at least six months under current conditions to move the Elk Hills Naval Reserve into full production and that the capacity of the Reserve to move to full production at the start of any hostilities had to be improved. The State Department wanted NATO to address the issue of oil planning because of its obviously critical role in the event of an East-West war.[10]

U.S. military and civilian officials in the early 1950s continued to perceive the eastern Mediterranean and Middle East as a British sphere of influence and a British strategic responsibility, especially given the level of U.S. commitments in other regions of the world. Secretary of Defense Robert Lovett informed the National Security Council at the end of 1951 that although the United States maintained naval and air forces in the Mediterranean, "in the event of Soviet aggression against Kuwait, Saudi Arabia, and Bahrein ... these naval and air forces cannot be considered capable by themselves of providing an effective defense of the ... areas." Although American officials perceived their relationship with Saudi Arabia as special, they were conscious of the need for collective action in the region in the event of hostilities and, to that end, in the early 1950s they worked with Great Britain, France, and Turkey to establish a Middle East command as a "focal point" for the defence of the area, but without the commitment of actual U.S. forces, since under the U.S. war plans approved at that stage, U.S. forces were not available for "specific commitment" to defend Kuwait, Saudi Arabia, or Bahrein. The Defense Department noted that "exclusive of the defense of the United States and support of the United Nations effort in Korea," the primary military commitment of the United States was the defence of Western Europe.[11]

Iran tended to be treated as a distinct challenge by U.S. officials, in part because the British oil industry was the sole operator there early in the 1950s. Any developments in Iran that affected the supply of oil and fuel to Great Britain, however, would invariably affect the United States as well; thus the presence of the Soviet Union on the Iranian border and increasing internal political turmoil in Iran in the 1950s became a source of intense concern to American policymakers. In 1951 the CIA estimate indicated that the loss of Iranian oil production and of the refinery at Abadan, with a twenty-seven million metric tons capacity per annum, would temporarily undermine economic activity in Western Europe and impose severe economic hardships on Great Britain even in peacetime. The CIA report indicated that if Iran were lost, "at least six months would be required to place marginal plants in operation, to change the composition of refinery output, to alter tanker routings, and to complete the redistribution of crude oil among the other refineries." The CIA estimated that, although the lost oil could be replaced over time from other sources, the financial impact on Britain would be far more difficult to reverse, if it could be accomplished at all. The CIA evaluation did place the relative positions of Great Britain and the United States in perspective. Even if Britain were to lose all of its control over Middle East production, British companies would still own about 35 percent of available world crude-oil production outside the Soviet Union, the United States, and Canada, in comparison with u.s. companies, which would own approximately one half of crude production outside the Soviet Union, the United States, and Canada. By 1950 u.s. companies controlled 100 percent of Saudi Arabian production, 23.7 percent of Iraqi production, 50 percent of Kuwait production, and 23.8 percent of Qatar production. This was in comparison to 61.5 percent in the Caribbean exporting area (included Venezuela and Mexico), and 100 percent of u.s. and Canadian production. Nonetheless, a loss of all Middle East supplies for Western Europe not only would affect Europe but also would require rationing in the United States. The CIA stressed that although the Middle East presently produced only 18.4 percent of non-Soviet oil, its proven reserves were more than 44 percent of non-Soviet sources, and its relative importance would likely increase. It is hardly surprising, therefore, that one of the first official foreign trips Secretary of State John Foster Dulles took was to Riyadh to meet with King Ibn Saud to assure the Saudis of American friendship and collaboration.[12]

Given the identified importance of Middle East oil to the West in general and of Iran in particular to Great Britain in the 1950s, it was inevitable that threatened instability in Iran would result in concerted action by both powers to protect their national security interests. Whether or not the United States was determined to displace Great Britain in Iran is open to debate, but there is little question that the primary objective of u.s. policy was to offset any Soviet influence, and achieving that goal required political stability and a pro-Western government firmly entrenched in Iran. The American ambassador informed the State Department in early 1950 that the Russians were significantly strengthening their political presence in Teheran, with a view to obtaining their long-term goal of access to the sea, but that Iran had to date succeeded in "staying outside the iron curtain," and had also not shown any signs of being intimidated by the Soviets. The British, on the other hand, he suggested, were determined to take a hard line in negotiating the Anglo-Iranian interests.[13] If the British could not ensure stability then the United States would.

The Iranian challenge in the early 1950s was twofold. One challenge was that most of the Middle East countries were seeking a higher take on oil revenues. The second and more serious threat to both u.s. and British interests was the emergence at the end of the 1940s of a strongly nationalistic group in the Iranian parliament led by Dr Mohammed Mossadegh, whose main platform became nationalization of the Anglo-Iranian Oil Company. British government and Anglo-Iranian officials took a hard line in negotiating with the Iranians, yielding reluctantly and belatedly to the same 50/50 sharing agreement that Saudi Arabia concluded with Aramco; but in early 1951 the Iranian Parliament nationalized Anglo-Iranian following the violent removal of the Prime Minister and his ultimate replacement by Mossadegh. British officials and the Truman administration differed over their reading of the challenge posed by Mossadegh and the potential resolution, with Truman and Dean Acheson opposed to confrontation, especially the use of force, and primarily focused on the need to keep Iran in the Western camp while at the same time securing the oil resources for the West. As much as they were concerned about the precedent posed by nationalization, as long as the oil continued to flow and was under Western administration, it was not of fundamental importance whether the operations were owned by the British or the Iranians. It was also critical to avoid driving an otherwise anti-Communist Mossadegh into the arms of the Soviets, who were already encroaching on Iranian territory.[14] The Truman administration remained firm in its commitment to a compromise in Iran to the end, but while negotiations foundered, the Iranian economy sank deeper into depression, Mossadegh's political situation became increasingly precarious, forcing him to depend more heavily even if reluctantly on the Tudeh (Communist) party in parliament, and the Churchill government's desire for an interventionist solution intensified. That interventionist approach had to await Eisenhower's election, the appointment of John Foster Dulles as Secretary of State, and a more sympathetic response to collaboration between the CIA and British authorities with the goal of removing Mossadegh.

With Mossadegh's political support already unravelling, the Shah, whom the U.S. ambassador at one stage described as "a little too Westernized for an oriental country,"[15] by decree removed him from office, and the Iranian army, with the British and Americans empathetic bystanders, restored power to the Shah. Mossadegh's removal did not in itself resolve the oil dispute, however, which lingered on through 1954, with Anglo-Iranian and British government officials still determined to regain their assets and control, but with the Shah increasingly willing to strike a deal with the Americans to get the oil flowing again and to reinvigorate the Iranian economy. The Eisenhower National Security Council showed no ambiguity about the importance of Iran. It indicated in early 1954 in a review of United States policy toward Iran that "because of its key strategic position, oil resources, vulnerability to intervention or armed attack by the USSR, and vulnerability to political subversion, Iran must be regarded as a continuing objective of Soviet expansion." The loss of Iran, the report concluded, would constitute a "major threat to the security of the entire Middle East."[16] If any groups benefited from the agreement that was ultimately struck it was u.s. private and national interests: Iranian oil remained in principle nationalized, but four of the major u.s. firms together acquired a 40 percent interest in the government company. British interests received more than £200 million over the next two decades. The u.s. private sector and the u.s. government had effectively supplanted the British in Iran, at least in terms of real power, within the space of four years. Robert Eakens, then chief of the Petroleum Staff in the State Department, later commented that the negotiations led by the u.s. government with Mossadegh resulted in the American companies acquiring the 40 percent interest in the Iranian consortium. Eakens indicated that "one thing our petroleum division always fought for was giving the American oil companies an equal opportunity." The State Department, he suggested, preferred to have several companies and several nationalities involved in producing countries to minimize risk.[17] In the process of consolidating the position of u.s.-based companies in the region, national security considerations also triumphed over any concerns the Justice Department had that the consortium established in Iran challenged American antitrust regulations. At a meeting of the National Security Council on 14 January 1954, over which President Eisenhower presided, the Council agreed to "advise the Attorney General that the security interests of the United States require that United States petroleum companies participate in an international consortium to contract with the Government of Iran ... on terms which will protect the interests of the western world in the petroleum resources of the Middle East."[18]

EGYPT, ISRAEL,
AND THE SUEZ CRISIS

Differences in approach to the Middle East during the early Cold War years between Great Britain and the United States, which were evident in the protracted negotiations over the nationalization of Anglo-Iranian Oil, were even more acute in their responses to the growing tensions between Israel and its Arab neighbours and the continuing rise of nationalism among the Arab nations in the region. The crisis that emerged over the Suez Canal in the mid-1950s was far more complex than either British or American concern about the security of access to regional oil resources. Both powers were concerned about Soviet designs in the area; but they were also competitors in their own right for hegemony in a region that had been a British sphere of influence for most of the twentieth century. Both British and American leaders sought to come to terms with the emergence of a powerful middle class in countries such as

Egypt and the desire of Arab leaders to achieve economic modernization and to exercise a higher degree of control over their economies in general and their natural resources in particular. From the British and American perspective Arab nationalism also presented an opportunity for the Soviet Union to increase its influence in the Middle East and potentially to threaten security of access to oil resources, a threat that was viewed by Anthony Eden and Harold Macmillan, then Chancellor of the Exchequer, as an issue over which Britain would be prepared to go to war.[19]

The emergence of Gamal Abdel Nasser in Egypt and his ascension to power following a coup in 1952 marked a critical turning point in Anglo-American relations in the area. Prior to the coup, British and Egyptian forces were engaged in conflict over the Egyptian government's demand that British troops be withdrawn from the Suez Canal zone, and in the aftermath of the conflict the increasingly ineffectual and traditionally pro-British King Farouk was removed from power, with the compliance of American officials. The rise of Nasser provided U.S. officials with the opportunity to increase American influence in the region, and they took full advantage of the opportunity by dealing directly with Nasser.[20] Nasser consolidated his control during the first Eisenhower administration, with the support of U.S., British, and Saudi Arabian economic aid. As Nasser negotiated a several hundred million dollar fund to finance the Aswan dam project, he went too far for both the British and the Americans. In 1955, failing to obtain the arms he sought from the United States, he negotiated a large arms deal with Czechoslovakia, and the following year the Egyptian government recognized the People's Republic of China. In so doing he fundamentally alienated powerful interest groups in the United States. With a presidential election looming that fall, the Eisenhower administration now backed away from its support for the Aswan dam project, opening the way for the Soviet Union to fill the gap. Nasser also moved quickly to nationalize the Suez Canal, a step that threatened to cut British access to the Persian Gulf and Asia. As much as the Eisenhower administration viewed the nationalization of the canal with the same alarm as the British, neither Dulles nor Eisenhower was prepared to see action taken that might drive Nasser and other Middle East countries into the Soviet camp. When Israel invaded Egypt in late October, followed by French and British intervention, the Eisenhower administration condemned the action before the UN Security Council, leaving Anthony Eden initially shocked and then angry at what he viewed as a fundamental betrayal designed to undermine the British position in the region and further entrench the United States.[21] This interpretation was reinforced when the Eisenhower administration succeeded early in 1957 in having Congress pass a joint resolution pledging the United States to provide economic and military assistance to countries in the Middle East to protect their "territorial integrity" and assist them in resisting "armed aggression" by nations under communist control.[22]

The Suez crisis highlighted the vulnerability of Western Europe as well as the United States to interruptions of oil supply from the Middle East. The Eisenhower administration's opposition to the Anglo-French and Israeli military actions against Egypt protected the United States against a direct Arab oil embargo but it did not prevent Saudi Arabia from embargoing sales to Britain and France, or Syria from temporarily shutting down the pipeline through Syria in mid-1956. The oil crisis in the mid-1950s was relatively short-lived, but it underlined the strategic vulnerability of the Western powers to political decisions in the Middle East as well as the need for effective collaboration among the Western governments and the private sector in the event of similar emergencies. The crisis provided some support for conservationist measures in the United States and prompted efforts to expand Western hemisphere production. The political influence of domestic producers in the United States was also reinforced in the course of the crisis by decisions of the Texas Railroad Commission designed to maintain price stability in the face of pressures to increase production to replace the European shortfall.[23] These were important lessons for subsequent U.S. administrations.

Although the Middle East remained highly unstable in the 1950s, the Eisenhower administration's actions during the Suez crisis contributed to consolidating Nasser's political position in Egypt and his credibility throughout the Arab world. By early 1958 the United States was once again providing economic aid to Egypt, and Nasser in turn continued to suppress communist influence in Egyptian politics. The U.S. position during the crisis also enhanced critical American relations with Saudi Arabia. By the end of the Eisenhower administration, although the U.S. position in the Middle East remained tenuous, the developments in Iran and Egypt in particular had served to strengthen American private and public power in the region.

LATIN AMERICAN TRENDS

The nationalism that emerged in the Middle East in the 1950s and influenced American policy and private sector interests mirrored strong nationalist sentiments in Latin America. Latin American countries were at least a generation ahead of their Middle East counterparts, however, in seeking to increase national control over foreign oil companies and to increase the revenues derived from their natural resources. All Latin American producing countries had state oil companies by the 1950s, with Pemex in Mexico providing the most powerful symbol of national power in natural resource development in the region, even though Venezuela, still adhering to the private sector model, generated a higher percentage return for the national treasury from the oil sector, and its pre-1950 50/50 profit-sharing arrangement had provided the inspiration for Middle East producers.

During the dictatorship of Colonel Marcos Pérez Jiménez (1953–58), American policymakers and the private sector enjoyed close and cooperative relations with Venezuela. Latin America was overshadowed in U.S. policy during the first decade of the Cold War by the primary focus on Europe and Asia. Other than the apparent influence of communism in Colombia in the late 1940s at the time of the *Bogotazo,* and the 1954 intervention in Guatemala, neither communism nor the Soviet Union appeared to have any significant presence in the region, at least until after the Castro revolution in Cuba. Neither the Eisenhower nor the Pérez Jiménez administrations expressed particular concern about human rights. Venezuela during the dictatorship was stable, pro-American in foreign and investment policies, and prosperous, at least in the case of Venezuelan elites. By 1957 Venezuela's exports to the United States represented one-quarter of the value of exports from all of Latin America, and U.S. direct investments in the country increased during the 1950s from $993 million to more than $2.5 billion. Venezuelan oil production also increased dramatically in the 1950s and early 1960s, from 130 million barrels in 1950 to 334 million in 1960 and 363 million in 1965.[24] With the overthrow of Pérez Jiménez in 1958, however, and the dramatic anti-American riots that greeted Vice-President Nixon in Caracas and elsewhere on his Latin American tour that year, the Eisenhower administration became more sensitive to the rising tide of anti-Americanism and the frustration with the lack of American economic aid to the region. The administration also grew more restive over the potential threat that such sentiments, fuelled by massive poverty and rising expectations, posed to the stability of the region and to American interests. The return of Romulo Betancourt to mainstream Venezuelan politics in 1958, and his election as President in early 1959, promised both democratic reforms and stability, but by the end of the 1950s Venezuela was no longer the Venezuela of Pérez Jiménez.[25] At the end of 1958 the provisional Venezuelan government retroactively increased corporate taxes, which directly affected the oil industry. U.S. operating companies, including Creole Petroleum and Standard Oil of New Jersey, as well as the Eisenhower administration, vigorously protested the action. Although production and exports were not affected, the companies and the U.S. government viewed the tax measures as a violation of the 50/50 arrangement that had been in place since the late 1940s.[26]

Most significant for the long term was the appointment of Juan Pablo Pérez Alfonso as minister of mines and hydrocarbons in the new regime.

A former minister of development, Pérez Alfonso had spent years developing expertise on oil industry issues and emerged as the leading Venezuelan authority on the industry within the Acción Democrática party. He was strongly influenced by development theories articulated most persuasively in the 1950s by Raul Prebisch, the Argentine economist whose ideas dominated the un Economic Commission for Latin America. Prebisch stressed the trade disadvantages of nations that depended on raw materials production and export and encouraged the development of economic policies that would stimulate industrialization.[27] Although oil prices remained relatively stable in this period, Pérez Alfonso sought to gain more state control over oil prices. To that end he established a commission on hydrocarbons, modelled on the highly effective Texas Railroad Commission, which he had studied extensively; the mandate of the Venezuelan commission was to monitor the extent to which private sector companies operating in Venezuela were obtaining maximum prices for Venezuelan oil exports. The commission was overwhelmed by the task of regulating the multinational oil firms.

In 1959 British Petroleum, followed by Standard Oil, decided to reduce prices, stimulating the producing countries to go further, with Abdulah Tariki of Saudi Arabia and Perez Alfonso of Venezuela taking the lead; in 1960 they collaborated with the major Middle East producing countries to establish the Organization of Petroleum Exporting Countries (opec), representing an astounding 80 percent of global crude oil exports. The stated objective was to identify mechanisms to stabilize prices through production control.[28] opec evoked little concern among u.s. officials or American multinationals in the 1960s, although it did bring about a greater sense of caution on the part of the companies and an awareness of the need to consult more fully with the people of the countries in which they operated. Some u.s. officials evinced a remarkably naïve perspective on the initial Venezuela-Middle East initiative. The director of the Office of International Resources, for instance, informed the Deputy Director of the Office of South American Affairs in the State Department in late 1957 that it was likely the Venezuelans were attending the Arab League conference in Cairo "reluctantly."[29] Ecuador was the only other Latin American country to join the producers' cartel, and it ultimately withdrew. Additional challenges included achieving consensus on policy among the Middle East producers, restraining nationalism in the relatively new producers in the region, such as Libya, and preventing conflict among the Arab states, such as that between Iraq and Kuwait, from decreasing the capacity of opec to be effective. Pérez Alfonso himself was critical of the ineffectiveness of opec by the time he resigned in 1963 as minister of mines and hydrocarbons.

Venezuela was clearly the most important actor in U.S.-Latin American oil relations in the 1950s and 1960s. Venezuela was also by 1960 still a far more important source of oil imports into the United States than the Middle East. In 1960 Mexico exported only 6 million barrels of oil to American markets (out of its 99 million barrels of production), in comparison with 44 million from Canada, 120 from the Middle East, 117 from the Netherlands East Indies, and 334 from Venezuela.[30] African production was yet to be a factor for the United States. Mexico demonstrated no weakening in its commitment to strong state control over foreign investment in natural resource development. Colombia, having established Ecopetrol as a state enterprise in the late 1940s to operate the Tropical Oil concession that had reverted to the nation, nonetheless remained open to foreign investment in the oil industry. At the end of the 1950s only Canada in the Western hemisphere appeared to offer significant potential.

CANADA AND U.S. OIL IMPORT QUOTAS

Canadian oil resources and production assumed considerably more economic and strategic significance for the United States after the Leduc development in the late 1940s and the occasional threats to the security of American supplies from Venezuela and the Middle East during the Truman and Eisenhower presidencies. Petroleum relations between the two nations in those years need to be viewed in the context of the larger considerations of the Cold War, since oil was clearly only part of the strategic means to a political, economic, and military end, i.e., the containment of Soviet-bloc communism and the maintenance of a strong American political economy and military capability.

Canadian and American policies and interests appeared to move ever closer together in this period as they joined in the alliance and continued various forms of military cooperation into the postwar years. American government considerations of establishing a more integrated resource development for Canada and the United States during the early Cold War foundered on the shoals of Canadian realism and domestic politics. High level discussions were held in 1948 with a view to the elimination of trade barriers between the two countries, an initiative that assistant secretary of state for economic affairs, Willard Thorpe, believed provided a "unique opportunity of promoting the most efficient utilization of the resources of the North American continent and knitting the two countries together, an objective of United States foreign policy since the founding of the Republic." Among the proposals considered was one that would have ensured "in the event that one country is subject to military attack, continued free access to the products of the other." The 1948 talks were aborted, but in the mid-1950s, in the context of bilateral discussions of the impact on Canada of the national security clause of the U.S. Trade Agreements Act, senior U.S. officials stressed – in a meeting with, among others, C.D. Howe and Lester Pearson – that the U.S. government considered North America a "strategic unit."[31]

U.S. administrations in the Cold War period showed a distinct tendency to take for granted the availability of Canadian resources for continental and international security purposes. Thus little consideration was given to Canada in the early 1950s when the National Security Council debated a national petroleum program for the United States. The lack of attention to Canada at this stage was partly because its resources were taken for granted, but more importantly because Canada was not a significant supplier of U.S. energy requirements before the Middle East crisis over Suez. In 1951 Canadian oil exports were only .6 percent of total Canadian production, and they remained between 2 and 3 percent until the Suez crisis, when exports rose to 12.9 percent of production in 1955, to 24.7 percent in 1956, and to more than 30 percent the following year. In 1955, 66 percent of that export was destined for the West coast of the U.S., and the remainder for the Mid-West. That remained the pattern until 1958, when the Mid-West began to receive the bulk with the completion of the pipeline to the area and to eastern Canada. The first major pipeline was completed under Imperial Oil, linking western Canada and Sarnia, Ontario, in 1950; by 1953 Wisconsin and Michigan were served by the line, and before the decade's end it reached Toronto. Not until late in the 1960s did the pipeline specifically serve the major Chicago metropolitan area.[32] Noting the dramatic expansion of Canadian oil production and the increase of proved crude oil reserves from one-half billion barrels in 1949 to almost 2 billion by 1953, the Assistant Secretary of State for Economic Affairs informed the Director of the Office of Defense Mobilization that it was anticipated that reserves and production would continue to increase "thereby further adding to this important nearby source of oil."[33]

National Security Council thinking in the early 1950s continued to stress the importance of Western hemisphere resources (including Canadian-based aluminum and nickel, 93 percent of the U.S. supply coming from Canadian sources) and the importance of minimizing restrictions on imports of hemispheric oil and gas into the U.S. This acceptance ran against the long-standing position of the domestic U.S. oil industry but was consistent with the idea that "the long-standing plan of the United States and Canada [is] to share their resources in time of war on a continental rather than on a national basis."[34] Within a few years the Eisenhower administration moved toward import restrictions precisely for security reasons, and this policy direction had clear implications for the Canadian industry.

The Eisenhower administration became convinced in the course of the 1950s that the main problem of national security involving oil was no longer U.S. corporate access to foreign sources – since the companies were now well established in the Middle East and nationalistic challenges had been weathered in Iran (where the five U.S. majors entered the traditionally British-dominated consortium in 1954) and in Latin America – but rather the effect on the domestic industry of imported oil. Concerned about the impact of imports on national security, President Eisenhower announced the formation of a cabinet committee to study the question in 1955, following a report to Eisenhower by the director of the Office of Defense Mobilization suggesting that national security was being threatened. That cabinet advisory committee recommended that a voluntary limit should be established on oil imports into the U.S. to ensure that the domestic fuels situation was not impaired, "endangering the orderly industrial growth which assures the military and civilian supplies and reserves necessary to the national defense." This task force noted that imports had risen to 9.4 percent of total U.S. crude oil consumption by 1954 from the 1946 figure of 4.7 percent and that most of the imports were by U.S. companies. The one dissenter on the advisory committee was John E. Warren of the First National City Bank of New York, who argued that import restrictions reduced the capacity of foreign producers to purchase U.S. goods and also resulted in price increases in the U.S., primarily on the east coast. He might have added, as the Nixon administration report on oil imports noted in 1970, that oil imports into the U.S. from Western hemisphere countries also caused smaller dollar outflows from the U.S. because those exporting nations had a higher capacity to purchase U.S. goods than Middle Eastern supplies.[35]

Warren's caution was not heeded. The import controls were introduced on a voluntary basis (in keeping with the laissez-faire ideological orientation of President Eisenhower and the Republican Party in the 1950s), but when voluntary restraint failed to bring results, the administration in 1959 imposed restraints by executive order. Under the voluntary program it was determined that imports of non-Canadian and non-Venezuelan crude oil brought into Oil Districts I–IV should not significantly exceed the proportion that these imports bore to domestic production in those districts in 1954 (a year in which Canadian oil exports were just beginning to gain momentum).[36] This initiative was taken under the authority of the Trade Agreements Extension Act of 1954, section 2 of which prohibited any decrease in duty on any article if such reduction would threaten domestic production needed for national defence.[37]

Canada was excluded from the application of the mandatory import restrictions by the provision that exempted imports overland, thus not allowing transport via the Great Lakes. The Canadian exemption was stipulated in part because of the influence of the major companies handling Canadian exports; as well, Canadians protested strongly against the restrictions. American government circles were also genuinely concerned that, given the importance of Canadian exports to the Canadian economy, restraint would be counterproductive in economic and strategic terms. Finally, the regulations favoured the type of u.s. company based in Canada, i.e., the large international companies with refining capacity in the United States, thus eliminating the newer overseas producing firms without such refining capacity.[38]

In the late 1950s and the 1960s, u.s. officials expressed concern about the reliance of eastern Canada on oil imports largely from South America; it was perceived that in the event of a crisis that curtailed shipments from what were seen as less reliable sources, the u.s., as an ally of Canada, would have to supply those depleted eastern markets, thus endangering u.s. security of supply. For a variety of market reasons, the major companies operating in western Canada preferred to ship oil to the u.s. markets in the West and Mid-West rather than to supply the Montreal refineries from Canadian sources. From the companies' perspective this was a commercial consideration; from the perspective of u.s. government officials, it was an issue of national security; but this dispute was not readily resolved.

CHAPTER ELEVEN

From OPEC to the Iranian Revolution

In the course of the 1960s U.S. dependency on offshore oil supplies increased to the point that its armed forces obtained 40 percent of its fuel requirements from foreign sources. In 1960 oil and natural gas constituted 48 percent of world energy consumption; that figure rose to 63 percent in 1970 and 67 percent in 1975. Between 1960 and 1975 U.S. energy consumption doubled, and reliance on imports increased from 23 percent to 39 percent.[1] Until the major oil shock of 1973 oil production was high and prices low, and consumers took advantage of comparatively low gasoline prices in the United States and elsewhere to fill the ever-expanding network of roads and highways in America with cars, while the petrochemical industry began to produce a wide range of consumer goods in plastic. United States industrial and military developments and consumerism combined with the economic recovery of Europe, the modernization of the Japanese economy, and the decline of coal as a source of energy to generate ever-increasing demand for oil. The arrival in the marketplace of major new exporting countries such as Libya, and the Soviet export of surplus oil to Western Europe served further to keep prices low.[2]

A number of factors intervened over the two decades from the Kennedy administration to that of Jimmy Carter to intensify the debate over international oil policy and to bring a sense of crisis to the United States and the other consuming nations. The most important development was the impact of the Arab-Israeli relationship in the Middle East on production, supply, and prices. Until the early 1970s official complacency about oil supplies was considerable. Clarence Nichols, special assistant to the Assistant Secretary of State for Economic Affairs, informed a Congressional committee in late 1961 that short of a major war it was unlikely that the United States would be cut off from access to foreign oil, in part because of the large and growing number of oil-producing countries that were single export economies and depended on that export for their economic prosperity.[3]

Nichols also observed that the Soviet Union had significantly increased its oil production in the course of the 1950s to almost 3 million barrels a day in 1960, with projected production of 4.8 million by 1965. Its capacity to export a significant portion of its production was also enhanced by the completion in the 1960s of pipelines to ports on the Baltic and Black seas, with most of its production reaching the more accessible markets of Western Europe. Nichols noted that although Soviet exports to Western Europe were driven primarily by economic considerations, in the case of exports to developing nations the Soviet Union had been prepared to make economic sacrifices to penetrate their markets, using such methods as barter trade and acceptance of local currencies. Nichols cautioned that such tactics could serve to increase the dependency on the Soviet Union of some developing countries, at the same time that Soviet exports to the "free world" had the effect of reducing revenues for other producers, and in the case of third world producers undermining their efforts to advance economically.[4]

In the early 1960s, especially with the establishment of OPEC, United States and British officials intensified an already close working relationship on oil-related issues. The governments of the two countries adopted a policy of neutrality and non-commitment toward OPEC from its inception, although by late 1965 the State Department and the British Government were at least considering modifying that policy in light of the recognition accorded OPEC by some international organizations and individual countries.[5] Leroy Stinebower, Treasurer of Standard Oil of New Jersey, made it clear in a conversation with State Department officials in mid-1962 that the formation of OPEC was an understandable response by the Middle East producing countries to surplus production, intense competition in the market, and lower prices. George Pearcy, Executive Assistant to the President of Standard Oil of New Jersey, stressed that OPEC had to be taken seriously.[6] Over the next few years American officials reviewed their attitudes towards OPEC, concluding that it was desirable to establish a working relationship with the organization in an effort to advance U.S. interests. American officials in Kuwait noted that although OPEC was "ostensibly" opposed to the interests of U.S. oil companies, certain OPEC objectives – production and price stability and a degree of uniformity of oil legislation among the producing countries – were in the long-term interest of some American oil companies. Officials wondered, for instance, whether there were "one definable U.S. oil company interest on which the U.S. government can afford to hang a petroleum policy." They further suggested that they viewed OPEC as a "manifestation of a strong historic trend toward economic nationalism in Arab and other developing countries" and that the Western countries had little hope of either directing or opposing the trend; that their sense was the OPEC was "mellowing with age"; and that a working relationship rather than formal recognition of OPEC might be in the best interests of the United States and the companies. Although corporate and government reaction to OPEC was mixed in the early years, more astute foreign observers such as former World Bank President and New York lawyer John McCloy advised President Kennedy that the oil companies might need to negotiate in concert with OPEC, which would involve relaxing antitrust regulations.[7]

Both American and British officials were also sensitive to the changing environment in which the multinational companies operated in the increasingly nationalistic producing countries and were anxious to develop policies that would offset the potential price and supply impact of that altered environment. Their experience in Iran in the 1950s and their dependency on imports made the British feel especially vulnerable. American officials appear to have believed the private sector strong enough to deal with the producing country governments at least in the short term; they were, in any event, as they had been historically, reluctant to "intervene diplomatically in disputes between American oil companies and foreign governments." To do so, a State Department official contended, would "undermine the responsibilities of the companies themselves." At the same time, it was suggested that the government should maintain frequent contact with the companies in case of conflict between them and a producer. It was ambiguous, therefore, what would transpire in the event of a serious conflict.[8]

The British and Americans identified a commonality of interest in protecting sources of oil in the early 1960s. To that end they held consultations during the Kennedy administration, beginning with bilateral talks in early 1961, and they met approximately every two years thereafter to compare perspectives, share information, and attempt to adopt a common approach. At one of the first meetings, in February 1961, Lord Hood, Minister in the British Embassy, stressed the strategic importance of oil to Britain, pointing out that the earnings from the two major companies that were wholly or partially British controlled were important to the British international payments position. Lord Hood also stressed that the main challenges included the demands of the producing countries for a larger share of earnings, in some cases promoting nationalization, and the specific issue of the movement of Soviet oil into Western markets. Large-scale infusions of Soviet oil into European markets at below market prices, perceived as a Cold War initiative, presented a serious challenge to Western companies marketing Middle East oil, and the producing countries were unwilling to entertain any price reductions that would decrease state revenues. Lord Hood contended that both American and British officials needed to provide "political guidance" to the oil companies and government backing "when free world oil was threatened." Foy Kohler, then Assistant Secretary for European Affairs, agreed with Lord Hood on his assessment of the challenges but indicated that American antitrust laws made it difficult for the u.s. government to provide political guidance to private firms, although government officials did discuss these issues with company officers.[9]

The informal bilateral Anglo-American meetings on oil policy continued through the Kennedy and Johnson years, and although differences in the strategic interests and priorities of the two countries emerged from time to time, in general the collaboration was productive. They reached an agreement in April 1963 on strategic matters in the Persian Gulf. At the June 1963 meeting they agreed to maintain a stance of neutrality and non-recognition of OPEC. At a meeting in Washington in late January 1964 Sir Geoffrey Harrison, Deputy Undersecretary of State in the British Foreign Office, noted that since the 1963 meetings the two countries had been able to closely align their approaches to petroleum issues in Indonesia, Peru, and Ceylon. Sir Geoffrey was also optimistic that OPEC would not survive because of what he described as an "unholy alliance" among Venezuela, Indonesia, and Iraq. From his perspective Middle East oil continued to be more important to Britain than to the United States. The British government was not concerned solely with the possibility that oil would be cut off from the region but rather with the continued availability of supplies at reasonable prices. Sir Geoffrey thought that there would be considerable pressure on the companies to accept a lower return on investments in the Middle East, and the British government feared that any confrontation between the companies and the producing governments in the region would lead to a confrontation between governments and an escalation of Arab nationalism, an eventuality they were anxious to avoid. John Kelly, the American Assistant Secretary for Mineral Resources in the Department of the Interior, concurred, adding that both countries considered that it was no longer possible to "brush OPEC under the rug," although the u.s. government through 1963 did not send even an observer to OPEC meetings.[10]

Although the two major powers worked in close consultation there were definable differences in approach and in their respective interests in the Middle East especially. The British continued to view the Middle East as their sphere of influence. That perspective was not shared by American officials. The difference was evident in the early 1960s, during the Kennedy and early Lyndon Johnson administrations, over policy toward Iraq. In late 1961 the Iraq government passed Law 80, which in effect took back more than 99 percent of the Iraq Petroleum Company's original concession. Shortly thereafter the Iraq government drafted legislation to establish the National Iraqi Oil Company to develop areas that were expropriated from the Iraq Oil Company under the 1961 law. American companies held a 23.75 percent interest in the Iraq Oil Company. The American Ambassador in Iraq interpreted the Iraqi initiative as part of a larger effort to drive the British out of the Persian Gulf and Aden; if the British were to take too hard a line, such action could run counter to U.S. interests in the region.[11]

Secretary of State Dean Rusk informed American Embassy officials in Iraq, on reflection, that it was important that U.S. companies that were not part of the IPC not be given the impression that the U.S. government favoured them taking advantage of Law 80 and seeking new concessions in Iraq. At that stage several American companies, including Phillips, Pauley, Murphy, Sinclair, Continental, and General Exploration, had expressed interest. The State Department perspective was that these and other interested companies might be "privately" informed that it was in the interest of all the companies and the U.S. government to come to a mutually acceptable settlement of any dispute over the IPC and that during negotiations the companies should refrain from making offers to the Iraq government for onshore concessionary areas. Rusk indicated that the U.S. government would encourage other governments whose firms had an interest in the region to pursue a similar approach, and that in the event the companies ignored the advice and took up concessions from the Iraq government, the U.S. government would continue to support the IPC claim.[12]

Any American hopes that Iran might break with OPEC or be expelled failed to be realized. The U.S. embassy in Saudi Arabia strongly recommended against any U.S. government intervention with the Saudis in an effort to have OPEC accept Iran's more moderate position, on grounds that the Iranian government was perceived as pro-U.S. Embassy officials also thought that if OPEC proved resilient the private companies needed to be encouraged to consider whether a more compromising position on the state share of revenues might not be a more productive means of gaining the support of moderate Arab sentiment. This could provide them all with a degree of peace and stability in the industry and the region for a longer period, such as the more than a decade that the 50/50 formula Aramco agreed to with Saudi Arabia in 1950 had endured.[13]

Beyond the Anglo-American relationship, some bureaucratic differences existed within the U.S. government over oil policy, primarily involving rivalry between the Department of the Interior and the Department of State. The primary differences had been over import policy, with Interior tending to favour restriction of imports, but by the mid-1960s the two departments were largely in agreement that national security required minimizing imports from areas considered to be even slightly unreliable over the long term. As Andrew Ensor observed following the November 1965 Anglo-American meetings on oil issues, this meant "everywhere but Canada."[14]

Serious U.S. concern was also expressed at the 1965 Anglo-American meetings that labour issues in the Persian Gulf area could become a considerable challenge to the companies and to national interest. U.S. officials were concerned that Middle East governments were unwilling to recognize that labour was a challenge and that the companies persisted in viewing labour's interests as politically motivated rather than an indication of legitimate economic goals. They were apprehensive that if labour's concerns were not addressed the movement could be captured by radical and politically oriented groups such as the United Arab Republic (UAR)-dominated Arab Federation of Petroleum Workers, which had made significant advances in Kuwait. The feeling was that Arab nationalism was a serious and growing threat to Western interests, in particular in Syria and the UAR. American officials contended that the ideas of radical nationalist Abdullah Tariki had considerable popular appeal in the Arab world, as well as those of Faisal Mazidi in Kuwait, who promoted the ultimate local government control of the industry. British and American government officials concurred that it was preferable for Western challenges to Arab nationalist propaganda to target the more extreme ideas rather than to focus on what was considered the more "sophisticated" approach taken by OPEC. Arab nationalist propaganda at that stage was being countered through liaison group consultations involving both governments and the companies.[15]

In the ever-important Iran in the mid-1960s, the Shah regularly expressed concern that if oil revenues did not meet expectations and if the companies did not provide the anticipated growth in revenues from their operations he might have to change his approach to their operations. In the Shah's discussions with American embassy officials in early 1966 he stressed the importance for the free world of "maintaining a militarily secure and economically prosperous Iran" and said that much of the stability in the Gulf region relied on Iranian leadership. The Shah also observed that the Soviet Union continued to make inroads among Arab states through such measures as discounted prices for the sale of MIG-21s. At the same time, U.S. officials expressed concern over Iran's barter deals with Eastern Bloc countries and urged Iranian leaders to remember that their predominant market was with the free world countries. The Shah was particularly concerned over Nasser's ambitions in the Persian Gulf area as the 1967 crisis unfolded. American officials reported that Iranian security forces believed that Nasser had designs on the oil-rich Iranian province of Khuzestan, which contained a substantial ethnic Arab population. From the U.S. perspective the conclusion in 1967 of a substantial Soviet-Iranian arms agreement was more worrying than Nasser's ambitions in Iran. That agreement, combined with an Iranian agreement with Britain to purchase missiles and naval equipment, broke the long-term monopoly held by the United States over supplying and training Iranian armed forces in the Cold War years. The Shah firmly believed that Iran had to be strong enough militarily to deal with Iraq and Egypt without U.S. intervention. The Shah informed CIA director Richard Helms in their meeting on August 23 that with the gradual withdrawal of Britain from the Persian Gulf the only free world partners capable of filling the vacuum were Iran and Saudi Arabia. On the Arab-Israeli dispute, the Shah took the view that he could not publicly oppose a Muslim cause and that, although he considered Nasser dangerous and aggressive, an issue other than Israel would have to be found to stop him.[16]

American officials were undecided in the months leading up to the 1967 Arab-Israeli war on how to deal with Nasser and Egypt. National Security Advisor Walter Rostow informed President Johnson in February that American efforts over the previous five years had been unsuccessful in winning Nasser over and weaning him through economic aid from both his Eastern bloc ties and his extremist position on relations with Israel and the moderate Arab states. As Rostow pointed out, "Nasser more and more sees us behind all his troubles in the Middle East ... One key question is whether abandoning the field would result in unchallenged Soviet influence or whether Nasser's own interest in maintaining his independence would bring him back to the West." Rostow concluded that he was "reluctant to close this door" in light of the influence Nasser exercised in the region and the damage he could do if completely cut off from Western aid. Rostow cautioned that Nasser could cut off the U.S. right to important overflights or turn the Arab boycott into a more significant weapon against American trade, "stir up more trouble for Israel ... or even trigger the nationalization or harassment of our oil companies."[17]

The deterioration of the political situation in the Middle East in the spring of 1967 leading up to the June 1967 Arab-Israeli war contributed to considerable concern in U.S. oil policy circles. On the eve of the war there were also still important unresolved contractual issues affecting American companies in the Middle East, the most pressing being the ongoing dispute between the Iraq government and the Iraq Petroleum Company over the 99 percent of the IPC that had been withdrawn from the company and the 0.5 percent that could be retained. State Department officials were optimistic that the appointment of President Arif as Prime Minister to replace Naji Talib and the appointment of a moderate cabinet might make it possible to resolve the disagreement with IPC.[18]

The Arab-Israeli conflict intervened to complicate the resolution of such contract disputes.

In May the Petroleum Security Subcommittee of the Foreign Petroleum Supply Committee recommended that the Department of Defense seek alternative sources for imports from Persian Gulf refineries. As close to the outbreak of war in the Middle East as late May 1967, the Foreign Petroleum Supply Committee, the members of which were top level Department of the Interior officers and executives of major American companies, was inactive, since its role was to deal with crises, the previous occasion being the Suez crisis in 1956. Nonetheless, a permanent subcommittee, the Petroleum Security Subcommittee, also composed of senior Interior officials and senior technical people from the oil companies, was meeting regularly during this period.[19] The strategic importance of the Middle East to the U.S. military was reflected in the fact that the 200,000 b/d purchased from those refineries at the time represented 80 percent of all oil used by U.S. military forces in the Pacific. Officials anticipated that in the event of a Middle East war and any embargo or other curtailment of supplies from the region, the best-case scenario was the loss of only two pipelines and the worst case would be the closure of the Suez Canal and the loss of all Arab oil. The Department of the Interior calculated that they could tolerate the loss of two of the five major regional producers but that the loss of Kuwait and Saudi Arabia together would cause serious disruptions and any more would also affect Europe and Japan.[20]

State Department officials were concerned not only about oil supply but also about the general stability of the Middle East and the capacity of Nasser to influence regime change in the more vulnerable countries. These were Saudi Arabia and Jordan in particular, but also Kuwait and Libya if the Egyptian armies made a good showing against Israeli forces or if Israel succeeded in occupying territory in Jordan, Egypt, Syria, and Lebanon. Either scenario could further excite Arab nationalism and play to Nasser's advantage. American oil companies were extremely concerned about the U.S. position in the Arab-Israeli conflict. Aramco's Washington representative, John Pendelton, for instance, informed the State Department in late May that Saudi Petroleum Minister Sheikh Zaki Yamani had told Aramco's vice-president that if the U.S. directly supported Israel "Aramco can anticipate being nationalized, if not today, then tomorrow. If the U.S. does not stay out of this conflict, the U.S. is finished in the Middle East."[21]

When the war broke out in June King Faisal informed the head of Aramco in Saudi Arabia, R.I. Brougham, that the Arabs and Israelis could no longer live together. Although King Faisal did not, according to the report, make a direct reference to oil policy, he made it clear that the major powers, in particular the United States, must remain aloof from the conflict because any assistance for Israel would result in retaliatory measures by the Arab states. Concerns were not limited to the oil companies. John McCloy, then Chairman of the Ford Foundation and the Council on Foreign Relations, and a former president of the World Bank, informed Dean Rusk in early June that the President of Amherst College and Chairman of the Board of American University in Beirut, Calvin Plimpton, had indicated that any stand by the United States in favour of Israel would severely damage the U.S. position in the region. McCloy was also a member of the board of Chase Manhattan Bank and Allied Chemical Company, both of which had substantial investments in Iran.[22]

The Oil Ministers' conference meeting in Baghdad at that time unanimously passed two resolutions. They first declared that Arab oil would be denied to any countries directly or indirectly "committing aggression or participating in aggression on sovereignty of any Arab state or its territories or its territorial waters, particularly Gulf of Aqaba." The second resolution was explicit about the consequences for the oil companies of any nation engaging in such aggression. Such aggression, the resolution stated, would result in the Arab states making the assets of the nationals of aggressor nations subject to the laws of war. "This includes assets of oil companies." The resolution also called on all Islamic and friendly oil producing countries, especially Iran, to cooperate in preventing oil from reaching Israel.[23]

On June 5 war broke out between Israel and the UAR, Syria, and Jordan. Egypt claimed that U.S. warplanes had participated in attacks on Egypt, and on June 6 Iraq took the lead among the Arab oil producers in embargoing the flow of oil to both the United States and the United Kingdom. Although Saudi oil minister Yamani indicated he was aware that the Egyptian allegation was without foundation and that the contention was propagated by Cairo, he felt he had to wait for an "appropriate time" to say so publicly. In the interim Aramco officials were concerned not only about the embargo but also about potential attacks on their oil installations. In Kuwait, officials insisted on assuming immediate control of shipping communications to prevent the shipment of oil to British or American destinations, but oil company officials did not anticipate confiscation of their assets and cooperated fully with the Kuwaiti government. Algeria and Bahrein also prohibited the export of oil to the United States or the United Kingdom. Iraq ordered the Iraq Petroleum Company not only not to export but also to cease operations, as did the Libyan government with all foreign operators. The Trans Arabian Pipeline of Aramco was closed, as was the Suez Canal.[24] The government of Colonel Muammar Qadaffi in Libya had already in 1971 unilaterally set the stage for price increases by other Middle East producers, but the Arab-Israeli conflict solidified their resolve as well as leverage with the companies.[25] Throughout the crisis Venezuelan officials adamantly resisted the pressures of other OPEC members to embargo oil to the United States in solidarity with the Arab states.[26] Official American protests against these policies and denials of the charges of aggression against the United States met with little success in the Arab world. CIA director John McCone noted in the midst of the crisis that friendly Arab states such as Saudi Arabia and Lebanon were restrained from taking a more moderate line towards the foreign companies as well as Britain and the United States under pressure from Iraq and Syria. Lebanon, McCone contended, would have been willing to open the Tapline (Trans-Arabian Pipeline) and get the oil flowing again were it not for fear of the popular reaction by groups "whipped up by Cairo propaganda." McCone was also convinced that the danger of "expropriation, expulsion and nationalization of American interests" were real and to be taken seriously in Washington.[27]

Oil company officials were also concerned that company collaboration among themselves and with the Western governments during the crisis not lead to antitrust action. Companies involved with the U.S. Foreign Petroleum Supply Committee, established in 1950 under the Defense Production Act, had protection under the antitrust laws and the Federal Trade Commission Act. They were concerned that if they were involved in collaboration with the OECD Oil Committee they should receive similar protection. The Departments of State and Interior did not, however, approve the establishment of an Anglo-American company committee.[28]

Both European officials and some U.S. representatives in European capitals in the midst of the Arab-Israeli conflict feared that the United States was treating Europe's oil supply problems as a strictly European problem. The American embassy in Bonn, for instance, informed the State Department in late June that Germany expected American and other foreign oil companies at least to recognize their obligations arising from their "dominant position" in the German market, "even if this requires changes or dislocations in the normal production and marketing patterns in the U.S." "It is unfair," the cable contended, "that our companies take the cream of profits from their operations in the German market in good times, and not give them their fair share of oil and shipping in time of crisis."[29]

Undersecretary of State Nicholas Katzenbach replied to the Embassy in Bonn that until there was a change in policy to determine that the oil supply situation represented a national security emergency for the United States, the companies could not collaborate to deal with the European markets without risk of violating antitrust regulations, although that issue was being addressed by the parties involved, specifically by the Department of the Interior, Office of Emergency Planning, and the Attorney General. Katzenbach added that, although Europe and Japan, but not the United States, were directly affected by the embargo, they were U.S. allies and thus a threat to their security constituted a threat to U.S. security as well. He did not add, but might have, that the U.S. was using two to three hundred thousand barrels of oil a day from the Middle East in its Vietnam operations. Shell Vietnam, controlled by London, provided one half of the entire oil supply for Vietnam. The oil was purchased by the United States for its military operations.[30]

On 1 August Saudi oil minister Yamani met in New York with oil company officials to discuss the Middle East situation. At the meetings Yamani stressed that the struggle in the Middle East was one between socialist and conservative Arab states and that it had been primarily the position of Saudi Arabia at the May oil ministers' meeting in Baghdad that had prevented the group from adopting a resolution nationalizing the oil industry. Yamani also indicated that the larger goal was to reduce American power to influence the course of events in the region and in particular to reduce the capacity of the United States to provide assistance to Israel. Yamani also indicated earlier that the political climate in the region would have to stabilize before Saudi Arabia could risk lifting the embargo against the United States, although with the late July decision of Iraq to lift the embargo on all countries except the United States, Britain, and West Germany, the position of even the hard liners was softening. In August Libya resumed direct oil exports to West Germany without public announcement; Abu Dhabi was continuing to export to the U.K.; Bahrain was allowing sales to Britain and the United States; by mid-August Shell was resuming unrestricted production in Muscat and Oman; and King Faisal announced at the beginning of September that Saudi Arabia would resume the flow of oil to all countries. For these concessions the moderate Arab states paid a substantial price to the identified "victims of Zionist aggression." Egypt was to receive approximately $266 million and Jordan $112 million.[31]

As the 1967 crisis wound down in late August, National Security Advisor Walter Rostow and other U.S. government officials met with executives from Standard Oil of California, Standard Oil of New Jersey, Texaco, Mobil, Gulf, Continental, and Aramco to review the situation. The corporate leaders remained very concerned that the Arab moderates were highly vulnerable and that thirty years of building an industry in the region was threatened, along with billions of dollars in investments and contributions to the U.S. balance of payments. The executives expressed the strong desire that American government officials would do all they could publicly to support the moderate Arab states.[32]

Although the immediate crisis ended without serious damage to

either the companies or the interests of the United States, it was evident
to all parties at the end of 1967 that the larger challenge remained of balancing the interests of the Middle East producers with those of the consuming nations and the foreign companies operating in the region. Nor
was the relationship between the more moderate and the more radical
Arab states resolved, not only over their attitudes and policies toward
the oil industry and the West but also over the place of Israel in the
region. In an indication of the ongoing commitment of the Arab oil producers to shape their own destiny, in early 1968 Saudi Arabia, Kuwait,
and Libya, meeting in Beirut, agreed to establish an Organization of Arab
Petroleum Exporting Countries, headquartered in Kuwait, with membership open only to those other Arab nations whose basic source of
income was oil. Iraq decided not to join the new organization but rather
to coordinate its oil policies within the Arab League, a far more radical
group.[33]

Had the United States, other Western powers, and Japan needed a
warning about their energy security, the 1967 war had provided it, even
though the crisis was short-lived and caused little disruption for the
United States. The crisis also reinforced the degree to which the private
companies operating in the Middle East were vulnerable to the political
dynamics in the Arab world and the difficulties that even the moderate
Arab governments had in holding more radical elements in check.
Nonetheless, the United States emerged from the 1967 war thinking that
its security was sound as long as Western hemisphere supplies were
available. But there was a heightened awareness of the extent to which
U.S. security depended on not only the availability of adequate supplies
for North American industrial and military operations in an emergency
but also adequate supply for the major allies in Western Europe and
Japan. President Johnson's Secretary of the Interior, Stuart Udall, commented in the aftermath of the Arab-Israeli conflict that the "relationship
between our national security and adequate supplies of oil is clear. On
this score it suffices to point out that oil is practically the sole source of
energy for transportation – both civilian and military."[34]

THE NIXON YEARS

The larger context for American security at the end of the 1960s was the
continuing challenge of Soviet-American relations and the deepening
international and domestic crisis associated with the Vietnam War. That
prolonged war contributed not only to a domestic political problem but
also to increased demand for oil for industrial and military use and to a
serious balance of payments problem for the United States. Unlike the
Middle East dynamic, oil resources were not a significant factor in the

Vietnam theatre itself, in spite of the high demand for petroleum products occasioned by the war effort. Vietnam had no proven onshore reserves, but there were potential offshore resources, and although neither South nor North Vietnam had established offshore concessions, a number of neighbouring countries had done so in the Gulf of Siam and South China Sea. The lack of resource development made Vietnam totally dependent on imports, which in the late 1960s and early 1970s drained $30 million annually from limited resources. In an effort to attract foreign oil companies to develop offshore resources in late 1970 the South Vietnamese National Assembly implemented legislation establishing the terms under which companies would operate in exploration and exploitation of possible offshore deposits. Several of the multinational firms, including Shell, Caltex, and Esso, were involved in marketing oil products in Vietnam, and they supplied the area from refineries primarily in the Persian Gulf and Singapore. By 1971 Esso had expressed to the State Department an interest in Vietnam's offshore oil potential. To that point no agency of the U.S. government had provided South Vietnam with technical or financial assistance for oil exploration.[35]

The Vietnam War until 1975 occupied much of America's energy and resources. Insofar as oil policy was concerned, however, the Middle East held centre stage, even if American oil interests in other parts of the world were challenged as producing countries became increasingly nationalistic, most notably in the Latin American context in Peru, where the military junta that came to power in 1968 nationalized the Talara oil refinery and subsequently nationalized Gulf Oil's operations. Increasing tensions and crises in the Middle East, in particular between Israel and the Arab nations in 1967 and 1973, led to an oil shock far more serious than that triggered by the Anglo-Iranian conflict and Suez crisis in the 1950s. The international community had only begun to recover from the 1973 Arab oil embargo that followed the Arab-Israeli war in 1973 when the Soviet Union invaded Afghanistan in 1979 and the Shah was driven from power in Iran by radical Muslim fundamentalists, creating yet another energy crisis in the United States. OPEC also proved to be more cohesive and influential in determining levels of production and world prices than had been anticipated by Western government and company officials at the time of the organization's birth in the 1960s.

The Nixon administration was aggressive on a broad front in foreign policy. Owing in part to the effective working relationship between President Nixon and Henry Kissinger, first as National Security Advisor and then as Secretary of State, the administration moved towards détente with the Soviet Union and engagement with the People's Republic of China. At the same time the administration faced a range of crises internationally and ultimately domestically, the latter destroying the Nixon presidency. In spite of the primary focus of u.s. officials on the Middle East, at least in terms of oil policy, North America played an increasingly important role as a source for u.s. energy from the 1960s on, not only for oil but also for hydro-electricity and natural gas. u.s. oil imports from Canadian sources increased steadily, from 4.9 percent of total u.s. oil imports in 1958 to 11.7 percent in 1962, and 18.7 percent by 1967; by that time Canadian exports significantly exceeded those from the Middle East, which in 1967 represented only 8.3 percent of total u.s. imports.[36] In spite of that increased export from Canadian sources to the u.s. market, in 1968 it was an estimated 1.7 million barrels/day of the maximum efficient reservoir capacity in Alberta was shut in because of restricted access to the u.s. market.

With u.s. domestic production lagging behind demand and with only a 5 percent rate of growth in the United States in 1970,[37] the Nixon administration was clearly optimistic about Canadian potential for long-term development and supply; it was noted in 1970 that at only $2.90/barrel even "modest sized" Arctic reserves could be developed, including potential reserves in the sedimentary areas of the Canadian Arctic and in the tar sands, which it was estimated at that time contained over 300 billion barrels of economically recoverable reserves. The administration believed that the possibilities for short-term expansion of Canadian production were only "modest" and that significant increases in Canadian production would require production from tar sands and the expansion of pipeline facilities for delivery to the u.s. Significantly, the Nixon administration study concluded that the import-control program initiated by President Eisenhower was of little real importance for the "oil security of the free world" or more specifically for the u.s., North America, or the Western hemisphere. In one extreme scenario outlined by the Nixon cabinet task force, the reallocation pattern assumed that the u.s. and Canada would receive no oil from either the Eastern hemisphere or from Latin America because naval warfare prevented oceanic shipping; in that case, adequate prices would be essential to ensure development of a sufficient continental supply.

The Nixon administration Cabinet Task Force on Oil Import Control and National Security focused on measures that would limit reliance on Eastern hemisphere imports to no more than 10 percent of requirements. The task force was confronted by the perennial problem of balancing national security considerations with political and diplomatic factors. The administration, especially the Department of State, was also concerned that strict quotas on imports from friendly nations would adversely affect diplomatic relations. They recommended that policy should be based on a broader range of factors, including: political stability of the supplying area; economic interdependence; and the degree of vulnerability to transport interference. The task force noted that it made little sense to favour sea shipments from Mexico over Great Lakes shipments from Canada, although they suggested that Caribbean shipments were likely as secure as Gulf Coast movements and more secure than shipments from either Alaska or Canadian Arctic islands. The task force concluded that Canada could be considered more reliable than any other foreign supplier.[38] Observing that Canadian imports were not counted as eligible inputs for the calculation of quota allocations, to discourage Canadian imports under the overland exemption, the task force concluded that since Canadian imports were secure there was no reason to treat them differentially from domestic American inputs.[39]

Secretary of Defense Melvin Laird found the report overly optimistic about the nation's capacity to respond to a military crisis; consequently, the Defense Department was willing to endorse the report only with the adoption of the recommendations to create a high-level inter-departmental management and control organization, chaired by the Office of Economic Preparedness and involving Defense membership. The Secretary of Defense's position reflected the persistence of the view of the previous twenty years that domestic resource development was essential, that domestic exploration had to be maintained minimally at current levels, and that import restrictions be modified only gradually when and if security needs were satisfied. The Pentagon stressed that the U.S. needed to look beyond 1980, when it was anticipated that Western hemisphere producing regions would decline.[40]

Clearly, by the early 1970s the Nixon administration was acutely aware that a higher degree of reliance on Western hemisphere resources was needed, as well as efforts to reduce reliance on imports as a whole. State Department officials noted that although increased reliance on Western hemisphere resources made policy sense, the constant increase in U.S. demand made the sufficiency of Western hemisphere supplies uncertain, and they projected that the increased supplies over the next decade would have to come primarily from the Middle East and West Africa.[41] They also were sensitive to the growing demand for oil products from other nations, in particular in Asia and Europe. Officials projected a doubling of demand for oil in Western Europe in the 1970s, with an even larger increase in Japanese demand. "In the future," noted one senior department official in 1972, three years before the first North Sea oil came on line after several years of expensive development, "we may have to join the Europeans and the Japanese in the search for oil in the Eastern Hemisphere to cover our own needs at home. Under such circumstances, the policies of Europe and Japan, as well as the policies of the producing countries, will have a significant impact on our interests."[42]

President Nixon indicated in the course of a review of oil import policy in 1970 that the appropriate offices in his administration agreed that "a unique degree of security can be afforded by moving toward an integrated North American energy market." He reported in 1970 that he had instructed the State Department to "explore more fully the possibility of reaching an agreement with Mexico," and added that he had given similar instructions to the department to "examine with Canada measures looking toward a freer exchange of petroleum, natural gas, and other energy resources between the two countries." At the same time, the administration established a limit of 395,000 barrels of crude and unfinished oil into Districts I-IV for the remainder of 1970, while discussions proceeded with a view to achieving a freer exchange. Nixon noted that Venezuelan and other Latin American suppliers had "proven to be dependable sources of oil during the crises we have experienced since the Second World War."[43]

Since Venezuelan oil exports were not transported overland to u.s. markets, Venezuela did not meet the criteria for exemption from the import control program, a development that caused considerable consternation in Venezuelan political and economic circles. Venezuelan President Rafael Caldera raised that concern in his 1970 address to the u.s. Congress during an official visit. He stressed that the Venezuelan economy depended heavily on petroleum exports and observed that as a result of u.s. policy exports to the United States had declined in recent years. "Our people cannot understand," he informed the assembled congressional representatives, "being made the object of discriminatory treatment." To Caldera, the treatment of Venezuelan oil exports was not a simple commercial issue but rather "a condition for the fulfilment of the development programs of a neighboring and friendly country and a key to the direction that future relations between the United States and Latin America will take." Although Caldera focused on oil in his remarks, he couched his concerns in the larger context of the challenges faced by Latin American producers and exporters of raw materials, and the picture he painted of the consequences for Latin America of restricted access to u.s. markets was a grim one, echoing a longstanding grievance on the part of most Latin American nations. "How many schools and hospitals will close," he asked, "how many workers be dismissed, how much pain be inflicted, how many rebellions engendered in peace-loving nations, by the reduction of a single cent per pound of coffee, bananas, lead, or copper."[44]

What Caldera did not mention was that u.s. investment in the Venezuelan oil industry had stagnated during the 1960s. Between 1960 and 1969 total u.s. investment in Venezuela increased only from $2.6 to $2.7 billion, although Venezuela enjoyed healthy economic growth during that period. U.S. officials attributed the lack of increased American investment in the Venezuelan oil industry to Venezuela's increasingly nationalistic policies. In 1959 Venezuela announced that it would approve no new oil concessions. In 1970 Venezuela raised taxes on the oil companies to 60 percent and established the precedent that reference prices would thereafter be fixed unilaterally by the government. U.S. officials estimated that close to 80 percent of revenues produced by the oil industry went to the Venezuelan government, the highest proportion among the major world producers. From 1960 to 1968 depreciation and amortization of fixed assets in the oil industry exceeded new investments in every year. In 1968 there were new investments in desulphurization plants. Although little new U.S. private investment in the Venezuelan oil industry occurred during the 1960s, considerable amounts of oil earnings were reinvested in the manufacturing sector.[45]

The Nixon administration responded to Canadian and Venezuelan concerns with some modification of the oil import program, on the recommendation of the Oil Policy Committee, chaired by General George A. Lincoln, Director of the Office of Emergency Preparedness, by increasing the level of imports of oil in Districts I-IV by 100,000 b/d. Although the Canadian limit of 395,000 b/d, a limit well below actual import levels, was to remain in place for the balance of the year, the Oil Imports Appeals Board was mandated to consider petitions from users of Canadian oil if they experienced "exceptional hardship." The administration also mandated that 40,000 b/d of No. 2 fuel oil be allocated to independent deep water terminal operators, which would place them in a position comparable to refineries operated by the major integrated companies, since No. 2 fuel oil was a major source of heat for homes and small businesses in New England and the Middle Atlantic states. The policy required that the No. 2 fuel oil be drawn from Western hemisphere sources in keeping with the preference for Western hemisphere oil recommended for reasons of national security by the Cabinet Task Force. As the administration indicated, the modification of policy was intended in part to "strengthen U.S. petroleum trade with Venezuela and the other Latin American countries.[46] General Lincoln indicated that the revised policy would not "adversely affect national security," but he expressed serious concern about the longer term. He indicated that "we face the growing danger of not having adequate supplies from reasonably secure sources ... National security must be a central consideration in working out that overall policy."[47]

In the mid-1970s Senator Henry M. Jackson's Committee on Inland and Insular Affairs reported on the geopolitics of energy that, in spite of the major political obstacles involved, "an energy effort in Canada" seemed to be "an obvious priority."[48] This observation followed the establishment in the late 1960s of the Canadian National Energy Board and the effort to establish more national controls over exploration, development, and marketing of Canadian resources. The Canadian initiative and the harder line by OPEC resulted in significant price increases in the 1970s for oil and natural gas exported from Canada to the U.S.; for instance, between 1977 and 1981 the border prices for export gas increased from C$1.94 to $4.94 per MMBTU. In spite of price increases, during the Arab oil embargo Canadian oil product exports to the U.S. increased from approximately 42,000 barrels/day in the pre-embargo period to almost 47,000. A subcommittee of the Senate Foreign Relations Committee observed after the OPEC embargo in 1973 that, given the high percentage of U.S. oil imports originating in Canada and the high percentage of U.S. direct foreign oil investment in Canada at the time (in 1973, $5.9 billion of a total $29.6 billion), it was important "to persuade the Canadian Government to delay implementation of its announced objective of curtailing exports to the United States." In 1975 the Canadian National Energy Board recommended to Cabinet border price increases on natural gas, increases that were implemented against U.S. objection; ultimately, at U.S. urging, the increases were implemented not on a differential basis affecting only the U.S. market, but on all export gas.[49]

Although the oil crises of the 1970s increased interest in Western hemisphere sources of supply, the focus of policymakers remained the Middle East. In the 1970s the oil-producing countries increasingly flexed their economic muscle, primarily to increase their share of profits from oil production but also in response to political challenges. This combination of politics and economics was evident early in the decade in Syria's interruption of the flow of oil through the Tapline from Saudi Arabia to the Mediterranean in mid-1970, contributing to high tanker rates for the balance of the year. In September that year Libya increased the tax rate on its producing companies to 55 percent. Iran and Kuwait followed suit later in the year, and in December OPEC, meeting in Caracas, set 55 percent as the minimum tax rate among its members and authorized an embargo against any company that did not accept the rate. The following year Libya negotiated with a group of Western oil companies on its own behalf and that of Saudi Arabia, Algeria, and Iraq, resulting in an increase of prices on oil delivered to the Mediterranean from $2.55 to $3.45 a barrel and an increase in the tax rate to 60 percent of posted price. At the end of the year it nationalized the British Petroleum Company concession. Shortly thereafter Iraq nationalized the Iraq Petroleum Company's concession that was owned by BP, Royal Dutch Shell, Compagnie Française des Petroles (CFP), Mobil, and Standard Oil of New Jersey (Exxon), and OPEC threatened to penalize those companies if they sought to increase production elsewhere to offset their losses in Iraq. A few months later OPEC approved a plan providing for 25 percent government ownership of all Western oil companies operating in Kuwait, Qatar, Abu Dhabi, and Saudi Arabia, with the intent to increase the percentage of ownership to 51 percent by 1983.

In 1972 the major companies accepted OPEC's demands for participation, or part ownership, in the companies' operations, and U.S. officials anticipated this would result in slightly higher prices.[50] In Iran, in 1973 the otherwise pro-Western Shah first announced that the 1954 operating agreement with the consortium of companies would not be renewed on its expiry in 1979; he then agreed to nationalize all assets in return for a guaranteed twenty years of access to Iranian oil production. Nationalizations continued elsewhere. In 1973 Libya nationalized the Bunker Hunt concession and acquired 51 percent of the concessions held by nine other foreign companies: Esso, Libya/Sirte, Mobil, Shell, Gelensberg, Texaco, SoCal, Libyan-American, and Grace. In Africa, Nigeria acquired 35 percent participation in the concession operated jointly by Shell and BP, and Libya acquired 51 percent of the Occidental Petroleum Company concession and of the Oasis consortium. When several U.S. companies balked at the 51 percent state control they were nationalized. In 1974 Kuwait and Qatar increased their shares in the BP-Gulf Oil concession to 60 percent; Nigeria increased its share of control in all concessions to 55 percent, and Saudi Arabia, Abu Dhabi, and Kuwait increased their level of participation in Aramco to 60 percent. Throughout this short period OPEC kept driving up the price of oil, an increase of 5.7 percent in April 1973 and an 11.9 percent increase in June of that year, all before the outbreak of the fourth Arab-Israeli war in October that year.[51] In Latin America, Venezuela, with the passage of a new hydrocarbons law, moved increasingly towards the nationalization of unexploited concession areas by 1974 and of their residual assets by 1983.

During 1973 the Nixon administration became increasingly aware of Egyptian President Anwar Sadat's aggressive intentions towards Israel, as well as of his efforts, consistent with the line Nasser had previously pursued, to push Saudi Arabia towards a harder line against Israel. The major U.S. oil companies in the region pressed the administration to adopt a less pro-Israeli position. Nonetheless, although Nixon had received considerable support from oil interests in his presidential campaigns and was prepared to meet with and listen sympathetically to the companies' concerns, their efforts to shift the administration towards a more pro-Arab position had little impact.[52] In any event the administration could have done little to prevent the October 1973 attack on Israel by Egypt and Syria. The Yom Kippur war had a far more dramatic impact on the United States than had the short-lived 1967 Arab-Israeli conflict. The day after the outbreak of the Arab-Israeli war in October, Iraq nationalized the shares in the Basrah Petroleum Company held by Exxon and Mobil, and a few weeks later OPEC oil ministers agreed to use oil as a weapon in the war, thus mandating a cut in exports and recommending an embargo against "unfriendly" states. Before the end of October a number of Arab states, including Saudi Arabia and Libya, embargoed oil exports to the United States and mandated a cut in production. The embargo against the United States remained in effect until the following June and continued thereafter against the Netherlands, South Africa, Rhodesia, and Portugal. By the end of the year production was increased but the posted price for crude was raised from $5.12 to $11.65 a barrel.

The Nixon administration increasingly sought to balance its support for Israel against the pressure from the other leading Middle East states, although publicly the President insisted that the United States was neither pro-Israel nor pro-Arab but pro-peace. At the end of December Nixon wrote to Sadat pledging that his second presidential term "will be remembered as the period in which the United States developed a new and productive relationship with Egypt and the Arab world."[53] Henry Kissinger had nothing but praise for the role the Shah of Iran played during the Arab-Israeli conflict. He noted in his memoirs that the Shah aided Western Europe, never used oil as a weapon, and declined to join the embargo; and that Iran was the only country bordering on the Soviet Union during the 1973 conflict that refused to allow the Soviet Union to use its air space. The Shah was critical to the U.S. position in the early 1970s, especially as Saudi Arabia wavered in its orientation. Nixon visited the Shah in 1972 in an effort to reinforce the relationship. As Kissinger noted, 15,000 Soviet troops were still in Egypt at that time; the USSR also had friendly relations with Iraq, which was the recipient of modern Soviet weapons, and had increased its influence in the Sudan and Algeria.[54]

As the international oil crisis spread and the domestic situation became more critical, the Nixon administration took the lead in bringing together the major consuming industrial nations. Domestically the Nixon administration called on Americans to turn down their thermostats, reduce driving speeds, and exercise conservation with lighting. Before the end of 1973 Sunday gasoline station closings were in effect and in December the President created the Federal Energy Office in the Executive Office to coordinate efforts to deal with the oil embargo and to allocate supplies of crude and refined oil products. The administration also imposed a two-tier price ceiling on crude oil sales: production of oil produced at or below 1972 levels from existing wells would be sold at March 1973 prices plus 35 cents; new oil would be sold at uncontrolled prices. By executive order the President also tripled the offshore acreage available for oil and gas leases and established the Office of Energy Conservation; with the outbreak of war that fall he pressed for Congressional action to relax environmental regulations.[55]

Thirteen industrial nations sent representatives to the February 1974 Washington Energy Conference, which sought to develop a collaborative approach among the main consuming countries. At the conference, Secretary of State Henry Kissinger presented the Nixon administration's "Project Independence" plan, which was designed to make the United States self-sufficient in energy. Speaking at a press conference in early January 1974 with newly appointed head of the Federal Energy Office William Simon, Kissinger stressed that the energy crisis represented a basic challenge for the entire international community and that the price increases imposed by OPEC could have a revolutionary impact on the world economy, affecting the balance of payments of all the advanced industrial nations as well as the less developed consuming nations. In January 1974 the Energy Office established a fuel allocation program for propane, butane, motor gasoline, aviation fuels, residual fuel oil, lubricants, and petrochemical feedstocks, among other commodities. Over the next few years this temporary office assumed increasing importance and was absorbed first into the Federal Energy Administration, which in turn was folded into the Department of Energy established by President Carter in early 1977, shortly after taking office. One of the several key responsibilities of the Federal Energy Administration was to assess energy policy alternatives and the capacity of the country to liberate itself from dependence on foreign supplies; in this role it contributed to the shaping of foreign policy as well as domestic policies.[56]

In 1974 the main consuming nations met in Paris to establish the International Energy Agency. The following year the major oil exporting companies met with leading consuming nations, including countries of Western Europe, the United States, and Japan, and several major developing nations that did not export oil, including India, Brazil, and Zaire, in an effort to address the impact of high energy costs on the international economy. As with many international efforts to bridge the interests of developing and developed nations in the 1970s, the conference foundered over the fundamentally divergent perspectives of their respective interests. Nonetheless, the main product of these and other talks was the establishment by the OECD (Organization for Economic Cooperation and Development) of a fund to assist industrial nations affected by high energy costs, and shortly thereafter the IMF, with collaboration from both industrial and oil-exporting countries, established a fund to provide loans to countries that were too wealthy to qualify for no-interest loans but too poor to meet current interest charges.

Nixon administration policy towards the embargo shifted between behind the scenes diplomacy and some sabre rattling in public. In a press conference in early January 1974 Kissinger, responding to a question, indicated in what seemed a veiled threat that the administration was not contemplating "specific measures at this moment." A few days later Secretary of Defense James Schlesinger warned, to the outrage of Arab countries, that reprisals were possible. It was not until mid-March 1974 that the first major break occurred, when seven of the nine Middle East nations engaged in the embargo agreed to lift the restrictions, only two weeks after the indictments had been issued for John Mitchell, Bob Haldeman, John Erlichman, and several others in the Watergate scandal. The President's capacity to achieve either domestic or foreign policy goals evaporated, although Kissinger continued his shuttle diplomacy in the Middle East in an effort to have full troop disengagement between Israel and Syria. The oil embargo crisis was nonetheless winding down at a cost to the United States that the President estimated at $15 billion during the first quarter of 1974 alone.[57]

Following Richard Nixon's resignation in the midst of the Watergate scandal, his successor and former vice-president Gerald Ford signed the Energy Policy and Conservation Act at the end of 1975, established the Strategic Petroleum Reserve, and approved regulation of oil prices. To build the Petroleum Reserve, crude oil was placed in underground storage accessible to tankers and pipelines so that oil could easily be drawn on in the event of another oil embargo. By the end of 1978 the reserve was to contain 150 million barrels of crude oil, with the objective of increasing the volume to 500 million by 1982. From 1975 through 1978 prices remained relatively stable, even if comparatively high relative to the 1960s, with Saudi Arabia and the United Arab Emirates selling at $12.09 a barrel and the other OPEC exporters setting their price at $12.70. In the period leading up to the Iranian revolution, Iran and Saudi Arabia took a more moderate stance on relations with the United States and other Western countries, but the political situation in Iran became critical in 1978. By September of that year, confronted by increasing rioting and the anti-Shah movement led by Muslim fundamentalists, the Shah felt compelled to place the country under military rule in an effort to suppress the opposition. Early the next year he left the country for the last time.

THE CARTER YEARS

President Jimmy Carter sought to address the energy issue from the outset of his presidency. Defining the energy crisis in terms coined by William James a century earlier, Carter presented the issue to the American people as the "moral equivalent of war." Carter noted at the time and subsequently in his memoirs that the lessons had not been learned from the oil crises of 1973 and earlier. If dependency on imported oil had been a problem in 1973, when imports accounted for 35 percent of American consumption, it was more so by 1977, when imports had risen to 50 percent of American requirements. As Carter noted, "we were the only developed nation without an energy policy, and our total energy consumption was at a record high."[58]

Carter's National Energy Plan, which he presented to Congress in April 1977 and which led to the establishment in August that year of the Department of Energy Organization Act, strongly emphasized the national security implications of the energy situation. President Carter and Congress concurred that the United States faced an increasing shortage of non-renewable energy sources, that the increased dependence on foreign supplies threatened national security as well as the health, safety, and welfare of American citizens, and that a strong national energy program was needed to meet present and future energy requirements "consistent with overall national economic, environmental and social goals." With the passage of the legislation establishing the Department of Energy, Carter symbolically appointed former Secretary of Defense James Schlesinger as the first Secretary of Energy, and later that fall he signed the National Energy Act, which included several subsets of legislation: the National Energy Conservation Policy Act; the Powerplant and Industrial Fuel Use Act; the Public Utilities Regulatory Policy Act; the Energy Tax Act; and the Natural Gas Policy Act. The collective goal was in part to establish a favourable tax environment to encourage research and development of domestic and alternative energy sources.[59]

In the last few months of 1978 Iranian production declined radically to a twenty-seven-year low while overall OPEC production increased and OPEC planned on a phased-in price increase of 14.5 percent in 1979. OPEC continued to raise prices during 1979 and Saudi Arabia moved to export more of its production independent of Aramco, further affecting prices in the midst of an oil glut in the market. In mid-November, with the Shah-installed government in collapse, the Carter administration embargoed Iranian imports into the United States; in return Iran cancelled all contracts with U.S. oil companies. By the end of the year Saudi Arabia had raised the price of crude to $24 a barrel. As the Carter administration, in its final year before giving way to Ronald Reagan's conservative Republican government, struggled with the twin challenges of attempting to liberate Americans being held hostage in Teheran and yet another energy shock, Iraq invaded Iran, setting the stage for an extended war that was costly in terms of human and material loss and severely compromised the position of the United States in the region.

In a national television address in mid-1979, President Carter indicated that the U.S. was working closely with Mexico and Canada in the development of energy policies; although it was anticipated that Canadian oil production would decline, the administration was counting on sharing Canada's hydroelectric power and natural gas; Carter expressed hope that by 1985 the Alaska natural gas pipeline would enable Alaskan and Canadian natural gas to displace almost 7,000 bb/d of imported oil. In early 1980 he told a White House briefing that for three years the administration had been working on energy security; "How," he asked, "can we remove the debilitating vulnerability which now afflicts our country because we are so heavily dependent on foreign oil?" In April of that year he signed the Crude Oil Windfall Profits Tax, and two months later he signed the Energy Security Act of 1980.[60]

The Iranian revolution, the taking of American hostages at the U.S. Embassy, and Iran's export of revolution through Hezbollah led to economic retaliation by the Carter administration. The administration established sanctions in 1980 and froze Iranian assets in the United States, but in spite of the sanctions Iran continued to export oil to the United States through much of the 1980s, until the Reagan administration, determined to weaken Iran in its war with Iraq, also sanctioned the import of Iranian oil and imposed controls over the sale of any military equipment to Iran.[61]

Outside the Middle East the Carter administration sought to focus on hemispheric supplies as well as conservation measures. Carter's efforts to stress the commonality of United States and Canadian interests came at the same time that the Liberal Government of Pierre Trudeau initiated the National Energy Policy (NEP). The Canadianization provisions of the NEP ran directly counter to the traditional American thrust toward continentalism in the use of natural resources. The Liberal government stressed the substantial capital outflows of dividend and interest payments from the Canadian oil industry in the 1970s and the need for Canadians to reap more of the economic benefits from this resource industry; the target was to make Canadian oil and gas production 50 percent Canadian owned by 1990, to discourage foreign investment, to encourage exploration and development on federal rather than provincial lands, to establish a tax system that would facilitate Canadian investor entry into the industry, and to use Petro-Canada (created in 1976) as a vehicle for Canadian participation and direction.[62] In March 1981 the Department of State formally protested to the Canadian Government against the general direction of the NEP and implied possible retaliation against Canadian investments in the United States. During his March 1981 official visit to Canada, President Reagan pointedly stressed that the direction of the U.S. was towards deregulation of the private sector. At a press conference shortly before leaving Washington, President Reagan, responding to a question on the Canadianization of the oil industry, indicated that he was "determined that the proper goal for us must be energy independence in the United States, not that we would take advantage of either of our neighbours there with regard to energy supplies." Undersecretary of State for Economic Affairs, Myer Rashish, was more pointed in his comments on the NEP, referring to it as "discriminatory ... favouring domestic investment." Rashish emphasized that it was the national security implications of American reliance on imported oil that were of most concern, and stressed the importance of the strategic petroleum reserve on the domestic side and the International Energy Agency on the multinational side in reducing the vulnerability of the U.S. to sudden shocks in the supply of oil.[63] The private oil companies were even more outspoken in their criticism of the NEP.[64]

By the end of the 1970s U.S. oil interests continued to be threatened by increasing domestic demand, the consolidation of nationalist controls in the Middle East as well as in North and South America, and the continued tensions associated with the Cold War. A number of these issues presented acute challenges during the Carter, Reagan, and George Bush, Sr, presidencies, as these American administrations sought to confront the challenge posed by dependence on foreign supplies of energy, the instability of the international order, and the threat of economic nationalism. In hindsight, by the end of the 1970s the old international order in the oil industry, dominated by a small number of major international oil firms exercising a high degree of control over development and markets, had been largely destroyed. The cumulative events of the Iranian and the Suez crises in the 1950s, followed by the establishment of OPEC in the 1960s, the 1967 Arab-Israeli war and then the Yom Kippur war, and the subsequent embargo, contributed to the destruction of that old order, in which Great Britain and the United States had been the largely unchallenged hegemonic powers. The decline of the old order was not solely the result of the rising power of OPEC, but rather the consequence of a complex range of factors including: OPEC; the U.S. becoming a net importer of oil; the increasing crisis of the U.S. balance of payments in the 1960s; the significant movement of the independent oil companies into territory traditionally dominated by a small number of majors; the arms race; and the resurgence of the Western European and Japanese economies. American-based oil companies nonetheless remained a major force in the global oil industry and their protection was a priority of U.S. foreign policy. The importance to the U.S. economy of those companies was hardly surprising given that in 1972 oil companies generated only slightly less than 49 percent of all U.S. foreign profits.[65] It was also not surprising that collectively the industry exercised massive political power in Washington, even if the traditional differences between domestic and international producers persisted. President Nixon was only partially correct when he wrote in his memoirs that "the predicament of the 1970s was the result of short-sighted government policies compounded by decades of wasteful habits."[66]

CHAPTER TWELVE

From Oil Shocks
to Oil Wars

The years between the Iranian revolution and the early twenty-first century were dramatic ones in international relations and in United States foreign policy. The Iranian revolution and the fall of the Shah reinforced the unpredictability of both domestic and international politics in the Near and Middle East. The Iranian transformation also unleashed an Islamic fundamentalist revolution that had an immediate and significant impact within the region and also on relations between Middle East countries, the United States, and Western Europe. Two decades separated the Iranian revolution from the events of 11 September 2001, but in hindsight there was a clear path between the two. Hatred for the West and in particular for the u.s. presence in the Middle East boiled over in 1979–1980, then simmered until the al-Qaeda-inspired attacks on American interests around the world and then on the World Trade Center towers and the Pentagon on that early morning in September 2001. In East-West relations the 1980s and early 1990s brought both confrontation and collaboration as Mikhail Gorbachev's policies of Perestroika and Glasnost softened the Soviet position toward the West. Unable to meet the challenges of a lost war in Afghanistan in the 1980s or the costs of a renewed arms race with the United States, the Soviet Union and the Communist regime collapsed in 1991, radically altering the face of international politics and the direction of the Central Asian and East European nations that had been dominated by the Soviet Union for most of the century.

Ronald Reagan came to the presidency in early 1981 towards the end of the Iranian crisis and during the Soviet buildup in its war against anti-Communist forces in Afghanistan. By the time Reagan was inaugurated oil prices had already reached unprecedented levels. The Iranian revolution had contributed to a decline of 3.9 million b/d of crude oil from Iran alone. Although a significant portion of the lost production was picked up by other Persian Gulf producers, with the Iran-Iraq war in 1980 many of those other countries also cut production. The result was that, although Saudi Arabia continued to increase production, by 1981 OPEC production overall was down 7 million b/d from its 1978 level.[1] Throughout 1980–81 OPEC-set crude oil prices fluctuated between $32 and $38 a barrel. The Iran-Iraq war itself had little noticeable impact on already high prices, in spite of the damage to oil tankers (including Saudi and Kuwaiti tankers), refineries, pipelines, and producing fields. The failure of the war to have a major impact on global prices derived in part from the Saudis' increase in exports in the first year of the Reagan administration. In addition, the Reagan administration took steps to stimulate investment and production. In one of his first acts after inauguration, President Reagan lifted any remaining domestic controls on oil prices and allocations and later in the year he reduced the windfall profits tax.[2]

Although the Iran-Iraq war in the 1980s was not in itself decisive in altering oil supply and prices, it contributed to the general instability in the region and was massively costly to both nations and to their oil industries. Both emerged from the conflict having suffered significant loss of life and with major international debt, although Iraq was overwhelmingly the main beneficiary of financial support from the Arab oil producing nations, themselves alarmed by the revolutionary zealotry of Iran's leadership.[3] Iraq's economic situation in the 1980s and 1990s became increasingly desperate as a result of massive debts accumulated from the Iran-Iraq war (approximately $97 billion in reparations payments to Iran and $299 billion in repair and reconstruction following the war), as well as the loss of revenue during the period of UN-imposed sanctions.[4]

The war was also, understandably, a security concern to the Reagan administration, especially by 1985–86 when Iran appeared to be making military gains. Determined to avoid any closure of the sea lanes in the region, President Reagan sent Vice-President George Bush to Saudi Arabia, Oman, and Bahrain to stress the commitment of the United States to their economic and military security and their common interests in ensuring that the free flow of oil was not hampered.[5]

While they lasted, the high prices of the first half of the 1980s were a significant stimulus to exploration and production in the non-OPEC countries. In the United States more efforts were made at conservation, including extending the life of marginal wells. Until prices declined once again, the higher domestic prices for petroleum products also stimulated exploration and development in the continental United States. High prices also encouraged technological advances to enhance secondary and tertiary recovery capability.

Consuming nations pressed vigorously in their search for energy sources that would substitute for those derived from and controlled by

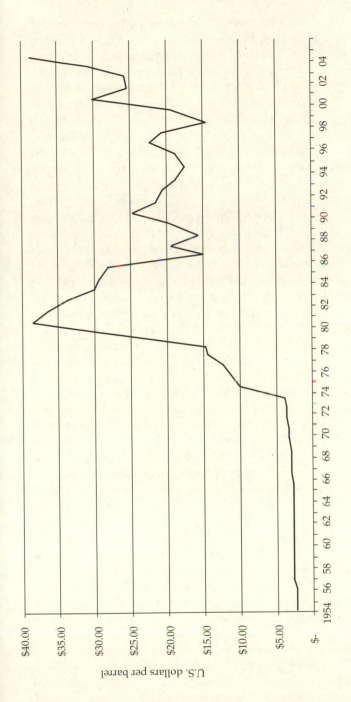

Figure 3

Spot Crude Prices (West Texas Intermediate) for a Fifty-Year Period, 1954-2004 (in actual current prices)

Source: United States Department of the Interior Minerals Management Service, Minerals Revenue Management (from *Oil and Gas Journal Energy Database*) http://www.mrm.mms.gov (accessed 15 August 2004); "International Petroleum Encyclopedia, 2001," *Oil and Gas Journal Online Research Centre* http://orc.pennnet.com/home.cfm (accessed 25 August 2004); see also British Petroleum, *BP Statistical Review of World Energy*, 53rd Edition, 15 June 2004 www.bp.com (17 August 2004)

*2004 statistics are an average of monthly crude prices from January through July.

Middle East producers. In turn, the development of alternative sources of supply outside OPEC control, in particular the North Sea, the Alaskan North Slope, and Mexico, increased the share of non-OPEC world production and contributed to a price decline in the course of the decade. By 1985 non-OPEC production had risen to 69 percent of world output in comparison to 50 percent at the outbreak of the Iranian revolution in 1978. Non-OPEC production increased from 14 million b/d in 1976 to 23 million b/d in 1985.[6] OPEC's share of U.S. oil imports also declined during the next several years, from 82 percent before the Iranian crisis to 41 percent. The increasing inability of OPEC to control its own members also contributed to the price decline. Saudi Arabia and other OPEC producers attempted to maximize their revenues by cutting production to sustain higher prices (close to $34 a barrel), but with increased production elsewhere OPEC was not able to maintain that level. Prices did not decline appreciably until 1983, when they stabilized at between $28 and $29 per barrel. In 1985 OPEC changed its tactics; between June and December 1985 OPEC it increased its production from a twenty-year low of 13.7 mb/d to 18 mb/d, and to 20 mb/d by mid-1986, contributing to a glut in crude oil and a price war that in 1986 drove prices down more than 50 percent. Throughout 1987 and 1988 OPEC members failed to reach effective agreements on production and price levels, with the result that actual production often exceeded OPEC quotas, serving to depress prices further. As analysts indicated, the circumstances in the international oil industry at the end of the first Reagan administration were in marked contrast to those that the Nixon, Ford, and Carter presidencies had had to confront. For Reagan's second term the world scene witnessed low prices, a major market surplus and a fragmented OPEC.[7]

During the 1980s, in part responding to the high prices early in the decade and in part reflecting changing consumer patterns and government regulations, the world demand for petroleum also declined. Between 1980 and 1985 world oil demand declined 5 percent. In the United States by 1983 oil consumption had fallen to 1971 levels. In contrast, in Asia the modernization and expansion of industrial capacity increased the demand for petroleum products, particularly for use in the production of steel, petrochemicals, and the mining of metals. Market conditions and the removal of export controls in the United States also stimulated the export of petroleum products by American producers to such areas as Central and South America and the Far East, which fifteen years earlier had not been the destination for American exports.[8]

When U.S. consumers enjoyed the return of comparatively low prices in the second half of the 1980s little hope remained for a rigorous enforcement of conservationist measures. President Reagan's conviction that policy should be driven strictly by the market placed a damper on those

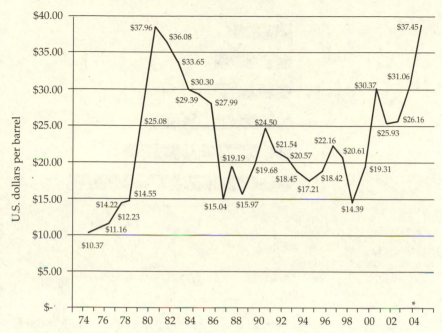

Figure 4

Spot Crude Prices (West Texas Intermediate) for a Thirty-Year Period, 1974-2004 (in actual current prices)

Source: United States Department of the Interior Minerals Management Service, Minerals Revenue Management (from *Oil and Gas Journal Energy Database*) http://www.mrm.mms.gov (accessed 15 August 2004); "International Petroleum Encyclopedia, 2001," *Oil and Gas Journal Online Research Centre* http://orc.pennnet.com/home.cfm (accessed 25 August 2004); see also British Petroleum, *BP Statistical Review of World Energy*, 53rd Edition, 15 June 2004 www.bp.com (17 August 2004)

*2004 statistics are an average of monthly crude prices from January through July.

who advocated either increased conservation or, once again, import restrictions. Reagan consistently opposed the development of an energy plan, contending that a combination of market forces and increased allocations to the Strategic Petroleum Reserve would be the most effective protection against a subsequent oil crisis. The one exception to Reagan's market-driven approach was in the area of nuclear energy, with the justification that a free market did not exist in that sector. A clear indication of Reagan's approach to energy policy was his appointment as Secretary of Energy of James Edwards, a dentist and former governor of South Carolina, who publicly stated that one of his goals was to abolish the Department of Energy, "bury it once and for all."[9]

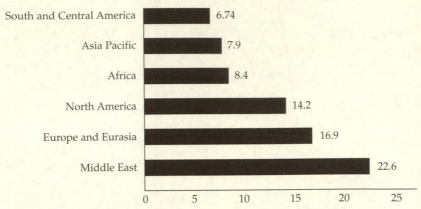

Figure 5
Distribution of Production by Region, 2003
million barrels per day
Source: British Petroleum, *BP Statistical Review of World Energy*, 53rd Edition, 15 June 2004 www.bp.com (17 August 2004)

A wasteful consumer culture was reinvigorated and the lessons of the previous decade apparently forgotten. Between 1985 and 2000 the demand in the United States for petroleum products increased by almost 4 mb/d, and the economy appeared buoyant, with industrial production strong and unemployment low. The Department of Energy reported that between 1986 and 1988 the overall energy intensity of the economy, which is taken to be a reflection of energy conservation, did not increase.[10] As in the past, independent oil producers and the state governments where they operated, confronted with the post-1986 price collapse and reduced domestic production, pressed hard for import restrictions late in the 1980s, on the traditional grounds that imports threatened national security. William Martin, Deputy Secretary of Energy, a former executive director of the National Security Council and a Reagan appointee, was convinced that in spite of administration opposition and its preoccupation with the Iran-Contra affair, the issue of energy security needed to be addressed. The result was the preparation of the 1987 study "Energy Security: A Report to the President." The report was much broader than the oil-import question, addressing the need for policy on alternative transportation fuels and electricity generation reforms, as well as suggesting that the USSR was moving ahead of the United States in oil production. The report languished, however, with only the security agencies expressing interest.

For security reasons the Reagan administration continued to restrict the export of crude and refined oil products from the United States. The administration did lift the restriction on the export of refined products in 1981, but kept strict controls over the export of crude oil. The circumstances under which crude oil could be exported were exceptional and limited. They included exports from Alaska's Cook Inlet, exports to Canada for consumption, exports in connection with refining or exchange of strategic petroleum reserve oil, and exports of poor quality California heavy oil, which was useful primarily for bunker fuel or asphalt production. An export licence was required to export to any destination, including Canada, any refined products derived from oil obtained from the Naval Petroleum Reserve.[11]

Saddam Hussein's Iraq, post-revolution Iran, and the volatile nature of Middle East politics remained persistent challenges for President Reagan's successors: George H.W. Bush, Bill Clinton, and George W. Bush. The end of the Iran-Iraq war did not bring stability to the region. The major military machine that Saddam Hussein had built during the war, with the support of the United States, remained a significant threat to its neighbours, and Saddam had territorial ambitions in areas that were long claimed to be part of Iraq. On 2 August 1990 Saddam Hussein sent Iraqi forces into Kuwait, taking control of the Rumailah oil field in the process. The George H.W. Bush administration responded quickly, deploying troops to Saudi Arabia and building a coalition force designed to drive Iraqi forces from Kuwait as well as to defend neighbouring countries from potential Iraqi aggression. The United Nations imposed an embargo on the export and sale of crude and refined oil products derived from either Iraq or occupied Kuwait. In response to the fear of supply shortfalls similar to those experienced following the Iranian revolution, short-term prices for crude oil and refined oil products rose sharply for the third time in seventeen years.[12] In the short period from late July 1990 to the end of August, the world price of oil shot up from a modest $16 a barrel to $28, and by late September reached $36. In mid-August 1990 Secretary of Energy James Watkins announced plans to increase domestic oil production and decrease consumption to offset the loss of Iraqi and Kuwaiti oil on the international market.[13] With u.s. troops attacking Iraqi military targets in early 1991, Watkins began to draw on the Strategic Petroleum Reserve, with the first oil reaching commercial buyers in early February. Despite the defeat of Hussein's forces and their withdrawal from Kuwait, Kuwait oil fields were extensively damaged as retreating Iraqi forces set fire to them. The result was that Kuwait product exports did not return to prewar levels until 1993; however, during the war and its immediate aftermath Iran and Saudi Arabia released stocks to take advantage of market demand and increased prices.[14]

In spite of the war, the extensive damage to Kuwaiti oil fields, and the curtailment of Iraqi oil exports, the conflict did not have a long-term negative impact on prices or global production. Optimism in the market could be seen as early as October 1990, when the United Nations first approved the use of force to remove Iraqi forces from Kuwait. In addition, the global oil market was more agile in 1990 than it had been in 1979, and the expansion of production in non-OPEC areas since that time provided a means to offset the more than 4 mb/d of oil that was lost with the embargo on Iraqi and Kuwaiti production.[15]

In the aftermath of Iraq's invasion of Kuwait, in August 1990, prior to the U.S.-led coalition invasion of Kuwait and Iraq, the United Nations Security Council adopted resolution 661, imposing comprehensive sanctions on Iraq. Directly following the end of the Gulf War in 1991, the UN Secretary General sent an inter-agency mission to Iraq to assess the humanitarian needs of Iraq and Kuwait resulting from the war and economic sanctions. In 1995, in an effort to combine assistance to the Iraqi people with a punitive approach to the Saddam Hussein regime, the UN passed resolution 986, which established the Oil-for-Food Program. The program began in late 1996 following the conclusion of a memorandum of agreement between the Iraq government and the UN. During the life of the highly controversial program, which was terminated in late November 2003 with U.S. and British forces occupying Iraq, 3.4 billion barrels of Iraqi oil valued at approximately $65 billion were exported. Of that amount 72 percent of the proceeds were allocated to humanitarian assistance – including food, medicines, and medical equipment – and the balance to Gulf War reparations through a compensation fund. Minor allocations covered the UN administrative and operational costs of the program and the UN weapons inspection program. The UN expanded the program over the years to allow for infrastructure rehabilitation, including electricity generation facilities and distribution, agriculture and irrigation, education, water and sanitation, transport, and telecommunications. Several billion dollars were also allocated to enable Iraq to acquire spare parts and equipment for the oil industry.[16]

The mid-1970s forecasts by many academics and government officials – that by the mid-1980s demand for Persian Gulf and other OPEC-produced oil would reach 50 mb/d, that prices would rise to more than $40/bbl, and that dependence on Saudi Arabia would be intensified – were not realized. On the contrary, by the mid-1990s the price of oil was about $23/bbl and Saudi Arabia was experiencing economic as well as political and cultural problems associated in part but not exclusively with the Islamic fundamentalist movement. Saudi stability continued to be an uncertain variable in international political and economic circles. It had weathered the Mecca Mosque affair in 1979 as well as riots in its eastern regions the following year, but the increasing impact of more radical elements in the country and the region during the 1980s and 1990s raised questions about its future.[17] Nonetheless, in 1999 Saudi Arabia led the producing nations in a movement to reduce production and raise prices, reflecting its capacity to influence the international oil market. This contributed to considerable consumer distress in the United States and other consuming nations, and pushed the Clinton administration into active lobbying with the Saudis and other Middle East producers.[18]

The Iranian regime also remained a pariah in the course of the 1990s, even with the deterioration of the American relationship with Iraq. The negative U.S. attitude to Iran derived in large part from Iran's export of revolution and terrorism, targeted in particular at U.S. and Israeli interests. In 1995 the Clinton administration, following the introduction of legislation in the Senate, sanctioned all trade with Iran and forbade the foreign subsidiaries of U.S.-based companies from trading in Iranian oil. President Clinton moved forward at the same time to encourage American companies to construct oil and natural gas pipelines from Central Asian producing fields through Afghanistan to the Persian Gulf, thus bypassing Iran. The sanctions imposed on Iran by the Clinton administration had a significant impact on some U.S. firms, in particular Conoco, which was at the time negotiating with the Iranian government. There was thus predictable opposition to the sanctions from the private sector, including such prominent individuals as Richard Cheney, former Congressman and Secretary of Defense under George H. W. Bush. Between his service in the Reagan administration and his appointment as vice-president in the George W. Bush administration, Cheney served as the CEO of Halliburton Corporation, a global energy services, manufacturing, and engineering corporation active in more than one hundred countries, including the Middle East. The Iran and Libya Sanctions Act threatened U.S. sanctions against foreign companies investing more than $20 million in Iran, although the legislation was not enforced against foreign companies. It was even stricter in its application to U.S.-based corporations, prohibiting any investment in Iran. In subsequent years the U.S. Treasury Department permitted two American companies, Chevron and Coastal, to import crude oil from Iran.[19]

The Middle East was not the only area of interest in energy policy circles during the Reagan and the subsequent Bush administrations. The Soviet Union was one of the world's major oil producing powers, not only supplying its domestic demand but also exporting significant quantities of crude and refined products to Western Europe and Latin America as well as crude oil to the Far East. American officials viewed any expansion of Soviet energy markets in Western Europe as a security threat. Reagan administration officials were particularly concerned early in the 1980s over the decision by Chancellor Helmut Schmidt's West German government to finance construction of a natural gas pipeline from

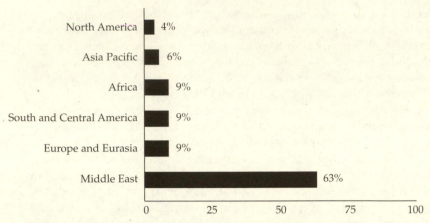

Figure 6
Distribution of Proved Reserves
percentages
Source: British Petroleum, *BP Statistical Review of World Energy*, 53rd Edition, 15 June
2004 www.bp.com (17 August 2004)

Siberia to Western Europe, greatly increasing Russian gas sales in the
West and, from a U.S. perspective, creating a dangerous dependence on
Soviet supplies. Testifying to Congress, Richard Perle, then Assistant Secretary of Defense for international security policy, contended that the
pipeline and increased West European dependence on Soviet natural gas
exports would "weaken the alliance politically and militarily," increase
the Soviet "advantage," and threaten "the unity and purpose on which
our collective security ultimately depends."[20] President Reagan strongly
advanced this perspective at the 1981 G-7 summit in Ottawa, offering to
assist Western Europe with alternative sources of energy if they would
back away from the Soviet deal, but Schmidt was not to be deterred from
what Europeans saw as a positive arrangement, not only from a geopolitical perspective but also in terms of the major opportunities it provided for European producers of pipe and equipment. In spite of the
harsh and ill-conceived export ban that President Reagan imposed on
sales of oil and gas equipment to the USSR and on U.S. subsidiaries abroad
in 1982, Russia and the Europeans proceeded to complete the project by
the end of the decade. For President Reagan the hard line approach was
costly: he had to fire Secretary of State Alexander Haig for his opposition
to the economic sanctions, and the measures greatly alienated West European leaders.[21]

Beset by economic challenges it could not meet, drained from its costly
and failed war in Afghanistan, confronted by internal political challenges

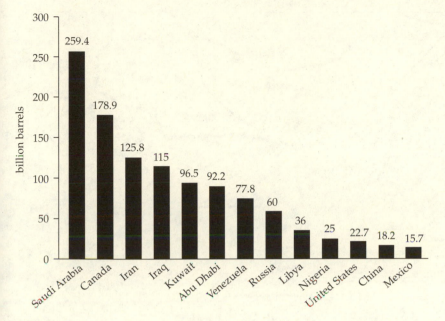

Figure 7
World Oil Reserves: Estimated Proved Reserves at 1 January 2004
Sources: "Worldwide Look at Reserves and Production," *Oil and Gas Journal* 101, no. 49 (22 December 2003): 43-44; see also Energy Information Administration, *International Energy Outlook 2004* www.eia.doe.gov/oiaf/ieo/pdf/oil.pdf (accessed 18 August 2004)

that could not be contained, and led by the reformist Mikhail Gorbachev, the Soviet Union at the end of 1991 dissolved into its formerly united socialist republics. The collapse of the Soviet regime caused both optimism and caution among Western oil companies faced with the opportunities and challenges of liberalizing investment potential in Russia itself as well as in the newly independent Central Asian states. Azerbaijan, Kazakhstan, Turkmenistan, and Uzbekistan together had proven oil reserves of 25 billion barrels (with possible reserves of 85 billion), in comparison with 139 billion for Iran and Russia, 17 billion for the North Sea, 22 billion for the United States, and 471 billion for the Arabian peninsula. The area was seen to have significant development potential, even though the region was fraught with high levels of risk for investors. The risk has been accentuated by the number of countries and interests competing for resources in a region where borders have been not only blurred but hotly disputed, regulatory regimes are not in place, and transportation routes run through areas of civil and military strife. The Caspian has also been seen, like the Persian Gulf, as an area of East-West, or at least Russian-

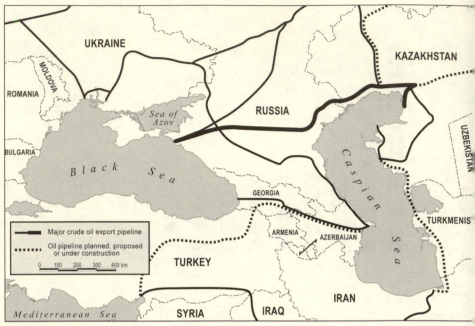

Figure 8
Caspian Sea Region Resource Developments
Created by Robin Poitras

United States competition for hegemony.[22] Chevron moved quickly in the early 1990s into the Tengiz oil field in Kazakhstan, which by 2001 was exporting oil over a pipeline to the Russian Black Sea port of Novorossiysk for subsequent export to Western Europe and the United States. Amoco established a presence on the Caspian Sea in the Azeri oil field. The Caspian Pipeline Consortium was a joint venture among several governments (Russia, Kazakhstan, and Oman) and several private sector companies (including Chevron, ExxonMobil, and LukArco).[23] In the 1990s the United States Export-Import Bank and the World Bank also provided financial support in an effort to revive the Russian oil industry,[24] especially to replace obsolete technology and to improve secondary recovery methods.

In 2001 Jan Kalicki, former Clinton administration Ombudsman for Energy and Commercial Cooperation with the Newly Independent States, recommended that the United States develop an energy policy towards the Caspian region in particular, given the massive oil resources of the former Soviet republics and neighbouring countries. Kalicki contended that the Bush administration was neglecting the potential of the region in contrast to the more aggressive approach taken by President Clinton. He argued that the United States should "strengthen its policy toward the Caspian by giving the highest level of support to the cooperative development of regional energy reserves and pipelines." Kalicki underlined the vulnerability of supply as long as the pipeline transport ran through Russian territory and depended on Russian lines. Equally undesirable in his view would be dependence on Iranian routes. With the objective of improving the diversity of export routes as well as pipeline control, in 2001 the United States, Turkey, Georgia, Kazakhstan, and Azerbaijan concluded a memorandum of agreement to transport oil across the Caspian to the Baku-Tbilisi-Ceyhan pipeline (BTC), controlled by the BP-led Azerbaijan International Operating Company. Kalicki further contended that it was especially important that the United States encourage "the construction of multiple pipelines to ensure diverse and reliable transportation of Caspian energy to regional and international markets." To Kalicki, the development of Caspian resources was in the interest not only of the private sector, which had an opportunity to realize significant profits, but also of the West in general, since economic development in the region would facilitate political stability as well as reduce reliance on Russia.[25] Nonetheless, foreign investment in the oil and other sectors of the former Soviet economy has been fraught with challenges associated with an unstable regulatory regime, widespread corruption, regional wars, and civil strife.

Energy considerations were also important in the negotiation and conclusion of the 1988 Free Trade Agreement (FTA) between the United States and Canada. Canadian energy resources had historically been generally open to foreign investment, although screening procedures were put in place when Trudeau's Liberal government established the Foreign Investment Review Agency in 1973, along with a national oil company, Petro-Canada. Confronted with the need to import increased amounts of Saudi oil into Eastern Canada in the midst of the Arab oil boycott, the Trudeau government put in place plans to construct a pipeline from the Alberta oil fields and also set price controls on Canadian oil. Under the arrangement, much to the chagrin of American officials and importers, Canadians would pay the controlled price for domestically produced crude oil; Canadian exports to the United States would be sold at world prices.[26]

The Canadian policies implemented in the context of the Arab oil embargo of 1973 were moderate, as was the American reaction, in contrast to the response to Trudeau's subsequent establishment of the National Energy Policy (NEP) after his return to office in 1980. By the time the Trudeau government inaugurated the NEP Ronald Reagan occupied the White House, and the response of the Reagan administration to what were perceived to be discriminatory as well as nationalistic controls over Canadian sources of energy was both immediate and blunt. Canadian policies were seen to run against traditional U.S. preference for an open door for investment and trade, in particular with its neighbour, Cold War ally, and major trading partner. The NEP also offended the anti-statist, free market ideology of the Reagan government. Building on the policies of the 1970s, the NEP established a two-price system for oil, with one price for domestic and another for international sales, as well as separate prices for oil from wells developed before 1973 and those developed after 1973. The stated objective of the NEP was to increase Canadian ownership of oil to 50 percent by 1990. Following formal protests by Secretary of State Alexander Haig, which President Reagan repeated during his official visit to Ottawa in 1981, and which were vigorously asserted by the new American ambassador to Canada, Paul Robinson, the Trudeau government backed away from the NEP. With the defeat of the liberal government, the newly elected Prime Minister, Brian Mulroney, shelved the policy.[27]

Although protectionist and nationalistic sentiments existed in both countries in the 1980s, especially in the U.S. Congress, most Canadian-American trade was free of duties even before the conclusion of the FTA, and both American and Canadian governments wanted to ensure equality of access to each other's markets. The U.S. in particular sought non-discriminatory access to Canadian energy sources, and Canada sought secure market access for Canadian manufacturing, agriculture, and energy exports to the U.S. The main principle underlying chapter 9 of the FTA, as in the GATT (General Agreement on Trade and Tariffs), was the national treatment principle; that is, that the laws and regulations of each should not discriminate between foreign and domestic energy goods on the basis of nationality, a principle that runs directly counter to much of U.S. foreign oil strategic thinking since World War II. Nonetheless, under the agreement, that principle was to be binding on U.S. federal energy bodies, the National Energy Board in Canada, and state/provincial agencies. As the U.S. Statement of Administrative Action indicated to Congress, this would preclude discriminatory internal taxes or a domestic rule in either nation imposing an internal quantitative requirement that a specified portion of an energy good be supplied from domestic sources.

The only significant change in U.S. procedure required by the FTA was to allow Canada access to a maximum of 50,000 b/d of Alaskan oil that had previously been restricted from export under the U.S. Export Administration Act of 1979. Article 904 stipulated that while either country might restrict energy exports if required to conserve resources or to deal with a short-supply situation, as permitted under GATT, it could do so only if the restriction did not reduce the proportion historically available, impose a higher export than domestic price, or disrupt the normal channels of supply or the mix of energy products supplied to the other country. Article 906 recognized the importance of government incentives for oil and gas resource development in view of the security implications, and neither country was required to eliminate such incentives, although the domestic oil and gas industry in the u.s. could seek relief under u.s. trade laws. Finally, Article 907 set out the national security exceptions applicable to energy goods. The grounds under which national security exceptions might be invoked are more restricted than under the GATT; in the FTA such restrictions can be imposed only if necessary to permit the supply of a military establishment, to fulfill critical defence contracts, to respond to armed conflict, to assure non-proliferation, or to respond to direct threats of disruption in the supply of nuclear materials for defence purposes. The Reagan administration statement of administrative action to Congress stressed that the objective of the restrictions in article 907 were to ensure continued access to Canadian energy sources.[28]

As important as Canada became after the 1970s to u.s. foreign energy policies, American policymakers continued to focus on the larger strategic picture, and so did West European countries. In late 2001 the Committee on Sustainable Energy of the United Nations Economic Commission for Europe (UNECE) issued a press release entitled "Concern about energy security is growing." The committee observed that the "increased sense of vulnerability" derived from rising energy import dependence, higher costs of new incremental energy supplies, increased dependence on OPEC and Middle East oil, longer supply routes, uncertainty over what full market liberalization would entail, and the "potential for social unrest and ethnic strife in a number of producing and transit countries." The UNECE press release noted the added concerns over energy-related environmental problems and the need to factor in the danger of terrorist attacks on energy installations in the aftermath of the events of September 11 in the United States.[29]

In its 2001 analysis of the energy outlook the International Energy Agency reached cautiously more optimistic conclusions, indicating that the reserves of oil, natural gas, coal, and uranium are "more than adequate to meet projected demand growth at least until 2020." At the same time it suggested that a massive investment in energy production and transportation infrastructure was needed if those resources were to be effectively exploited. It noted that, for oil, the ability and willingness of Middle East producers to exploit lower-cost reserves was a source of uncertainty and that in the case of natural gas, the cost of supply and the "impact of technology" would be critical. The report concluded, rather optimistically, that "beyond 2020, new technologies such as hydrogen-based fuel cells, clean coal burning and carbon sequestration hold out the prospect of abundant and clean energy supplies in a world largely free of climate destabilizing carbon emissions."[30] It is difficult to envisage such a rosy situation in such newly industrializing states as China.

Another major development in the industry in the 1990s was a significant merger movement among the companies in their quest to rationalize operations, including consolidating their downstream operations. Joint ventures, both domestically and with foreign companies in their overseas operations, proved another way for companies to reduce costs without the complications of full mergers. Domestically the result was that the number of major U.S. energy companies declined to ten from nineteen at the beginning of the decade. One of the most striking mergers was between Mobil and Exxon, which resulted in the creation of the largest publicly traded corporation in the world. In 2001 there was also a major merger of Chevron and Texaco; Gulf Oil had already been acquired by Standard Oil of California (SoCal).[31]

In terms of political power and influence within the American context, as Louis Turner has ably argued, not only the oil industry has to be taken into consideration but also major companies in associated industries. He appropriately identified Bechtel, the San Francisco-based construction and engineering firm that was close to several departments in the Reagan and Bush administrations and has had long-standing operations in Saudi Arabia. As Turner noted, in the 1980s Bechtel was simultaneously working with the Department of State, the Pentagon, and the Department of Energy. Bechtel's extensive global engineering expertise – it had dealt effectively with putting out the oil well fires in Kuwait in 1991 – and political connections enhanced its ability to obtain government contracts in the aftermath of the American invasion of Iraq in 2003. In April 2003 the company acquired an initial contract worth over $34 million from USAID. Halliburton withdrew from the bidding in the context of concern over favouritism because of Vice-President Cheney's ties to the company. Yet Bechtel also had close ties to the Bush administration at the time the contract was tendered. Two of its executives were associated with the administration. One of its senior vice-presidents, John Sheehan, was a member of the Defense Policy Board, established to advise the Secretary of Defense, Donald Rumsfeld, who himself had been a member of the Bechtel board. Sheehan, a former marine corps general, was the manager of petroleum and chemical operations for Bechtel. Riley Bechtel, Bechtel's chairman, was at the time a George W. Bush appointee to the Export Council, which advises the President on international trade policy.[32]

In the early twenty-first century governments and international agencies are taking a much broader approach to issues pertaining to energy security. Access to oil reserves of course remain one of the main concerns, and the United States under the George W. Bush administration has seen

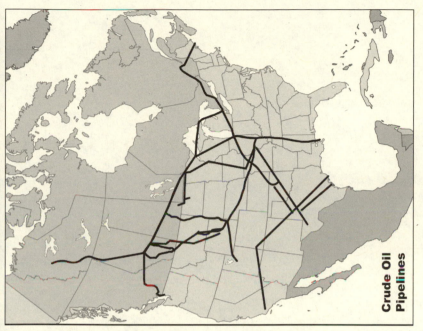

Crude Oil Pipelines

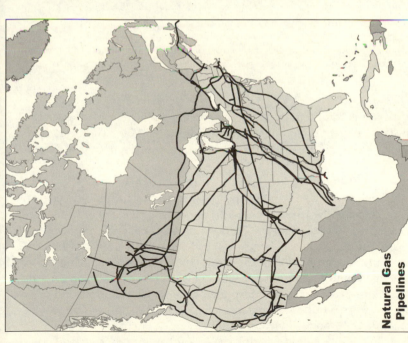

Natural Gas Pipelines

Figure 9

Canada–u.s. Natural Gas and Oil Pipelines

Source: Courtesy of the Canadian Association of Petroleum Producers, Calgary

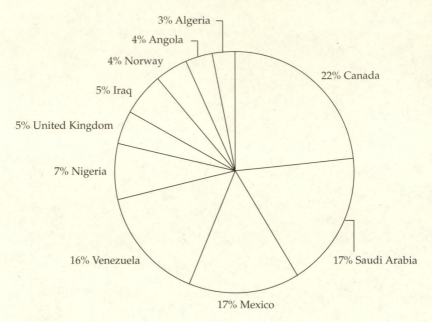

Figure 10
Imports of Crude Oil and Petroleum Products into the United States, 2002,
by country of origin
Source: Energy Information Administration, *Petroleum Supply Annual 2003, Vol. 1,*
Table 21, page 55.
http://www.eia.doe.gov/pub/oil_gas/petroleum/data_publications/petroleum_su
pply_annual/psa_volume1/current/pdf/table_21.pdf (accessed 5 August 2004)

a return to the traditional policy focus on expanding supply; hence the
controversial intention to open a portion of the Alaskan Wildlife Refuge
to development and the overtures to Iran to normalize Iranian-u.s. relations.

In May 2001 President Bush proposed the development of a National
Energy Policy in what was described as a means to address the energy
challenges facing the United States. To review the challenges systematically, the President appointed a National Energy Policy Group, chaired
by Vice-President Richard Cheney and including the secretaries of all the
major cabinet departments, the director of the Office of Management and
Budget, the Deputy Chief of Staff for Policy, the Director of Intergovernmental Affairs, and the Assistant to the President for Economic Policy.

The task force produced an extensive report in May 2001 entitled "Reliable, Affordable and Environmentally Sound Energy for America's
Future." In the international realm, the task force strongly recommended

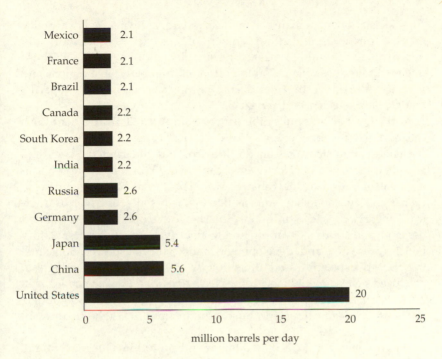

Figure 11
Leading World Oil Consumers, 2003
(includes all countries that consumed more than 2 million bb/d)
Source: Energy Information Administration, *Top World Oil Tables: Non-OPEC Fact Sheet* http://www.eia.doe.gov/cabs/topworldtables3_4.html (accessed 15 August 2004)

strengthening America's global alliances and adopting measures to reduce reliance on imported oil and to a lesser extent natural gas, the only two energy sources in which the United States was not self-sufficient by 2001. The report noted that in 1999 the United States consumed 25 percent of all world oil produced in that year and relied on imports for 52 percent of its energy needs, with 50 percent of those imports coming from the Western hemisphere and 24 percent from the Middle East. In the Western hemisphere, Canada was the largest single supplier of u.s. oil imports, meeting 14 percent of u.s. demand. The report underlined the concern of its authors that by 2020 an estimated 54–67 percent of world oil supply would be derived from the Middle East. Consistent with previous liberalization policies, the expressed administration goals were to increase the importance of the Western hemisphere and to encourage Middle East producers to open their energy sectors to private foreign investment.[33]

In the aftermath of the report President Bush called on Congress to pass legislation to enhance American security. Bush's energy policy focused on a significant expansion of electricity generation and improved distribution to meet increasing demand. The policy was also intended to reduce reliance on imported oil from less stable regions and to focus more on North America and the Western hemisphere, in particular Canada, Mexico, and Venezuela.

At the Quebec Summit of the Americas in April 2001 President Bush called for the development of a North American energy plan. To that end the energy ministers of Canada, Mexico, and the United States had already established the North American Energy Working Group to facilitate collaboration at the cabinet level. The group had a mandate to exchange views and share information on factors affecting North American energy policies, programs, market developments, anticipated demand, and sources of supply, and to identify issues such as regulatory policies, research and development, and technical specifications that might need to be addressed. In its first two years of existence the group produced several reports, including *North America – The Energy Picture* in 2001 and *North American Energy Efficiency, Standards and Labeling* in late 2002. At the same time, the Bush administration sought to increase domestic oil production.

On 11 September 2001, only a few months after the Quebec Summit, al-Qaeda-inspired terrorists flew hijacked commercial airliners into the two towers of the World Trade Center and the Pentagon, with a fourth aircraft crashing in Pennsylvania. While Americans and their allies wept over the loss of life, parts of the Muslim world clearly celebrated the violation of the world superpower. For the United States, the world had undergone a dramatic change. Traditional concerns about such issues as a secure supply of oil at reasonable prices now paled in comparison with the threat of direct terrorist attacks on American soil, and energy security concerns increased once again. Analysts had commented on the vulnerability of United States energy well before the events of September 11. Writing in 1982 in *Brittle Power – Energy Strategy for National Security*, a volume that was part of a study by the U.S. Federal Emergency Management Agency, Amory and L. Hunter Lovins contended that "massive attacks by nuclear-armed missiles are not this country's only strategic problem. National security is threatened not only by hostile ideology but also by misapplied technology; not only by threats that America heedlessly – and needlessly – has imposed on itself. Despite its awesome military might, the United States has become extremely vulnerable, and is becoming more vulnerable, to the simple, low technology disruption of such vital infrastructure as energy supply, water, food, data processing, and telecommunications." Ominously, they forecast almost 20 years before that "terrorism, technical mishap, or natural disaster that dam-

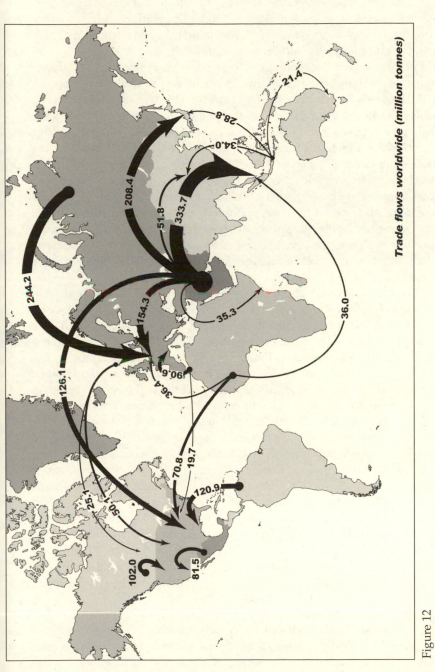

Figure 12

Major Oil Trade Movements

Source: Canadian Association of Petroleum Producers

aged the domestic energy system could be nearly as devastating as a sizeable war. Covert paramilitary or nonmilitary attacks on key infrastructure are so cheap, safe and deniable that they may prove a fatally attractive instrument of surrogate warfare."[34]

The Persian Gulf has remained a focus regardless of potential oil developments in Alaska, the former Soviet Union, or elsewhere in the world. The George W. Bush administration's decision in 2003, with Great Britain as its chief ally, to invade Iraq to remove Saddam Hussein and his regime from power, clearly had oil security as a contextual even if not a primary causal factor. Kenneth Pollack, director for Persian Gulf Affairs on the National Security Council in 1995–96 and 1999–2001, effectively underlined this reality. Pollack wrote that the issue is not the price of gasoline at the pump in the United States or which oil company acquires oil rights and contracts, or even the extent to which the United States imports oil from the region; rather, he suggested, the critical factor is that "the global economy built over the past 50 years rests on a foundation of inexpensive, plentiful oil, and if that foundation were removed, the global economy would collapse."[35]

As noted earlier, there has been considerable debate over the extent to which Russia and the former Soviet republics can alter the balance of power in the oil industry.[36] Since the end of the Cold War Russia and the newly autonomous republics have attracted considerable attention, but there is no reason to assume that oil production and export from those areas will rival that from the Gulf states or alter the balance of oil power. Considerable reserves lie in Russia itself, offshore in the Arctic region, in the Sakhalin Island area, and in the Russian Caspian Sea. Estimates have also placed the potential of the Kashagan offshore field at approximately 22 billion barrels of oil, which represents twice the reserves of Alaska's Prudhoe Bay. Nonetheless, as analysts have noted, even taking into consideration the combined reserves of Russia and the former Soviet republics, those reserves do not approximate the more than 262 billion barrels of proven reserves in Saudi Arabia alone. In addition, the Middle East resources are far more important to the American and European markets than Russian and Caspian resources. Even in Western Europe, which draws more on Russian production than does the United States, Russian/Caspian production is unlikely to do more than supplement Middle East supplies, and the same could be applied to the Asian markets.[37]

A further consideration in the aftermath of the American war in Iraq is the role of post-Saddam Hussein Iraq in the Middle East and in world oil circles. It has been suggested that the removal of Saddam Hussein does not alter the importance and position of Iraq in the region, given the traditional power rivalries that have existed between Iran and Iraq. An independent Iraq, freed from u.s. political controls and military occupation, needs to be sufficiently strong to defend its security from Iran, which has a nuclear weapons program, and a militarily strong Iraq will in the future be just as capable of posing a threat to Kuwait and Saudi oil fields as it was at the time of the first Gulf War. As one analyst correctly suggested, "American victory over Saddam will do little to affect this basic dynamic, because it stems less from the nature of Iraq's leadership than from simple geopolitics."[38]

The identification of energy security as a high priority among policy-makers has not been limited to Europe and North America, of course, nor to the period since September 11. The vulnerability to terrorist attack of oil and natural gas pipelines as well as hydro-electric transmission lines, has been a consistent problem in Colombia, for instance, over the past two decades, as it was in such countries as El Salvador during the 1980s civil war. Of even more significance is the increased concern over energy supplies and security that has emerged in Asia in recent years and that will become more acute as economic development progresses. The Japanese senior vice-minister for foreign affairs, Seishiro Eto, told a seminar on energy security in Asia in March 2001 that the region's economic growth required an increase in its supply of energy from outside the region. He suggested that by 2020 Asia was expected to account for 35 percent of world energy demand, making the region the leading energy consumer in the world. China, he noted, has been a net importer of oil since 1993, and the IEA has observed that China's oil imports over the next decade are expected to increase rapidly and surpass many countries in the OECD, while its imports of natural gas will increase as it seeks to address environmental impact.[39] In the 1990s China diversified its sources of crude oil supply: in 1990 it drew 39 percent of its supply from the Middle East and 61 percent from Asia-Pacific suppliers; by 1997 reliance on the Middle East had risen to over 47 percent, but Asia-Pacific had dropped to 26 percent, with Africa providing almost 17 percent and other sources providing almost 10 percent.[41] Japan is far more dependent on Middle East resources than the u.s., with 24 percent derived from Saudi Arabia, 23 percent from the UAE, 10 percent from each of Iran and Kuwait, 9 percent from Qatar.[41] Even Malaysia and Indonesia, major producers, will likely become net importers within a decade or so. Each of these countries will need to rely more heavily on Middle East exports. Given transportation distances, supply will be vulnerable to the vagaries of natural disasters as well as sabotage. To offset that vulnerability, Eto indicated that Asian countries should continue to diversify their sources of energy, in particular natural gas and renewable energy, because of their lesser impact on the environment. He pointed as an example to discussions of the development of Siberian and Sakhalin natural gas resources and the construction of a natural gas pipeline in Asia. Eto noted further that few Asian countries, Japan and South Korea being the exceptions, had effective stockpiling systems in place to cope with short-term energy shocks. Japan, for instance, which is a member of the IEA, stockpiles approximately 160 days' supply of oil.[42]

It is evident that concern about energy security in the post September 11 environment is part of a larger historical cycle of concern about the vulnerability of supplies of energy. Much of that traditional concern has focused on oil and on broader geopolitical considerations relating to the stability of the world system, the stability of individual political regimes, and the security of transportation routes. The present concern is clearly much broader, not only covering those traditional issues but also focusing far more sharply on the vulnerability of our entire energy sector to terrorist actions. There is every indication that the instability evident in the world order at the moment, as well as in individual regions and countries that are important sources of energy, will be the norm for the foreseeable future. We are unlikely to witness in the short term any significant stabilization in Iraq or Saudi Arabia in the Middle East, in Africa, or in Asia. It is also evident that the competition for energy sources is going to become even more intense in the future, with the growing demands of such emerging new economies as China.

Reflections on the Past and Present

Some years ago in a provocative study, *Lessons of The Past*, Ernest R. May outlined the need for historical perspective on the part of policymakers and the potential contribution of academics to the shaping of that perspective.[1] Policymakers in the United States and the other major Western industrial nations, as well as in such major emerging powers as China, have now had almost a century of experience with the challenges associated with energy dependency to learn the lessons of the past. The history of United States foreign oil policy since World War I reveals clearly that lessons learned are not necessarily lessons applied. Whether it has been a failure of political will or of vision, some eighty years after policymakers in the 1920s debated the issue of oil dependency, the United States is no closer to a solution to its dilemma. It might be suggested that in the years since the beginning of the Reagan administration in 1981 the United States has become more rather than less vulnerable. It has twice chosen to use massive military force to secure its hegemony in the Middle East, and the results have reinforced the reality that military supremacy alone does not provide any guarantee of effective control or support in the region.

In late 2003, the thirty-year anniversary of the Arab oil embargo against the United States, *The Economist* ran as its cover title and lead editorial "The End of the Oil Age."[2] It suggested that "a generation after the embargo began, the facts seem plain: the world remains addicted to Middle Eastern oil." Yet the journal was responding in part to an earlier and seemingly paradoxical comment by former Saudi oil minister Sheik Zaki Yamani that "the Stone Age did not end for lack of stone, and the Oil Age will end long before the world runs out of oil." Yamani contended that something fundamental had transpired since the 1973 embargo to weaken the position of producing countries such as Saudi Arabia, not least of all the advances in clean energy technology, from wind power to hydrogen fuel cells and bioethanol. Although *The Economist* suggested that technological advances were a cause for optimism, it also concluded that such optimistic results were not imminent, in part because the alternative technologies were not sufficiently advanced and in part because governments such as that of George W. Bush and American politicians in Congress have continued to focus on increasing oil supplies and oil security rather than on making significant investments in alternative energy research and development. *The Economist* leader asserted that "By introducing a small but steadily rising tax on petrol, America would do far more to encourage innovation and improve energy security than all the drilling in Alaska's wilderness." The authors noted that, in spite of expansion of Russian and Caspian resources, the geological reality remained that Saudi Arabia held two-thirds of the world's proven oil reserves. They might have specified "traditional" reserves, since the editorial did not mention the Canadian tar sands, which have the potential to match Saudi Arabia in volume, if not in cost of recovery, and which have the added advantage to the United States of being more secure politically and strategically. As *The Economist* stressed, not only has the Middle East, in particular Saudi Arabia and the members of OPEC, been questionable in terms of security and political reliability, dependence on oil imports from OPEC members since the 1973 embargo has resulted in the transfer of approximately U.S.$7 trillion from American consumers to producers, and that figure does not include the costs of two wars against Iraq, the postwar peace building effort, or the basic cost to the United States of maintaining a constant military presence in the region long after the end of the Cold War was supposed to produce a peace dividend.

The views advanced in *The Economist* in the fall of 2003 seemed contradictory. On the one hand its editorial advocated state investment in alternative energy technologies and a modest petrol tax; on the other hand, the authors of the special report on OPEC advanced several basic arguments reinforcing the importance of the market over state controls. As they contended: "OPEC's power was enhanced by stupid policies pursued by western governments, then reduced by wiser policies of energy conservation, and now is making an alarming comeback." The authors faulted the Nixon administration, for instance, for imposing price controls in 1971 in the context of a major balance of payments problem and prior to the Arab oil embargo of 1973. The price controls, the authors argued, restricted producers from passing cost increases on to consumers, and this in turn resulted in the major international companies reducing imports to the United States. The authors also found fault with Congress for its decision in 1973, in the midst of the Arab oil embargo, to legislate the regional allocation of oil within the United States, again leading to "panic and hoarding."[3]

The history of the evolution of United States foreign oil policy reflects this ongoing tension between a tendency to rely on market forces and efforts of the state to control those forces in the interest of consumers and national security. In the midst of what was thought to be one of the first national oil crises in 1973–74, the Senate Foreign Relations Committee established a subcommittee to inquire into the history and operations of the multinational oil companies. It began groping for an answer to the basic question posed in frustration by people in gasoline lines, in Congress, and in the White House: What had gone wrong? Why was the United States – the world's major domestic producer of oil and oil products, whose multinational oil companies spanned the globe – suddenly confronted with an apparent shortage of a vital domestic strategic and industrial resource? Members of the Senate Foreign Relations Committee concluded that the crisis was the product of the failure to develop a coherent and aggressive oil policy. Yet that conclusion begged the larger question: Why?

Even the standard historical literature on American foreign oil policy suggested a conclusion divergent from that of the committee. Case studies of oil policy in Latin America, the Middle East, and the East Indies, among other areas, indicated that since World War I the United States had pursued a vigorous policy to ensure the access of American corporations to the oil resources of the globe and to protect national interests once established. The evidence suggested that pre-1950s policy was more cohesive than the Senate Foreign Relations Committee had detected, but that the policies of the earlier years contained within them the potential seeds from which would grow the challenges of the Cold War years. All the evidence suggests a high degree of consistency in policy goals, in other words policy on a macro level, even if the tactics shifted from time to time to meet the exigencies of the moment. Just as the major international oil companies have been concerned with ensuring access to reserves and the capacity to control their share of the international market, so American policymakers have been concerned with ensuring that American industry, the American military, and the American consumer have had secure and reliable access to oil products at reasonable prices.

The first edition of this study, written more than twenty years ago in the context of high oil prices and the Iranian revolution, grew out of a desire to test the conclusions of the Foreign Relations Committee, to trace the evolution of policy in what were the critical three decades of the century for the establishment of American hegemony, to identify the main actors and their ideas, and above all to explore the relationship between the state and the private sector in the development of policy. This second and extended edition has taken the analysis to the present.

The picture that emerges continues to be a complex one, but the issues of security of supply, alternative sources of supply, and alternative sources of energy have remained constant, even though a significant shift of focus to the Middle East and the Caspian Sea region has occurred since World War II, and even though the larger international order has dramatically changed with the end of the Cold War. In an effort to explain policy formation, analysts have identified the inherent weaknesses of capitalism, the power of corporate elites, state interventionism in the "natural" workings of the market, bureaucratic conflicts, and the socioeconomic background of policymaking officials. As much as these divergent interpretations are often contradictory, they all underline the difficulties that faced policymakers, in the years since World War I, in their efforts to establish coherent policies. In spite of the obstacles, the record suggests that foreign oil policy goals have been, in general, attained, although at considerable cost in lives and material, especially during the two Iraq wars fought by the Bush presidencies. The oil policies developed over the past century emerged within the framework of long-established foreign policy and domestic political traditions, involving a blend of Jeffersonian liberalism with the statism of twentieth-century reformers. The latter, from the Progressives of the World War I and 1920s era, through the efforts of Harold Ickes during and immediately following World War II, to the Carter presidency and the establishment of the Department of Energy, sought to stabilize, systematize, and control political and economic processes, to impose the will of the state on the private sector, at the same time being restrained by the strong strand of conservative, antistatist thought that runs through American political thought.

The tension between these two traditions was critical to an understanding of the formation of policy. That tension was reflected in the rejection of the proposals in the 1920s for a United States government-controlled oil corporation and in the Reagan administration's efforts in the 1980s to kill the Department of Energy. The establishment of a state oil company – something that might have played a role akin to that played by the Tennessee Valley Authority – was an idea that was widely discussed in government circles in the 1920s, advanced by such peripheral reformers as Mark Requa, and to some extent picked up during and immediately following World War II by Secretary of the Interior Harold Ickes. There was considerable recognition in the predepression decade that the emergence of the United States as a major military and economic power made a higher level of state intervention in the private sector essential, to enable American firms to compete internationally. From that awareness grew what historians have appropriately referred to as the associational state, characterized by a high level of state coordination and support for the activities of the private sector in the belief that such an approach was in the long-range national interest.

Policymakers in the immediate aftermath of World War I did not hesitate to identify oil as of vital strategic importance to the United States, especially in the context of a postwar oil shortage scare. Policy formation during that early decade was facilitated by the coincidence of objectives and needs on the part of government officials and the major companies, led by Standard Oil of New Jersey. The companies were ready for major expansion of their operations after the war – in exploration, development, and marketing – and government officials increasingly perceived that expansionism as essential to the national interest. With officials concerned with the potential oil shortage, as well as with the threat of nationalization in Mexico and its reality in the Soviet Union, it was a short step to what historian John DeNovo identified as the development of an aggressive international oil policy. Historians have tended to suggest that such an aggressive policy was short-lived, that with the end of the threatened oil shortage, the development of major new domestic resources, such as the east Texas fields, and the onset of depression conditions that resulted in an oil surplus until the late 1930s, both corporate and government officials relaxed their vigilance. I suggest that there was a higher degree of continuity than is often assumed.

Policymakers and companies involved in the international sphere, as distinct from purely domestic producers, consistently placed a high premium on the acquisition of foreign reserves, the breaking down of traditional spheres of interest of competing international powers, particularly those of Great Britain and the Netherlands, and the containment of nationalism. Those challenges remained remarkably similar in the aftermath of World War II, especially when the location of oil resources coincided with regions where the United States was anxious to block Soviet expansion. The first crisis came in Iran during the Truman and Eisenhower presidencies with the initial removal from power of the Shah, the emergence of Mossadegh, and the nationalization of the Anglo-Iranian Oil Company. As this study indicates that was only the beginning of the basic challenges posed by nationalism to policymakers and companies in the Western developed countries. Even before the establishment of OPEC in the 1960s, it had become clear to policymakers and companies that the days of unrestricted private enterprise in the development of overseas oil resources were gone. Producing country governments, conscious of the enormous wealth to be derived from their natural resources and determined to ensure that the "state take" was substantial, established state oil companies, nationalized private sector companies, increased royalty levels, and in some instances blocked foreign companies from developing their oil resources. Mexico was the first to move in this direction prior to World War II, although the Soviet Union had confiscated foreign companies during the Russian Revolution, and other producing countries were mindful of both the example and the response the Mexican actions evoked from the British and American companies. During the 1920s the administrations of Warren G. Harding, Calvin Coolidge, and Herbert Hoover always stopped short of identifying any flag companies. Yet it was also clear, given the international power of a small group of corporations, including the old Standard Oil group, the Texas Company, Gulf Oil, and Royal Dutch Shell and Anglo-Persian (subsequently British Petroleum) among foreign companies, that power would flow towards a small number of firms. Consequently, the main triumphs of the decade included the temporary containment of Mexican nationalism on oil policy, the American breakthrough in the Middle East with the conclusion of the Red Line Agreement among the companies (with State Department sanction), the corporate stabilization associated with the Achnacarry Agreement on marketing, and the strengthened United States position in the Netherlands East Indies. The diplomacy surrounding such agreements drew the United States into the development of a global policy, involving areas of the world in which it had previously had limited strategic and economic interests. In traditional spheres of interest, such as Latin America, the growing importance of oil introduced a critical dimension to international relations.

Equally important were the domestic consequences of an identification of petroleum security as a major foreign policy objective. The newly created office of the assistant secretary of war, for instance, devoted considerable attention to petroleum as part of its planning for industrial mobilization in the event of war. The fear of an oil shortage early in the decade stimulated President Coolidge to establish the Federal Oil Conservation Board and planners to show more concern for the cautious development and management of the Naval Petroleum Reserves. Even the end of this first threat of oil shortage by mid-decade did not alter the basic thrust of policy to ensure equality of access to foreign resources and conservation at home. Clearly increased domestic production, international stabilization, and depression-induced price declines for oil products after 1929 reduced the sense of urgency that had characterized the earlier years in the decade, but this early experience was critical in establishing the basic parameters in which policy was subsequently developed. The conservationism, nationalism, and aggressive internationalism thus carried over into the Hoover and Roosevelt presidencies.

In the formulation of policy prior to World War II, a broad consensus developed, involving Congress, the international oil companies, and officials of the departments of state, war, commerce, navy, and interior, as well as the White House. Significantly, this was one area of interwar foreign policy to which all of the presidents contributed. Presidential and congressional support was conditioned by both the power of the major companies and economic conditions, which favoured the compliance, if not the active support, of the non-integrated domestic corporations with an expansionist foreign oil policy. Thus nationalist sentiments tended to override isolationist ones, as United States policymakers and corporate interests sought to ensure that they were not left behind in the international struggle for raw materials. Although academic analysts have been correct in identifying the extent to which international cooperation became important in the development of oil policy, especially between the United States and Great Britain, it would be erroneous to conclude that Britain yielded to American pressures to gain access to its spheres of interest for other than pragmatic reasons. British policymakers saw international competition as counterproductive and, given the realities of the international power balance after World War I, likely to lead to British loss.

The nature of policy objectives may not have significantly altered during the Hoover and pre-Depression Roosevelt years, but the circumstances in which policy evolved underwent dramatic changes. One of the main contributions of the decline in economic prosperity after 1932 was to heighten the cooperation among the major companies and to exacerbate conflict with the domestic producers, as markets dwindled and domestic companies found themselves increasingly concerned with competition from crude oil imported by the major companies. The development of the rich east Texas oil fields contributed substantially to the problems of domestic and international overproduction. The economic problems faced by the industry contributed to further incentive among the majors to conclude international marketing arrangements and among the domestic producers to obtain a tariff on imported oil. Although the Hoover administration's voluntaristic domestic policies proved generally unsuccessful in curbing the problems faced by the industry, the administration adopted a more vigorous policy abroad in support of both the national interest and United States nationals. At the same time, the Federal Conservation Board continued to emphasize the strategic and economic significance of conserving oil.

Heightened nationalism abroad, reflected in both restrictive legislation relating to the operation of American firms and higher tariffs, impeded the easy realization of American foreign policy objectives. Such was the challenge presented, for instance, in Colombia to Standard Oil of New Jersey and Gulf Oil subsidiaries, in Chile to Jersey Standard and the Union Oil Company of California's marketing interests, and in Argentina to Jersey Standard, as each nation moved towards tighter controls over foreign enterprise, an effort that in Argentina led to the formation of the first state oil enterprise in the hemisphere, ypf (Yacimientos Petrolíferos Fiscales). In each instance the Hoover administration sought not only to defend private interests but also to preserve the strategic interests of the United States in Latin America. It sought to counteract nationalism, to preserve the free enterprise model in oil development, and at the same time to gently pressure the companies to show flexibility and political sensitivity within the host societies. Moreover, contrary to the image of Anglo-American cooperation advanced by some historians, American policymakers sought, with more vigour than the companies at times, to provide a competitive edge for American interests over their foreign rivals.

As active as oil policy was in Latin America, from the 1930s forward the Middle East increasingly attracted diplomatic and corporate attention, even though the depression years witnessed a general surplus of oil on world markets. The temporary economic conditions failed to dull the desire of companies to be in a region on the ground floor or the concern of u.s. policymakers to protect their increasingly global vision of American national interest. In the Middle East, American power provided the entering wedge for American corporations, notably Gulf Oil, Standard Oil of California, and the Texas Company, in Kuwait, Bahrein, and Saudi Arabia in these years. Consequently, on the eve of World War II, American interests were poised for a dramatic expansion in this traditionally British sphere of interest.

An oil surplus during the depression decade and a tinge of anti-business sentiment may well have lulled the Roosevelt administration into complacency on the international stage and heightened the application of antitrust policies at home – to some extent, that is precisely what transpired. The realities of foreign and domestic developments fostered different results, however. The Bolivian expropriation of Standard Oil of New Jersey properties in 1937 and the sweeping nationalization in Mexico the following year dramatically underlined the vulnerability of American corporate and strategic interests even in an area perceived as a special sphere of United States influence. Developments in Bolivia and Mexico combined with the threat of similar action in Venezuela to produce not a new direction for United States policy but a firmer commitment from state and corporate officials to stabilize the international oil situation. For government officials, this required the delicate balancing of the olive branch and the sword, explicitly recognizing the right of a foreign state to nationalize American properties with payment of adequate compensation, but at the same time pressuring Bolivia and Mexico to remain in line. The war greatly complicated the realization of those objectives. With heightened demand for oil supplies to fuel the war, and with concern for continued security of supply after the war, American policymakers pursued a more muted line, much to the chagrin of the nationalized companies. For the next several years, the State Department and the White House sought to achieve a settlement for nationalized properties and to establish a rapport with Latin America that would reduce the likelihood of further expropriation.

The rift between the companies and government officials over the tactics to be pursued was deep and very real, but its importance in the development of foreign oil policy should not be exaggerated. To the companies, a hard line was viewed as critical for achieving a satisfactory settlement and for warning other states contemplating such action; to Roosevelt administration officials and more enlightened corporate officials, a hard-line response had to be sufficiently muted to avoid a widening of the crisis and to foster a sufficiently conciliatory attitude in Mexico to ensure the continued availability of Mexican oil in the event of a national emergency. More critical, given the growing importance internationally of Venezuelan production, was to guard against Venezuela emulating the Bolivian and Mexican measures. United States policy was successful in attaining its short-term objectives. Mexican oil remained available throughout the war, and in Venezuela and the Middle East the companies emerged from the war in a strengthened position. Such developments could not have been attained without active state involvement and support for the private sector in consolidating its international activities. At the same time policymakers were less successful from World War I through the Cold War in attempting to deflect efforts to establish state foreign oil corporations. Argentina's YPF, Mexico's Pemex, Colombia's Eco-petrol, and British government participation in British Petroleum bore witness to that failure, as well as to the extent that the United States was out of step with what would be the basic pattern of government participation in domestic and international petroleum development. That failure was less apparent in the late 1940s than it would become by the 1960s with the establishment of OPEC, but the existence of the critique at the time reflects the prescience of some officials and the myopia of others in anticipating postwar international oil realities.

Whether World War II marked a turning point in the nature of policy formulation and in the direction of that policy remains problematic. Winning the war was clearly the paramount objective of military and civilian planners through 1945, and for those concerned with oil, the primary concerns were immediate logistical ones, ensuring the availability of oil products to industry, to shipping, and to military operations. Beneath the primary objectives, however, even those agencies responsible for the coordination of the war effort – such as the Petroleum Administration for War and military supply departments, as well as State Department and White House officials – sought to reexamine the nature of international oil policy.

From that reevaluation emerged the Petroleum Reserves Corporation, but it was never popular with all segments of the bureaucracy or with the business community, and its projects for the Middle East as initially conceived were ultimately aborted. Planners also spawned the idea of an international agreement on petroleum development, one of the most promising initiatives late in the war; a broad international agreement on oil development was envisaged, consistent with the principles of the Atlantic Charter, assuring freedom of access to international raw materials. The agreement was to begin on a bilateral basis with an Anglo-American accord, but with the clear intent to broaden it ultimately to include the world's major producing and consuming nations. The failure of the United States to consummate this initiative by the end of the 1940s was one of the major failures of the Cold War and set the United States on an unfortunate path towards isolation from third-world producers.

The war also witnessed an increased interest in the development of offshore oil resources. Within territorial waters that issue created a lengthy federal-state jurisdictional conflict; outside territorial waters, the explicit assumption that Open Door principles should apply to the development of seabed minerals heralded an entirely new era of expansionism, conflict, and coexistence in the postwar years.

World war exigencies did inspire a pragmatic reconsideration of the direction and nature of American foreign oil policy. Whatever consensus for a more active state involvement in international petroleum development may have been patched together during the war quickly fragmented as wartime cooperation turned to Cold War conflict. The major and independent companies both reasserted their desire for nonintervention in the private sector as the war drew to a close. The wartime agencies that had contributed to the debate over new directions, such as the Petroleum Administration for War, were disbanded; officials who had contributed to the search for new directions, such as Harold Ickes, passed from the scene; the Anglo-American oil agreement died in the United States Senate. All were victims of company opposition, a surprisingly hostile if not lethargic Truman administration, and a State Department more committed to the continuation of private sector initiative. Among the few institutional legacies of the war, insofar as oil policy was concerned, were the petroleum division in the Department of State and an oil and gas division in the Department of the Interior, the latter having a considerably reduced impact on policy formation with the departure of the boat-rocking Harold Ickes.

This apparent complacency was founded in part on perceived American strength in the postwar world. American oil companies were well established internationally. In spite of the Mexican and Bolivian setbacks of the late 1930s, there was expansion in Venezuela combined with remarkable growth and consolidation in the Middle East and new discoveries in Canada's Alberta fields. The brief flurry of antitrust activity of the late 1930s was mirrored in the oil-cartel case of the 1950s, so well documented in recent years by Burton Kaufman.[4] But antitrust was not in vogue, and it seemed ill conceived at a time of global conflict with the Soviet Union to weaken the power of u.s. corporations overseas. More characteristic of the postwar era was the revitalization of business-government cooperation with the establishment of the Petroleum Advisory Council during the Korean War, bringing together once again government planners and the officers of the major international companies. In 1947 James Forrestal, secretary of defense, observed, in a remark that accurately captured the current mood, that "Calvin Coolidge was ridiculed for saying ... the chief business of the United States is business, but that is a fact."[5] Optimism, if not overconfidence, was also implicit at a twenty-eight-nation International Materials Conference held in 1951, through the cooperation of the Truman administration, Britain, and France; petroleum was not among the commodities identified as strategic raw material critical for defence and economic stability, suggesting that American policymakers had learned little from the lessons of the post-World War I years.[6]

The American oil industry at home and overseas appeared too healthy to cause either alarm or careful long-range planning. Domestically the oil industry was a "pacesetter" in the expansionist economy of the 1950s. By decade's end, more than half of the ten largest United States corporations were oil companies; the United States consumed 60 percent of world oil production; and oil was the single most important commodity by value in international trade. In 1957 Jersey Standard alone produced and refined approximately 15 percent of the world's crude oil.[7] All seemed to be a basis for complacency and confidence.

But unheeded beneath this surface lay causes for concern. The high level of domestic consumption of petroleum products for private, industrial, and military use was one. Except for 1920, the United States was a net exporter of oil from the turn of the century to 1939. Thereafter the importance of foreign oil supplies as a component of domestic supply was substantial. In the early 1950s President Eisenhower's Materials Policy Commission projected a 109 percent increase in petroleum demand by the 1970s, less than the anticipated increase of 291 percent for aluminum, but surprisingly accurate in retrospect. This provided adequate grounds for some officials to attempt to dispel the general mood of complacency.[8]

A second factor that was cause for concern, or should have been in retrospect, was what economist Mira Wilkins has accurately identified as the decline of the capacity of the major companies to control the international industry in the way they had before World War II. Reflective of that change, the 1990s saw a significant merger movement among the companies in their quest to rationalize operations, including the consolidation of their downstream operations. Joint ventures both domestically and with foreign companies in their overseas operations proved another way for companies to reduce costs without the complications of full mergers. Domestically, the result was that in the 1990s the number of major U.S. energy companies declined to ten from nineteen at the beginning of the decade. The major mergers included Mobil and Exxon, which resulted in the creation of the largest publicly traded corporation in the world. In 2001 Chevron and Texaco merged; Gulf Oil had already been acquired by Standard Oil of California (SoCal).[9]

Nor had the threat of nationalism and expropriation abroad disappeared. The United States weathered potential crises in Venezuela and Iran during the early years of the Cold War, but the events since the establishment of OPEC have dramatically underlined the accuracy of the Cassandra-like forebodings of the Federal Oil Conservation Board in the 1920s, of Harold Ickes during World War II, and of William S. Paley's Materials Policy Commission under President Eisenhower, when its report cautioned in 1952 that the world's nations were interdependent on raw materials and that the time had passed for the "spendthrift use of our rich heritage."[10] The oil crises from the time of the 1967 Israeli war through the 1973 Arab oil embargo and the Iranian revolution at the end of the decade took place in the context of the Cold War and confrontation between East and West but also in the context of a strong, emergent Arab nationalism and Islamic fundamentalism. The end of the Cold War reduced the Soviet-American conflict in such critical areas as the Middle East but certainly did not end Russian-American competition for oil resources in Central Asia, and in the Near and Middle East.

Nonetheless, the main challenge to the United States in those regions since the Iranian revolution has been not the remnants of Russian power but the strength of anti-Western, anti-American Islamic fundamentalism and its capacity to destabilize the region. Analysts have indicated that one of the problems that has confronted American policy and policy-makers in the Middle East since the recognition of Israel in the late 1940s is the tension between America's commitment to Israel and its determination to avoid alienating the Arab oil-producing states.[11] Walking that tightrope continues to be one of the main challenges for American policy in the twenty-first century.

Notes

INTRODUCTION

1 Examples include: Anderson, *Aramco, the United States and Saudi Arabia*; Miller, *The Search for Security*; Stoff, *Oil, War and American Security*; and Rabe, *The Road to OPEC*. More recent and comprehensive is Klare, *Resource Wars*. Yergin's *The Prize* remains the most comprehensive treatment of international oil politics, with particular focus on corporate policies. For an analysis of the emerging Caspian producing region see Forsythe, *The Politics of Oil*. See also Bull-Berg, *American International Oil Policy*. Conant, *The Oil Factor in U.S. Foreign Policy* is more focused on policy recommendations. On the origins and impact of Saudi policies in 1999–2000 see Gause, "Saudi Arabia Over a Barrel." See also Kohl, "Oil and National Security," in Kohl, ed., *After the Oil Price Collapse*, and Turner, *Oil Companies in the International System*.

2 Klare, see n1, provides considerable insight in this regard. Eckes, *The United States and the Global Struggle for Minerals*, remains the most useful overview, linking oil with other strategic resource issues.

3 See for instance, Kolko, *The Roots of American Foreign Policy*; and U.S. Congress, Senate, SFRC, *Report on Multinational Petroleum Corporations and Foreign Policy*.

4 Especially valuable for an understanding of state-private sector relations are the following: Hogan, *The Marshall Plan*; and Hogan and Paterson, eds., *Explaining the History of American Foreign Relations*, especially the chapter on "Corporatism." Leffler's *A Preponderance of Power* is valuable not only for the Truman years but also for an understanding of the broader contours of U.S. foreign policy.

5 *Historical Statistics of the United States*, 546, 548.

6 Darmstadter, *Energy in the World Economy*, 103.

7 Wilkins, *The Maturing of Multinational Enterprise*, 87, 88; Latin American data are from the Bureau of Foreign and Domestic Commerce, *Trade Information Bulletin*, no. 731 (Washington, DC, 1930), 18–19.

8 Ferrier, *The History of the British Petroleum Company*, 1–3, 543t.

9 Kolko, *The Roots of American Foreign Policy*, 9–17.

10 Cuff, "A Dollar-a-year Man in Government:"; Koistinen, "The Industrial-Military Complex in Historical Perspective"; Galambos, "The Emerging Organizational Synthesis"; and Hawley, "Herbert Hoover, the Commerce Secretariat, and the Vision of an Associative State." For company-government linkages in the Reagan-George W. Bush years see chapter 12.

11 Biographical information is drawn from the Department of State *Register*; the *Dictionary of American Biography*; *Who's Who in America*; *Who Was Who In America*; the George Bush Presidential Library; and the Carlyle Group website.

12 Krasner, *Defending the National Interest*. For a more detailed discussion of this important work, see Randall, "Raw Materials and United States Foreign Policy." Krasner's subsequent work also adds important insights into regime theory and adds to our understanding of international economic relations. See *Structural Conflict*; and Krasner, ed., *International Regimes*; and with Katzenstein and Keohane, *Exploration and Contestation in the Study of World Politics*.

13 Hoff Wilson, *American Business and Foreign Policy*, 189; Miliband has provided an insightful Marxist analysis of the role of the state in *The State in Capitalist Society*. Braeman in "The New Left and American Foreign Policy During the Age of Normalcy," argues that "the New Left interpretation of American foreign policy in the age of normalcy is … a case of ideology imposing an artificial simplicity upon a complex reality" (102). Braeman is correct that the relationship between the state and state actors on the one hand and the private sector on the other is a complex one. I continue to believe that the historical evidence supports the thesis that U.S. foreign policy in the 1920s and subsequently was driven primarily by security considerations and that in the case of oil policy the state and the private sector had a clear commonality of interest in promoting a liberal, capitalist world order that was, at least for American interests, open for trade and investment.

14 For the army position see file 483, Foreign Countries, South America, Planning Branch, Office of the Assistant Secretary of War, RG 107. The Report of the Federal Oil Conservation Board is from U.S. Senate, *American Petroleum Interests in Foreign Countries* (Washington, DC, 1946), 323. W.D. Andrews, president, Atlantic Refining Company, to the Bureau of Foreign and Domestic Commerce, 23 December 1927, file 312 General, RG 151.

15 Batten, ed., *Encyclopedia of Governmental Advisory Organizations*, 9th edition, 474–5.

CHAPTER ONE

1 DeNovo has provided the most satisfactory account of this early development of foreign oil policy. See "The Movement for an Aggressive Oil Policy Abroad, 1918–1920." Lane was a strong exponent of domestic conservation. See, for instance, his letter of 4 March 1919 to M.C. Robinson, director of oil conservation, U.S. Fuel Administration, box 453, Commerce Files, HHP.

2 Daniel Smith, *Aftermath of War: Bainbridge Colby and Wilsonian Diplomacy, 1920–21*, 46–7. Josephus Daniels, *Diaries*, Cabinet, entry for 28 February 1920, LC.

3 Requa, Manning, and Smith to Garfield, 28 February 1919, Fuel Administration file, box 518, Daniels Papers, LC. Requa, "The Petroleum Problem of the World," *Saturday Evening Post*. (30 October 1920). Requa identified Mesopotamia, Palestine, the Caucasus, and Russia as primary areas. Requa memorandum, 15 November 1920, box 454, Commerce Files, HHP.

4 *Summary of Facts and Recommendations Bearing Upon the Petroleum Policy of the United States* (1919), folder 614, box 32, Polk Papers, Yale University. Wilbur Carr, for the acting secretary of state, to Caribbean area legations, 31 May 1919, DS 800.6363/2a.

5 London *Times*, 3 July 1920; *Washington Post*, 18 November 1920; Lansing to British ambassador, 20 December 1919, FO 371, file 4564; Benson to Lansing, 22 August 1919, DS 800.6363/11.

6 DS 800.6363/89.

7 Dated 29 February 1920, DS 800.6363/95. See, as well, George Otis Smith, address to the New York meeting of the AIMME, February 1920, Pre-Commerce Papers, box 26, HHP.

8 Campbell to Lansing, 9 August 1919, DS 800.6363/10; Lansing to Campbell, 14 August 1919, DS 800.6363/10.

9 Adee to Bradley Staughton, 17 April 1920, DS 800.6363/95; American Embassy in Paris to DS, 3 May 1920, DS 800.6363/108; secretary of state to American ambassador, London, 5 May 1920, DS 800.6363/111a. The note was forwarded by Norman Davis to the Foreign Office, 12 May 1920, DS 800.6363/143. U.S. Congress, Senate, "Restrictions on Certain Petroleum Prospectors in Certain Foreign Countries," Senate document 272 (1920). American anxiety over oil supply paralleled that in Britain, which in 1920 sought to secure control over Royal Dutch Shell and reduce British dependence on foreign-produced oil. See Petroleum Department memorandum, FO 371, file 1331, vol. 5212, 101–4. For the reluctance of Jersey to expand without government support, see the memorandum of a conversation (Everit Sadler and Arthur Millspaugh), 3 August 1920, DS 800.6363/162.

10 Frost to Polk, 9 March 1920, folder 615, box 32, Polk Papers, Yale University.

11 American notes of 12 May and 28 May 1920; British reply of 9 August 1920, DS 800.6363/163.

12 U.S. Congress, Senate, 66th Cong., 2nd sess., Senate document no. 97 (1920); U.S. Congress, Senate, *Congressional Record* (17 May 1920), 7144; (17 January 1921), 1491. The reference to Phelan's proposal to Payne is from *Commercial and Financial Chronicle*, 22 May 1920. The BFDC reported that Standard Oil of California exported more than 10 million barrels of fuel oil to other countries, mostly Japan and China, in the first quarter of 1920 (file 312 General, RG 151). De Novo, "Movement for an Aggressive Oil Policy," 871. Colby to Senator Reid Smoot, 19 November 1920, DS 811.6363/216. On the Phelan proposal see, as well, DS 811.6363/25/46/328. De Novo, "Movement ..." 871-3.

13 Report of the British ambassador to the U.S., 26 November 1920, FO 371, vol. 4587, file 898, 105.

14 U.S. Congress, Senate, *Congressional Record*, 66th Cong., 3rd sess., 872, 1032-57. R.C. Lindsay, British Embassy in Washington, to Lord Curzon, 9 January 1920, FO 371, file 4564, 43-6.

15 SFRC, Multinational Petroleum Corporations and Foreign Policy, *Report*, 33.

16 Memorandum on the General Leasing Law, undated, folder: Oil, 1928, box 452, Commerce Papers, HHP. At this time Shell had two main producing subsidiaries in the U.S.: Shell of California and the Roxana Petroleum Corporation in the mid-continent. Only California Shell had an internal marketing system. Shell also controlled Ozark Pipeline Corporation, Matador Petroleum, Asiatic Petroleum (New York), New Orleans Refining, and three subsidiary shipping companies (FO 371, A 3623/177/45.

17 J.C. Van Eck, Shell Union Oil Company, New York to Sir Henri Deterding, 16 January 1924, Shell Papers; Hogan, *Informal Entente*, 165.

18 Leigh-Jones to Deterding, 29 December 1925, Shell Papers.

19 Foreign Office memorandum, "Acquisition by Foreigners of Mining and Oil Rights in British Dominions," 23 April 1920, FO 371, vol. 4564, 111; FO minute of 15 June 1920, same file, 117. Petroleum Department to undersecretary of state, vol. 5212, file 1331, 114-16. Geddes to Curzon, 22 January 1920, FO 371, A 904/177/45.

20 A.C. Veatch to Department of State, 26 January 1920, DS 800.6363/74. Canadian restrictions are discussed in Wilkins, *Maturing of Multinational Enterprise*, 156.

21 Colby to John Davis (U.S. ambassador to Britain), 23 November 1920, and Oil Note to Curzon, 22 November 1920, DS 800.6363/196a.

22 Millspaugh memorandum for Frost and Merle-Smith, 17 August 1920; Manning to Frost, 12 August 1920, 30 August 1920; Frost to Manning, 1 September 1920, DS 800.6363/276; /275. See as well Tulchin, *Aftermath of War*, 125. Merle-Smith to secretary of state, 11 March 1921, DS 800.6363/325.

23 Millspaugh memorandum, 19 February 1921, DS 800.6363/276.

24 Nash, *U.S. Oil Policy*, 53.

25 Hoover, for example, recommended to President Harding, 2 April 1921, that the department be asked to investigate foreign petroleum resources (box 452, Commerce Files, HHP).

26 U.S. Senate, *Congressional Record*, 67th Cong., 1st sess., 12 April 1921, 157ff. Fall's letter of 21 March 1921 to Lodge, outlining British restrictions on American oil interests, is in ibid., 162ff. In July, Fall was still pressing his position on international oil policy. At Cabinet on 15 July he read a memo on world oil production emphasizing the importance of imports (see DS 800.6363/324). See, as well, Geddes to Curzon, 29 April 1921; Andrews to Lodge, 27 April 1921, FO 371, A 3304/44/45. The British government held 5 million ordinary shares, 1000 preferred shares, and 199,000 debentures of Anglo-Persian.

27 DS letters of 6, 12 April 1921, DS 800.6363/243a.

28 April 1921 meeting of Foreign Oil Policy Committee of AIMME, box 452, Commerce Files, HHP.

29 Barneson to Hoover, 9 May 1921, box 454, Oil Conference, Commerce Files, HHP.

30 Bedford to Dearing, assistant secretary of state, 16 April 1921, DS 800.6363/257; Lufkin to Dearing, 20 April 1921, DS 800.6363/253. Millspaugh to secretary of state, 10 December 1921, DS 800.6363/333. There was evidently also support for such an initiative in the Department of Commerce. See the unsigned memorandum of 14 April 1921 in box 452, Commerce Files, HHP, proposing a British-American agreement for the "removal of obstacles to the international involvement of capital, and by the elimination of conditions and practices that unnecessarily delay the development of oil-bearing areas."

31 Letter of 10 June 1921, FO 371, A 4717/44/45.

32 Manning report to API, August 1921, DS 800.6363/295. On Cadman, see Rowland and Basil, Second Baron Cadman, *Ambassador for Oil, The Life of John, First Baron Cadman*. Shortly after his visit to the United States in late 1921 to speak to the API on international oil issues, Cadman resigned from government service, became technical adviser to the Anglo-Persian Oil Company (APOC) and the following year managing director of D'Arcy Exploration Company, the main exploration subsidiary of APOC. Cadman's speech to the API in Chicago was read in advance by the commercial secretary of the British Embassy. Cadman strongly opposed direct government involvement in the industry as "wasteful and ill advised expenditure" (FO 371, A 905/177/45).

33 Petroleum Department, memorandum, "Acquisition by Foreigners of Oil Rights in British Territory," May 1921, FO 371, W 4817/757/50. Sir Charles Greenway of Anglo-Persian and Bedford of Standard had already met on

this issue. Minutes of British Inter-Departmental Petroleum Committee, 30 June 1921, FO 371, W 8377/757/50. Lloyd-Greame report for Cabinet, 6 January 1922, FO 371, W 873/873/50.

34 Colonial Office memorandum, November 1921, marked "to be considered Colonial Office Policy," FO 371, W 12305/757/50. It is interesting that the hard line of the British Admiralty and Colonial Office paralleled that the of the U.S. Navy, which was extremely anxious to obtain additional fuel in 1921. See, for example, R.E. Coontz, acting secretary of the navy, to secretary of state, 20 April 1921, DS 800.6363/254. The British Admiralty obtained 40 percent of its requirements under contract with Anglo-Persian, the remainder under short-term contracts or yearly purchase from the U.S., Mexico, Trinidad, Borneo, Burma, and Scotland. FO memorandum by Sir P. Lloyd-Greame, 6 January 1922, FO 371, W 873/873/50. Memorandum, 23 October 1920, FO 371, A 4695/79/45.

35 Secretary of State Colby, for instance, wrote William Phillips in mid-1920: "It is not desired that the above views be interpreted as a special interest in behalf of any particular individual or corporation" (DS 856d.6363/12). Secretary of state to Phillips, 16 October 1920, DS 856d.6363/16. For a general statement of later department policy, see Kellogg to secretary of the navy, R.L. Wilbur, 29 June 1928, DS 811.6363/205.

36 DS memorandum, "Foreign Economic Interests in the Far East," box 128, Conference on the Limitation of Armaments, 1921–1922," RG 43. Production figures are drawn from BFDC, Special Circular no. 218, "Petroleum Trade of the Dutch East Indies," (1925), file 312, Dutch East Indies, RG 151; J.F. Jewell, U.S. Consul at Batavia, "Report on Mineral Oil Concessions and Rights in Netherlands India," 27 January 1920, DS 856d.6363/1. The best brief treatment of part of the story is Reed, "Standard Oil in Indonesia, 1898–1928."

37 Independent Petroleum Association, "Report of the Independent Petroleum Association of America," in SFRC, *A Documentary History of the Petroleum Reserves Corporation* (Washington, DC 1944), 105. Wilbur J. Carr to U.S. consul, 4 March 1920, DS 800.6363/95a; A.A. Adee, assistant secretary of state, to the U.S. minister in The Hague, 13 April 1920, FR, 1920, III, 264–6. BFDC memorandum, 18 September 1928, file 312, Dutch East Indies – 1928, RG 151; Colby to Phillips, 17 July 1920, DS 856d.6363/6.

38 4 September 1920, FR, 1920, III, 276; letters of 7 and 25 September 1920, in FO 371, A 3747/44/45. U.S. Congress, Senate, *Diplomatic Protection of American Property Abroad* (1945), 37; Nash, *U.S. Oil Policy*, 63.

39 Hughes to Phillips, 22 April 1921, FR, 1921, II, 536, 540–1. Standard Oil sent its associate general counsel and its European representative to lobby against passage of the Djambi concession bill. R. Graham, British ambassador to The Hague, to the FO, 24 May 1921, FO 371, A 3748/44/45.

40 File 312, Dutch East Indies, RG 151. W. de Beaufort, Netherlands, to

secretary of state, 27 September 1920, DS 800.6363/183. See as well FO 371, minutes of 21 June 1921, A 4497/44/45; FR, 1921, II, 529, 531; Hughes to Phillips, 31 March 1921, 12 April 1921, DS 856d.6363/71/72. Interview of 26 May 1921, box 176, Hughes Papers, LC. R. Graham to FO, 2 June 1921, A 4064/44/45. Wall and Gibb, *Teagle of Jersey Standard*, 204ff.

41 Foreign Office cable to The Hague, 27 June 1921, FO 371, A 4569/44/45.

42 Memorandum by A.S. Openheim, Royal Dutch Shell, The Hague, 13 July 1926, Shell Papers.

43 Andrews to de Kok (copy to Deterding), 4 October 1926, Shell Papers. Adrian Corbett, Shell Group, to J.S. Van Eyck, New York, 24 January 1927; Van Eyck to J.B. Kessler, 30 December 1927, Shell Papers.

44 Kessler to Richard Airey, New York, 16 February 1928; Agnew to H.W. Cole, British Petroleum Department, 7 May 1929, Shell Papers.

45 Report of the Petroleum Division, BFDC, to Standard Oil, 18 August 1922, file 312, Dutch East Indies, RG 151. Loomis to Hoover, 21 January 1924, box 452, Commerce Files, HHP; British Intelligence Notes, Malay Command, 21 May 1924, FO 371, F 2222/304/61; U.S. commercial attaché, Brussels, to chief of the minerals division, 3 August 1925, file 312, Dutch East Indies, RG 151. British consul general in Batavia to FO, 23 August 1927, FO 371, W 619/619/29; Lord Grenville, The Hague, to FO, 15 February 1928, FO 371, W 1440/619/29. FR, 1928, III, 399–406; Kellogg to secretary of the navy, 29 June 1928, DS 811.6363/205; U.S. Congress, Senate, Special Committee Investigating Petroleum Resources. *Hearings, Report of the Group on Petroleum Interests in Foreign Countries*, 79th Cong., 1st sess. (New York: Arno Press edition 1976), 381.

46 The best general treatments of American diplomacy in the area are DeNovo, *American Interests and Policies in the Middle East*; Shwadran, *The Middle East, Oil and the Great Powers*. The most recent scholarly study of Iraq oil is Stivers, "International Politics and Iraqui Oil, 1918–1928: A Study in Anglo-American Diplomacy." See also U.S. Congress, Senate, Subcommittee on Multinational Corporations, *Multinational Corporations and United States Foreign Policy, Hearings* (1974), part 8, 510 (referred to throughout the notes as SFRC, Multinational Corporations and Foreign Policy, *Hearings*).

47 Hoover to Hughes, 22 December 1921, Commerce Files, box 571, HHP.

48 For comments on Manning's influence, see W.H. Field, S. Pearson and Sons, to J. Ryder, New York, president, Amerada Petroleum Corporation, 17 September 1923, container 25, Venezuela folder, Pearson Papers. On Nelson, see Nelson memorandum, 15 February 1927, file 312, General/1927, RG 151; Nelson to assistant director, BFDC, 25 March 1927, "Proposed Remedy for Foreign Oil Monopolies," file 312 General, RG 151. On the Webb-Pomerene Act see Parrini, *Heir to Empire*.

49 McGrath to Klein, 15 April 1927; D.L. Harper to Guy Wellman, associate general counsel, Standard Oil of New Jersey, 11 November 1927, file 312

General, RG 151; James Moffett, Standard Oil of New Jersey, to Nelson, 28 December 1927, file 312 General, RG 151.

50 Board of Trade memorandum, "The Turkish Petroleum Company and Iraq Oil Policy," 4 February 1924. Treasury Department to the Anglo-Persian Oil Company, 28 February 1928; Anglo-Persian to Treasury, 15 March 1928, FO 371, W 2991/2991/50.

51 FO minute, James Morgan, 30 March 1927, FO 371, E 1439/104/65; secretary of state, FO, to undersecretary of state, Colonial Office, 23 April 1927, FO 371, E 1084/104/65. J.C. Clarke, Board of Trade, to Walter Samuel, Shell, 5 December 1922; Samuel to Clarke, 7 December 1923, Shell Papers.

52 Nicholls to the British Petroleum Department, 13 December 1922, 23 January 1923, Shell Papers.

53 Churchill letter of 1 February 1922, FO 371, E 1195/132/54; Deterding to Baldwin, 2 September 1922, E 10170/132/65; Baldwin's private secretary to Deterding, 4 September 1922, Shell Papers. Cowdray memorandum of conversation with Baldwin, 15 May 1923; Deterding to Colonel J.N. Boyle, 30 January 1922, folder: British Imperial Oil Company, container 44, Pearson Papers.

54 Teagle to Hughes, 9 November 1923; Teagle to secretary of state, 25 October 1923; Hughes to Teagle, 8 November 1923. Copies in box 454, Oil: Turkish Oil, 1922–1923, Commerce Files, HHP. Hughes to Coolidge, 31 October 1923; Coolidge to Hughes, 31 October 1923, file 20, Coolidge Papers, LC.

55 Hughes to Teagle, 22 August 1922; Teagle to Hughes, 25 August 1922, TPC folder, box 286, Commerce Files, HHP. Frost to Manning, 27 November 1922, DS 800.6363/205a, RG 59. Hoover stressed to Hughes that American access was a "matter of national pride." Hoover to Hughes, 19 August 1922, Commerce Files, box 286, HHP.   .

56 Nicholls to Teagle, 14 December 1923, Shell Papers.

57 FO minutes of 5 March 1924, FO 371, E 1785/13/65; Wellman to Nicholls, TPC, 19 December 1923, Shell Papers. Dulles memorandum of a conversation with Wellman, 22 January 1924, p. 30 of "Issues Concerning the Iraq Petroleum Company," March 1947, box 6, PD. Memorandum of 10 May 1923, p. 38 of "Issues Concerning the Iraq Petroleum Company."

58 Hughes to Kellogg (U.S. ambassador to Britain), 21 October 1924; Kellogg to the U.S. chargé in Britain, 20 April 1925, FR, 1925, II, 230–8; Foreign Office minutes, 14 March 1925, FO 371, E 2760/43/65; SFRC, Subcommittee on Multinational Corporations, Hearings, 1974, part 8, 498; Kellogg to Wilbur, 29 June 1928, FR, 1928, III, 396–8.

59 Draft agreement dated 23 August 1927, Shell Papers.

60 Notes of meeting of the groups, 18 March 1927; memorandum, general manager, TPC, 21 December 1926, Shell Papers.

61 Records of September 1927 meetings, Shell Papers.

62 For State Department support of the agreement see economic adviser, Department of State, memorandum, 13 April 1928, and correspondence of 16 April 1928, DS 890g.6363 T84/320, 321, RG 59, NA.

63 SFRC, *Report on Multinational Petroleum Corporations* (1975), 45–7. SFRC Subcommittee on Multinational Corporations, *Hearings* (1974), part 7, 24; Wall and Gibb, *Teagle*, 260; Larson, Knowlton, and Popple, *History of Standard Oil ... New Horizons*, 60. It was a profitable arrangement at least for Jersey Standard, which estimated that by 1937 its one-eighth share of the Iraq Petroleum Company was worth between $119 and $143 million on an initial investment of $13.9 million. SFRG Subcommittee on Multinational Corporations, *Hearings* (1974), part 8, 499–500.

64 SFRC, Subcommittee on Multinational Corporations, *Hearings* (1974), part 8, 30–4. Sampson, *The Seven Sisters*, 90. Ferrier, *The History of the British Petroleum Company* I, 463. As Ferrier indicates, the Achnacarry Agreement was preceded by an arrangement between Anglo-Persian and Royal Dutch Shell over outlets in the Far East and in Africa through the formation of the Consolidated Petroleum Company Ltd, as well as by the merger of Burmah Oil and Royal Dutch Shell Indian interests in 1927 in Burmah-Shell Ltd. The material on the Petroleum Export Association is drawn from a Department of Justice memorandum, 14 January 1952, file 60-57-140, RG 60. The author expresses his appreciation to Bennett Wall and Burton Kaufman for drawing this material to his attention. The corporation history of these years is most thoroughly treated by Wilkins, *The Maturing of Multinational Enterprise, 1914–1970*.

CHAPTER TWO

1 Memorandum of a meeting at the State Department of Merle-Smith, Frost, Millspaugh, and E. Sadler of Jersey Standard, among others, 12 January 1921, DS 800.6363/238.

2 Ibid. The question of petroleum in Soviet-American relations in the 1920s has received little attention from historians. The most perceptive analysis is that by Wilson, *Ideology and Economics: U.S. Relations with the Soviet Union, 1918–1933*. See also the brief account by E. Heymann, "Oil in Soviet-Western Relations in the Interwar Years."

3 Prizer to Hoover, 31 October 1922, box 485, Commerce Files, HHP.

4 A.C. Millspaugh memorandum, 3 May 1922, DS 861.6363/6. See, as well, Wilkins, *The Maturing of Multinational Enterprise*, 50. Gibb and Knowlton, *A History of Standard Oil: The Resurgent Years, 1911–1927*. U.S. trade commissioner, Constantinople, to Kennedy, 27 February 1920, file 312 Russia, RG 151.

5 Filene, *Americans and the Soviet Experiment, 1917–1933*, 106–8. Hoover ad-

dress to the International Chamber of Commerce, 15 May 1922, box 227, Commerce Files, HHP. Wilson, *Ideology and Economics*, 32. On the Sinclair question see G. Riddell to Klein, 27 February 1925, file: Oil-FOCB, Commerce Files, Official Files, HHP. Heymann, "Oil in Soviet-Western Relations," 307–8. U.S. Congress, Senate, *Report of the Group on Petroleum Interests in Foreign Countries* (Arno edition, 1976), 431. H.F. Sinclair to secretary of state, 12 May 1921, DS 861b.6363/7; DS to Sinclair, 27 September 1921, DS 861b.6363/39a; D.C. Poole, chief of Division of Russian Affairs, to undersecretary William Phillips, 26 September 1922, DS 861b.6363/39.

6 There is extensive correspondence on these questions between the companies and the Department of State. See, for example, Department of State memorandum prepared for Cabinet meeting, 12 March 1925, DS 861b.6363/116; Hughes memorandum, 3 June 1925, DS 861b.6363/131; A.C. Veatch, Sinclair vice-president, to secretary of state, 15 October 1924, DS 861b.6363/102; Hughes to Veatch, 20 December 1924, DS 861b.6363/106; Hughes to R. Crandall, Sinclair Exploration, 14 April 1923, DS 861b.6363/58; Hughes to Francis B. Loomis, Standard Oil of California, 19 May 1923, DS 861b.6363/70a; Bedford to Hughes, 1 December 1922, box 11, Hughes Papers, LC.

7 Hughes to the International Barnsdall Corporation, 30 January 1923, DS 861.6363/124a. On IBC, see U.S. trade commissioner, Riga, to BFDC, 28 September 1922, file 312 Russia, RG 151.

8 For the BFDC position, see G. Riddell memorandum, February 1925, and Riddell to Julius Klein, 27 February 1925, box 453, file: FOCB, Commerce Files, Official File, HHP. Advisory Committee, FOCB, to chairman Hubert Work, 26 February 1925, box 453, file: Oil-FOCB, Commerce Files, Official File, HHP.

9 Richard Washburn Child, U.S. ambassador to Italy, to secretary of state, 24 April 1922, DS 711.61/60.

10 Hughes to Child, 4 May 1922, DS 861.6363/54. Bedford to Hughes, 5 May 1922, DS 861.6363/63. Child reported 7 May 1922 that Lloyd George, head of the British delegation at Genoa, had assured him Shell had not reached an agreement with the USSR. Lloyd George also expressed the view that failure to reach a general agreement at Genoa would make it difficult to control the private interests anxious to participate in Soviet oil development.

11 Heymann, "Oil in Soviet-Western Relations," 307–10. In 1924 the Soviet Naptha Syndicate established a subsidiary in England.

12 Ibid., 314–15. Sampson, *Seven Sisters*, 87–9.

13 Tulchin, *Aftermath of War*, 133–4, contends that oil policy cannot be treated in Mexico as distinct from other policy considerations.

14 Ibid., 149–53.

15 U.S. Congress, Senate, *American Petroleum Interests in Foreign Countries* (1946), 335–7. Robert Smith, *The United States and Revolutionary Na-*

tionalism in Mexico, 1916–1932, 146. U.S. firms rapidly increased their share of Venezuelan production to 50 percent by 1929. See Rabe, "Anglo-American Rivalry for Venezuelan Oil, 1919–1929," 109, and *Road to* OPEC.

16 Information is for June 1921 (file: Oil Interests in Foreign Fields, Commerce Files, OF, HHP).

17 Wilson, *American Business and United States Foreign Policy*, 199–200. Data are drawn largely from Aguila Company folder, box 44, Pearson Papers. See also Giddens, *Standard Oil Company (Indiana): Pioneer of the Middle West*, 240–1.

18 Robert Smith, *Revolutionary Nationalism*, 89, 184–5, 235. Smith convincingly advances a structuralist argument, even though he notes that prominent Wilson administrators, such as George Creel, believed that Wilson's policy of nonrecognition of Obregón's government derived from industry pressure.

19 Bosques, *The National Revolutionary Party of Mexico and the Six Year Plan*, appendix IV.

20 Smith, *Revolutionary Nationalism*, 147–8. Jersey Standard prior to 1917 was very active in Mexico, controlling two-thirds of Waters Pierce Oil Company, which had a monopoly on the oil retail trade in Mexico (Mexican Eagle File, box 44, Pearson Papers). Before Pearson reached agreement with Shell, there had been extensive negotiations with Jersey in 1911–13 and 1916–18 on Aguila properties (file: Negotiations with Standard Oil, box 44, Pearson Papers). The provisions of Article 27 were incorporated in a general petroleum bill in 1921 (see FR, 1921, II, 439–46).

21 Lansing to President Wilson, 15 April 1917, DS 812.01/A.

22 U.S.-Mexican Commission, *Proceedings of the United States-Mexican Commission Convened in Mexico City, May 14, 1923* (Washington, DC 1925), 47–9 (copy in box 172, Hughes Papers, LC). The agreement was limited to the term of the current Mexican executive (U.S. Senate, *Diplomatic Protection* [Washington 1945], 67–9). For the Texas Company case see FR, 1921, II, 461–73. The other cases were instituted by the International Petroleum Company and the Tamiahua Petroleum Company.

23 Smith, *Revolutionary Nationalism*, 231.

24 Ibid., 255–7.

25 FR, 1927, I, 356–63. Lansing, Doheny, and Republican Senator Albert Fall were among the more prominent early spokesmen identifying Mexico with Bolshevism. See, for example, Josephus Daniels's comments, *Diary*, entry for 4 December 1919, Daniels Papers, LC. The congressional opposition to Kellogg's red-scare tactics came from progressives such as William Borah, George Norris, Burton Wheeler, and Robert LaFollette (see Smith, *Revolutionary Nationalism*, 238, 239n). For business and press opposition to intervention, see the *New York Times*, 5 January 1927, and the *Commercial and Financial Chronicle*, 15 January 1927.

26 Original draft of Hughes's instructions, 30 April 1923, box 172, Hughes Papers, LC. Glad, *Charles Evans Hughes*, 250. Fletcher to Carranza, 2 April 1918, box 29, Polk Papers. On the oil export tax see U.S. chargé to secretary of state, 8 June 1921, DS 600.127/175; C.J. Wrightsman, Independent American Oil Producers, to secretary of state, 19 June 1921, DS 600.127/185; Frederic Watriss to secretary of state, 7 July 1921, DS 600.127/211.

27 On the mission of the oil executives, see Teagle to Hughes, 18 August 1921, DS 611.127/394; minutes of meeting with Tampico managers, December 1921, DS 600.127/250; Teagle to Hughes, 11 May 1922, DS 812.512/2873.

28 Shipping Board report, appended to Millspaugh memorandum for the U.S. delegates to the Washington Conference, 1921, "The Petroleum Situation with Special Reference to the Far East," folder 25, box 130, Conference on the Limitation of Armament, 1921–22, RG 43, NA.

29 Cowdray memorandum, 13 April 1916; John Cadman, petroleum executive, to Cowdray, 8 January 1923, box 44, Pearson Papers. U.S. official concern with increased British involvement is reflected in Boaz Long, chief, Division of Mexican Affairs, 15 January 1919, Polk Papers.

30 Carlton Jackson, trade commissioner, Mexico City, to BFDC, 28 April 1921, folder: Oil, Mexican, box 454, Commerce Files, OF, HHP.

31 Doheny to Requa, 15 March 1918, box 29, Polk Papers.

32 FDR to J.B. Bowditch, Massachusetts, 18 April 1916, assistant secretary of the navy, OF, FDR Papers.

33 Tulchin, *Aftermath of War*, 130–1. Matthew Hanna, chief, Division of Mexican Affairs, memorandum, 11 July 1922, DS 812.6363/1228; Robert Olds, undersecretary of state, to commercial counsellor, British Embassy, 6 October 1927, DS 812.6363/2453/2454.

34 Kellogg to Sheffield, 29 October 1925, DS 5200/34a; 13 November 1925, DS 812.5200/50; 31 December 1925, DS 812.6363/1629. See also Smith, *Revolutionary Nationalism*, 232–4. On Sadler, see Wall and Gibb, *Teagle*, 188.

35 Kellogg to Coolidge, DS 812.6363/2152.

36 Schoenfeld to secretary of state, 7 August 1927, DS 812.6363/2339.

37 Smith, *Revolutionary Nationalism*, 256–7; Howard Cline, *The United States and Mexico* (New York, 1971), 210–12. U.S. Senate, *Diplomatic Protection* (1945), 71–2. For the revised petroleum law, see FR, 1928, III, 301–6.

38 Ovey to FO, 23 February 1928, FO 371, A 1793/38/26; Snow minute, 14 September 1928, FO 371, A 6407/38/26.

39 Mexican Eagle file, box 43; Mexico file, box 44, Pearson Papers.

40 Thompson, *Since Spindletop*, 74–5; Gibb and Wall, *Teagle*, 195.

CHAPTER THREE

1 Larson, Knowlton, and Popple, *History of Standard Oil ... New Horizons*, 148–9; Wilkins, *Maturing of Multinational Enterprise*, passim.

2 Wall and Gibb, *Teagle*, 261–5; Department of State meeting with John Frey (Department of Commerce), 9 July 1930, DS 800.6363/403.

3 J.B. Aug. Kessler, "Cooperative Plan for World Oil Industry," *World Petroleum* (October 1931), 564–7; Editorial, *World Petroleum* (October 1931), 561–2; Ames, "Anti-Trust Laws and the Petroleum Industry," *World Petroleum* (October 1931), 563. Wirt Franklin address, 15 January 1932; Teagle to Hoover, 7 December 1929, box 217, Oil Matters, Presidential Papers, HHP.

4 Doherty to Wilbur, 26 October 1931, box 520, Petroleum Regulation, RG 40, NA. The best general treatment of the domestic issues during the Hoover years is Nash, *United States Oil Policy*.

5 U.S. FOCB, *Sources of U.S. Oil Supply ... Report V to the President of the United States* (1932).

6 Address of November 1932, box 219, Oil Matters, Presidential Papers, HHP.

7 De Novo provides a thorough overview of these developments in *American Interests and Policies in the Middle East, 1900–1939*. For a discussion of the "As Is" arrangements and the implications of the expansion of Gulf and Standard Oil of California, see the justice department memorandum of 14 January 1952, file 60-57-140, RG 60, NA (courtesy of Bennett Wall).

8 F. Leavy, president, Eastern Gulf Oil, to secretary of state, 27 November 1931, DS 890B.6363 Gulf Oil Corporation/1; Stimson to Atherton, 3 December 1931, DS 890b.6363 Gulf Oil Corporation/5; Castle to Leavy, 3 December 1931, DS 890B.6363 Gulf Oil Corporation/7.

9 P.M. Roberts minute, 30 December 1931, FO 371, E 6350/325/91.

10 Sir Lancelot Oliphant, undersecretary of state for foreign affairs, to L.D. Wakely, India Office, 22 January 1932, FO 371, 261/121/91; George Randel, minute of meeting with Wakely, 30 January 1932, FO 371, E 1019/12/91; Government of India to India Office, 25 February 1932, FO 371. 1019/121/91.

11 March 1932, FO 371, E 1347/121/91; Dreyer to Oliphant, 14 March 1932, FO 371, E 1348/121/91 secretary of state to U.S. chargé in Britain, 26 March 1932, DS 890B.6363 Gulf Oil Corporation/46.

12 The secretary of state and Near East division officials met with Gulf Oil officials on 30 November 1931 at Mellon's request. Near East division memorandum, 30 November 1931, DS 890B.6363 Gulf Oil Corporation/2. Wallace Murray, Near East division, to undersecretary William R. Castle, Jr, 1 December 1931, DS 890B.6363 Gulf Oil Corporation/3. Chisholm, *The First Kuwait Oil Concession*, 131–4. Castel to Atherton, 2 April 1932, DS 890B.6363 Gulf Oil Corporation/50.

13 Chisholm, *Kuwait*, 134–5.

14 Sir John Simon to Atherton, 9 April 1932, FO 371, E 1733/121/91; on Cadman see FO 371, E 1870/121/91. For the revival of Anglo-Persian interest in Kuwait, see G.W. Rendel, FO minute, 26 July 1932, FO 371, E 3589/121/91.

Cadman to Oliphant, 31 December 1932, FO 371, E 25/12/91. FO minutes, 21 and 29 December 1932, FO 371, A 8510/3165/45.

15 Note of 6 September 1932, FO 371, E 4582/121/91. FO minute, 13 October 1932, FO 371, E 5295/121/91.

16 Rendel minute, 20 October 1932, FO 371, E 5410/121/91; E 5644/121/91. See also W.T. Wallace, Gulf Oil, to B.R. Jackson, APOC representative in the U.S., 8 September 1932, cited in Chisholm, *Kuwait*, 166–7; Rendel minute, 17 September 1932, FO 371, E 4670/121/90.

17 G. Laithwaite, India Office, to C.F. Warner, FO, 19 June 1933; Warner to Laithwaite, 29 June 1933, FO 371, E 3253/12/91. Colonial Office memorandum, 26 April 1933, FO 371, E 2422/12/91. Rendel minute, 28 March 1933, FO 371, E 1498/487/25.

18 Letter of 3 October 1932, cited in Chisholm, *Kuwait*, 167. Laithwaite to Warner, 11 December 1933, FO 371, E 7627/12/91.

19 Hamilton, *Americans and Oil in the Middle East*, 194. Laithwaite to Warner, 19 January 1933, FO 371, E 413/12/91. Chisholm, *Kuwait*, 174. FO minute, 11 December 1933, E 7627/12/91. Cadman to John Lloyd (APOC), 1 March 1933, cited in Chisholm, *Kuwait*, 176–7.

20 Rendel to C.F. Warner, 3 February 1933, FO 371, E 723/12/91.

21 Rendel minute, 4 March 1933, FO 371, E 1196/12/91.

22 Chisholm, *Kuwait*, xiv; Anderson, *Aramco, the United States and Saudi Arabia*.

23 Chisholm, *Kuwait*, 187–91.

24 U.S. Department of State, Near Eastern division, "Important Accomplishments in the Countries of the Near East, March 1929–February 1933," box 239, Stimson Papers, Yale University.

25 Ibid.; see also FR, 1931, II, 608.

26 Castle to Atherton, 27 November 1931, DS 890g.6363/306; British assistant undersecretary of state for foreign affairs to the American counselor, London, 23 December 1931, FO 371, E 6320/5/93.

27 Wilkins, *Maturing of Multinational Enterprise*, 114–16.

28 Wilkins, "Multinational Oil Companies in South America in the 1920s," 415ff.

29 File 312, Argentina, 1924–25, 1926, RG 151, NA. Solberg, *Oil and Nationalism in Argentina*, especially 112ff. File 312, Bolivia, 1930, RG 151, NA.

30 Material on Colombia is based on my book, *The Diplomacy of Modernization: Colombian-American Relations, 1920–1940*.

31 DS memorandum of a meeting with Walter Teagle, President of Standard Oil, and E.T. Stannard, president, Kennecott Copper, 27 January 1939, DS 825.6363/175.

32 DS, "Review of Questions of Major Interest in the Relations of the United States with the Latin American Countries 1929–1933," box 239, Stimson Papers, Yale University.

33 Stuart Grumman, Latin American Division, memorandum for Edwin C. Wilson, chief of division, 10 November 1931, DS 825.6363/90½.

34 DS memorandum, Joe Stinson for Edwin Wilson, 15 February 1932, DS 825.6363/93.

35 U.S. officials appeared convinced, for instance, that the Soviet Union had financially supported political revolt in Mexico in 1928–9. See Ralph Easley, National Civic Federation, to Hoover, 17 July 1929, box 993, Foreign Affairs, Countries File, Russia, Presidential Papers, HHP. Evidently Mathew Wol and General Samuel McRoberts had raised this issue. Investigation showed that the Amtrog Trading Corporation had spent $9 million in support of revolution in Mexico in 1928–9.

36 Ibid.; see, as well, memorandum of State Department meeting, 23 November 1931, DS 825.6363/82. DS, "Review of Questions."

37 DS 825.6363/122/130.

38 See, for example, Stuart Grumman memorandum of conversation with T.A. Shone, first secretary, British Embassy, Washington, 21 May 1932, DS 825.6363/124. Jersey's attorney informed the department that Shell and Jersey were working "shoulder to shoulder" in opposition to the bill (DS 825.6363/77). Jersey also claimed, however, that the Chilean government would grant a contract to an English promoter (DS, "Review of Questions").

39 DS, "Review of Questions."

40 Ibid.

41 DS 825.6363/150.

CHAPTER FOUR

1 Anderson, *The Standard-Vacuum Oil Company and United States East Asian Policy, 1933-1941*.

2 The most thorough assessments of Roosevelt-era relations with Latin America are Gellman, *Good Neighbor Diplomacy: United States Policies in Latin America, 1933-1945*; Wood, *The Making of the Good Neighbor Policy*.

3 There are useful career outlines of department figures in Gellman, *Good Neighbor Diplomacy*, passim and the Department of State, *Register*, various years.

4 Memorandum of 26 March 1934, Lieutenant-Colonel Charles Harris, "Strategic Commodities," file 71; Harris memorandum, 8 March 1935, box 1037, file 470.1/129.8, RG 107, NA.

5 See the minutes of a meeting of Commodity Committee, 38, Petroleum Products, with the Army-Navy Munitions Board, 6 February 1934, file 322, RG 107.

6 See, for example, department correspondence with major companies in 1935 and discussion of a conference on oil in early 1936 with industry executives, box 1037, file 470.1/129.8, RG 107.

7 Harris letter of 18 March 1938 to Reserve Major Verne Austin, California, file 470.1/129.8, RG 107.

8 Rutherford to chairman, Energy Resources Committee, 17 October 1941, box 1037, file 470.1/129.8, RG 107. For the post-World War II shift in thinking, see the files of the Plans and Operations Division, P & O 370.01, case file 19, 31 October 1947, RG 107.

9 Nash, *United States Oil Policy*, 128–9.

10 Ibid., 139–41. Wall and Gibb, *Teagle*, 283–4. Teagle also served on the Business Advisory Council and was chairman of the Industry Advisory Board, although he disliked many aspects of the New Deal. For opposition to the tariff, see Daniel Roper to M. Logan, chairman, Senate Committee on Mines, 29 June 1935, and S. Bland, House Committee on the Merchant Marine, 18 July 1935, both in file 82272/1, RG 40. Hull to Johnson and Johnson reply, 9 August 1933, DS 811.6363/243A/245.

11 Hawley, *The New Deal and the Problem of Monopoly*, 213–16.

12 Ibid.; Nash, *Oil Policy*, 150–2.

13 Nash, *Oil Policy*, 153. Harold Stephens, assistant attorney general, to Roosevelt, 24 February 1934, Official Files, 277, FDRL.

14 Nash, *Oil Policy*, 156. Mira Wilkins, for example, stresses the importance of joint oil industry ventures in the foreign sector during the 1920s. See *The Maturing of Multinational Enterprise*, 212.

15 See boxes 1, 7, OF 1092, FDRL.

16 Ickes to Roosevelt, 30 March 1934, box 10, OF 1092-A, FDRL. For the role of Charles Leith in stimulating official interest in resource management, see Eckes, *The United States and the Global Struggle for Minerals*.

17 Platt letter of 15 February 1935; Landreth to Platt, 23 February 1935; W.K. Cadman, Wichita, to Platt, 23 February 1935; Sutho to Ickes, 22 January 1935, all in container 218, secretary of the interior file, Ickes Papers. Ickes's public statements that had prompted Platt's invective were in a *Saturday Evening Post* article, 16 February 1935.

18 Container 218, secretary of interior file, Ickes Papers.

19 Office of the Solicitor, Department of the Interior, box 39, RG 48 NA.

20 Moffett to Roosevelt, 4 January 1937. The White House passed Moffett's letter along to Ickes. Secretary of the interior file, container 218, Ickes Papers.

21 Swanson statement, 3 November 1937, secretary of the interior file, container 218, Ickes Papers.

22 Roosevelt to Ickes, 21 December 1937, file 82272/1, RG 40; A. Dye, director, Bureau of Foreign and Domestic Commerce, 20 January 1938, file 312 General, 1938, RG 151.

23 Hull to Ickes, 1 October 1938, box 8, PD, RG 59.

24 Department of State memorandum, 12 August 1938, box 8, PD, RG 59.

25 Roosevelt to chairman of the House Committee on Interstate and Foreign Commerce, 22 July 1939, box 2824, file I-188, RG 48. See, as well, Ickes, *The Secret Diary of Harold Ickes*, vol. 3.

26 U.S. commercial attaché, Tokyo, to BFDC, 27 June 1934, file 312 Japan, RG 151. See also Wilkins, *Maturing of Multinational Enterprise*, 230ff. The most thorough treatment of this issue is Anderson, *The Standard Vacuum Oil Company and United States East Asian Policy*.

27 Ickes, *Secret Diary*, vol. 1, 192; FO minute, 8 September 1934, FO 371, F 5436/1659/23.

28 C.W. Orde minute, September 1934, FO 371, F 5468/1659/23; Deterding to Teagle, 10 September 1934, FO 371, F 5473/1659/23; A.W. Randall minute, 19 September 1934, FO 371, F 5563/1659/23; Randall minute, 22 September 1934, FO 371, F 5666/1659/23; Sir R. Clive (British ambassador to Japan) to FO, 27 September 1934, FO 371, F 5792/1659/23. Clive to FO, 8 October 1934, FO 371, F 5999/1659/23. For the U.S. protest to Japan of 30 November 1934, see FO 371, F 7615/1659/23.

29 Orde minute, 30 October 1934, FO 371, F 6426/1659/23; British secretary of state for foreign affairs, Cabinet memorandum, "Oil Position in Japan and Manchuria," 20 November 1934, CAB/24/251. Orde minute, 11 December 1934, FO 371, F 7300/1659/23.

30 Anderson, *Standard Vacuum*, 71–103; Wilkins, *The Maturing of Multinational Enterprise*, 232–3.

31 H.K. Rutherford, director, Office of Planning, U.S. Department of War, 15 November 1939, box 1037, file 470.1, RG 107.

32 The standard English treatments of the Mexican expropriation are Wood, *The Making of the Good Neighbor Policy*; Meyer, *Mexico and the United States in the Oil Controversy*, trans. Muriel Vasconcelos. On Bolivia, see Klein, "American Oil Companies in Latin America: The Bolivian Experience," 47–72; Wood, *Making of Good Neighbor Policy*; and Gellman, *Good Neighbor Diplomacy*.

33 Laurence Duggan (chief, Latin American division) memorandum of meeting with Thomas Armstrong, Jersey Standard, 27 September 1938, DS 824.6363 ST 2/287.

34 See Department of State instructions to U.S. missions in the three countries and to the American delegate to the Chaco Peace Conference, 17 September 1937, DS 824.6363 ST 2/172.

35 Carlos Calvo, for whom the doctrine was named, was a distinguished Bolivian jurist, who was ironically also the Standard Oil attorney in La Paz in 1937 until he was expelled from the country (it was later learned) for his opposition to the expropriation decrees. See Wood, *Making of Good Neighbor Policy*, 175.

36 Ibid., 168. Hull memorandum of meeting, 11 April 1939, box 57, Hull Papers.

37 Department of State memorandum, undated, DS 824.6363 ST 2/607.

38 Mooney to Hull, 28 April 1937, DS 824.6363 ST 2/117.

39 Sumner Welles, undersecretary of state, to Green Hackworth, legal adviser, 8 November 1937, DS 824.6363 ST 2/189. Armstrong to Welles, 22 Novem-

ber 1937, DS 824.6363 ST 2/204. Armstrong to Welles, 28 April 1938, DS 824.6363 ST 2/255. Duggan memorandum of meeting with Armstrong, 27 September 1938, DS 824.6363 ST 2/287. The fullest official company statement came in a pamphlet published privately by Standard Oil of Bolivia, *Confiscation: A History of the Oil Industry in Bolivia*.

40 Armstrong to Hackworth, 8 May 1939, DS 824.6363 ST 2/355.

41 Memorandum of meeting of Holman, Armstrong, Palmer (for Standard Oil), with Hackworth, Donovan, and Butler of state, 28 April 1939, DS 824.6363 ST 2/375. It was Undersecretary Sumner Welles who had urged the need for a meeting. Welles to Ellis Briggs (American Republics), 19 April 1939, DS 824.6363 ST 2/373. See also box 85, Petroleum file, Hull Papers, LC.

42 DS 821.6363 ST 2/376/384/394.

43 Memorandum of 11 January 1940; DS 824.51/989½/1009.

44 Armstrong to Duggan, 16 January 1940, DS 824.6363 ST 2/432. Armstrong to secretary of state, 13 November 1940; Welles to William Farish, SO, 13 December 1940, DS 824.6363 ST 2/495A. Welles to Philip Bonsal, 26 February 1941, DS 824.6363 ST 2/526.

45 W.F. Farish to Bonsal, 19 February 1941; Bonsal to Daniels, 8 March 1941, DS 824.6363 ST 2/536/538. Bonsal to Duggan, 18 September 1941, DS 824.6363/197.

46 Dawson to secretary of state, 26 February 1942; 2 March 1942, DS 800.6363 ST 2/577/580; Warren Pierson, president Export-Import Bank, to Don Luis Fernando Guochalla, Bolivian ambassador to the United States, DS 824.6363 ST 2/578. In April, Bolivia paid $1,729,375 to Standard Oil of New Jersey.

47 Townsend to Max Thornburg, petroleum adviser, 19 April 1943, DS 824.6363/265. Department of State memorandum, July–August 1943, DS 824.6363/278. Wood, *Making of Good Neighbor Policy*, 288.

48 There is extensive literature on the Mexican expropriation. In addition to some of the works cited earlier, students may wish to consult more recent doctoral dissertations: Ring, "American Diplomacy and the Mexican Oil Controversy, 1938–1943"; Baldridge, "Mexican Petroleum and United States Mexican Relations"; Stegmaier, "From Confrontation to Cooperation: The United States and Mexico, 1938–1945." A perceptive recent analysis is that of Koppes, "The Good Neighbor Policy and the Nationalization of Mexican Oil: A Reinterpretation."

49 Research and Analysis Branch Report no. 2099, "Foreign Investments in Latin America," RG 59, NA.

50 There are useful sketches of these events in Gellman, *Good Neighbor Diplomacy*, 51–5; Cline, *The United States and Mexico*; and Wood, *Making of Good Neighbor Policy*. The companies expropriated were Standard Oil of New Jersey and California, Sinclair, Cities Service, South Penn Company, and Royal Dutch Shell. Those excluded because they had reached settlements with Mexican labor were Gulf Oil, New England Oil, Seaboard Oil,

and Globe Petroleum. See Wilkins, *The Maturing of Multinational Enter-prise*, 228.

51 Gellman, *Good Neighbor Diplomacy*, provides the best brief overview of internal department positions (see 51–3).

52 Ring, "American Diplomacy and the Mexican Oil Controversy."

53 Ibid., 186–7.

54 Hull memorandum of a meeting with Lindsay, 30 March 1938, 19 August 1938, box 58, Hull Papers. Feis memorandum, 14 April 1938, box 80, Hull Papers. Welles to Mexican ambassador, 29 June 1938, Welles file, box 106, Daniels Papers.

55 W.R. Davis was active throughout this period in attempting to gain control of the Mexican oil export market. There were even rumors that he was pro-viding funds to finance a new organization of Mexican petroleum and metallurgical workers, thus ingratiating himself with both the Mexican government and labor at the same time that he won few friends among the American oil companies. Daniels to Secretary of Commerce Daniel C. Roper, 29 September 1938, box 99, Daniels Papers. Thomas Lockett, U.S. commercial attaché, Mexico City, to Daniels, 5 December 1938, box 657, Daniels Papers.

56 W.B. Richardson, National City Bank, to Daniels, 4 February 1939, box 657, Daniels Papers. Hoover to Berle, 29 September 1939, DS 862.20213/1803.

57 McCoy report, 14 September 1939, box 657, Daniels Papers.

58 This was the course of events anticipated in 1940 by the Mexican undersecretary of state for foreign affairs, Ramón Beteta. See the transcript of an interview, 8 February 1940, with Betty Kirk, box 657, Daniels Papers.

59 The company negotiators, Patrick Hurley and Donald Richberg, carried with them to Mexico letters of introduction from Sumner Welles. Daniels to his son, 17 December 1938, box 657, Daniels Papers, LC.

60 Welles to Daniels, 31 August 1939, Welles file, box 106, Daniels Papers, LC. See as well Ring, "American Diplomacy and the Mexican Oil Controversy," 198, 215; Wood, *Making of Good Neighbor Policy*, 232–3.

61 Richberg's address of 14 April 1939; Farish to Richberg, 1 December 1939; Farish to secretary of state, 10 August 1939, all in box 80, Hull Papers, LC. See also Richberg's memorandum of 11 May 1939 criticizing company policy, cited in Ring, "American Diplomacy ...," 190–7, and his letter of resignation to Teagle, 17 February 1941, box 2, Richberg Papers, LC. Richberg's thoughts on business-government relations are outlined in his 1943 publication, *Government and Business Tomorrow: A Public Relations Program*.

62 Duggan memorandum of conversation, 19 June 1939, FR, 1939, V, 680–3. Welles memorandum, 20 July 1939, FR, 1939, V, 686–7.

63 Daniels to Hull, 26 July 1938, box 61, PSF, Diplomatic, FDRL, Hyde Park.

64 Wood, *Making of Good Neighbor Policy*, 254–9; Hull memorandum, 18 November 1942 box 60, Hull Papers. The *London Financial Times* reported on 23 November 1942 that the resumption of British diplomatic relations with Mexico would "counteract pro-Axis, anti-Allied sentiments in Mexico."

65 Wood, *Making of Good Neighbor Policy*, pp. 250–1; Hull to Messersmith, 6 August 1941, box 221, interior file, Ickes Papers, LC.

66 Wilkins, *The Maturing of Multinational Enterprise*, 238–9; Wood, *Making of Good Neighbor Policy*, 263; Knudson, "Petroleum, Venezuela, and the United States: 1920–1941." Knudson's thesis is especially useful for a study of oil in relation to the reciprocal trade agreement with Venezuela.

67 Hull memorandum of conversation with the Netherlands foreign minister and minister to Washington, 2 February 1942, box 60, Hull Papers, LC. For the details of the Venezuelan settlement, see Wood, *Making of Good Neighbor Policy*, 276.

68 F. Corrigan (U.S. ambassador to Venezuela) to secretary of state, 5 February 1940, DS 831.6363/1173; Ruth Knowles, Office of Petroleum Coordinator for War, to Ickes, 11 September 1941, DS 831.6363/1252.

69 Corrigan to Hull, 30 December 1939, DS 740.00111 Neutrality Patrol/57. Duggan memorandum, 29 March 1940, DS 831.6363/1198½. Department of State memorandum, 26 June 1939, DS 831.6363/1141.

70 Department of State Memorandum, 7 June 1940, DS 831.6363/1207. Welles to Corrigan, 2 April 1941, DS 831.6363/1226. Memorandum of conversation with Gulf president, 19 April 1941, DS 831.6363/1238.

71 Knowles to Ickes (note 68 above).

CHAPTER FIVE

1 Holland to Ickes, 22 July 1940; Ickes to Roosevelt, 1 August 1940, box 219, Ickes Papers, LC. The standard and official history of the PAW is John Frey and H. Chandler Ide, *A History of the Petroleum Administration for War, 1941–1945*.

2 Ickes to Roosevelt, 29 December 1941, Interior file, box 219, Ickes Papers, LC: Ickes to Leo Crowley, 24 November 1943, Petroleum Board folder; Henry Wallace to Ickes, 18 December 1942, Foreign Petroleum Policy Committee folder, box 1612, E-326, RG 169, NA.

3 C.V. Barry to Max Thornburg, 25 February 1942, Foreign Petroleum Policy Committee folder, box 1612, E-326, RG 169, NA. Record of Cabinet meeting for 15 May 1942, box 1, Francis Biddle Papers, FDRL. William R. Boyd, Jr to Stephen Early (president's secretary), 11 September 1942, OF 4435 B, FDRL. Boyd explicitly complained about the conflicts among the federal agencies. See also John M. Blum, *The Price of Vision*, 81. Thornburg to Dean Acheson (assistant secretary of state), 16 February 1942, DS 800.6363/541 1/2.

4 Knox and Petterson to/Harold Smith (director of the budget), 7 September 1942, Oil folder, office safe files of Secretary of War Henry Stimson, Modern Military Records Branch, NA.

5 Ickes tells his own version of these events in *Fightin' Oil*. Stoff, *Oil, War and American Security*, provides a sympathetic account of Ickes's activities relating to the Middle East during the war. The forthcoming second volume of Linda Lear's biography of Ickes covers these years.

6 The reference to Davies's abilities is from a letter to Harry Hopkins, stockpiling oil folder, box 328, Harry Hopkins Papers, FDRL.

7 Ickes to Fortas, 25 April 1944, PRC file, Davies Papers. DeGolyer to H.R. Cullen (Quintana Petroleum Company), 5 May 1944, PRC file, Davies Papers, HSTL. Wall and Gibb, *Teagle of Jersey Standard*, 202. On Duce, Crampton, and Hawkins, see the justice department memorandum of 23 January 1952, file 60-57-140, RG 60.

8 Ickes to the Honorable Jennings Randolph, House of Representatives, 15 November 1943; Ickes to Kirchwey, 18 January 1944, petroleum administration file, box 2829, I-188, RG 48, NA.

9 This breakdown of personnel is from box 2828, Department of the Interior file I-188, RG 48.

10 Frey and Ide, *The Petroleum Administration for War*, 253. Ickes, *Fightin' Oil*, 144, 77–9. For the justice department's postwar position see W.B. Snyder to Morison, 14 January 1952, file 6-57-140, RG 60 (courtesy of Bennett Wall).

11 Petroleum Administration for War, "Petroleum in War and Peace," papers presented by the PAW before the U.S. Special Senate Committee to investigate Petroleum Resources (1945), 40–1.

12 Ickes to Rudolph Spreckles, 10 October 1940; Independent Petroleum and Consumers Association to Ickes, 26 September 1940; interior folder, box 219, Ickes Papers, LC. See also the *Washington Star*, 4 September 1940.

13 Frey and Ide, *History of the Petroleum Administration for War*, 22–3; Ickes, *Fightin' Oil*, 143; on the development of the petroleum attaché program see Thornburg to Laurence Duggan and Emiliano Collado, 25 February 1942; Duggan to Sumner Welles, 10 February 1942, DS 800.6363/541 1/2.

14 Frey and Ide, *History of the Petroleum Administration for War*, 272. G.M. Richardson Dougall, "The Petroleum Division," October 1944, box 48, Harley Notter lot file, RG 59, NA.

15 Dougall, "The Petroleum Division."

16 Feis, *Three International Episodes Seen from E.A.*, 120. There is also information on Thornburg in U.S. Congress, Senate, Special Committee Investigating the National Defense Program, *Hearings*, Part 41, *Petroleum Arrangements with Saudi Arabia*, 80th Congress, 1st session, 1948; Hull, *The Memoirs of Cordell Hull*, II, 1517. Stoff, *Oil, War, and American Security*, provides a sound account of Thornburg's activities, although he tends to exaggerate antibusiness sentiment within the Department of State.

17 Office of the Petroleum Adviser to the director of the budget, 11 October 1941, folder: foreign oil policy, 1941–42, box 8, PD.

18 Ickes to Thornburg, 29 January 1942, interior file, box 220, Ickes Papers, LC. Ickes Diaries, vol. 41, 6200, 6217–18 (all references to the Ickes Diaries are to the unpublished microfilm version in the Library of Congress unless otherwise indicated). Dougall memorandum; Thornburg to Milo Perkins, 25 February 1942, Foreign Petroleum Policy Committee folder, box 1612, E-326, RG 169, NA.

19 Dougall memorandum; Welles's note of 3 December 1941, and Thornburg to Wallace Murray, undated, DS 800.6363/501 1/2.

20 Thornburg memorandum, 18 May 1942, DS 800.6363/690 1/2.

21 Hawkins to Dean Acheson, 9 January 1942, DS 800.6363/514 1/2.

22 Walter C. Ferris memorandum, "United States Foreign Oil Policy," attached to Thornburg to P. Bonsal, Division of American Republics, 1 April 1942, DS 800.6363/579 1/2.

23 Thornburg to Welles, 23 March 1942, DS 800.6363/579 1/2.

24 Thornburg memorandum, 23 November 1942, box 7, folder: Latin American Petroleum Policy, 1942, PD.

25 DS 800.6363/770.

26 Ferris memorandum, 24 March 1942, DS 800.6363/579 1/2.

27 File 5-1-11, box 48, records of the secretary of the navy, James Forrestal, RG 80, NA; memorandum by the director of the Naval Transportation Service for the Combined Military Transportation Committee, 23 February 1942, Combined Chiefs of Staff, file 463.7 (2–23–42), RG 218, NA. The members of the board were Brigadier-General Walter B. Pyron (war department liaison officer); Captain A.F. Carter (navy department petroleum liaison officer); Brigadier-General T.J. Hanley, Jr (army air force); Captain R.L. Mabon (Navy Bureau of Supplies and Accounts); Brigadier-General C.P. Gross (Army Transportation Service) Captain E.J. Foy (Naval Transportation Service).

28 See, for example, Carter to Secretary of the Navy Frank Knox, 17 January 1944, Army-Navy Petroleum Board, file 14/1, RG 334, NA.

29 P.M. Jester, Near Eastern division, memorandum of meeting, 11 January 1943, folder: Petroleum Policy Study Group, 1943, box 19, PD.

30 Thornburg memorandum, 15 January 1943, folder: Petroleum Policy Study Group, 1943, box 19, PD.

31 Wright memorandum for Philip Bonsal and Herbert Feis, 14 January 1943, folder: Petroleum Policy Study Group, 1943, box 19, PD.

32 Acheson to Berle, Welles, and Hull, 26 February 1943, folder: Committee on International Petroleum Policy, PD.

33 Feis memorandum, 11 January 1943, DS 800.6363/1091, RG 59, NA.

34 Dougall, memorandum "The Petroleum Division" October 1944, box 48, Harley Notter Lot file, RG 59, NA; Feis, *Three International Episodes ...*, 110–12.

CHAPTER SIX

1 James A. Moffett to Roosevelt, 16 April 1941, box 69, file 36-1-30, James Forrestal Papers, RG 80, NA. Moffett was at the time chairman of the board of Caltex and the Bahrein Petroleum Company. He had spoken with Roosevelt earlier on 9 April. See, as well, the State Department memorandum, 21 April 1941, box 68 PSF, Roosevelt Papers, FDRL. The Saudi Arabian developments are thoroughly detailed in Anderson, *Aramco, the United States and Saudi Arabia*, and Miller, *Search for Security*.

2 Frank Knox to Roosevelt, 20 May 1941, box 68, PSF, Roosevelt Papers, FDRL. W.S. Rodgers to Jesse Jones, 20 May 1941; Jones to Moffett, 11 August 1941, box 69, file 36-1-30, Forrestal Papers, RG 80, NA. Memorandum of a conversation between Cordell Hull and Lord Halifax (British ambassador to the U.S.), 7 May 1941, folder: Great Britain, box 58, Hull Papers, LC. Harry Hopkins to Jesse Jones, 14 June 1941, box 68 PSF, Roosevelt Papers, FDRL.

3 Plans and Operations Division (OPD) memorandum, April 1942, war department general staff, OPD 004, commercial enterprise and projects, case 19, RG 165, NA. Miller, in *Search for Security*, correctly identifies the American perception of the area in the early 1940s as one in which the United States recognized the primacy of British interests.

4 Longhurst, *Adventure in Oil: The Story of British Petroleum*, 106–8; SFRC, Multinational Petroleum Corporations and Foreign Policy, *Report* (1975), 38.

5 General Walter B. Pyron to Robert Patterson, undersecretary of war, 5 June 1942, folder: petroleum-gas, oils, no. 1, Patterson Papers, RG 80, NA.

6 Jester memorandum for the Foreign Oil Policy Committee, 2 February 1943, DS 800.6363/1107 1/2; Dean Acheson comments in the committee meeting of 2 March 1943, DS 800.6363/1113 1/2. See also Acheson to Adolf Berle, Sumner Welles, and Cordell Hull, 26 February 1943, Committee on International Petroleum Policy folder, PD.

7 Thornburg to Welles, 18 February 1943, DS 800.6363/1101 1/2; Feis to Welles, 21 January 1943, DS 800.6363/1087.

8 Walter Pyron memorandum, 27 February 1943, Foreign Petroleum Policy Committee folder, box 134, Patterson Papers, LC.

9 Pyron to Patterson, 23 April 1943, Foreign Petroleum Policy Committee folder, box 134, Patterson Papers, LC.

10 Joseph E. Pogue to Feis, 11 January 1943, DS 800.6363/1104; Pogue to Hornbeck, 14 April 1943, DS 800.6363/1155. Hornbeck brought Pogue's correspondence to the attention of Feis.

11 SFRC, Multinational Petroleum Corporations and Foreign Policy, *Report* (1975), 38–9, 42.

12 Minutes of the meeting of 22 February 1943 of the Foreign Petroleum Policy Committee, committee folder, box 19, PD.

13 Bonsal to Thornburg, 25 February 1943; Bonsal to Feis, 1 March 1943,

Petroleum Reserves Corporation folder no. 1, box 1, PD. Feis's comment is from Blum, ed., *The Price of Vision: The Diary of Henry A. Wallace, 1942–1946*, 198. See, as well, the Dougall report, "The Petroleum Division," Harley Notter lot files, box 48, RG 59, NA. Minutes of the meeting of the committee on International Petroleum Policy, 5 March 1943, folder, PRC no. 1, box 1, PD. Berle's statement is from a letter of 24 March 1943, DS 800.6363/1145.

14 Unsigned memorandum, Department of State, 6 June 1944, "The Position of the Department of State on the Petroleum Reserves Corporation," DS 800.6363/2-644, PRC folder no. 1, box 1, PD; Thornburg to Hull, 27 March 1943, DS 800.6363/1141 1/2. See as well petroleum folder, box 85, Hull Papers, LC.

15 Committee on International Petroleum Policy, report to the secretary of state, 22 March 1943, PRC folder no. 1, box 1, PD.

16 Thornburg to the secretary of state, 27 March 1943, DS 800.6363/1141 1/2.

17 Hull to Roosevelt, 30 March 1943, OF 56c, Saudi Arabia, Roosevelt Papers, FDRL; "The Position of the Department on the Petroleum Reserves Corporation," DS 800.6363/2-644.

18 ABC 679, section 1, file 5-2-43, RG 319, NA.

19 Henry Stimson, *Diaries*, entries for 4 and 8 June 1943, vol. 43, 94–5, Yale University Library.

20 Admiral William D. Leahy, chief of staff, to Roosevelt, 8 June 1943, PRC folder no. 1, box 1, PD.

21 Stoff, *Oil, War and American Security*, argues convincingly that the British had no such designs on Saudi Arabia.

22 Minutes of the meeting of the Joint Chiefs of Staff, 8 June 1943, CCS 463.7, file 5-31-43, RG 218, NA.

23 Stimson, *Diaries*, entries for 8 and 11 June 1943, vol. 43, 104, 107–8. Bullitt was not pleased with the proposed government stock acquisition in Aramco and advised the president against it. See SFRC, *Documentary History of the Petroleum Reserves Corporation*, 5, 6–8.

24 "The Position of the Department on the Petroleum Reserves Corporation," DS 800.6363/2-644; Cordell Hull memorandum, 14 June 1943, PRC folder no. 1, box 1, PD. William Leahy *Diaries*, vol. 3, 120, entry for 11 June 1943, LC. For the meeting of 11 June involving Feis, James Byrnes, Stimson, Knox, Ickes, and Boykin Wright, see SFRC, *Documentary History of the Petroleum Reserves Corporation*, 7. Ickes to Roosevelt, 10 June 1943, PRC file, box 21, Davies Papers, HSTL.

25 Alling memorandum, 14 June 1943, PRC folder no. 1, box 1, PD.

26 Ickes to Roosevelt, 10 June 1943, PRC file, box 21, Davies Papers, HSTL. Feis suggested that Roosevelt did not realize he had an option between a stock purchase in Aramco and a contractual agreement to purchase Saudi Arabian

oil. Feis expressed the view in "The Position of the Department on the Petroleum Reserves Corporation" (DS memorandum).

27 Wallace Murray memorandum, 3 November 1943, DS 800.6363/11-343. SFRC, *Documentary History of the Petroleum Reserves Corporation*, 41. Ickes to Alvin Wirtz, 5 November 1943, PRC file, box 21, Davies Papers, HSTL. Ickes, *Diaries*, 8422 (references to the Ickes Diaries are to the unpublished microfilm copies in the LC).

28 Murray memorandum; Murray to Edward Stettinius, 4 November 1943, DS 800.6363/11-343.

29 James C. Sappington, Office of the Petroleum Adviser, Department of State, to Murray, 30 November 1943, PRC folder, box 1, PD.

30 Loftus to Steinbower, 8 December 1943, PRC folder, box 1, PD.

31 Hull to Leahy, 15 December 1943; Hull to Ickes, 13 November 1943, PRC folder, box 1, PD.

32 Ickes, *Diaries*, 8570.

33 Foreign Operations Committee, "A Foreign Oil Policy for the United States," November 1943, box 159, Ickes Papers, LC. The companies also agreed to maintain a crude-oil reserve for the United States government of one billion barrels or 20 percent of crude-oil reserves.

34 Petroleum Administration for War press releases, 6 February 1944, box 221, Ickes Papers, LC. Negotiations leading to the agreement are discussed in Ickes, *Diaries*, 8578–94, and in the minutes of the meeting of PRC directors, 27 January 1944, folder 2845, file I-188, RG 40, NA.

35 Ickes, "We're Running out of Oil," *American Magazine* (January 1944); Ickes, *Diaries*, 8826, 8630; see also the diary entry for 20 February 1944, 8664–5.

36 *Washington Post* (7 February 1944); *New York Times* (6 February 1944); *Time* (14 February 1944), 79. The *New York Herald Tribune* expresed reservations in a 14 March editorial: "The Basis for an Oil Policy." The *Post* contended prophetically on 12 February that instead of leading to international complications, as some of the critics in industry suggested would occur, government participation was "more likely to avert future trouble. For if this country ever finds itself dependent upon foreign oil ... all of us will look to the Government to see that those needs are met." The press response was more complex than some analysts have suggested. See for instance Stoff, *Oil, War and American Security*, 140.

37 Ickes, *Diaries*, 8594–5, 8605.

38 Charles Rayner to secretary of state, 5 February 1944, DS 800.6363/2-544.

39 Ibid.

40 Research and Analysis Branch, "Problems of Legal, Political, and Administrative Nature Concerning the Arabian Oil Agreement," 12 February 1944, report no. 1897, RG 59, NA.

41 Research and Analysis Branch, "Comments on a Foreign Petroleum Policy of the United States," 24 February 1944, report no. 2014, RG 59, NA.

42 Coe to Leo Crowley, director FEA (Foreign Economic Administration), 16 February 1944; Pike to Lauchlin Currie, 28 February 1944, folder: Saudi Arabia, box 819, E-129, RG 169, NA.

43 H.D. Collier report to stockholders, Standard Oil Company of California, PRC file, Davies Papers.

44 A copy of the March resolution is in OF 4436-b, Roosevelt Papers, FDRL. See, as well, PIWC, *United States Foreign Oil Policy and Petroleum Reserves Corporation: An Analysis of the Effect of the Proposed Saudi Arabian Pipeline* (1944); SFRC *Documentary History of the Petroleum Reserves Corporation*.

45 Abe Fortas to Ickes, 22 February 1944, Interior file, box 221, Ickes Papers, LC. Fortas to Lindley Beckworth, House of Representatives, 24 February 1944, box 1, series 225, RG 234 (Reconstruction Finance Corporation), NA. Ickes, *Diaries*, entry for 11 March 1944, 8703.

46 Zook to Ickes, 3 March 1944, file I-188, folder 2845, RG 48; Zook, "The Proposed Arabian Pipe Line: A Threat to Our National Security," 28 April 1944, in PIWC, *United States Foreign Oil Policy ...*; Independent Petroleum Association of America, "An Analysis of the Effect of the Proposed Saudi Arabian Pipeline," in SFRC, *Documentary History of the Petroleum Reserves Corporation*, 88–119.

47 Carter to Boyd, 18 February 1944, PRC file, Davies Papers, HSTL.

48 SFRC, *Documentary History of the PRC*, 72–9.

49 George A. Miller, "U.S. Foreign Policy for Oil," *Mining and Metallurgy* (March 1944). Miller's article was based on an interview with Lovejoy.

50 Brown to Stimson, 15 March 1944, ABC 679 (5-2-43), section 2, RG 319, NA.

51 Roosevelt to Ickes, 30 May 1944; the letter is in Ickes, *Diaries*, entry for 28 May 1944, 8941–55. Roosevelt to Ickes, 12 June 1944; Roosevelt to Senator Francis Maloney, 12 June 1944, PRC file, box 21, Davies Papers, HSTL. Andrew Carter to secretary of the navy, 17 June 1944, file 36-1-30, box 69, RG 80, NA.

52 Charles Rayner to Undersecretary of State Stettinius, 5 May 1944, DS 800.6363/1656. James Forrestal, acting secretary of the navy, memorandum of a conversation with Stettinius, 5 May 1944, PRC folder no. 3, box 1, PD. Forrestal indicated that little would be lost as far as the present war was concerned by postponing the Saudi pipeline, "but the main thing is to keep our feet on the ground in concessions in that area." See also the memorandum, "Justification of Trans-Arabian Pipeline,' 8 June 1944, PRC file, box 1, Davies Papers, HSTL (unsigned).

53 U.S. Congress, Senate, Special Committee Investigating the National Defense Program, Subcommittee Concerning Investigations Overseas, *Report, Section 1 – Petroleum Matters*, S. report 10, part 15, 78 Cong., 2nd sess. (1944).

See Riddle, *The Truman Committee: A Study in Congressional Responsibility*.

54 U.S. Congress, Senate, Special Committee Investigating Petroleum Resources, *American Petroleum Interests in Foreign Countries, Hearings*, 79 Cong., 1st sess. (1945); *Hearings, Petroleum Requirements – Postwar*, 79 Cong., 1 sess. (1946).

55 Special Committee Investigating the National Defense Program, *Report*, 550.

56 Ibid., 514–16.

57 Leo Crowley to Hugh Fulton, chief counsel, Truman committee, 10 February 1944, DS 800.6363/1632; Charles Rayner to Hull, 9 February 1944, DS 800.6363/2-944.

58 The other members of the committee were Tom Connally, Texas (chairman of the Senate Foreign Relations Committee); Joseph O'Mahoney, Wyoming; Edwin Johnson, Colorado; Scott Lucas, Illinois; Burret Maybanks, South Carolina; Arthur Vandenburg, Michigan; E.H. Moore, Oklahoma; Owen Brewster, Maine; Chan Gurney, South Dakota; Robert M. LaFollette, Jr, Wisconsin.

59 U.S. Congress, Senate, Special Committee Investigating Petroleum Resources in Relation to the National Welfare, *Final Report*, 80 Cong., 1st sess. (1947), 3. Maloney to Ickes, 14 June 1944, PRC file, box 21, Davies Papers, HSTL.

60 The story of the corporate reorganization is briefly recounted in Stoff, *Oil, War and American Security*, 195–208. The quotation is from the SFRC, *Multinational Petroleum Corporations and Foreign Policy, Hearings*, part 4, 2. Harold Ickes, *An Oil Policy: An Open Letter to the Members of the Congress of the United States* (30 May 1947), 3.

61 The terms are those of Hogan, *Informal Entente*, and Stoff, *Oil, War and American Security*.

62 One of the most useful analyses of the limitations imposed on policymakers in a liberal structure is that of Katzenstein, ed., *Between Power and Plenty: Foreign Economic Policies of Advanced Industrial States*, 881–7.

CHAPTER SEVEN

1 Of the known oil reserves in the United States in 1943, 93 percent were state and privately owned; 4.8 percent were on the public domain (box 2829, I-188, Petroleum Administration, RG 48, NA).

2 Leahy to the asscretary of the navy, 14 January 1939, file JJ7-11/L14-1 (390106), RG 80, NA. On drilling activities see Ickes to Donald M. Nelson (chairman, War Production Board), 1 May 1943, records pertaining to PAW and interagency committees, Petroleum Board documents of 14 April 1943, RG 253.

3 President Roosevelt assured the secretary of the navy before the war that he would "always be ready to do what I can to protect these reserves from exploitation and to guard against the adoption of policies that would adversely affect them" (letter of 20 April 1938, FDR OF 56c: Elk Hill folder, 1933-40, FDRL).

4 On the tidelands, see Bartley, *The Tidelands Oil Controversy*, and Nash, *United States Oil Policy 1890-1964*, 190-4. See as well Charles Edison, acting secretary of the navy, to the director of the budget, 12 August 1939, file NA (A-1)/N-13 (360724-67), RG 80, NA. Leahy to Roosevelt, 5 July 1938, FDR OF 56c: Elk Hill, FDRL; *Los Angeles Times*, 21 February 1939.

5 Frank Knox to Roosevelt, 28 May 1943 and 15 July 1943; Roosevelt to Knox, 31 May 1943; Ickes to Roosevelt, 2 July 1943, 6 September 1943, and 7 September 1943, FDR OF 56c, Elk Hill, 1941-4, FDRL. The House Committee on Naval Affairs appointed a subcommittee, chaired by London Baines Johnson, to investigate the Elk Hills contract. See Carl Vinson to Roosevelt, 8 November 1943, FDR OF 56c, Elk Hill, 1941-4, FDRL. Major General Thomas Handy, assistant chief of staff, memorandum, 3 July 1943, case 70 OPD 463.7, RG 165, NA.

6 Daniels to Roosevelt, 7 July 1943, FDR OF 56c, Elk Hill, 1941-4, FDRL.

7 Stimson, *Diaries*, vol. 45, entry for 22 November 1943, 51-3. Charles Rayner to Edward Stettinius (undersecretary of state), 13 November 1943; Stettinius to Hull, 16 November 1943; Hull to Ickes, 31 January 1944, folder: Reserves, General, box 2, PD.

8 Deputy Administrator's Personal File, 1941-46, Arabian and National Oil Policy, Petroleum Administration for War, RG 253, NA.

9 Ickes to Roosevelt, 4 March 1944, FDR OF 56c, Elk Hill, 1941-4, FDRL.

10 Statement of Attorney General Francis Biddle before the House Naval Affairs Committee, 8 December 1943 (folder: Congressional Testimony, box 1, Biddle Papers, FDRL; Frank Knox to Roosevelt, 13 January 1944, FDR OF 56c, Elk Hill, 1941-4, FDRL.

11 Daniels to Roosevelt, 22 February 1944, FDR OF 56c, Elk Hill, 1941-4, FDRL.

12 F.S. Bryant, director and vice-president, Standard Oil of California, to James Forrestal, secretary of the navy, 19 June 1944, file 36-1-11, box 70, RG 80, NA; Roosevelt to Daniels, 12 June 1944, FDR OF 56c, Elk Hill, 1944, FDRL; Ickes to the acting secretary of the navy, 23 June 1944, FDR OF 56c, Elk Hill, 1944, FDRL; Bruce Brown, assistant deputy administrator, PAW, memorandum, 24 June 1944, deputy administrator's personal file, 1941-46, Elk Hills Naval Petroleum Reserve no. 1, RG 253, NA.

13 *New York Times*, 2 July 1944, III, 5:6; ibid., 14 February 1945, 20:3.

14 There were several dimensions to Canol and several modifications in the project during its brief history. Canol No. 1 was the Norman Wells development and pipeline to Whitehorse and the refinery. Canol No. 2 was a pipeline from Skagway to Whitehorse; Canol No. 3 involved a gasoline

pipeline between Whitehorse and Watson Lake: Canol No. 4 was a crude-oil and gasoline pipeline from Whitehorse to Fairbanks; No. 5 was a gasoline pipeline between Fairbanks and Tannana, Alaska. See Finnie, *Canol, The Subarctic Pipeline and Refinery Project*; Diubaldo, "The Canol Project in Canadian-American Relations," 179–95; U.S. Congress, Senate, Committee on National Defense, Report no. 10, part 14, *The Canol Project* (1944); Army Service Forces, Office of the Commanding General, Control Division, Administrative Management Branch, historical file, 1941–1946, *Reference Data, Canol Project*, 2 vols (RG 160, NA).

15 Army Service Forces, *Canol Project*, historical files, RG 160, NA.

16 Committee on National Defense, report no. 10, part 14, *The Canol Project*, conclusions, 7; *New York Times*, 9 January 1944, 17:1; Riddle, *The Truman Committee*, 117–18.

17 Diubaldo, "The Canol Project," 180.

18 Army Service Forces, *Canol Project*, Historical files, RG 160, NA; Stimson, *Diaries*, 1 October 1943, vol. 44, 163–4, 177; Leahy to Byrnes, 26 October 1943, Army Staff Plans and Operating Division, 463.7, Canol, RG 319, NA; Stimson, *Diaries*, 9 December 1943, vol. 45, 106–8, contains a memorandum on the Canol project by Robert Patterson.

19 Appendix to the Joint Chiefs of Staff, Report by the Joint Production Survey Committee, Somervell to chief of staff, 22 July 1943; Patterson to director of the budget, 27 July 1943, RG 160, NA.

20 Memorandum of a conference held in the office of the secretary of war, 9 December 1943, at the request of Senator Truman. Those present included Stimson, Patterson, Generals Robins, Peckham, Pyron, Mr Amberg, Frank Knox, Admiral Horne, Ickes, Davies, Donald M. Nelson and Mr Whitney of the War Production Board. Army Service Forces, *Reference Data, Canol Project*, historical file, 1941–46, RG 160, NA.

21 Truman committee, report no. 10, part 14, 16; Roosevelt to Donald M. Nelson, 17 November 1942 and Nelson to Roosevelt, 24 November 1942, FDR OF 4435, FDRL; Ickes to Frank Knox, 18 April 1944, box 2829, file I-188, Petroleum Administration, RG 48, NA; Ickes to Colonel Frederic A. Delano, Carnegie Institution, 5 October 1943, 1 January 1944, interior file, container 221, Ickes Papers, LC.

22 Knox to Roosevelt, 10 March 1944, file 36-1-1, box 70, RG 80, NA.

23 Forrestal to Roosevelt, 31 March 1945, FDR OF 56c, Elk Hill, 1944, FDRL.

24 *New York Times*, 6 May 1944, 17:3; Diubaldo, "The Canol Project," 188.

25 Diubaldo, "The Canol Project," 189–90.

26 James Forrestal to President Truman, 22 January 1946, file 36-1-1, box 70, RG 80, NA.

27 Ickes to President Truman, 4 February 1946; Truman to Forrestal, 24 January 1946, file 36-1-1, box 70, RG 80, NA.

28 Box 218, Ickes Papers, LC.

29 Roosevelt memorandum for the attorney general, 17 January 1939, FDR OF 56c, Elk Hill, 1933–40, FDRL.

30 Roosevelt memorandum to the attorney general, the secretaries of state, navy, and interior, 1 July 1939, box 218, Ickes Papers, LC; attorney general to the assistant secretary of the navy, 10 july 1939, file NZ8 (A-1) N1-13 (360724-84), RG 80, NA. (The members of the committee were as follows: Norman Littell, assistant attorney general; Newman Townshend, acting assistant solicitor general; Green Hackworth, legal adviser, Department of State; Captain H.A. Stuart, director, Naval Petroleum Reserves; Leslie McNemar, Office of the Judge Advocate General (Navy); Nathan Margold and Henry Edelstein, both of the Department of the Interior.) See, as well, Thurman Arnold to Roosevelt, 21 August 1939, FDR OF 56c, Elk Hill, FDRL.

31 These developments are discussed in detail in Bartley, *Tidelands*, 101–2; Nash, U.S. Oil Policy, 190–2; file NZ8 (A) N-1-13 (360724-84), RG 80, NA.

32 Claude Swanson, secretary of the navy, to Roosevelt, 6 March 1939, file NZ8 (A-1) /N1-13 (360724-54), RG 80, NA.

33 U.S. Congress, House, *Hearings before the House Judiciary Committee Relative to the Establishment of Title of the United States to Certain Submerged Lands Containing Petroleum Deposits*, House Joint Resolution 181, 76th Cong. 1st sess., 22 and 23 March 1939. U.S. Congress, Senate, *Hearings before the Committee on Public Lands and Surveys on Senate Joint Resolution 83, Relative to the Establishment of a Naval Petroleum Reserve in the Submerged Lands Along and Adjacent to the Coast of the State of California*, 27, 28, 29 and 30 March 1939. Stuart's testimony is on pp. 46–54, 417–21.

34 Senate, *Hearings before the Committee on Public Lands ... Resolution 83*, 55.

35 Ibid., 69.

36 Biddle to Roosevelt, 9 June 1944; Roosevelt to Ickes, 12 June 1944; Ickes to Roosevelt, 21 June 1944; Ickes to Biddle, 21 June 1944, FDR OF 56c, Elk Hill, 1940, FDRL.

37 Biddle memorandum for Roosevelt, 9 December 1944; Ickes to Roosevelt, 13 December 1944; Biddle to Roosevelt, 21 December 1944, FDR OF 56c, FDRL. See as well boxes 1 and 3, Biddle Papers, FDRL. Increasing State Department interest is reflected in Breckinridge Long, memorandum, 15 July 1944, Protection of Marine Resources folder, box 54, Hull Papers, LC.

38 Bartley, *Tidelands Oil*, 159–61, 192–3.

39 322 U.S. 19.

40 Truman's veto message is in U.S. Congress, Senate, Senate Document No. 139 (Washington 1952). For the conflict that occasioned Ickes's resignation see Blum, *The Price of Vision*, 440–1, and Miller, *Plain Speaking. An Oral Biography of Harry S. Truman*, 226–7.

41 U.S. Congress, Senate, Senate Joint Resolution 13, 83rd Cong., 1st sess., 14 May 1953, 4953 and 1 June 1953, 5842.

42 Ickes to Stettinius, 31 January 1945, DS 811.0145/1-3145, RG 59, NA.

43 Joseph Grew, acting secretary of state, to Ickes, 31 March 1945, DS 811.0145/1-3145. Joint memorandum for the president, "Resources of the Continental Shelf and Coastal Fisheries," 22 January 1945, DS 811.0145/1-2245.

44 Ickes and Grew to Truman, 30 April 1945, DS 811.0145/5-445.

45 James F. Byrnes, secretary of state, to Ickes, 27 August 1945, DS 811.0145/6-2845, Ickes to Byrnes, 28 August 1945, DS 811.0145/8-2845.

46 Eugene Dooman, Office of the Assistant Secretary of State, to William Phillips, 15 June 1945, DS 811.0145/6-1545. *New York Times*, 29 September 1945, 2:2. See, as well, U.S. Congress, Senate, Special Committee Investigating Petroleum Resources, *American Petroleum Interests in Foreign Countries, Hearings*, 79th Cong., 1st sess., (1946).

47 U.S. *Congressional Record*, 83rd Cong., 1st sess., 1 August 1953, 10955.

CHAPTER EIGHT

1 Stoff, *Oil, War and American Security* is the most recent exponent of the international cooperation thesis. The contention that the Anglo-American oil agreement was a self-interested United States effort to "break further British supremacy in the Middle East" is advanced by Joyce and Gabriel Kolko, *The Limits of Power: The World and United States Foreign Policy, 1945–1954*, 70–3. The Kolkos overstate their thesis, failing to recognize the extent to which American officials perceived cooperation with Britain and British-Dutch companies as a most effective means by which to achieve stability in the area and to counteract Soviet ambitions. United States oil policy in the Middle East in this period is deftly treated by Anderson, *Aramco, the United States and Saudi Arabia*, and Miller, *Search for Security: Saudi Arabian Oil and American Foreign Policy, 1939–1949*.

2 Feis, "The Anglo-American Oil Agreement," 1174.

3 See the report prepared by the Army-Navy Petroleum Board, "Rehabilitation of Petroleum Resources in Netherlands East Indies, Status as of 15 November 1943," file CCS 463.7 (7-11-42); Admiral Horne to JCS, 13 March 1943, file CCS 463.7 (3-13-43); A.F. Carter memorandum for the Commanding General Army Service Forces, 20 April 1944, file CCS 463.7, RG 218.

4 Walter C. Ferris memorandum, "Iran and the Atlantic Charter," 24 March 1942, DS 800.6363/579½.

5 John Jernegan memorandum, "American Policy in Iran," 23 January 1943, FR (1943), IV, 325–35.

6 For example, Lytle, who devotes much of his 1975 OAH paper to an effort to explain this inconsistency in United States policy.

7 Paul Atkins, letter of 29 April 1943, folder 7, box 1, Atkins Papers, Yale University Library.

8 Wallace Murray memorandum, 23 August 1943, Iran folder, box 52, Hull

Papers, LC; P. Parker, Standard-Vacuum Oil Company, to the secretary of state, 20 October 1943, DS 381.6363/808.

9 James Byrnes to the secretary of the navy, 20 August 1943; Carter to Byrnes, 30 August 1943, Oil folder, Stimson Safe File, RG 107.

10 Thornburg memorandum, 13 October 1942, Latin American folder, box 1, PD.

11 Thornburg memorandum for Herbert Feis, 26 May 1943, folder; Committee on International Petroleum Policy 1943, box 19, PD.

12 Ferris memorandum, 18 March 1942, folder: Petroleum Policy Study Group 1943, box 19, PD.

13 Dougall memorandum, "The Petroleum Division," box 48, Harley Notter Lot file, RG 59, NA.

14 Wright to Feis and Philip Bonsal, chief, Division of American Republics, 14 January 1943, folder: Petroleum Policy Study Group 1943, box 19, PD.

15 Smyth memorandum for Feis, 15 January 1943, folder: Petroleum Policy Study Group 1943, box 19, PD.

16 Feis to Hull, 22 March 1943, DS 800.6363/3-2243; Feis, "The Anglo-American Oil Agreement," 1178.

17 Folder: Special Committee on Postwar Petroleum, box 28, PD.

18 Knox to Hull, 24 May 1943, PRC folder no. 1, box 1, PD.

19 Unsigned memorandum, 18 June 1943, PRC folder no. 1, box 1, PD.

20 Stoff, Oil, War and American Security, advances this thesis most systematically, 113–16.

21 Ickes wrote the Washington Post, 10 August 1944, that the underlying purpose of the pipeline idea was to get Britain and the United States together, and it had achieved its purpose (interior file, box 221, Ickes Papers, LC).

22 Butler minute, 18 August 1943, FO 371, A7590/32/45.

23 Sir William Brown to Sir D. Scott, 13 August 1943, FO 371, A7590/32/45.

24 The United States was especially insistent on reaching agreement. Note, for example, the letter from the American ambassador to Britain to Anthony Eden, 20 August 1943, FO 371, A7590/32/45, requesting an immediate reply to the American request of 1 June concerning enemy-occupied territories.

25 Wilkinson's statement is in a lengthy letter to Sir William Brown, 2 September 1943, FO 371, A9286/3410/45. See, as well, Ickes, Diaries, entry for 29 August 1943, 8117–25.

26 Nevile M. Butler Minute, 28 September 1943; Sir R.I. Campbell, British chargé in Washington, to the Foreign Office, 28 September 1943, FO 371, A9193/3410/45.

27 Herbert Feis, memorandum of a conversation with Jackson, 1 October 1943, box 3, PD. Jackson made similar remarks earlier to James F. Duce of PAW. Duce memorandum, 13 August 1943, DS 800.6363/1281.

28 Jackson to Sir William Fraser, 25 August 1943, FO 371, A9194/3410/45.

29 Jackson to Colonel Blake Taylor, British Embassy, Washington, 31 August 1943, FO 371, A9194/3410/45.

30 Sir William Fraser to Orville Harden, vice-president, Jersey Standard, 25 August 1943, DS 800.6363/1316. Anglo-Iranian and Jersey were also contemplating in mid-1943 the formation of a jointly owned subsidiary in the Bahamas (Sumner Welles, acting secretary of state, to the American Embassy, London, 16 August 1943, DS 800.6363/125A). Nor were the majors united in their support of Jackson's interpretation. Sir Frederick Godber of Shell thought private agreement in the Middle East should precede government involvement (Butler minute, 20 October 1943, FO 371, A9286/3410/45).

31 FO cable to Washington Embassy, 12 October 1943, FO 371, A9194/3410/45; FO minute, 13 October 1943, A9286/3410/45.

32 FO minute, 8 October 1943, FO 371, A9286/3410/45.

33 Butler minute, 1 October 1943, FO 371, A9286/3410/45.

34 Cable of 21 October 1943, FO 371, A9286/3410/45.

35 British Embassy to the Foreign Office, 29 October 1943, FO 371, A9835/3410/45.

36 Butler minute, 30 October 1943; 1 November 1943, FO 371, A9835/3410/45.

37 Geoffrey Lloyd to Churchill, 22 October 1943, FO 371, A10103/3410/45. Hull to Halifax, 2 December 1943, DS 800.6363/1388a; Hull to Roosevelt, 8 December 1943, DS 800.6363/1423. On Churchill's decision not to approach Roosevelt, see R.M.A. Hankey, FO, to Sir William Brown, 15 November 1943, FO 371, E7226/2551/65.

38 Foreign Office to British Embassy, Washington, 25 November 1943, E7226/2551/65.

39 Wilkinson to F. Starling, Petroleum Department, 5 December 1943, E7792/3710/45.

40 Brigadier General Boyken Wright to the secretary of war, 30 November 1943, cited in the U.S. SFRC, *Documentary History of the Petroleum Reserves Corporation*, 41–4. PWC-33, memorandum of 22 February 1944, Harley Notter Lot file, RG 59, NA.

41 One of the more valuable recent studies of this period is Lytle, "Oil and Conflict in Iran, 1943–1946," Organization of American Historians, and Lytle, "American-Iranian Relations, 1941–1947 and the Redefinition of National Security."

42 Committee memorandum, 12 October 1946, cited in FR (1946), VII, 529–32.

43 For the exchange of cables between Churchill and Roosevelt of 20 and 25 February 1944, see cables folder, box 4, PD.

44 *Financial Times*, 3 March 1944; *Manchester Guardian*, 9 March 1944.

45 Stettinius to Roosevelt, 12 February 1944; Stettinius to Hull, 15 February 1944, DS 800.6363/1534; /1535. Ickes, *Diaries*, entry of 19 February 1944, 8657.

46 Ickes, *Diaries*, 8669–71. Knox to Hull, 11 January 1944, box 3, PD.

47 Loftus memorandum, 15 January 1944, box 1, PD.

48 Acheson to Rayner, 18 March 1944; Rayner to Boyd, 20 March 1944, box 3,

PD. Memorandum of Technical Committee meetings, 12, 13 April 1944, Anglo-American Agreement file, folder 5, RG 253.

49 This analysis is based on the minutes of meetings and supporting documentation in oil folder I, Anglo-American Oil Treaty file, box 13, Ralph Davies Papers, HSTL.

50 Folder 2, Anglo-American Oil Treaty file, box 13, Davies Papers, HSTL.

51 Rayner to Hull, 15 March 1944, DS 800.6363/1583.

52 Memorandum of 26 July 1944, Anglo-American Agreement folder, box 1, PD.

53 Stoff, *Oil, War and American Security*, 171.

54 Minutes of joint session no. 5, 22 April 1944, folder 7, Anglo-American Oil Agreement files, RG 253; Rayner memorandum to the secretary of state, 15 May 1944; Haley memorandum, 19 May 1944, folder: Memoranda on Oil Agreement, 1944, box 20, PD. Rayner to secretary of state, 27 May 1944, folder: Anglo-American Oil Agreement, box 1, PD.

55 Peckham to secretary of war, 4 May 1944; Pyron to secretary of war, 4 May 1944, Oil folder, Stimson Safe File, RG 107, NA.

56 DS 800.6363/1624; Hogan to Ickes, 21 March 1944, DS 800.6363/1594.

57 Ickes, *Diaries*, entry for 23 April 1944, 8826–35.

58 Brown to Rayner, 4, 15 May 1944, DS 800.6363/1668 and /1669. Hill's statement was 29 April 1944, Anglo-American Oil Agreement folder, box 20, PD.

59 Report of the Stettinius mission to London, "Cartels," 29, box 87, Hull Papers, LC.

60 Rayner to Hill, 12 May 1944, Anglo-American Oil Agreement folder, box 20, PD.

61 Pew to Hull, 23 August 1944, and 11 September 1944; Pew to Connally, 17 August 1944, DS 800.6363/2344 and /9-1144.

62 Rayner memorandum, 15 September 1944, petroleum agreement folder, box 1, PD.

63 Loftus memorandum of a conversation with Thornburg, 14 September 1944, box 1, PD. Harden to Rayner, no date, folder: Memos, petroleum agreement 1944, box 20, PD.

64 "Cartels: What Shall We Do about Them," *Harper's Magazine*, 189 (November 1944), 570–8. Emphasis in the original.

65 Rayner memorandum, 24 October 1944, DS 800.6363/10-2444; Loftus memorandum, 30 October 1944, box 1, PD. Joseph Pogue, a vice-president of Chase National Bank of New York, provided consistent support for the agreement in 1944 and 1945, attempting to convince the independents of its merits. Speaking before the Interstate Oil Compact Commission on 7 October 1944, Pogue suggested that the scarcity of oil was not a problem; the purpose of the agreement was to provide "orderly and efficient development" of those resources, "avoiding on the one hand those repressive forces

which make for an inadequate supply, and preventing on the other ... the hasty exploitation of rich deposits" (folder: petroleum 1944, box 201, Long Papers, LC.)

66 Sappington to Rayner, 13 November 1944, box 1, PD. There is a copy of the Montana resolution in DS 800.6363/2-1345. The views of the independents were fully embodied in a 31-page publication of the Independent Petroleum Association of America, *The Anglo-American Petroleum Agreement. An Analysis of Its Effect on Our Constitutional Form of Government and the Domestic Oil Industry* (Washington 1944).

67 There is an analysis of these revisions in Ethel Dietrich, Board of Economic Warfare (BEW), to Frank Coe, BEW, 13 December 1944, folder: Commodities – Petroleum, E-128, RG 169, NA.

68 Frey and Ide, *History of the Petroleum Administration for War*, 281-2. The agreement had also met with a hostile reaction in Senate. Political pressures compelled Roosevelt to submit the agreement to Senate as a treaty rather than implement it as an executive agreement, and when Breckinridge Long and Charles Rayner met with Tom Connally and two members of the special Senate committee investigating petroleum resources, Senators Maloney and Moore, it was clear that the agreement faced major hurdles. Long noted, following the meeting on 10 August 1944, that the Senate Foreign Relations Committee members now believed the nature of the agreement to be more significant. They also raised the issue that would plague the agreement during its protracted consideration, that it opened the way to control over domestic American production (Long memorandum, folder: Petroleum, 1944, box 201, Long Papers, LC).

69 Minutes of meeting, Petroleum Industry War Council, 25 October 1944, file S-195, I-5, RG 253, NA. Wendell Berge, assistant attorney general, to Robert Hardwicke, PAW counsel, 2 December 1944; Hardwicke to Berge, December 1, 1944, Anglo-American Oil Treaty file, folder 5, box 13, Ralph Davies Papers, HSTL.

70 Memorandum for Davies, 21 November 1944, Anglo-American Oil Treaty file, folder 2, box 13, Davies Papers, HSTL.

71 Minutes of meeting, PIWC, 6 December 1944, file S-195, I-5, RG 253, NA.

72 Rayner memorandum, 1 December 1944, DS 800.6363/12-144. Stettinius to Roosevelt, 4 January 1945, PSF 115, Anglo-American Agreement folder, FDRL.

73 Rayner to secretary of state, 17 August 1944, DS 800.6363/8-1744.

74 Stenographic record, minutes of meeting, 18–19 April 1945, file S-199, legal division, miscellaneous reports, National Oil Policy Committee folder, RG 253, NA.

75 Memorandum, 2 February 1945, folder: Memoranda, President's Committee, box 20, PD. Feis memorandum, 9 February 1945, of a conversation with

Darlington, folder: Petroleum–personal, box 23, Feis Papers, LC.

76 Statement of 22 February 1945, file 36-1-30, box 69, Forrestal Papers, RG 80, NA.

77 Ickes, *Diaries*, entries for 3 March 1945, 29 April 1945, 9578, 9679.

78 Rayner to Acheson and Clayton, 6 February 1945, folder: Anglo-American Oil Agreement 1945, box 4, PD. E.S. Mason memorandum for Clayton, meeting of Cabinet Oil Committee, 20 February 1945, DS 800.6363/2-2145. Ickes to Roosevelt, 12 March 1945, PSF, box 115, folder: Anglo-American Oil Agreement, FDRL.

79 Grew to Roosevelt, 21 March 1945, DS 800.6363/3-2145. Roosevelt to Ickes, 24 March 1945, PSF, box 115, folder: Anglo-American Oil Agreement, FDRL.

80 Folder: Standard Oil Company, 1933–1944, OF 663, Roosevelt Papers, FDRL.

81 Stenographic record, minutes of the National Oil Policy Committee, 18–19 April 1945, file S-199, legal division, miscellaneous reports, RG 253, NA.

82 Folder: Standard Oil Company, 1933–1944, OF 663, Roosevelt Papers, FDRL.

83 *Wall Street Journal*, editorial, 8 February 1945.

84 Hamilton memorandum for Francis Biddle, February 1945, Anti-Trust cases and cartels 1945, box 1, Biddle Papers, FDRL.

85 John Blum, ed., *The Price of Vision*, 250–1.

86 Ibid., 464n, for the appointment of Clark. Wallace's impression of Roosevelt's approach is on p. 409. The Leavell memorandum is 23 July 1945, DS 800.6363/7-2445. At the time he wrote, the Arabian-American Oil Company was negotiating with the British for a pipeline right of way across Trans-Jordan and Palestine (Raymond Hare, first secretary, U.S. Embassy, London, to secretary of state, 15 May 1945, DS 800.6363/5-1545). More generally on cartels is U.S. Senate, Committee on Military Affairs, Subcommittee on War Mobilization, *Cartels and National Security, Report* (16 November 1944); *Part II: Analytical and Technical Supplement*.

87 Stenographic record, minutes of National Oil Policy Committee, 18–19 April 1945, file S-199, legal division, miscellaneous reports, RG 253, NA.

88 B.F. Haley, Department of State, to W. Clayton, 17 May 1945, DS 800.6363/5-1745.

89 Folder: Mission for Economic Affairs, progress report, 1944–45, box 33, PD. Sappington memorandum of Conversation, 20 June 1945, box 4, PD. Sappington to secretary of state, 1 August 1945, DS 800.6363/8-145.

90 SFRC, *Petroleum Agreement with Great Britain, Hearings* (1947), 99.

91 23 June 1945.

92 "Changes in Anglo-American Petroleum Agreement," Anglo-American Oil Treaty File, folder 2, box 3, Davies Papers, HSTL. See also Rayner's explanation of the agreement to John C. Wiley, U.S. ambassador to Colombia, 23 January 1946, DS 800.6363/12-2845.

93 Ickes, *Diaries*, entry for 6 October 1945, 10,016. *The Nation* contended that the agreement "served to underwrite the well-established Anglo-Dutch-

American monopoly of the international oil trade and to render fairly meaningless … references … to 'equal opportunity.' " (6 October 1945).

94 Circular letter of 30 August 1945 to American oil company representatives in London, Anglo-American Oil Treaty file, folder 5, box 13, Davies Papers, HSTL.

95 Holman to Clayton, 6 September 1945, DS 800.6363/9-645; Clayton to Holman, 12 September 1945; Harden to Clayton, 11 September 1945, DS 800.6363/9-1145.

96 C.M. Pigott, State Department, memorandum to J.A. Ross, 29 December 1945, DS 800.6363/12-2945. This general issue is thoroughly treated in Gardner, *Sterling Dollar Diplomacy. The Origins and Prospects of Our International Economic Order.*

97 Stoff, *Oil, War and American Security*, 190.

98 British Foreign Office to the United States ambassador, London, 31 August 1946, DS 800.6363/9-946. Victor Butler, British petroleum representative in the U.S., to Ralph Davies, 30 October 1945, Anglo-American Oil Agreement file, folder 5, box 13, Davies Papers, HSTL.

99 Memorandum of conversation, John Loftus and Louis Hyde, adviser to John Winant, 6 November 1946, folder: Anglo-American Oil Agreement, box 20, PD.

100 Boyd to Acheson, 3 February 1947, DS 800.6363/2-347. Boyd to Secretary of State Byrnes, 2 December 1946, DS 800.6363/246.

101 W.B. Heroy, PAW, to Davies, 8 February 1946, Anglo-American Oil Treaty file, folder 5, box 13, Davies Papers, HSTL.

102 25 January 1946, Anglo-American Oil Treaty file, folder 3, box 13, Davies Papers, HSTL.

103 Hardwicke to Davies's assistant, 12 August 1946, Anglo-American Oil Treaty file, folder 6, box 14, Davies Papers, HSTL.

104 Draft dated 1 May 1946, Anglo-American Oil Treaty file, folder 3, box 13, Davies Papers, HSTL.

105 Hawkins to Hardwicke, 31 July 1946, Anglo-American Oil Treaty file, folder 6, box 14, Davies Papers, HSTL.

106 Zook to Robert S. Kerr, 6 August 1946, Anglo-American Oil Treaty file, folder 3, box 13, Davies Papers, HSTL.

107 Davies memorandum of a conversation with Acheson and Clayton, 25 April 1946, Anglo-American Oil Treaty file, folder 6, box 14, Davies Papers, HSTL.

108 Draft prepared by PAW official Samuel Botsford, 7 January 1946, Anglo-American Oil Treaty file, folder 3, box 13, Davies Papers, HSTL.

109 W.B. Heroy for Davies, 12 February 1946, Anglo-American Oil Treaty file, folder 5, box 13, Davies Papers, HSTL.

110 Gardner to secretary of the interior, 12 April 1946, Anglo-American Oil Treaty file, folder 6, box 14, Davies Papers, HSTL.

111 Holman to Loftus, 3 September 1946, folder: Industry, Standard Oil Company, New Jersey, box 9, PD.

112 Zook press release, 1 November 1946; Jacobsen to Hardy, 2 November 1946; Davies to Zook, 14 November 1946; Pogue to Hardy, 4 November 1946 (Anglo-American Oil Treaty, folder 6, box 14, Davies Papers, HSTL).

113 SFRC, *Petroleum Agreement with Great Britain, Hearings* (1947), 155.

114 Anglo-American Oil Treaty file, folder 6, box 14, Davies Papers, HSTL.

115 Davies to L.B. Wolters, Compagnie Financiere Belge des Petroles, 16 June 1947, Anglo-American Oil Treaty file, folder 6, box 14, Davies Papers, HSTL.

116 Eckes, *Global Struggle for Minerals*, 138.

117 Based on Divine, *Second Chance: The Triumph of Internationalism in America during World War II*, and Schoenebaum, ed., *Political Profiles: The Truman Years*.

118 SFRC, *Petroleum Agreement with Great Britain, Hearings*. Moore's statement is on 17; McCarthy, 67–71; Boyd, 85; Hill, 145.

119 Ibid., 38, 40–2, 43, 105–7, 109, 110–11, 112.

120 Clayton letter to American Petroleum Institute, 20 January 1947, cited in ibid., 18. Acheson's statement is on 22–3.

CHAPTER NINE

1 Research and Analysis Branch, OSS (Office of Strategic Services), Report no. 3408, 26 September 1945, "The Treatment of U.S. Oil Interests in Countries in Eastern Europe," RG 59, NA.

2 U.S. military representative, Allied Control Commission, "The Rumanian Oil Industry," Bucharest, 15 April 1945, Rumania file, RG 165, NA. Pearton, *Oil and the Romanian State*, 295, 295n. See, as well, Ickes to Leahy, 1 March 1945, file I-88, Petroleum Administration, box 2829, RG 48, NA.

3 Pearton, *Romanian State*, 241–4.

4 Crowley to secretary of state, 6 October 1944, file E-129, box 818, folder: Rumania, RG 169, NA. Ickes to Hull, 29 September 1944; Ickes to Stettinius, 9 January 1945; Ickes to Byrnes, 30 August 1945, file I-88, Petroleum Administration, box 2830, RG 48, NA; Pearton, *Romanian State*, 275; Department of State memorandum, 11 March 1946, folder: Rumania, 1945–7, box 15, PD.

5 William Donovan, director of Office of Strategic Services, to Joint Chiefs of Staff, 28 November 1944, file OPD 336 Russia, case 121, and case 16, Rumania, RG 165, NA.

6 Major General J.E. Hull, assistant chief of staff, to the assistant secretary of War, 7 December 1944, reporting on a discussion with Cavendish Cannon, director of Southern European Affairs, Department of State, OPD 336 Russia, case 187, RG 165; Joseph Grew to Ickes, 2 May 1945, file I-88, Petroleum Administration, box 2830, RG 48, NA.

7 U.S. Department of State, *The Conference of Berlin* [the Potsdam Conference], (Washington 1960), vol. I, 371. Grew to Ickes, 27 January 1945, file I-188, Petroleum Administration, box 2829, RG 48, NA.

8 McCollum to Darlington, 30 July 1945; Darlington, 2 August 1945, folder: Rumania, 1941–5, box 15, PD.

9 Research and Analysis Branch, Report 3314, "Rumanian-Soviet Economic Collaboration on Petroleum under the Agreement of May 8, 1945," RG 59, NA.

10 Grew to U.S. Embassy in Moscow, 29 June 1945, file OPD 463.7, case 8(2); Clayton to secretary of war, 6 July 1945, RG 165, NA.

11 State Department memorandum, "Use of American Property by Satellite Countries for Reparation," attached to Grew to secretary of war, 6 July 1945, file OPD 463.7 Rumania, case 8(2), RG 165, NA.

12 Roosevelt to Churchill, 11 March 1945, cited in W. Averell Harriman and Elie Abel, *Special Envoy to Churchill and Stalin, 1941–1946*, 425–6.

13 U.S. Department of State, *The Conference of Berlin*, vol. 1, 371. Harriman to secretary of state, 29 June 1945, cited in ibid., 943.

14 Ibid., vol. II, 737–8.

15 Pauley to secretary of state, 20 July 1945; secretary of state to Ickes, 6 July 1945; Davies to Pauley, 13 July 1945, cited in ibid., vol. II, 1382; vol. I, 945–7.

16 Pearton, *Romanian State*, 281.

17 Ibid., 276–8. Larson, Knowlton, and Popple, *History of Standard Oil ... New Horizons, 1927–1950*, 568. Department of State memorandum, "The Present Status of the Rumanian Oil Industry," 12 December 1945, folder: Rumania, 1945–7, box 15, PD.

18 Memorandum of 12 September 1947, folder: claims 1947, box 15, PD.

19 Larson, et al., *History of Standard Oil ... New Horizons*, 777.

20 Department of State memorandum, 25 February 1946, "Negotiations with the Russians for the Return of the Maort Properties," OPD 004, case file 3, Hungary, RG 319, NA. The file also contains Vishinsky's reply to Kennan's letter of 13 March 1946.

21 Larson, et al., *History of Standard Oil ... New Horizons*, 570–3.

22 Ibid., 730–1.

23 Schmitt, *Mexico and the United States, 1821–1973*, 188.

24 That decision was contained in a State Department memorandum signed by President Truman 13 October 1945, FR, 1945, IX, 1161.

25 Acheson to Walter Thurston, 27 August 1946; memorandum of 23 August 1943, DS 812.6363/8-2746.

26 Ibid.

27 The reference is to Laurence Duggan, former chief of the Division of American Republics, who at this time was serving as a consultant for Jersey Standard on the Mexican situation. Everett DeGolyer served as adviser to Pemex.

28 Thurston to secretary of state, 10 January 1947, DS 812.6363/1-1047; 21 January 1947, DS 812.6363/1-2147.

29 Secretary of state to Thurston, 31 October 1947, DS 812.6363/10-3147; Thurston to secretary of state, 12 December 1947, DS 812.6363/12-1247.

30 Thurston to Undersecretary of State Robert Lovett, 30 September 1947, DS 812.6363/10-647. Lovett forwarded a copy to his counterpart at the navy department.

31 Thurston to secretary of state, 16 April 1948, DS 812.6363/4-1648. In February Thurston returned to the U.S. for consultation. Indicative of the continued importance given to the Mexican situation, he met on 17 February with the National Security Resources Board (FR, 1948, IX, 612–16).

32 Thurston to secretary of state, 24 August 1948, DS 812.6363/8-2448; Charles Bohlen to Senator Wherry, 14 June 1948, DS 812.6363/6-348.

33 FR, 1948, IX, 612–16.

34 Dougall memorandum, 1944, box 48, Harley Notter Lot file, RG 59, NA.

35 Secretary of state to the American chargé in Caracas (Dawson), 7 January 1946, DS 831.512/1-346.

36 Dawson to the secretary of state, 10 January 1946, DS 831.512/1-1046.

37 Larson, et al., *History of Standard Oil ... New Horizons*, 622; Lieuwen, *Petroleum in Venezuela: A History*, 104–5. Betancourt provides one perspective on these events in *Venezuela, Oil and Politics*.

38 U.S. ambassador in Venezuela (Corrigan) to secretary of state 3 June 1946, DS 831.6363/6-346.

39 Cable of 23 May 1946, DS 831.6363/5-2346.

40 *Public Papers of the Presidents of the United States: Harry S. Truman*, II, 1946 (Washington 1952), 233–5. For 1946 considerations of U.S. arms sales to Venezuela and for the establishment of a military mission, see FR, 1946, XI, 1306–22.

41 Secretary of war to secretary of state, 7 June 1946; state to war, 17 June 1946, DS 831.6363/6-746. See, as well, Strong memorandum, 3 June 1946, OPD, 091 Venezuela, case file 5, RG 319.

42 Memorandum of 10 July 1946, OPD, case file 48, RG 165. Later in the year the intelligence staff prepared a "Study of Communist Activities in Venezuela with Reference to Possible Curtailment of Oil Supply to the United States" (OPD 350.05, TS, 6 November 1946, case 38, RG 165).

43 Larson, et al., *History of Standard Oil ... New Horizons*, 623–7, 727; Corrigan to secretary of state, 8 November 1946, DS 831.6363/11-846.

44 Byrnes to the U.S. Embassy, Caracas, 10 January 1947, DS 831.00/1-747.

45 Memorandum of meeting of 17 July 1947 involving the director of the American Republics division, G-2 (Intelligence) for the American Republics, and commander Edgar Thompson, Office of Naval Intelligence, among others (DS 831.00/7-1747).

46 Secretary of state, circular telegram to diplomatic representatives in Argentina, Bolivia, Brazil, Chile, Colombia, Ecuador, Mexico, Peru, Venezuela, 26 March 1948, DS 810.6363/3-2648.

47 Appendix I of IADB minutes of 24 February 1948, enclosure I, acting secretary of state to diplomatic representatives in the American Republics, 14 April 1948, DS 810.6363/4-1448.

48 Ibid., enclosure II.

49 Plans and Operations Division 463, case file 6, RG 319.

50 Memorandum by Lt-Colonel Pettison, 5 May 1948, Plans and Operations Division 463, case file 6, RG 319.

51 Forrestal to secretary of state, 24 April 1948, OPD 463, case file 15/4, RG 319.

52 Memorandum of 13 July 1948, OPD 463, case file 15/7. Lt-General A.C. Wedemeyer, director, OPD, for the chief of staff, 18 June 1948, OPD 463, case file 6/16, RG 319.

53 A 1948 public opinion poll indicated that 70 percent of the Venezuelan population supported nationalization. Memorandum for the army chief of staff, 12 November 1948, OPD case file 15/21, RG 319. Lieuwen, *Petroleum in Venezuela*, 106–7; Larson, et al., *History of Standard Oil ... New Horizons*, 279-80; Betancourt, *Venezuela*, 134–8.

54 Romualdi, *Presidents and Peons: Recollections of a Labor Ambassador in Latin America*, 443.

55 Loftus memorandum, "Suggested Approach to Middle East Oil Situation," 4 March 1947, DS 800.6363/3-447.

56 FR, 1945, VIII, 534; Mark Lytle, "American-Iranian Relations, 1941–1947 and the Redefinition of National Security."

57 Paterson, *Soviet-American Confrontation: Postwar Reconstruction and the Origins of the Cold War*, 174–206.

58 FR, 1944, V, 470.

59 Paterson, *Soviet-American Confrontation*, 177–9; FR, VII, 289–326; II, 685–6; 1946, VI, 734.

60 FR, 1946, VII, 518, 524, 549.

61 FR, 1947, V, 890–2.

62 Paterson, *Soviet-American Confrontation*, 206n; Department of State memorandum of conversation, 3 February 1947, folder: Standard Oil Company (New Jersey), box 9, PD.

63 Miller, *Search for Security*, 177–8; Paterson, *Soviet-American Confrontation*, 182–3.

64 Hogan, "The Search for a Creative Peace: The United States, European Unity, and the Origins of the Marshall Plan," 267–86.

65 Miller, *Search for Security*, 178. Walter Jensen, *Energy in Europe, 1945-1950*.

66 The general question of sterling in international relations in this period is treated effectively by Gardner, *Sterling Dollar Diplomacy*. See also U.S. Congress, Senate, Select Committee on Small Business, *The Impact of Monopoly and Cartel Practices on Small Business*, 82 Cong., 2nd sess. (1952).

67 FR, 1945, VI, 122–204. *Oil Forum* 3 (March 1949): 115–18. Department of state memorandum, "The Sterling Oil Problem," 27 April 1949, DS 800.6363/4-2749. *Oil Forum* 3 (August 1949): 335–6. Larson, et al., *History of Standard Oil ... New Horizons*, 705–6.

68 The most perceptive recent studies in this area are Miller, *Search for Security*, 173–203, and Anderson, *Aramco*, 167–80.

69 Department of State circular, "Instructions on Petroleum Reporting," 26 April 1946, DS 800.6363/72046, and Loftus to Eugene Holman, president of Jersey Standard, 20 July 1946, same file.

70 Department of State to U.S. ambassador, London, 16 March 1946, folder: Transjordan, box 6, PD, NA. Loftus to Henderson, 5 February, 1946, FR, 1946, VII, 18–22.

71 Shechtman, *The United States and the Jewish State Movement: The Crucial Decade, 1939-1949*.

72 Henderson to secretary of state, 26 May 1948, FR, 1948, V, 15. Anderson, *Aramco*, 170–1. For the Department of Defense position see Millis, ed., *The Forrestal Diaries*, 344–9, 356–65. File CCS 600.6 Middle East (1–26–46), Joint Chiefs of Staff, general files, 1948, RG 218, NA.

73 Anderson, *Aramco*, 173–4.

74 Henderson to undersecretary of state, Robert Lovett, 24 September 1947, DS 690F. 119/9-2447. Marshall to secretary of commerce, 15 September 1948, FR, V, 45–7. For the opposition of the American independent oil companies see the *Oil and Gas Journal* (4 October 1947): 40, and U.S. Congress, Senate, *Congressional Record*, 11 March 1949, 81 Cong., 2nd sess., 2222–5. Miller, *Search for Security*, 84, 195–9.

75 The best studies of these developments are Anderson, *Aramco*, and Miller, *Search for Security*. State Department concern over the implications of the Palestine question for American oil and other interests in the Middle East is reflected in a communication to the American Embassy in London, 16 March 1946, box 6, PD.

76 Larson, et al., *History of Standard Oil ... New Horizons*, 734–5; Thompson, *Gulf since Spindletop*, 101; SFRC, Multinational Petroleum Corporations and Foreign Policy, *Report* (1975), 45, 46–9; Anderson, *Aramco*, 145. On the marketing agreements of 1947, see the Department of Justice memorandum, 14 January 1952, file 60-57-140, RG 60. I would like to thank Professor Bennett Wall for bringing this justice department document to my attention.

77 J.E. Taylor, Anglo-Iranian, to J.W. Boyle, Anglo-Saxon Petroleum Company, 22 January 1946, Shell Papers, file MEP/17. Minutes of the group

meeting, London, 9 May 1946, Shell Papers, file MEP/42. Near East Development Corporation to the Anglo-Saxon Petroleum Company, Ltd, 3 October 1946, cited in SFRC, Multinational Petroleum Corporations and Foreign Policy, *Report* (1975), 51.

78 SFRC, Multinational Petroleum Corporations and Foreign Policy, *Report* (1975), 150–1.

79 Department of State memorandum, "Issues Concerning the Iraq Petroleum Company as Raised in the French Note of January 13, 1947," 6 March 1947, box 6, PD. Solicitors for the CFP (French Company in IPC) to the Anglo-Saxon Petroleum Company, 27 December 1946; J.W. Boyle reply, 31 December 1946; Boyle to the Near East Development Corporation, 17 December 1946. Boyle indicated that although Anglo-Saxon did not agree with the legal conclusions of the Near East Development Corporation, the former did not intend to take legal action (see file MEP/17 Shell Papers). The D'Arcy Group's legal opinion was that the group agreement was abrogated between the parties when France came under German control in 1940 (J.E. Taylor to Near East Development Corporation, 16 December 1946, DS 800.6363/1-1347).

80 Loftus to Davies, 21 April 1944, box 2, PD.

81 Loftus memorandum, 4 March 1947, DS 800.6363/3-447; Loftus memorandum, 31 December 1946, box 2, PD.

82 Letters to the companies are attached to a Loftus memorandum, February 1947, box 2, PD. For government-company discussions see, as well, memorandum of conversation, 3 December 1946. FR, 1946, VII, 40–3, and Anderson, *Aramco*, 152–4.

83 For justice department views, see memorandum by W.B. Watson Snyder, 14 January 1952, file 60-57-140, RG 60.

84 SFRC, Multinational Petroleum Corporations and Foreign Policy, *Report* (1975), 55. Memorandum by C.F. Dalington, Socony-Vacuum, and Minutes of the Board of Directors, Socony, 11 March 1947, cited in SFRC, Multinational Petroleum Corporations and Foreign Policy, *Hearings* (1974), part 8, 160–6.

85 For the French protest, see French ambassador, Henri Bonnet, to secretary of state, 4 January 1947, FR, 1947, V, 627–9, and 13 January 1947, DS 890.6363/1-447. American note of 10 April 1947, FR, 1947, V, 657–60. Anderson, *Aramco*, and Miller, *Search for Security*, provide detailed accounts of the financial dimensions of the 1947 arrangements. The agreement is also discussed in a justice department memorandum by W.B. Watson Snyder to the assistant attorney general, 14 January 1952, file 60-57-140, RG 60.

86 SFRC, Multinational Petroleum Corporations and Foreign Policy, *Report* (1975), 52–4.

CHAPTER TEN

1 Memorandum of Conversation (Nitze), September 19, 1952, *Foreign Relations*, IV (1952–54), 610–13.
2 On the antitrust dimensions of policy see: Memorandum by the Assistant Secretary of State for Economic Affairs (Thorpe) to the Secretary of State, 31 March 1952, and Secretary of State to the Chairman of the Federal Trade Commission, 25 April 1952, Memorandum of Discussion at the 116th Meeting of the National Security Council, 30 April 1952; President Truman to Chairman of the Federal Trade Commission, 5 June 1952, *Foreign Relations*, I (1952–54), 1259–76; Report by the Departments of State, Defense and Interior, 6 January 1953, Foreign Relations, IX (1952–54), 637–48. The standard secondary treatment of the issue is Kaufman, *The Oil Cartel Case*.
3 On Venezuela see Rabe, *The Road to* OPEC; on Saudi Arabia, see Anderson, *Aramco, the United States and Saudi Arabia*; for a broader and detailed analysis see Yergin, *The Prize*, especially 446–54.
4 *Foreign Relations*, I (1951), 967.
5 Thorpe to Secretary of State, 3 January 1951, *Foreign Relations*, I (1951), 966–7.
6 "A National Petroleum Program," report to the President, 13 December 1951, *Foreign Relations*, I (1951), 978ff; see also National Security Council Document 97, "A National Petroleum Program," 28 December 1950, *Foreign Relations*, I (1950), 489.
7 Thorpe to Acheson, 3 January 1951, *Foreign Relations*, I (1951), 966–8. There is relatively little academic work on the Petroleum Administration for Defense. See Brown, *Oil Men in Washington*.
8 Nestor Ortiz, Petroleum Policy Staff, to the Acting Chief of the Petroleum Policy Staff, 21 March 1951, *Foreign Relations*, I (1951), 909.
9 Memorandum, Walter Walmsley, 29 November 1951, *Foreign Relations*, I (1951), 970–1. Document was marked "Top Secret."
10 Thorpe to Webb, 11 December 1951, Foreign Relations, I (1951), 971–4. See the "Interim Report by the National Security Council on a National Petroleum Program," *Foreign Relations*, I (1951), 978–92.
11 Lovett Memorandum, 11 December 1951, *Foreign Relations*, I (1951), 974–5.
12 CIA, "Interest of the United States in the Development of the Petroleum Resources of the Near and Middle East," 8 January 1951, *Foreign Relations*, V (1951), 268–76. Memorandum of Conversation, Riyadh, 18 May 1953, *Foreign Relations*, IX (1952–54), 96–105.
13 Kolko, *Confronting the Third World*.
14 U.S. Ambassador in Iran (Wiley) to Secretary of State, 30 January 1950, *Foreign Relations*, V (1950), 459–60.

15 American Ambassador to Secretary of State, 30 January 1950, *Foreign Relations*, V (1950), 463.

16 NSC, "United States Policy Toward Iran," 2 January 1954, *Foreign Relations*, X (1952–1954), 865–9.

17 Oral history interview with Robert H.S. Eakens, Austin, exas, 13 June 1974, Harry S. Truman Presidential Library.

18 NSC, "Memorandum of Discussion at the 181st Meeting of the National Security Council, Washington, 14 January 1954," *Foreign Relations*, X (1952–1954), 907–8. See also *Foreign Relations*, I (1952–1954), 1259–378 on the development of U.S. policy regarding the applicability of antitrust legislation to international petroleum companies.

19 Yergin, *The Prize*, 485–86.

20 Kolko, *Confronting the Third World*, 71–2.

21 Eden, *Full Circle*, 540.

22 Department of State, *Bulletin* (28 January 1957), 128.

23 Yergin, *The Prize*, 487–97.

24 U.S. Department of Commerce, *Business Statistics 1961*, 106–13; U.S. Senate, Committee on Foreign Relations, Subcommittee on Multinational Corporations; U.S. Bureau of Mines, *Minerals Yearbook*, 1950–70.

25 *Foreign Relations*, V (1958–60), 917

26 Rabe, *The Road to OPEC*, 155–6. The Eisenhower administration view is reflected in *Foreign Relations*, V (1958–60), 918.

27 For Prebisch's ideas see Prebisch, *Change and Development*; Werner Baer, "The Economics of Prebisch and ECLAC," in Nesbit, ed., *Latin America.*

28 Rabe, *Road to OPEC*, 159–60. For Alfonso's account, see *Petroleo y dependencia.*

29 Armstrong to Sanders, 19 November 1957, Foreign Relations, VII (1955–57), 1162–4.

30 U.S. Department of the Interior, Bureau of Mines, *Minerals Yearbook 1961.*

31 Willard Thorpe to Undersecretary of State, Robert Lovett, 8 March 1948, U.S. Department of State, *Foreign Relations*, IX (1948), 406–10; Memorandum on Meeting of 26 September 1955 of U.S.-Canada Committee on Trade and Economic Affairs, *Foreign Relations*, IX (1955), 152–3.

32 Shaffer, *Canada's Oil*, 150.

33 Canadian Petroleum Association, *Statistical Yearbook – 1971* (Calgary, 1972), 75, 101; Canada, Royal Commission on Energy, *Second Report* (Ottawa, 1959), 32, 37. Assistant Secretary of State to Director of Office of Defense Mobilization, 30 March 1954, *Foreign Relations*, I (1952–54), 1140.

34 National Security Council Memorandum, 16 October 1953; National Security Council Document 163/1, 24 October 1953; National Security Council document 97/6, "Statement of Policy," all of which are found in *Foreign Relations*, I (1952–54), 1020–61.

35 U.S. Cabinet Task force on Import Control, *The Oil Import Question*, 43–4.

36 *The Oil Import Question*, 165–77.

37 Ibid., 2–3; Appendix c-2, 182–4.

38 For a thorough discussion of these factors see Shaffer, *Canada's Oil* and *The Oil Import Program*.

CHAPTER ELEVEN

1 *The Oil Import Question*, 83; u.s. Senate, Committee on Interior and Insular Affairs (chair, Henry M. Jackson), *Geopolitics of Energy*, Energy publication no. 95–1 (Washington, 1977), 9–10.

2 Statement by C.W. Nichols, Special Assistant to the Assistant Secretary of State for Economic Affairs, to House Select Committee on Small Business, 21 November 1961, Department of State, *Bulletin*, XLVI, no. 1175 (1 January 1962), 31–4.

3 Ibid.

4 Ibid., 33.

5 George Ball Memorandum, u.s. Policy toward the Organization of Petroleum Exporting Countries, 24 November 1965, *Foreign Relations*, XXXIV (1964–1968), 333; Department of State Circular to Certain Posts, 22 December 1965, *Foreign Relations*, XXXIV (1964–1968), 334–40.

6 Memorandum of Conversation, 20 July 1962, *Foreign Relations*, IX (1961–1963), 794–5.

7 Howard Cottam, U.S. Embassy in Kuwait to Department of State, 14 March 1966, *Foreign Relations*, XXXIV (1964–1968), 344–5. On McCloy, see Sampson, *The Seven Sisters*, 167–8.

8 *Foreign Relations*, XXXIV (1964–1968), 315–16.

9 Memorandum of Conversation, U.S.-UK Bilateral Talks, 13 February 1961, *Foreign Relations 1961–1963*, vol. IX, 752–54. For the perspective of Standard Oil of New Jersey on the impact of Soviet oil exports see Memorandum of conversation between Dean Rusk and Rathbone of SONJ, 18 July 1961, *Foreign Relations*, IX (1961–1963), 762–4.

10 Memorandum of Conversation, 29 January 1964, *Foreign Relations*, XXXIV (1964–1968), 317–19.

11 Telegram from Embassy in Iraq to the Department of State, 7 February 1964, *Foreign Relations*, XXXIV (1964–1968), 320–1.

12 Rusk to Embassy in Iraq, 13 April 1964, *Foreign Relations*, XXXIV (1964–1968), 324–5.

13 U.S. Embassy, Jidda, 12 April 1964, to the Department of State, *Foreign Relations*, XXXIV (1964–1968), 321–4.

14 Cited in a memorandum from Fried to Solomon, 8 February 1966, *Foreign Relations*, XXXIV (1964–1968), 332.

15 Department of State Memorandum, u.s./u.k. Oil Talks, 22 December 1965, *Foreign Relations*, XXXIV (1964–1968), 338.

16 American Embassy, Iran, to Department of State, 20 January 1966, *Foreign Relations*, XXXIV (1964–1968), 342–3 and 6 January 1966, 341. Intelligence Memorandum, "The Shah of Iran and His Policies," 5 June 1967, *Foreign Relations*, XXII (1964–1968), 380–4; U.S. Embassy in France to Department of State, Averell Harriman reporting on private conversation with the Shah, 5 June 1967, 384–6; Helms Memorandum, 23 August 1967, 419–20. The Shah's official visit to Washington took place August 22–24. During that time he had two meetings with President Johnson, meetings with the Vice-President and Dean Rusk, a meeting with members of the Senate Foreign Relations Committee, and a meeting with American business leaders.

17 Rostow to Johnson, 14 February 1967, *Foreign Relations*, XVIII (1964–1968), 763–64. The President met that day with, among others, Rostow, Assistant Secretary of State Nicholas Katzenbach, and Secretary of Defense Robert McNamara.

18 Editorial Note, *Foreign Relations*, XXXIV (1964–1968), 379.

19 Memorandum, director of the Office of Fuels and Energy, Bureau of Economic Affairs (Oliver), 23 May 1967, *Foreign Relations*, XXXIV (1964–1968), 417.

20 Memorandum from the Director of the Office of Fuels and Energy, Department of State (Oliver) to the Deputy Assistant Secretary of State for Economic Affairs (Fried), 23 May 1967, *Foreign Relations*, XXXIV (1964–1968), 416.

21 Memorandum, 24 May 1967, *Foreign Relations*, XXXIV (1964–1968), 419–20. The attached notations suggest that the memo was seen by both the Secretary of State and President Johnson. Yamani was educated in law at Cairo, New York University, and Harvard before returning to Saudi Arabia to practice law. He was also a member of the board of Aramco. See Sampson, *The Seven Sisters*, 164.

22 McCloy to Rusk, 5 June 1967 and editorial notes, *Foreign Relations*, XXXIV (1964–1968), 421.

23 U.S. Embassy, Iraq, to Department of State, 6 June 1967, *Foreign Relations*, XXXIV (1964–1968), 422.

24 Editorial note, *Foreign Relations*, XXXIV (1964–1968), 423–24; Dean Rusk to Secretary of the Interior (Udall), 8 June 1967, 426.

25 On Qadaffi see Arabinda Ghosh, OPEC, 60.

26 Editorial note, *Foreign Relations*, XXXIV (1964–1968), 472–73.

27 Memorandum of a Briefing by Director of the Central Intelligence Agency, McCone, 29 June 1967, *Foreign Relations*, XXXIV (1964–1968), 452–56.

28 Manager of Government Relations Department, Standard Oil of New Jersey, to Assistant Secretary of the Interior for Mineral Resources, 8 June 1967, and editorial notes, *Foreign Relations*, XXXIV (1964–1968), 424–5.

29 U.S. Embassy, Bonn, to Department of State, 23 June 1967, *Foreign Relations*, XXXIV (1964–1968), 445–6.
30 Department of State to Bonn Embassy, 24 June 1967, *Foreign Relations*, XXXIV (1964–1968), 446–8. On the use of Middle East oil in the U.S. war in Vietnam, see Memorandum of a Briefing by Director of the Central Intelligence Agency, McCone, 29 June 1967, 452–6. Although it casts little light on U.S. policy, Louis Wesseling, *Fuelling the War*, gives an excellent account from the perspective of the director of Shell Vietnam.
31 Editorial Note, *Foreign Relations*, XXXIV (1964–1968), 466–7, 469.
32 Rusk, circular Telegram to Certain Posts, 25 August 1967, *Foreign Relations*, XXXIV (1964–1968), 470–1.
33 U.S. Embassy in Lebanon to Department of State, 17 January 1968, *Foreign Relations*, XXXIV (1964–1968), 475–6.
34 U.S. Department of State, *American Foreign Policy: Current Documents – 1967* (Washington, 1967), 1121.
35 David M. Abshire, Assistants Secretary for Congressional Relations to J. William Fulbright, Chair, Senate Foreign Relations Committee, 10, February 1971, 27 February 1971, Department of State, *Bulletin*, LXIV (5 April 1971), 491–2.
36 Shaffer, *The United States and the Control of World Oil*, 132.
37 Address by Philip Trezise, Assistant Secretary of Economic Affairs, to the 1970 Convention of the Pacific Coast Gas Association, Portland, Oregon, Department of State, *Bulletin*, LXIII (26 October 1970), 479.
38 *The Oil Import Question*, 37–70.
39 Ibid., 81.
40 Ibid., 132.
41 Statement by William Casey, Under Secretary for Economic Affairs, to the Senate Committee on Interior and Insular Affairs, May 1, 1973, Department of State, *Bulletin*, LXVIII, no. 1770 (28 May 1973), 702–6.
42 Undersecretary of State John Irwin, "The International Implications of the Energy Situation," presented to House of Representatives Committee on Interior and Insular Affairs, 10 April 1972, Department of State, *Bulletin*, LXVI (January–June 1972), 626–31.
43 Department of State, *Bulletin*, LXII (30 March 1970), 427.
44 Department of State, *Bulletin*, LXII (29 June 1970), 798.
45 Robert McClintock, U.S. Ambassador to Venezuela, address to Venezuelan Association of Executives, 18 February 1971, Department of State, *Bulletin*, LXIV (19 April 1971), 522–8.
46 Department of State, *Bulletin*, LXIII (6 July 1970), 7.
47 Department of State, *Bulletin*, LXIII (28 September 1970), 360.
48 *Geopolitics of Energy*, 20.
49 U.S. Congress, Senate, Senate Foreign Relations Committee, Subcommittee on Multinational Corporations, *Multinational Oil Corporations and United States Foreign Policy. Report* (Washington, 1975), 4, 7–8.

50 Department of State, *Bulletin*, LXVI (January–June 1972), 629. Note that the British Government by 1975 controlled almost 70 percent of BP shares. See Sampson, *The Seven Sisters*, 201, note.

51 U.S. Department of Energy, Energy Information Administration, "World Oil Market and Oil Price Chronologies, 1970–2003," www.eia.doe.gov/emeu/cabs/chron.html.

52 Yergin, *The Prize*, 596. Sampson, *The Seven Sisters*, cites Rawleigh Warner of Mobil as indicating that Nixon and Kissinger were willing to listen but they did not alter their direction as the result of corporate pressures, 206.

53 Nixon, *Memoirs*, 986–7.

54 Kissinger, *White House Years*, 344–6, 1262–4; on the 1973 energy crisis, see Kissinger, *Years of Upheaval*, 854–95.

55 Nixon, *Memoirs*, 983. Kissinger's press conference, 10 January 1974, Department of State, *Bulletin*, LXX (4 February 1974), 109–22.

56 U.S. Department of Energy, "The Atomic Century: Historical Collection of Declassified and Released Documents," Part II: "The Federal Energy Administration," http://www.dpi.anl.gov; Federal Energy Administration, *Project Independence*; Federal Energy Agency, *Annual Reports*; De Marchi, "Energy Policy Under Nixon: Mainly Putting Out Fires," in Goodwin, ed., *Energy Policy in Perspective*; Bromley, "The Economic Crisis," in *American Hegemony and World Oil*.

57 Kissinger, *Years of Upheaval*, 891; Nixon, *Memoirs*, 987.

58 Carter, *Keeping Faith*, 91.

59 Grossman, *Encyclopedia of the U.S. Cabinet*, I, 248–9. Arabinda Ghosh suggests in *OPEC* that the Nixon administration's response to the crisis reflected anger, confusion, and frustration. He is especially critical of Kissinger, who, he claims, acted towards the Arab producers as though "the Visigoths had arrived at the gates of imperial Rome." 149.

60 For Carter's statements see: U.S. Department of State, *American Foreign Policy: Basic Documents, 1977–80*, 287–8; 290–1.

61 Clarke, *Against All Enemies*, 102.

62 Canada. Department of Energy, Mines and Resources, *The National Energy Program, 1980*, 17–18, 19, 39, 47, 49, 51.

63 U.S. Department of State, "Note on National Energy Program to the Government of Canada," 5 March 1981; Reagan press conference, 6 March 1981, *American Foreign Policy, Current Documents 1981*, 639; Rashish, "Approach to Foreign Economic Issues," *Department of State Bulletin* (October 1981), 40–6.

64 See, for instance, the blistering editorial in the *Oil and Gas Journal*, 79 (26 January 1981), citing from a report of the Department of Energy, Mines and Resources that Canadian ownership had in any event risen between 1971 and 1979 from 22.4 to 38.5 percent.

65 Bromley, "The Economic Crisis," 138, 140, 142. Bromley indicates that

the majors' share of non-Communist-bloc oil declined from 82 percent in 1963 to 32 percent by 1974.

66 Nixon, *Memoirs*, 982.

CHAPTER TWELVE

1 U.S. Department of Energy, *Petroleum Chronology of Events, May 2002*, www.eia.doe.gov.

2 Executive Order 12287, Decontrol of Crude Oil and Refined Petroleum Products, 28 January 1981, *http://www.reagan.utexas.edu/resource/speeches/1981*. President Reagan also proposed transferring Department of Energy responsibilities to the Department of Commerce but Congress did not act on the proposal.

3 See Telhami et. al., "Does Saudi Arabia Still Matter?" On the impact of the Iran-Iraq war see Viorst, "Iraq at War."

4 U.S. Department of Energy, Energy Information Administration, "Energy Situation Analysis Report 3 January 2002," *http://www.eia.doe.gov/security*. Iraq's debt estimates are from Abbas Alnasrawi, *The Economy of Iraq*, 159.

5 Viorst, "Iraq at War," 362.

6 Stagliano, *A Policy of Discontent*, 44.

7 Ibid., 45.

8 Ibid.

9 In 1990 Congress enacted additional authority for drawing on the SPR following the EXXON Valdez oil spill. The provision allowed no more than 30 million barrels to be withdrawn over a period of sixty days and only when the SPR is at 500 million barrels or more. The drawdown under this provision is permitted in the event of a situation that constitutes or is likely to constitute a "domestic or international supply shortage of significant scope or duration." See Bamberger, "Strategic Petroleum Reserve," CRS Issue Brief. For a perceptive analysis of the 1987 energy security report and the Reagan administration, see Kohl, "Oil and National Security," in Kohl, ed., *After the Oil Price Collapse*, 151–2. On the Reagan administration's non-interventionist approach on energy policy during his first administration, including the discussion of James Edwards, see Katz, *Congress and National Energy Policy*, 153–69. See also U.S. Department of Energy, *Securing America's Energy Future*.

10 U.S. Department of Energy, *Petroleum Chronology of Events, May 2002*, *www.eia.doe.gov*.

11 Testimony of Roger Majak, Assistant Secretary of Commerce, to the House of Representatives Subcommittee on Energy and Power, 19 October 2000, U.S. Department of Commerce, Bureau of Industry and Security.

12 American oil or oil service companies active in Iraq at the time of the

first Gulf War included Mobil, Pullman-Kellogg, Halliburton, and Howe-Baker Engineering. Chevron and Coastal were interested in purchasing Iraqi crude. American companies active in Kuwait at the time of the Iraqi invasion included Chevron, Getty Oil, Gulf Oil, Mobil, and Texaco.

13 Department of Energy, DOE Timeline 1981–1990, History Division, http://ma.mbe.doe.gov.

14 U.S. Department of Energy, Energy Information Agency, *World Oil Market and Price Chronologies: 1970–2003*, www.eia.doe.gov/emeu/cabs/chron.html.

15 Majak testimony, see n9 above.

16 UN, Office of the Iraq Program Oil for Food website. There is considerable controversy over what portion of the UN funds were actually used for the stated purposes as opposed to being siphoned off by corrupt officials, including Saddam Hussein and other members of the Baathist regime.

17 Gannon, "A Global Perspective on Energy Security," 6 December 1996, *http://www.cia.gov*. One of the best analyses of energy security in the 1980s is Fried and Blandin, eds, *Oil and America's Security*. On the Middle East see especially Quandt, "The Middle East Factor," in Fried and Blandin. More extensive analysis is provided by Bull-Berg, *American International Oil Policy*. Conant, *The Oil Factor in U.S. Foreign Policy*, is more focused on policy recommendations. On the origins and impact of Saudi policies in 1999–2000 see Gause, "Saudi Arabia Over a Barrel."

18 See n17.

19 Clarke, *Against All Enemies*, 103. Conoco merged with Phillips Petroleum in 2002 to become Conoco-Phillips. See Thompson, *A Brief History of Major Oil Companies*.

20 U.S. Senate, "Proposed Trans-Siberian Natural gas Pipeline," Committee on Banking, Housing and Urban Affairs, 97th Congress, 1st session (12 November 1981).

21 Cited in Stagliano, *A Policy of Discontent*, 54, 55.

22 Klare, *Resource Wars*, 109–37.

23 Kalicki, "Caspian Energy at the Crossroads," 122. The data on reserves is drawn from BP *Statistical Review of World Energy* and the U.S. Geological Survey, *World Petroleum Assessment*, cited in Kalicki, 123.

24 U.S. Department of Energy, Petroleum Chronology of Events, May 2002, www.eia.doe.gov.

25 Kalicki, "Caspian Energy at the Crossroads," 120–1. U.S. concern over reliance on Russian oil pipelines also applied to the transport of regional natural gas. For an earlier perspective on the region see Blank, "Energy, Economics, and Security in Central Asia: Russia and Its Rivals." Blank wrote that "whoever controls the energy economy will determine the destiny of the region," v.

26 On FIRA and oil price controls see Granatstein and Bothwell, *Pirouette*, 86. For the United States reaction see Thompson and Randall, *Canada and the United States*, 256–7.

27 Thompson and Randall, *Canada and the United States*, 266–9.

28 U.S. Department of State, The United States–Canada Free Trade Agreement Implementation Act, *Statement of Administrative Action* (1988).

29 UNECE, "Concern about energy security is growing," Geneva, 22 November 2001, http://www.unece.org.

30 International Energy Agency, "World Energy Outlook: 2001 Insights," http://www.iea.org.

31 U.S. Department of Energy, Petroleum Chronology of Events, May 2002, *www.eia.doe.gov*. On industry restructuring see also Bull-Berg, *American International Oil Policy*, 175.

32 Turner, *Oil Companies in the International System*, 222. George Schultz, Treasury Secretary under Richard Nixon, served as president of Bechtel for seven years until 1981, when Ronald Reagan appointed him Secretary of State. While Secretary of State, Schultz assisted Bechtel with a proposal to Saddam Hussein to construct an oil pipeline from Iraq through Jordan to Aqaba. The proposal failed and Schultz returned to the Bechtel Board when he left government. Casper Weinberger was the general counsel for Bechtel and served on its board from 1975 until 1981 when he became Reagan's Secretary of Defense. On Bechtel's links to government officials see Associated Press Online, 18 April 2003. None of this is to suggest that Bechtel did not have the requisite expertise to undertake the project. To the contrary, the company had a half century of extensive experience in the region. In 1947 it began an expedited industrialization of the entire Persian Gulf, with a particular focus on Saudi Arabia, where it built a railroad, power plants, and refineries as well as the thousand mile Trans-Arabian pipeline, Tapline, linking oil fields in Saudi Arabia with the Lebanese port Saidon. See also Knight Ridder/Tribune News Service, 8 June 2003.

33 Report of the National Energy Policy Group (Washington, 2001), chapter 8, "Strengthening Global Alliances."

34 Lovins and Lovins, "Reducing Vulnerability," in *Brittle Power*, 173.

35 Pollack, "Securing the Gulf," 3.

36 Telhami et al., 170.

37 Gannon; Telhami et al., 168.

38 Pollack, 5, 9. Pollack suggests that the American military presence in the Gulf states is, perhaps ironically, one of the major impediments to regional stability and that a reduction or even total withdrawal of U.S. military forces from the area would reduce hostility to the United States even if it would remove the deterrence factor against Iran and make it difficult to respond quickly to crises in the area. He suggests that a

return to the earlier "over the horizon" or offshore military presence might be appropriate.

39 Eto, "Asian Energy Security." International Energy Agency, "China's Quest for Energy Security," http://www,iea.org/public/studies.

40 "Diversification of Chinese Oil Import Sources," http://www.iea.org/public/studies/china.

41 U.S. Department of Energy, Energy Information Administration, "Energy Situation Analysis Report 3 January 2002," http://www.eia.doe.gov/security.

42 Eto, "Asian Energy Security." http://www.mofa.go.jp.

CONCLUSION

1 May, *Lessons of the Past.*
2 *The Economist*, 25–31 October 2003.
3 *The Economist*, 25–31 October 2003, 61.
4 Kaufman, *The Oil Cartel Case.*
5 Wittner, *Cold War America*, 115.
6 Eckes, *The United States and the Global Struggle for Minerals*, 168ff.
7 Wittner, *Cold War America*, 115–16.
8 Eckes, *The United States and the Global Struggle for Minerals*, 179, 274–5.
9 Wilkins, "The Oil Companies in Perspective," 160.
10 Cited in Eckes, *The United States and the Global Struggle for Minerals*, 178.
11 Bull-Berg, *American International Oil Policy.* See especially chapter 6, "Oil and Security Policy: The American Dilemma."

Bibliography

MANUSCRIPT SOURCES

National Archives, Washington, DC, and Federal Records Center, Suitland, Maryland

RG 40 – General Records of the Department of Commerce

RG 43 – Records of International Conferences

RG 48 – General Records of the Secretary of the Interior

RG 59 – General Records of the Department of State (DS); includes the following lot files: Petroleum Division Lot File; Harley Notter Lot File; Leo Pasvolsky Lot File; Research and Analysis Branch, Office of Strategic Services

RG 60 – Records of the Department of Justice

RG 80 – Records of the Department of the Navy

RG 107 – Records of the Office of the Secretary of War

RG 120 – Records of the Federal Trade Commission

RG 151 – General Records of the Bureau of Foreign and Domestic Commerce (BFDC)

RG 160 – Records of the United States Army Service Forces

RG 165 – Records of the Department of War, General and Special staffs

RG 169 – Records of the Foreign Economic Administration

RG 218 – Records of the Joint Chiefs of Staff

RG 234 – Records of the Reconstruction Finance Corporation

RG 253 – Records of the Petroleum Administration for War (PAW)

RG 319 – Records of the Plans and Operations Division, Department of W (OPD)

RG 334 – Records of Interservice Agencies; includes the Army-Navy Petroleum Board and the Petroleum Reserves Corporation (PRC)

Presidential Papers

Calvin Coolidge Papers, Library of Congress
Herbert C. Hoover Papers (HHP), Herbert Hoover Presidential Library, West
  Branch, Iowa
Ronald Reagan Papers, Ronald Reagan Presidential Library, Simi Valley, Cal-
  ifornia
Franklin D. Roosevelt Papers, Franklin D. Roosevelt Presidential Library,
  Hyde Park, New York
Harry S. Truman Papers, Harry S. Truman Presidential Library, Indepen-
  dence, Missouri

Papers of the Secretaries of State

Charles Evans Hughes Papers, Library of Congress
Cordell Hull Papers, Library of Congress
Henry S. Stimson Papers and Diaries, Yale University

Personal Papers

Paul Atkins Papers, Yale University
Adolf Berle, Jr, Papers, Roosevelt Library
Tom Connally Papers, Library of Congress
Francis P. Corrigan Papers, Roosevelt Library
Josephus Daniels Papers, Library of Congress
Ralph Davies Papers, Truman Presidential Library
Herbert Feis Papers, Library of Congress
James Forrestal Papers, National Archives
Harry Hopkins Papers, Roosevelt Library
Harold Ickes Papers, Library of Congress
Julius Krug Papers, Library of Congress
William Leahy Papers and Diary, Library of Congress
Breckinridge Long Papers, Library of Congress
Arthur C. Millspaugh Papers, Yale University
Henry Morgenthau, Jr, Papers and Diaries, Roosevelt Library
Robert Patterson Papers, Library of Congress
Franklin Polk Papers, Yale University
Donald Richberg Papers, Library of Congress
Henry Wallace Papers, Roosevelt Library
Ray Lyman Wilbur Papers, Hoover Presidential Library
John G. Winant Papers, Roosevelt Library

Great Britain

Public Record Office: Foreign Office Political Files, FO 371; Colonial Office; Admiralty; Cabinet minutes and memoranda

Private Collections: Shell Group of Company Records (Shell Papers), Shell Centre, London; S. Pearson and Son Papers (controlled the Amerada Corporation in the United States and the Mexican Eagle Oil Company in Mexico), Science Museum Library, London

GOVERNMENT DOCUMENTS AND PUBLICATIONS

Bamberger, Robert. "Strategic Petroleum Reserve." CRS Issue Brief for Congress, National Library for the Environment, 2 August 2001.

Canada. Department of Energy. Mines and Resources. *The National Energy Program, 1980.* Ottawa, 1980.

Canada. Royal Commission on Energy. *Second Report.* Ottawa, 1959.

Majak, Roger, Assistant Secretary of Commerce. Testimony before the House of Representatives Subcommittee on Energy and Power, United States Department of Commerce, Bureau of Industry and Security, 19 October 2000.

Mexico. Mexico's Oil. Mexico City: Government of Mexico, 1940.

Petroleum Industry War Council (PIWC). *United States Foreign Policy and the Petroleum Reserves Corporation: An Analysis of the Effect of the Proposed Saudi Arabian Pipeline.* Washington, 1944.

Schnabel, James F. *The History of the Joint Chiefs of Staff: The Joint Chiefs of Staff and National Policy, Vol. I, 1945–1947.* Washington: Historical Division, Joint Chiefs of Staff, 1979.

Tracie, R.G. "History of the Naval Petroleum Reserves." Unpublished, U.S. Department of the Navy, 1938.

U.S. Army Service Forces, Office of the Commanding General, Control Division Administrative Management Branch, Historical File, 1941–1946. *Reference Data, Canol Project.* 2 vols (RG 160, NA).

U.S. Bureau of the Census. *Historical Statistics of the United States from Colonial Times to 1957.* Washington: GPO, 1960.

U.S. Bureau of Foreign and Domestic Commerce. *Trade Information Bulletin,* no. 731. Washington: GPO, 1930.

U.S. Bureau of Mines. *Minerals Yearbook,* 1950–1970.

U.S. Cabinet Task Force on Oil Import Control, *The Oil Import Question: A Report on the Relationship of Oil Imports to the National Security.* Washington: GPO, 1970.

U.S. Congress. *Congressional Record, 1919–* .

U.S. Congress. House of Representatives. House Judiciary Committee. *Hearings Relative to the Establishment of Title of the United States to Certain Submerged Lands Containing Petroleum Deposits.* 76th Cong., 1st sess. 1939.

U.S. Congress, Senate. Committee on Foreign Relations (SFRC). *Documentary History of the Petroleum Reserves Corporation, 1943–1944.* Washington: GPO, 1974.

– *Petroleum Agreement with Great Britain and Northern Ireland. Hearings.* 2–25 June 1947. 80th Cong., 1st sess. 1947.

U.S. Congress. Senate. Committee on Foreign Relations (SFRC). Subcommittee on Multinational Corporations and United States Foreign Policy. Hearings. 93rd. Cong., 2nd sess. 1973–74.

– *Report on Multinational Petroleum Corporations and Foreign Policy.* 93rd Cong., 2nd sess. 1975.

U.S. Congress. Senate. Committee on Military Affairs. Subcommittee on War Mobilization. *Cartels and National Security. Report. Part 11: Analytical and Technical Supplement.* Washington: GPO, 1944.

U.S. Congress. Senate. Committee on National Defense. Report no. 10, part 14. *The Canol Project.* Washington: GPO, 1944.

U.S. Congress. Senate. Committee on Public Lands and Surveys. *Hearings on S. J. Resolution 253, a bill authorizing the Attorney General with the concurrence of the Secretary of the Navy to release claims of the United States upon certain assets of the Pan American Petroleum Co. and the Richfield Oil Co. of California.* Washington: GPO, 1933.

– *Hearings on Senate Joint Resolution 83, Relative to the Establishment of a Naval Petroleum Reserve in the Submerged Lands Along and Adjacent to the Coast of the State of California.* 76th Cong., 1st sess. 1939.

U.S. Congress. Senate. "Restrictions on Certain Petroleum Prospectors in Certain Foreign Countries." Senate document 272 (1920).

U.S. Congress. Senate. Select Committee on Small Business. *The Impact of Monopoly and Cartel Practices on Small Business.* 82nd Cong., 2nd sess 1952.

U.S. Congress. Senate. Senate document no. 139. Washington, 1952.

U.S. Congress. Senate. Senate Foreign Relations Committee. Subcommittee on Multinational Corporations. *Multinational Oil Corporations and United States Foreign Policy: Report.* 1975.

U.S. Congress. Senate. Special Committee Investigating the National Defense Program. *Additional Report, Overseas Investigations, Section 1, Petroleum Matters.* S. Report 10, part 15. 78th Cong., 2nd sess. 1944.

– *Hearings, part 41, Petroleum Arrangements with Saudi Arabia.* 80th Cong., 1st. sess. 1948.

U.S. Congress. Senate. Special Committee Investigating Petroleum Resources in Relation to the National Welfare. *Diplomatic Protection of American Petro-*

leum Industries in Mesopotamia, Netherlands, East Indies, and Mexico. 79th Cong., 1st sess. 1945.

– *Final Report*. 80th Cong., 1st. sess. 1947.

U.S. Congress, Senate. *Restrictions Imposed on Citizens of the United States in Prospecting, Acquiring, and Developing Petroleum Lands Abroad*. Senate document 272, 66th Cong., 2nd sess. 1920.

U.S. Congress. Senate. Temporary National Economic Committee. Investigation of the Control of Economic Power. Monograph 39, *Control of the Petroleum Industry by Major Oil Companies*, by Roy C. Cook. 76th Cong., 3rd sess., Senate Committee Print, 1941.

– *Investigation of the Concentration of Economic Power. Description of Hearings and Monographs of the* TNEC. 76th Cong., 3rd sess. 1941.

– Monograph no. 39A: *Review and Criticism on Behalf of Standard Oil (New Jersey) and Sun Oil Company of Monograph no. 39, with Rejoinder by the Monograph Authors*. 76th Cong., 3rd. sess. 1941.

U.S. Department of Commerce. Bureau of Foreign and Domestic Commerce (BFDC). *American Direct Investments in Foreign Countries 1936*. Washington: GPO, 1938.

– *Business Statistics*. 1961.

– *Commerce Reports*. 1920– .

– *Foreign Capital Investments in Russian Industries and Commerce*. Miscellaneous series no. 124 (1924).

– *Trade Information Bulletin* 1930–.

U.S. Department of Energy. "The Atomic Century: Historical Collection of Declassified and Released Documents, Part II: "The Federal Energy Administration." http://www.dpi.anl.gov.

– DOE *Timeline, 1981–1990*. History Division, DOE. http://ma.mbe.doe.gov.

– *Petroleum Chronology of Events*. May 2002. www.eia.doe.gov.

– *Securing America's Energy Future: National Energy Policy Plan*. July 1981.

U.S. Department of Energy. Energy Information Administration. "Energy Situation Analysis Report, 3 January 2002." http://www.eia.doe.gov/security.

– "World Oil Market and Oil Price Chronologies, 1970–2003." www.eia.doe.gov/emeu/cabs/chron.html.

U.S. Department of Energy. Federal Energy Administration. *Project Independence: A Summary*. Washington: GPO, 1974.

U.S. Department of Energy. Federal Energy Agency. *Annual Reports*.

U.S. Department of State. *American Foreign Policy: Current Documents – 1967; 1981*. Washington: GPO, 1967; 1981.

– *American Foreign Policy: Basic Documents, 1977–80*. Washington: GPO, 1983.

– *Biographic Register*. Washington: GPO (title and years vary).

– *Bulletin*. 1957–.

- "Note on National Energy Program to the Government of Canada." 5 March 1981.
- *The Conference of Berlin* (The Potsdam Conference). 2 vols. Washington: GPO, 1960.
- *Papers Relating to the Foreign Relations of the United States.* 1919–.
- *Postwar Foreign Policy Preparation, 1939–1945.* Washington: GPO, 1949.
- *Proceedings of the United States-Mexican Commission Convened in Mexico City,* 14 May 1923. Washington: GPO, 1925.
- U.S. Federal Oil Conservation Board (FOCB). *Sources of the U.S. Oil Supply, 1918–1931. Report V to the President of the U.S.* Washington: GPO, 1932.
- U.S. Federal Trade Commission. *Report on Foreign Ownership in the Petroleum Industry.* Washington, 1923.
- U.S. President. *Public Papers of the Presidents of the United States: Harry S. Truman.* 8 vols. Washington: GPO, 1961–6.
- U.S. Senate. Committee on Banking, Housing and Urban Affairs *Proposed Trans-Siberian Natural Gas Pipeline.* 97th Cong., 1st sess. 1981.
- Committee on Interior and Insular Affairs. Chair, Henry M. Jackson. *Geopolitics of Energy.* Energy publication No. 95–1, Washington: 1977.
- Report of the Federal Oil Conservation Board. *American Petroleum Interests in Foreign Countries.* Washington: GPO, 1946.

International Organizations

International Energy Agency. "World Energy Outlook: 2001 Insights." http://www.iea.org.
- "China's Quest for Energy Security." http://www.iea.org/public/studies.
- "Diversification of Chinese Oil Import Sources." http://www.iea.org/public/studies/china.
United Nations. Office of the Iraq Program Oil for Food. http://www.un.org/Depts/oip/.
United Nations Economic Commission for Europe. Press Release. "Concern about Energy Security is Growing." Geneva, 22 November 2001. http://www.unece.org.

NEWSPAPERS, MAGAZINES, AND TRADE JOURNALS

American Magazine
Chicago Sun
Commercial and Financial Chronicle
The Economist
Financial Times (London)
Foreign Affairs

Knight Ridder/Tribune News Service
London Times
Los Angeles Times
Manchester Guardian
Mining and Metallurgy
The Nation
National Geographic Magazine
National Petroleum News
New Republic
New York Herald Tribune
New York Journal of Commerce
New York Times
Oil and Gas Journal
Oil Forum
Oil World (California)
Petroleum Register
Saturday Evening Post
Texas Oil Journal
Time
Wall Street Journal
Washington Post
Washington Star

MEMOIRS AND PERSONAL ACCOUNTS

Alfonso, Pérez. *Petroleo y dependencia*. Caracas: Sintesis Dosmil, 1971.

Betancourt, Romulo. *Venezuela, Oil and Politics*. Boston: Houghton Mifflin, 1978.

Blum, John, ed. *From the Morgenthau Diaries*. 2 vols. Boston: Houghton Mifflin, 1967.

– ed. *The Price of Vision: The Diary of Henry A. Wallace, 1942–1946*. Boston: Houghton Mifflin,1973.

Carter, Jimmy. *Keeping Faith: Memoirs of a President*. London: St James Place, 1982.

Child, Richard Wasburn. *A Diplomat Looks at Europe*. New York: Duffield, 1925.

Connally, Tom, and Alfred Steinberg. *My Name Is Tom Connally*. New York: Crowell, 1954.

Connelly, William. *The Oil Business as I Saw It: Half a Century with Sinclair*. Norman: University of Oklahoma Press, 1954.

Cronon, E. David, ed. *The Cabinet Diaries of Josephus Daniels*. Lincoln: University of Nebraska Press, 1963.

Daniels, Josephus. *The Wilson Era: Years of War and After, 1917–1923*. Chapel Hill: University of North Carolina Press, 1946.

Dawes, Charles. *Journal as Ambassador to Great Britain*. Westport, Conn.: Greenwood, 1970.

Deterding, Sir Henri. *An International Oilman*. London 1934 (microfilm, Library of Congress).

Grew, Joseph. *Turbulent Era: A Diplomatic Record of Forty Years, 1904–1945*. 2 vols. Boston: Houghton Mifflin, 1952.

Harriman, W. Averell, and Elie Abel. *Special Envoy to Churchill and Stalin, 1941–1946*. New York: Random House, 1975.

Hoover, Herbert. *The Memoirs of Herbert Hoover*. 2 vols. New York: Macmillan, 1952.

Hughes, Charles Evans. *The Pathway of Peace: Representative Addresses Delivered during His Term as Secretary of State*. New York: Harper, 1925.

Hull, Cordell. *The Memoirs of Cordell Hull*. 2 vols. New York: Macmillan, 1948.

Ickes, Harold. *Autobiography of a Curmudgeon*. New York: Reynal and Hitchcock, 1943.

– *Fightin' Oil*. New York: Knopf, 1943.

– *An Oil Policy: An Open Letter to the Members of the Congress of the United States*. 30 May 1947.

– *The Secret Diary of Harold Ickes*. 3 vols. New York: Simon and Schuster, 1954.

Kaufman, Burton. *The Oil Cartel Case: A Documentary Study of Antitrust Activity in the Cold War Era*. Westport: Greenwood, 1978.

Kissinger, Henry. *White House Years*. Boston: Little, Brown, 1979.

Leahy, William. *I Was There*. New York: McGraw-Hill, 1950.

Miller, Merle. *Plain Speaking: An Oral Biography of Harry S. Truman*. New York: Berkly Medallion, 1973.

Millis, Walter, ed. *The Forrestal Diaries*. New York: Viking, 1951.

Nixon, Richard. *The Memoirs of Richard Nixon*. New York: Grosset & Dunlap, 1978.

Richberg, Donald. *Government and Business Tomorrow, Public Relations Program*. New York: Harper, 1943.

Romualdi, Serafino. *Presidents and Peons: Recollections of a Labor Ambassador in Latin America*. New York: Funk and Wagnalls, 1967.

Rosenman, Samuel I., ed. *The Public Papers and Addresses of Franklin Delano Roosevelt*. 13 vols. New York: Russell, 1938–50.

Rowland, John, and Basil, Second Baron Cadman. *Ambassador for Oil: The Life of John, First Baron Cadman*. London: Herbert Jenkin, 1960.

Truman, Harry S. *Memoirs*. 2 vols. Garden City, NY: Doubleday, 1955–6.

Tulchin, Joseph, ed. *The Autobiographical Notes of Charles Evans Hughes*. Cambridge: Harvard University Press, 1973.

Wilson, Sir Arnold T. *Mesopotamia, 1917–1920. A Clash of Loyalties. A Personal and Historical Record*. London: Oxford University Press, 1931.

SECONDARY SOURCES

Books

Adams, Frederick C. *Economic Diplomacy: The Export Import Bank and American Foreign Policy, 1934–1939.* Columbia: University of Missouri Press, 1976.

Alnasrawi, Abbas. *The Economy of Iraq: Oil, Wars, Destruction of Development and Prospects 1950–2010.* Westport: Greenwood, 1994.

American Council of Learned Societies. *Dictionary of American Biography.* New York: Scribner's, 1928–.

American Petroleum Institute. *Petroleum Facts and Figures.* New York: API, 1937.

Anderson, Irvine. *The Standard Vacuum Oil Company and United States East Asian Policy.* Princeton: Princeton University Press, 1975.

– *Aramco, the United States and Saudi Arabia: A Study of the Dynamics of Foreign Oil Policy, 1933–1950.* Princeton: University Press, 1981.

Bartley, Ernest. *The Tidelands Oil Controversy.* Austin: University of Texas Press, 1953.

Batten, Donna, ed. *Encyclopedia of Governmental Advisory Organizations*, 9th edition. Detroit: Gale Research, 1993.

Behrman, J. *Some Patterns of the Rise of Multinational Enterprise.* Chapel Hill: University of North Carolina Press, 1969.

– *U.S. International Business and Governments.* New York: McGraw-Hill, 1971.

Blair, John. *The Control of Oil.* New York: Pantheon, 1976.

Bosques, Gilberto. *The National Revolutionary Party of Mexico and the Six Year Plan.* Mexico: National Revolutionary Party, 1937.

Braeman, John, Robert Bremner, and David Brody. *Twentieth-Century American Foreign Policy.* Columbus: University of Ohio, 1971.

Brandes, Joseph. *Herbert Hoover and Economic Diplomacy.* Pittsburgh: University of Pittsburgh Press, 1962.

Bromley, Simon. *American Hegemony and World Oil.* University Park: Penn State University Press, 1991.

Brown, Bruce K. *Oil Men in Washington: An Informal Account of the Organization and Activities of the Petroleum Administration for Defense During the Korean War, 1950–1952.* n.l.: Evanil Press, 1965.

Bull-Berg, Hans Jacob. *American International Oil Policy: Causal Factors and Effect.* New York: St Martin's, 1987.

Burns, James MacGregor. *Roosevelt: The Soldier of Freedom.* New York: Harcourt, Brace, 1970.

Canadian Petroleum Association. *Statistical Yearbook – 1971.* Calgary: CPA, 1972.

Casson, Mark, ed. *The Growth of International Business.* New York: Allen and Unwin, 1983.

Chisholm, Archibald. *The First Kuwait Oil Concession Agreement.* London: Frank Cass, 1975.

Clarke, Richard. *Against All Enemies: Inside America's War on Terror.* New York: Free Press, 2004.

Cline, Howard F. *The United States and Mexico.* New York: Atheneum, 1971.

Conant, Melvin. *The Oil Factor in U.S. Foreign Policy, 1980–1990.* Lexington, Mass.: Heath, 1982.

Curry, George. *James F. Byrnes. Vol. XIV of The American Secretaries of State and Their Diplomacy,* Robert Ferrell and S.F. Bemis, eds. New York: Cooper Square, 1965.

Dallek, Robert. *Franklin D. Roosevelt and American Foreign Policy, 1932–1945.* New York: Oxford University Press, 1979.

Darmstadter, Joe. *Energy in the World Economy: A Statistical Review of Trends in the World Economy since 1925.* Baltimore and London: Johns Hopkins, 1971.

Davenport, Ernest, and Sidney Cooke. *The Oil Trusts and Anglo-American Relations.* London: Macmillan, 1923.

Davis, Vincent. *Postwar Defense Policy and the United States Navy, 1943–1946.* Chapel Hill: University of North Carolina Press, 1966.

DeGolyer, Everett. *Twentieth-Century Petroleum Statistics.* Dallas: DeGolyer and MacNaughton, 1946.

Denny, Ludwell. *We Fight for Oil.* Westport, Conn.: Greenwood, 1976 (1928).

DeNovo, John. *American Interests and Politics in the Middle East.* Minneapolis: University of Minnesota Press, 1963.

Divine, Robert A. *Second Chance: The Triumph of Internationalism in America during World War II.* New York: Atheneum, 1971.

Eden, Anthony. *Full Circle.* Boston: Cassel, 1960.

Eckes, Alfred, Jr. *The United States and the Global Struggle for Minerals.* Austin: University of Texas Press, 1979.

Fanning, L. *The Rise of American Oil.* New York and London: Harper, 1936.

– *American Oil Operations Abroad.* New York and London: McGraw-Hill, 1947.

– ed. *Our Oil Resources.* New York and London: McGraw-Hill, 1945.

Feis, Herbert. *Petroleum and American Foreign Policy.* Stanford: Food Foundation, 1944.

– *Three International Episodes Seen from E.A.* New York: Knopf, 1946 (reprint edition 1966).

Ferrier, Ronald W. *The History of the British Petroleum Company. Vol. 1. The Developing Years, 1901–1932.* Cambridge: Cambridge University Press, 1982.

Filene, Peter. *Americans and the Soviet Experiment, 1917–1933.* Cambridge: Harvard University Press, 1967.

Finnie, David H. *Desert Enterprise: The Middle East Oil Industry in Its Local Environment.* Cambridge: Harvard University Press, 1958.

Finnie, Richard. *Canol, the Subarctic Pipeline and Refinery Project*. San Francisco: Ryder and Ingram, 1945.

Fischer, Louis. *Oil Imperialsim*. New York: International Publishers, 1926.

Forsythe, Rosemary. *The Politics of Oil in the Caucasus and Central Asia*. Oxford: Oxford University Press and the International Institute for Strategic Studies, 1996.

Frey, John, and Chandler Ide. *A History of the Petroleum Administration for War, 1941–1945*. Washington: GPO, 1946.

Fried, Edward, and Nanette Blandin, eds. *Oil and America's Security*. Washington: Brookings, 1988.

Gaddis, John. *The United States and the Origins of the Cold War*. New York: Columbia University Press, 1972.

Gardner, Lloyd C. *Economic Aspects of New Deal Diplomacy*. Madison: University of Wisconsin Press, 1964.

– *Architects of Illusion: Men and Ideas in American Foreign Policy, 1941–1949*. Chicago: Quadrangle, 1970.

Gardner, Richard. *Sterling Dollar Diplomacy: The Origins and Prospects of Our International Economic Order*. New York: McGraw-Hill, 1969.

Gellman, Irwin. *Good Neighbor Diplomacy: United States Policies in Latin America*. Baltimore: Johns Hopkins University Press, 1979.

Gerig, Benjamin. *The Open Door and the Mandates System*. London: Allen and Unwin, 1930.

Gerretson, Frederik. *History of the Royal Dutch Shell, 4 vols*. Leiden: Brill, 1953–7.

Ghosh, Arabinda. OPEC, *The Petroleum Industry, and United States Energy Policy*. Westport: Quorum Books, 1983.

Gibb, George, and Evelyn Knowlton. *History of Standard Oil Company of New Jersey: The Resurgent Years, 1911–1927*. New York: Harper, 1956.

Giddens, Paul. *Standard Oil Company (Indiana), Oil Pioneer of the Middle West*. New York: Appleton, Century, Crofts, 1955.

Glad, Betty. *Charles Evans Hughes and the Illusions of Innocence: A Study in American Diplomacy*. Urbana: University of Illinois Press, 1966.

Goodwin, Craufurd, ed. *Energy Policy in Perspective: Today's Problems, Yesterday's Solutions*. Washington: Brookings Institution, 1980.

Granatstein, J. L., and Robert Bothwell. *Pirouette: Pierre Trudeau and Canadian Foreign Policy*. Toronto: University of Toronto Press, 1991.

Grossman, Mark. *Encyclopedia of the U.S. Cabinet*. Vol. I. Santa Barbara: ABC Clio, 2000.

Hamilton, Charles W. *Americans and Oil in the Middle East*. Houston: Gulf Publishing Company, 1962.

Hawley, Ellis. *The New Deal and the Problem of Monopoly*. Princeton: Princeton University Press, 1966.

Hewins, Ralph. *Mr. Five Per Cent: The Story of Calouste Gulbenkian*. London: Hutchison, 1957.

Hoff Wilson, Joan. *American Business and Foreign Policy, 1921–1933*. Lexington: University of Kentucky Press, 1971.

– *Ideology and Economics: U.S. Relations with the Soviet Union, 1918–1933.* Columbia, Mo.: University of Missouri Press, 1974.

– *Herbert Hoover, Forgotten Progressive.* Boston: Little, Brown, 1975.

Hogan, Michael. *Informal Entente: The Private Structure of Cooperation in Anglo-American Economic Diplomacy, 1918–1928.* Columbia: University of Missouri Press, 1977.

– *The Marshall Plan: America, Britain and The Reconstruction of Western Europe, 1947–1952.* New York: Cambridge University Press, 1987.

– and Thomas Paterson, eds. *Explaining the History of American Foreign Relations.* New York: Cambridge University Press, 1991.

Hornbeck, Stanley. *The United States and the Far East.* Boston: World Peace Foundation, 1942.

Hurewitz, J.C. *Diplomacy in the Near and Middle East: A Documentary Record, 1914–1956.* Princeton: Princeton University Press, 1956.

Ise, John. *The United States Oil Policy.* New Haven: Yale University Press, 1924.

James, Marquis. *The Texaco Story: The First Fifty Years, 1902–1952.* New York: The Texas Company, 1953.

Jensen, Walter. *Energy in Europe, 1945–1950.* London: Foulis, 1967.

Katz, James. *Congress and National Energy Policy.* New Brunswick and London: Transaction Books, 1984.

Katzenstein, Peter, ed. *Between Power and Plenty: Foreign Economic Policies of Advanced Industrial States.* Madison: University of Wisconsin Press, 1977.

Kaufman, Burton I. *The Oil Cartel Case: A Documentary Study of Antitrust Activity in the Cold War Era.* Westport, Conn.: Greenwood, 1978.

Kemnitzer, William. *Rebirth of Monopoly: A Critical Analysis of Economic Conduct in the Petroleum Industry of the United States.* New York and London: Harper, 1938.

Kent, Marion. *Oil and Empire: British Policy and Mesopotamian Oil, 1900–1920.* New York: Harper, 1976.

Kissinger, Henry. *Years of Upheaval.* Boston: Little Brown, 1982.

Klare, Michael T. *Resource Wars: The New Landscape of Global Conflict.* New York: Holt and Company, 2002.

Kohl, William, ed. *After the Oil Price Collapse.* Baltimore: Johns Hopkins, 1991.

Kolko, Gabriel. *The Politics of War: The World and United States Foreign* Policy, 1943–45. New York: Random House, 1968.

– *The Roots of American Foreign Policy: An Analysis of Power and Purpose.* Boston: Beacon Press, 1969.

– *Confronting the Third World: United States Foreign Policy 1945–1980.* New York: Pantheon, 1988.

– and Joyce Kolko. *The Limits of Power: The World and United States Foreign Policy, 1945–1954.* New York: Harper, 1972.

Krasner, Stephen D. *Defending the National Interest: Raw Materials Investments and U.S. Foreign* Policy. Princeton: Princeton University Press, 1978.

– *Structural Conflict: The Third World Against Global Liberalism.* Berkeley: University of California Press, 1985.

– ed. *International Regimes.* Ithaca: Cornell University Press, 1983.

– Peter Katzenstein and Robert O. Keohane, *Exploration and Contestation in the Study of World Politics.* Cambridge, Mass: MIT Press, 1999.

Krueger, Robert. *The United States and International Oil: A Report for the Federal Energy Administration.* New York: Praeger, 1975.

Larson, Henrietta, Evelyn Knowlton, and Charles Popple. *History of Standard Oil Company of New Jersey: New Horizons, 1927–1950.* New York: Harper, 1971.

Larson, Henrietta, and Kenneth Porter. *History of Humble Oil and Refining Company.* New York: Harper, 1959.

Lear, Linda. *Harold L. Ickes: The Aggressive Progressive, 1874–1933.* New York: Garland Publishers, 1981.

Lebkicker, Roy. *Aramco and World Oil.* New York: Russell Moore, 1952.

Leffler, Melvyn. *A Preponderance of Power: National Security, The Truman Administration and the Cold War.* Stanford: Stanford University Press, 1992.

Leighton, Richard. *Global Logistics and Strategy, 1943–45: The United States Army in World War II.* Washington: The Department of War, 1968.

– and Robert Coakley. *Global Logistics and Strategy, 1940–43: The United States Army in World War II.* Washington: The Department of War, 1955.

Leith, Charles, J.W. Furnass, and Cleona Lewis. *World Minerals and World Peace.* Washington: Brookings Institution, 1943.

Lenczowski, George. *Oil and the State in the Middle East.* Ithaca: Cornell University Press, 1960.

Lieuwen, Edwin. *Petroleum in Venezuela: A History.* Berkeley: University of California Press, 1954.

Liss, Sheldon B. *Diplomacy and Dependency: Venezuela, the United States and the Americas.* Salisbury, NC: Documentary Publications, 1978.

Longhurst, Henry. *A Short History of the Anglo-Iranian Oil Company.* London: n.p., 1948.

– *Adventure in Oil: The Story of British Petroleum.* London: Sidgwick and Jackson 1959.

Longrigg, Stephen. *Iraq, 1900–1950.* London: Oxford University Press, 1953.

– *Oil in the Middle East: Its Discovery and Development.* 3rd ed. London: Oxford University Press, 1968.

Louis, William R. *British Strategy in the Far East, 1919–1939.* London: Oxford University Press, 1971.

Lovins, Amory B., and L. Hunter Lovins. *Brittle Power: Energy Strategy for National Security.* Andover, MA: Brick House, 1982.

McLean, John, and Robert Haigh. *The Growth of Integrated Oil Companies.* Boston: Harvard School of Business Administration, 1954.

McNeill, William. *America, Britain and Russia: Their Cooperation and Conflict, 1941–1946.* London: Oxford University Press, 1953.

Maddox, Robert J. *William E. Borah and American Foreign Policy.* Baton Rouge, La.: Louisiana University Press, 1969.

Marshall, Herbert, Frank Southard, and Kenneth Taylor. *Canadian-American Industry.* New Haven: Yale University Press, 1936.

Matloff, Maurice. *Strategic Planning for Coalition Warfare, 1943–44: The United States Army in World War II.* Washington: The Department of War, 1959.

– and Edwin Smith. *Strategic Planning for Coalition Warfare, 1941–1942: The United States Army in World War II.* Washington: The Department of War, 1953.

May, Ernest R. *Lessons of the Past: The Use and Misuse of History in American Foreign Policy.* New York: Oxford University Press, 1973.

Meyer, Lorenzo. *Mexico and the United States in the Oil Controversy.* Trans. Muriel Vasconcelos. Austin: University of Texas Press, 1977.

Miliband, Ralph. *The State in Capitalist Society.* London: Quartet, 1969.

Miller, David Aaron. *Search for Security: Saudi Arabian Oil and American Foreign Policy.* Chapel Hill: University of North Carolina Press, 1980.

Morison, Elting R. *Turmoil and Tradition: A Study of the Life and Times of Henry L. Stimson.* Boston: Houghton-Mifflin, 1960.

Nash, Gerald D. *United States Oil Policy, 1890–1964.* Pittsburgh: University of Pittsburgh Press, 1968.

Neumann, William. *After Victory: Churchill, Roosevelt, Stalin and the Making of the Peace.* New York: Harper, 1967.

Nicholson, Harold. *Curzon: The Last Phase.* Boston: Houghton-Mifflin, 1934.

Nixon, Edgar B. *Franklin D. Roosevelt and Foreign Affairs.* 3 vols. Cambridge: Harvard University Press, 1969.

Notter, Harley. *Postwar Foreign Policy Preparation, 1939–1945.* Washington: Department of State, 1949.

O'Connor, Harvey. *Mellon's Millions: The Biography of a Fortune.* New York: John Day, 1933.

– *The Empire of Oil.* New York: Monthly Review Press, 1955.

– *World Crisis in Oil.* New York: Monthly Review Press, 1962.

Parrini, Carl. *Heir to Empire: United States Economic Diplomacy, 1916–1923.* Pittsburgh: University of Pittsburgh Press, 1969.

Paterson, Thomas. *Soviet-American Confrontation: Postwar Reconstruction and the Origins of the Cold War.* Baltimore: John Hopkins, 1973.

Pearton, Maurice. *Oil and the Rumanian State.* Oxford: Clarendon Press, 1971.

Penrose, Edith F. *Economic Planning for Peace.* Princeton: Princeton University Press, 1953.

Perkins, Dexter. *The Diplomacy of a New Age: Major Issues in United States Policy since 1945.* Bloomington: University of Illinois, 1967.

Pratt, Julius. "Cordell Hull," Vols XII and XIII in *The American Secretaries of State and Their Diplomacy*, edited by Robert H. Ferrell and S.F. Bemis. New York: Cooper Square, 1964.

Prebisch, Paul. *Change and Development: Latin America's Great Task*. New York: Praeger, 1971.

Puga Vega, Mariano. *El Petroleo Chileno*. Santiago: Editorial Andres Bello, 1964.

Quandt, William. *Saudi Arabia's Oil Policy: A Staff Paper*. Washington: Brookings, 1982.

Quint, Howard, and Robert Ferrell, eds. *The Talkative President: The Off-the-Record Press Conferences of Calvin Coolidge*. Amherst: University of Massachusetts Press, 1964.

Rabe, Stephen. *The Road to OPEC: United States Relations with Venezuela, 1919–1976*. Austin: University of Texas Press, 1982.

Randall, Stephen J. *Colombia and the United States: Hegemony and Interdependence*. Athens and London: University of Georgia Press, 1992.

– *The Diplomacy of Modernization: Colombian-American Relations, 1920–1940*. Toronto: University of Toronto Press, 1977.

Reynolds, P.A. *British Foreign Policy in the Interwar Years*. London: Longmans, 1954.

Riddle, Donald H. *The Truman Committee: A Study in Congressional Responsibility*. New Brunswick: Rutgers University, 1964.

Rippy, J. Fred. *British Investments in Latin America, 1822–1949*. Minneapolis: University of Minnesota Press, 1959.

Roberts, Glyn. *The Most Powerful Man in the World: The Life of Sir Henri Deterding*. New York: Covici-Friede, 1938.

Rondot, Jean. *La Compagnie Française des Petroles*. Paris: Plon, 1962.

Sampson, Anthony. *The Seven Sisters: The Great Oil Companies and the World They Shaped*. New York: Viking Press, 1975.

Sawyer, Herbert L. *Soviet Perceptions of the Oil Factor in U.S. Foreign Policy*. Boulder: Westview, 1983.

Schechtman, Joseph. *The United States and the Jewish State Movement: The Crucial Decade, 1939–1949*. New York: Herzl Press, 1966.

Schmitt, Karl M. *Mexico and the United States, 1821–1973*. New York: Wiley, 1974.

Schoenbaum, Eleanora, ed. *Political Profiles: The Truman Years*. New York: Facts on File, Inc., 1978.

Shaffer, Edward H. *Canada's Oil and The American Empire*. Edmonton: Hurtig, 1983.

– *The United States and the Control of World Oil*. London: Croon-Helm, 1983.

– *The Oil Import Program of the United States: An Evaluation*. New York: Praeger, 1968.

Shwadran, Benjamin. *The Middle East, Oil and the Great Powers*. New York: Praeger, 1955 (3rd ed. Jerusalem, 1973).

Smith, Daniel M. *Aftermath of War: Bainbridge Colby and Wilsonian Diplomacy, 1920–1921*. Philadelphia: American Philosophical Society, 1970.

Smith, Robert M. *The United States and Revolutionary Nationalism in Mexico, 1916–1932*. Chicago: University of Chicago Press, 1972.

Solberg, Carl. *Oil and Nationalism in Argentina*. Stanford: Stanford University Press, 1979.

Sprout, Harold, and Margaret Sprout. *Toward a New Order of Sea Power: American Naval Policy and the World Scene, 1918–1922*. Princeton: Princeton University Press, 1940.

Stagliano, Vito. *A Policy of Discontent: the Making of a National Energy Strategy*. Tulsa: Pennwell, 2001.

Staley, Eugene. *Raw Materials in Peace and War*. New York: Council on Foreign Relations, 1937.

Standard Oil Company of Bolivia. *Confiscation: A History of the Oil Industry in Bolivia*. New York: Standard Oil of New Jersey, 1939.

Stocking, George. *Middle East Oil*. Nashville: Vanderbilt University Press, 1970.

Stoff, Michael B. *Oil, War, and American Security: The Search for a National Policy on Foreign Oil, 1941–1947*. New Haven: Yale University Press, 1980.

Supple, Barry, ed. *Essays in British Business History*. New York: Clarendon Press, 1972.

Tanzer, Michael. *The Political Economy of International Oil and the Underdeveloped Countries*. Boston: Beacon Press, 1969.

Taylor, A.J.P. *English History, 1914–1945*. New York: Oxford University Press, 1965.

Thompson, Craig. *Since Spindletop: A Human Story of Gulf's First Half-Century*. Pittsburgh: Gulf Oil, 1951.

Thompson, John H., and Stephen J. Randall. *Canada and the United States: Ambivalent Allies*, 3rd edition. Athens: University of Georgia Press, 2003.

Tugwell, Franklin. *The Politics of Oil in Venezuela*. Stanford: Stanford University Press, 1975.

Tulchin, Joseph. The *Aftermath of War: World War 1 and United States Policy toward Latin America*. New York: New York University Press, 1971.

Turner, Louis. *Oil Companies in the International System*, 3rd edition. London: George Allen & Unwin, 1983.

Vanek, Jaroslav. *The Natural Resource Content of United States Foreign Trade, 1870–1955*. Cambridge: Harvard University Press, 1963.

Wall, Bennett H., and George S. Gibb. *Teagle of Jersey Standard*. New Orleans: Tulane University Press, 1974.

Wallace, Benjamin, and Lynn Edminster. *International Control of Raw Materials*. Washington, 1930.

Wesseling, Louis. *Fuelling the War: Revealing an Oil Company's Role in Vietnam*. London and New York: I.B. Taurus, 2000.

Who's Who in America and *Who Was Who in America*. Various editions. Marquis, 1899–.

Wilkins, Mira. *The Maturing of Multinational Enterprise: American Business Abroad from 1914 to 1970*. Cambridge: Harvard University Press, 1970.

Williamson, Harold F., et al. *The American Petroleum Industry*. Vol. II: *The Age of Energy*. Evanston: Northwestern University Press, 1963.

Wittner, Lawrence. *Cold War America: From Hiroshima to Watergate*. New York: Praeger 1974.

Wood, Bryce. *The Making of the Good Neighbor Policy*. New York: Columbia University Press, 1967.

Yergin, Daniel. *The Prize*. New York: Simon & Schuster, 1991.

Zeis, Paul. *American Shipping Policy*. Princeton: Princeton University Press, 1938.

Articles

Abrahams, Paul. "American Bankers and the Economic Tactics of Peace: 1919." *Journal of American History* 56 (1969).

Ames, C.B. "Anti-Trust Laws and the Petroleum Industry." *World Petroleum* (October 1931).

Blank, Stephen. "Energy, Economics, and Security in Central Asia: Russia and Its Rivals." Presented at Carlisle Barracks, March 1995.

Braeman, John. "The New Left and American Foreign Policy During the Age of Normalcy." *Business History Review* 57 (Spring 1983): 73–104.

Cuff, Robert. "A Dollar-a-Year Man in Government: George N. Peek and the War Industries Board." *Business History Review* 41 (Winter 1967).

DeNovo, John, "Petroleum and The United States Navy before World War I." *Mississippi Valley Historical Review* 41 (March 1955): 641–56.

– "The Movement for an Aggressive American Oil Policy Abroad, 1918–1920." *American Historical Review* 61 (July 1956): 854–76.

Diubaldo, Richard. "The Canol Project in Canadian-American Relations." *Canadian Historical Association, Historical Papers* (1977): 179–95.

Enos, J.L. "The Mighty Adversaries: Standard Oil Company (New Jersey) and Royal Dutch Shell." *Explorations in Entrepreneurial History* 10 (April 1958): 140–9.

Fanning, Leonard M. "Conservation Board Creation Epochal." *Oil and Gas Journal*, 29 January 1925.

Feis, Herbert, "The Anglo-American Oil Agreement." *Yale Law Journal 55* (August 1944) : 1174–90.

Fletcher, M.E. "From Coal to Oil in British Shipping." *Journal of Transport History*, 1975.

Galambos, Louis, "The Emerging Organizational Synthesis in Modern American History." *Business History Review* 44 (Autumn 1970): 279–90.

Gause, F. Gregory. "Saudi Arabia Over a Barrel." *Foreign Affairs* 79, no. 3 (May-June 2000): 80–94.

Hawley, Ellis. "Herbert Hoover, the Commerce Secretariat, and the Vision of an Associative State." *Journal of American History* 61 (June 1974): 116–40.

Heymann, Hans. "Oil in Soviet-Western Relations in the Interwar Years." *American Slavic and East European Review* 7, no. 4 (1948): 308–31.

Hogan, Michael. "The Search For a Creative Peace: The United States, European Unity, and the Origins of the Marshall Plan." *Diplomatic History* 6 (Summer 1982): 267–86.

Ickes, Harold. "We're Running Out of Oil." *American Magazine*, January 1944.

Jones, Geoffrey G. "The British Government and the Oil Companies, 1912–1924: The Search for an Oil Policy." *Historical Journal* 20 (1977).

– "The Oil Fuel Market in Britain, 1900–1914: A Lost Cause Revisited." *Business History* 20 (July 1978): 131–52.

Kalicki, Jan H. "Caspian Energy at the Crossroads." *Foreign Affairs* 80, no. 5 (Sept/Oct. 2001): 120–34.

Kaufman, Burton I. "Oil and Antitrust: The Oil Cartel Case and the Cold War." *Business History Review* 51 (Spring 1977): 35–56.

Kessler, J.B. "Cooperative Plan for World Oil Industry." *World Petroleum* (October 1931): 564–7.

Klein, Herbert, "American Oil Companies in Latin America: The Bolivian Experience." *Inter-American Economic Affairs* 18 (Autumn 1964) .

Klein, Julius. "International Cartels." *Foreign Affairs* 6 (April 1928): 448–58.

Koistinen, Paul. "The Industrial-Military Complex in Historical Perspective: The Inter-War Years." *Journal of American History* 56 (March 1970): 819–35.

Koppes, Clayton. "The Good Neighbor Policy and the Nationalization of Mexican Oil: A Reinterpretation." *Journal of American History* 69 (June 1982): 62–81.

Miller, George A. "u.s. Foreign Policy for Oil." *Mining and Metallurgy* (March 1944) .

Nordhauser, Norman. "Origins of Federal Oil Regulations in the 1920s." *Business History Review* 47 (Spring 1973): 53–71.

Pollack, Kenneth M. "Securing the Gulf." *Foreign Affairs* 82, no. 4 (July/August 2003): 2–16.

Rabe, Stephen. "Anglo-American Rivalry for Venezuelan Oil, 1919–1929." *MidAmerica* 58, no. 2 (April 1976): 97–109.

Randall, Stephen. "Raw Materials and United States Foreign Policy." *Reviews in American History* (September 1980): 413–18.

– "Harold Ickes and United States Foreign Petroleum Policy Planning, 1939–45." *Business History Review* 57, no. 3 (Fall 1983): 367–87.

Reed, Peter. "Standard Oil in Indonesia, 1898–1928." *Business History Review* 32 (Fall 1958): 311–37.

Sharp, Roger. "America's Stake in World Petroleum." *Harvard Business Review* 28 (September 1950): 25–41.

Smith, George Otis. "Where the World Gets Its Oil." *National Geographic Magazine* 37 (February 1920): 181–202.

Stivers, W. "International Politics and Iraqui Oil, 1918–1928: A Study in Anglo-American Diplomacy." *Business History Review* 55 (Winter 1981): 517–40.

Telhami, Shibley, et al. "Does Saudi Arabia Still Matter? Differing Perspectives on the Kingdom and Its Oil." *Foreign Affairs* 81, no. 6 (November-December 2002), 167–79.

Viner, Jacob. "National Monopolies of Raw Materials." *Foreign Affairs* 4 (July 1926): 585–600.

Viorst, Milton. "Iraq at War." *Foreign Affairs* 65, no. 2 (Winter 1986), 349–65.

Wilkins, Mira. "Multinational Oil Companies in South America in the 1920s." *Business History Review* 48 (Autumn 1974): 415–46.

– "The Oil Companies in Perspective." *Daedalus* (Fall 1975): 159–78.

Williamson, Harold F., and Ralph Andreano. "Integration and Competition in the Oil Industry." *Journal of Political Economy* 69 (August 1961): 381–5.

Wilson, D.A. "Principles and Profits: Standard Oil Responds to Chinese Nationalism, 1925–27." *Pacific Historical Review* 46 (November 1977): 625–47.

Dissertations and Unpublished Papers

Baldridge, Donald. "Mexican Petroleum and United States-Mexican Relations." ph d dissertation, University of Arizona, 1971.

Eto, Seishiro. "Asian Energy Security and Japan's Foreign Policy." Seminar on Energy Security in Asia, March 6, 2001. http://www.mofa.go.jp.

Fithian, Floyd. "Soviet-American Economic Relations 1918–1933: American Business in Russia during the Period of Non-recognition." ph d dissertation, University of Nebraska, 1964.

Knudson, David L. "Petroleum, Venezuela, and the United States, 1920–1941." ph d dissertation, Michigan State University, 1975.

Lytle, Mark. "American Iranian Relations 1941–1947 and the Redefinition of National Security." ph d dissertation, Yale University, 1973.

– "Oil and Conflict in Iran, 1943–1946." Paper presented to the Organization of American Historians, Boston, 1975.

Mannock, James. "Anglo-American Relations, 1921–1928." ph d dissertation, Princeton University, 1962.

Moore, Frederick. "Origins of American Oil Concessions in Bahrain, Kuwait, and Saudi Arabia." ph d dissertation, Princeton University, 1968.

Ring, Jeremiah. "American Diplomacy and the Mexican Oil Controversy, 1938–1943." ph d dissertation, University of New Mexico, 1974.

Seidel, Robert. "Progressive Pan Americanism: Development and United States Policy toward South America, 1906–1931." ph d dissertation, Cornell University, 1971.

Stegmaier, Harold. "From Confrontation to Cooperation: The United States and Mexico, 1938–1945." ph D dissertation, University of Michigan, 1970.

Thompson, Eric V. *A Brief History of Major Oil Companies in the Gulf Region.* Petroleum Archives Project, Arabian Peninsula and Gulf Studies Program, University of Virginia, np., nd. http://www.virginia.edu/igpr/apagoil-history.html

Walt, Joseph. "Saudi Arabia and the Americans, 1928–1951." ph D dissertation, Northwestern University, 1960.

Index